Research in Early Childhood for Sustainability

Sustainability is a global issue that urgently needs addressing, and for which the most serious consequences are for children and future generations. This insightful research text tackles one of the most significant contemporary issues of our time – the nexus between society and environment – and how early childhood education can contribute to sustainable living. By offering international and multidisciplinary research perspectives on early childhood education for sustainability, each chapter explores and investigates the complex topic of sustainability and its relationship to early childhood education. A particular emphasis that runs through this text is young children as empowered citizens, capable of both contributing to and creating change for sustainability.

The chapter authors work from, or are aligned with, a transformative education paradigm that suggests the socio-constructivist frameworks currently underpinning early childhood education require reframing in light of the social transformations necessary to address humanity's unsustainable, unjust and unhealthy living patterns. This research text is designed to be provocative and challenging; in so doing it seeks to encourage explorations of current understandings about early childhood education for sustainability, offers new dimensions for more deeply informed practice, and proposes avenues for further research in this field.

Julie Davis is Associate Professor in Early Childhood Education at Queensland University of Technology, Australia.

Sue Elliott is Senior Lecturer in Early Childhood Education at the University of New England, Australia.

Research in Early Childhood Education for Sustainability

International perspectives and provocations

Edited by Julie Davis and Sue Elliott

 Routledge
Taylor & Francis Group

LONDON AND NEW YORK

First published 2014
by Routledge
2 Park Square, Milton Park, Abingdon, Oxon OX14 4RN

and by Routledge
711 Third Avenue, New York, NY 10017

Routledge is an imprint of the Taylor & Francis Group, an informa business

British Library Cataloguing in Publication Data
A catalogue record for this book is available from the British Library

Library of Congress Cataloging in Publication Data
Research in early childhood education for sustainability : international
perspectives and provocations / edited by Julie Davis, Sue Elliott.
pages cm
1. Early childhood education—Research. I. Davis, Julie. II. Elliott, Sue.
LB1139.225.R45 2014
372.2107—dc23
2014001224

ISBN: 978-0-415-85448-1 (hbk)
ISBN: 978-0-415-85449-8 (pbk)
ISBN: 978-1-315-76749-9 (ebk)

Typeset in Bembo
by FiSH Books Ltd, Enfield

MIX
Paper from
responsible sources
FSC   FSC® C013056
www.fsc.org

Printed and bound in Great Britain by
TJ International Ltd, Padstow, Cornwall

Contents

List of illustrations   viii
List of contributors   x
Acknowledgements   xiv
Foreword by Daniella Tilbury   xv

An orientation to early childhood education for sustainability and
research – framing the text   1
JULIE DAVIS AND SUE ELLIOTT

CLUSTER 1
Ethics and values   **19**

1   Examining early childhood education through the lens of education
for sustainability: Revisioning rights   21
JULIE DAVIS

2   Belonging, value conflicts and children's rights in learning for
sustainability in early childhood   38
SOLVEIG HÄGGLUND AND EVA M. JOHANSSON

3   Learning from the wisdom of elders   49
JENNY RITCHIE

CLUSTER 2
Historical and sociocultural contexts   **61**

4   Intercultural dialogues in early childhood education for sustainability:
Embedding Indigenous perspectives   63
MELINDA G. MILLER

5   Perspectives on early childhood environmental education in Japan:
    Rethinking for a sustainable society   79
    MICHIKO INOUE

6   The role of early childhood education in building Singapore as a
    sustainable nation   97
    HUI-LING CHUA

7   Norwegian perspectives on ECEfS: What has developed since the
    Brundtland Report?   112
    BARBARA MARIA SAGEIDET

CLUSTER 3
Curriculum and pedagogy   125

8   Early childhood education for sustainability and natural outdoor
    playspaces: Researching change and theorizing about interfaces   127
    SUE ELLIOTT

9   An AuSSI early childhood adventure: Early childhood educators and
    researchers actioning change   143
    TRACY CHARLOTTE YOUNG AND AMY CUTTER-MACKENZIE

10 The Project Approach in early childhood education for sustainability:
    Exemplars from Korea and Australia   158
    OKJONG JI AND SHARON STUHMCKE

11 Valuing agency in young children: Teachers rising to the challenge of
    sustainability in the Aotearoa New Zealand early childhood context   180
    GLYNNE MACKEY

12 I want to do real things: Explorations of children's active community
    participation   194
    LOUISE GWENNETH PHILLIPS

13 Education for sustainability in Swedish preschools: Stepping forward
    or out-of-step?   208
    INGRID ENGDAHL AND EVA ÄRLEMALM-HAGSÉR

14 Innovative approaches to early childhood education for sustainability
    in England: Case studies from the field   225
    ROBERT BARRATT, ELISABETH BARRATT-HACKING, AND PAT BLACK

15 Early childhood education for sustainability in the United States of
    America   248
    LOUISE CHAWLA AND MARY RIVKIN

16 The Arts and education for sustainability: Shaping student teachers'
    identities towards sustainability   266
    LYNDAL O'GORMAN

17 Science in preschool – a foundation for education for sustainability?
    A view from Swedish preschool teacher education   280
    BODIL SUNDBERG AND CHRISTINA OTTANDER

18 Early childhood education for sustainability in the United Kingdom:
    Generating professional capital   294
    LOUISE GILBERT, MARY FULLER, SALLY PALMER, AND JANET ROSE

19 Expanding worlds of early childhood education for sustainability:
    Looking back, looking forward   309
    ANN FARRELL AND SUSAN DANBY

    Appendix 1: Transnational dialogues participants   314
    Appendix 2: Our chronology of selected key events, research and
                publications that chart the development of ECEfS   316

Index   324

List of illustrations

Figures

1.1	Five dimensions of rights for early childhood education in light of the challenges of sustainability	23
5.1	Education for sustainability: now and future	88
8.1	Banksia Childcare Centre outdoor playspace	130
8.2	Acacia Kindergarten outdoor playspace	131
8.3	The study starting point for Banksia Childcare Centre and Acacia Kindergarten	135
8.4	Study end point for Banksia Childcare Centre: nested systems	136
8.5	Study end point for Acacia Kindergarten: not yet fully nested systems	136
9.1	Thematic network for this study: the global theme, three organizational themes and their respective basic themes	150
10.1	Synthesizing the fields	161
10.2	An exciting moment: finding otter excrement	165
10.3	Children's drawing after finding an otter footprint	165
10.4	Front side of the Musim Stream animal map	167
10.5	Back side of the Musim Stream animal map	167
10.6	An otter badge	168
10.7	Child's collage about the rainforest	170
10.8	Child's construction – rubbish crane	173
10.9	A page from the children's book *Ways to Act for the Environment*	174
10.10	The transformative project approach	177
11.1	The dinosaur playground	187
11.2	Exploring the 'high hills'	187
11.3	Voting for the best swing	190
11.4	Sorting food scraps at the lunch table	191
12.1	Class display of signs children made to plead for support for the recovery of the Coxens' fig-parrot population	201
13.1	Child interviews were conducted employing this drawing by Anna-Karin Engström as a stimulus for conversations	215

13.2   Children visiting a local station for recycling paper, glass, plastic, etc.   217
15.1   The Lucy School in Middletown, Maryland, a Green Ribbon
       School, uses the surrounding farmland as an outdoor classroom and
       playground. The younger children enjoy much outdoor time   255
15.2   Dodge Nature Center Preschool, St. Paul, Minnesota   256
15.3   After four year olds at the Boulder Journey School visited the
       Civic Area and Boulder Creek greenway, many of their pictures
       and ideas recommended caring for the wildlife   260
16.1   Student self-portrait and artist's statement   272
16.2   Student self-portrait and artist's statement   273

Tables

5.1   A chronology of national Japanese early childhood education
       policies and curriculum guidelines 1899–2008   81
5.2   Results of CiNii Japanese academic database search for key words in
       whole publications and titles conducted in 2013   85
9.1   Descriptions of the four participating children's services   148
10.1   Existing sustainability practices at the kindergarten and additional
       practices introduced during the Rainforest Project   175
13.1   Knowledge content areas that describe sustainability   213

Boxes

14.1   A summary of early years provision in England   226
14.2   The sustainable schools framework in England (2006–2010)   232
14.3   EfS learning experiences for the early years   243

List of contributors

Eva Ärlemalm-Hagsér is a senior lecturer and researcher at the School of Education, Culture and Communication, Mälardalen University, Sweden. Her main interests are early childhood education for sustainability, preschool children's meaning-making and agency, child participation and the lived curriculum.

Elisabeth Barratt-Hacking is Director of Studies for the MA in Education in the Department of Education, University of Bath, UK. She has published widely in the field of environmental education. Her research interests relate to childhood and environment, children's voice and participation and the relationship between children and their local environment.

Robert Barratt is Professor of Education, Assistant Dean and Director of Education at Bath Spa University, UK. He has been involved in educational research for over 15 years. He has published widely in the international field of children's environmental education, participation and place-based education.

Pat Black is Head of Initial Teacher Education at Bath Spa University, UK. She has been involved in primary and early years teacher education for fifteen years; before this she was an early years practitioner. Her academic interests include education policy and teacher education.

Louise Chawla is a professor in the Environmental Design Program at the University of Colorado, USA, Co-editor of *Children, Youth and Environments*, and Associate Director of the Children, Youth and Environments Center. Her research relates to children's experiences of cities and nature.

Hui-Ling Chua is an adjunct lecturer in early childhood studies in Singapore who strongly advocates environmental education as authentic and relevant education for children. She is also currently a doctoral student at the University of South Australia researching Singapore children's engagement with the natural world.

Amy Cutter-Mackenzie is Director of Research for the School of Education, Southern Cross University, Australia. She is also Research Leader of the 'Sustainability, Environment and Education' (SEE) Research Cluster and Editor of the *Australian Journal of Environmental Education*.

Susan Danby's areas of expertise are in early years language and social interaction, childhood studies, and early literacy. She has published in the following areas: qualitative research, classroom discourse, helpline talk, gender, classroom interaction, early childhood education pedagogy, talk and interaction, children's work and play, and teacher-student interactions.

Julie Davis is Associate Professor in the School of Early Childhood, Queensland University of Technology, Australia, and has been teaching, advocating for, and researching in this field for over twenty years. She edited the first textbook on this subject, *Young Children and the Environment: Early Learning for Sustainability* (Cambridge University Press, 2010).

Sue Elliott is a long-term advocate of education for sustainability and natural outdoor playspaces. She lectures in early childhood education at the University of New England, Australia and is a recognized author. Her current focus is 'Bush Kinder', an Australian adaptation of Scandinavian forest schools.

Ingrid Engdahl is Director of Studies and Researcher at the Department of Child and Youth Studies at Stockholm University, Sweden. Her main interests are: early childhood education with a child oriented approach, focusing on infants and toddlers, and education for sustainability.

Ann Farrell is Professor of Early Childhood and Head of the School of Early Childhood at Queenland University of Technology (QUT), Brisbane, Australia. Her teaching and research expertise is in research ethics, children's rights to protection and participation, childhood and families studies, and children in the legal and criminal justice systems.

Mary Fuller is an experienced educational researcher focusing on individual differences and equity (race, class and gender) and an active participant in professional and research organizations. She recently led a project rated as outstanding on disabled university students' learning.

Louise Gilbert trained in health and education and has worked as a senior lecturer in early years at Bath Spa University, UK. She has published on transformational learning in higher education and is currently writing-up her doctoral research on the transference of Emotion Coaching into community educational practice.

Solveig Hägglund is Professor of Education at Karlstad University, Sweden. Her research includes social learning, bullying, peace education and children's rights. She is the former convenor of Children's Rights in Education, a network within the European Conference on Educational Research.

Michiko Inoue is a professor in the School of Early Childhood, Faculty of Education, Osaka Ohtani University, Osaka, Japan. She teaches biology and environment to preservice students studying early childhood and primary education. She is a leader in environmental education and education for sustainability at the early childhood level. More specifically, her interest is focused on conceptual understandings and the actual educational practices of educators in kindergartens and nursery centres.

Okjong Ji is a professor in the Early Childhood Education Department of Korea National University of Transportation, Korea. In 1993–1994, she visited the University of Illinois to study the Project Approach with Professors Lillian Katz and Sylvia Chard. In 2010–2011, she was Visiting Scholar at Queensland University of Technology, Australia, focused on early childhood education for sustainability. Currently, she is Vice President of Cheongju YWCA in Cheongju City, as supervisor of eight institutes for young children. She has published several books in Korean about the application of the Project Approach in early childhood education.

Eva M. Johansson is Professor of Education at the University of Stavanger, Norway. Her research involves questions on moral learning including national and international studies on how children experience and develop morality and how teachers approach such issues in their work.

Glynne Mackey is a senior lecturer in early childhood education at the University of Canterbury, New Zealand, teaching and researching in sustainability early childhood education. Her research explores ways in which young children participate in action within their communities.

Melinda G. Miller is a lecturer in the School of Early Childhood, Queensland University of Techology, Brisbane, Australia. Her teaching and research interests include cultural studies, ECEfS and action research. Melinda's doctoral thesis focused on embedding Indigenous perspectives in non-Indigenous educational contexts.

Lyndal O'Gorman is a senior lecturer in the School of Early Childhood, Queensland University of Technology, Brisbane, Australia. Lyndal's teaching and research examines the ways in which the Arts can offer preservice teachers and children new ways of understanding sustainability.

Christina Ottander is an associate professor in science education at Umeå University, Sweden. She has long experience of teacher education. Her research concerns socio-scientific issues and their ability to improve students' interest and learning, professional development, and science in preschool.

Sally Palmer is Course Leader in Early Childhood Studies at the University of Gloucestershire, UK. She is currently working on a range of research projects centred around learning for sustainable futures in the early years.

Louise Gwenneth Phillips is a lecturer in literacy education in the School of Education at University of Queensland, Brisbane, Australia, with twenty years of experience as a professional storyteller and early childhood teacher. Sustainability principles have been (and continue to be) at the core of her work with storytelling and early childhood education. Her current research focuses on explorations of young children's active citizenship, foregrounding young children's participation in society, and cultivating social responsibility.

Jenny Ritchie is currently Associate Professor in Early Childhood Teacher Education at Te Whare Wānanga o Wairaka (Unitec Institute of Technology), Auckland, New Zealand. Her teaching and research focus on cultural, environmental and social justice issues.

Mary Rivkin teaches preservice early childhood teachers at the University of Maryland, Baltimore County (UMBC), USA. She focuses on outdoor play and science education. She has recently revised her 1995 book *The Great Outdoors* (NAEYC).

Janet Rose is Programme Leader and Award Leader in early years childhood education at Bath Spa University, UK. She has recently co-written a book on the role of the adult in early years settings and is currently leading a research project on developing a community-wide, cross-disciplinary approach to promoting children and young people's resilience via the adoption of emotion coaching into practice.

Barbara Maria Sageidet, Associate Professor, Department of Early Childhood Education, University of Stavanger, Norway, has a background in botany, ecology, paleoecology and soil sciences, and a research focus on sustainability and inquiry learning in the kindergarten.

Sharon Stuhmcke is an early childhood teacher who has more than twenty years teaching experience with children from kindergarten to three years of age. Sharon has recently completed a doctorate in education for sustainability in early childhood education using a transformative project approach. Sharon's thesis was awarded an Executive Dean's Commendation (QUT) in 2012. Sharon currently teaches at Southbank Institute of Technology (SBIT), Brisbane, Australia.

Bodil Sundberg has a PhD in biology and long experience of teaching science at preschool and elementary teacher education. Bodil's research interests concern early years science education in relation to teacher education, ICT use, curriculum, and education for sustainability.

Tracy Charlotte Young received the 2010 Barbara Creaser Memorial Lecture award in recognition of her work as an advocate for early childhood environmental education. She is a lecturer at Swinburn University of Technology, Hawthorn, Australia. Her research is situated in early childhood education, with a particular interest in sustainability, ecological literacy and human-animal research.

Acknowledgements

As co-editors we recognise that we build on a history of committed practitioners who dared to begin 'greening' early childhood education several decades ago. We gratefully acknowledge the small, but now critical mass of international researchers who have contributed to this publication and have demonstrated their support for us as co-editors. In this publication they share diverse insights, commitment and expertise.

We continue to be inspired by what they offer, individually and collectively, in this text. We encourage others to participate in this endeavour to explore the multiplicities of early childhood education for sustainability research at this critical time on Earth. Creating sustainable and just futures for all motivates our ongoing work.

Foreword

The time has come to bring together two critical areas of research that are of great significance to the future of our planet and quality of life within it. Research studies into early childhood education have confirmed the importance of these formative years in the formulation of identity, willingness to learn, as well as engage, with the world. Extending research inquiries to consider questions around relationships and responsibilities that can shape more sustainable futures is of great interest to us all.

Education for sustainability is a relatively new field that has become a global movement in the space of a decade. A recent UN commissioned global review documents how this area of learning now features: in many national policies and is a formal responsibility of one or more national government agencies; in school inspections as well as reviews of quality of standards in formal and non-education; in strategic plans and programmes of regional and local governments; as well as in the priority lists of research funding councils and international aid agencies (UNESCO 2014 in print). As the UN announces a new Global Action Programme in Education for Sustainable Development (UNESCO 2014) identifying and addressing questions that have been deprived of attention becomes a priority. Early childhood education is one of several key areas that is yet to command international commitment and that deserves its place in the new global platform.

This book paves the way for international dialogue and strengthens arguments for investment, research and action in early childhood education for sustainability (ECEfS). It maps the landscape in ways that help us understand the roots and influences; locate current concerns and debates; and identify opportunities and future pathways for ECEfS. For example, it recognises that there is a body of research that has documented the role of environmental studies and outdoor education in the shaping of children's interest and attachment to nature but takes the discussions to a different level by asking questions about pedagogy, place, participation and ultimately how paradigm shifts towards more socially just and democratic education models can be attained. Authors do not shy away from complex questions such as the relationship between environmental education and education for sustainability or the place of indigenous perspectives and knowledge in early childhood education. Most visible across the chapters, is the perspective that children are social beings; learning must support the development of capabilities and encourage participation of young children in debates and experiences relating to international understanding, equity and social justice.

The text reminds us that early childhood education, through the education for sustainability lens, provides an interesting set of perspectives that have implications for mainstream educators – and not just for colleagues already engaged with sustainability. Underpinning the contributions in this book are diverse ideological perspectives and methodological frames that seek to challenge traditional notions of learning and the young learner. The book acknowledges children as thinkers, problem-solvers, social beings and agents of change moving away from engrained positions and the misperception that they are too young to formulate meaningful and owned responses to issues around them.

The authors of this text give presence to the role of families and communities in the theory and practice of early childhood education. This refreshing perspective is underpinned by a systems approach to understanding of education and sustainability. The book documents how sustainability is relevant to children, their families and the communities they grow up in. It presents a strong reminder of the right of every child to grow up in a healthy, just and participatory society and leaves the reader in no doubt of the potential and vital contribution of early childhood research to the future of people, places and planet.

Daniella Tilbury
November 2013
Chair, UNESCO Global Monitoring and Evaluation Expert Group (MEEG)
for the UN Decade in Education for Sustainable Development
Dean of Sustainability at University of Gloucestershire, UK

References

UNESCO ESD Section (2014) *Global Action Programme on Education for Sustainable Development*. Online. Available: http://www.unesco.org/new/en/unesco-world-conference-on-esd-2014/esd-after-2014/global-action-programme/ (accessed (12 January 2014).

UNESCO (2014 in print) *A UN Decade in Education for Sustainable Development: The Third Global Monitoring and Evaluation Report*. Paris: UNESCO.

An orientation to early childhood education for sustainability and research – framing the text

Julie Davis and Sue Elliott

A small group of thoughtful people could change the world. Indeed, it's the only thing that ever has.

(Margaret Mead, 1901–1978)

Introduction

This publication arose from the interests of the chapter authors, 'a small group of thoughtful people' almost all of whom participated in one or both Transnational Dialogues in Research in Early Childhood Education for Sustainability conferences, held in Stavanger, Norway in 2010 and Brisbane, Australia in 2011 (see Appendix 1 for a list of participants). These meetings were the first time that a critical mass of researchers from vastly different parts of the globe – Norway, Sweden, Australia and New Zealand at the inaugural meeting, with additional participants from Korea, Japan and Singapore attending the second – had come together to debate, discuss and share ideas about research and theory in the emerging field of Early Childhood Education for Sustainability (ECEfS). Some of the researchers who joined these Transnational Dialogues had met serendipitously at earlier conferences and meetings, or had corresponded via email, but many had never met face-to-face. Now a significant number are contributing authors to this book. It is a testament to these researchers' interest in this agenda that they mostly self-funded their travel and other costs to attend the Transnational Dialogues research meetings.

It is important to emphasize at the outset that a key focus of these meetings was to explore ECEfS from the perspective of young children as central – as thinkers, problem-solvers and agents of change for sustainability. We were not interested, for example, in discussing nature education or outdoor education – although we appreciate their value – except as these education approaches support or, indeed, may hinder thinking about children's capabilities to engage in sustainability issues and topics (Sundberg and Ottander, Chapter 17). We also wish to emphasize that viewing children as active agents of change does not imply that we see children as saviours for sustainability, tasked with doing the repair work that adults have created. Instead, the approach to ECEfS that we promote is one of children working authentically in the exploration of topics and issues of interest to them. This means working alongside their teachers, families and communities in solving problems, seeking solutions and taking action to 'make a difference', mostly within their local context (Ärlemalm-Hagsér and Engdahl, Chapter 13), but occasionally on a bigger stage (Ji and Stuchmke, Chapter 10 and Phillips, Chapter 12). We believe education that results in young children becoming 'worriers or warriors' for sustainability is inherently wrong. Nevertheless, in emphasizing a more critical, participatory orientation to environmental education/education for sustainability, we make no apologies.

What was determined by all members of the Transnational Dialogues group was that there was a need to engage even more researchers in the work of ECEfS. To date, the ECEfS field has primarily been the province of advocates and practitioners, that is, committed individuals working alone or within their organizations who have seen the relevance of environmental and sustainability issues for young children and their families, and the potential of early childhood education to contribute to healthy, just and sustainable societies, now and for the future. We recognized that research and researchers, too, have an important place.

The Transnational Dialogue participants included experienced, mid-career, and early career researchers, those underway with doctoral studies or yet to commence. The varied levels of research expertise and experience are reflected in these chapters. As co-editors, we view all contributions as equally valuable. A number of contributions take a strongly philosophical and theoretical lens to topics concerning young children and education for sustainability. Most chapters, however, focus on observations, analyses and critical reflections of early childhood practitioner curricula and pedagogical approaches – this is where the existing small modicum of research is located. Like Hart (2002), we consider practitioner research as 'knowing that comes from within the action' (p. 146) and as researchers we are 'exploring the possibilities of theorizing with [teacher] stories instead of about them' (p. 155). At the same time, we acknowledge that this practitioner focus is evidence of a nascent field where it has been early childhood practitioners, rather than theorists and researchers, who have driven the uptake of ECEfS. Now, however, we believe it is time to turn a more scholarly eye to what is being enacted and to explore approaches and practices more deeply and critically. Hence, we see this text as evidence that the field, more generally, is beginning to mature.

While most chapter authors come from the field of early childhood education, a few are more aligned with education for sustainability/environmental education, while a much smaller number are already working at the intersection of early childhood education and education for sustainability. What we share as a group is a range of perspectives and orientations to research and to the research focus at the heart of this book – young children and their actual and potential capabilities as agents of change for sustainability. As researchers, regardless of experience and perspectives, participants knew they had something extra to offer – their expertise as researchers – providing scholarly insights into the work of practitioners, applying critically-reflective lenses to curricula, pedagogies and assumptions, testing of ideas and theories, and presenting a sense for where ECEfS might fit or, indeed, go beyond norms and orthodoxies. This is a text, then, for both researchers and those whose primary interests lie in daily interactions with children, families and communities.

Building on historical threads

As noted, this group of authors builds on a history of advocacy and practice dating back to the early 1990s when a handful of early childhood practitioners and academics, mainly in the United States and Australia, recognized the links between emerging environmental issues and early childhood education. The foundational importance of the early years for the development of life-long pro-environmental attitudes (Tilbury 1994) and the unique affordances of early childhood education to foster environmental knowledge and skills capitalizing on children's innate curiosity about the world (Palmer 1995) was just beginning to be recognized. At this time, too, the new sociology of childhood (Corsaro 1997) and United Nations Convention on the Rights of the Child (UNCRC) (UNICEF 1989) were provoking early childhood educators to view children as active social agents with rights to participate in decision-making about matters relevant to them. The synergies between these shifting early childhood education paradigms and growing global environmental concerns thus inspired the emergence of early childhood environmental education.

In elaborating these historical threads, as chapter authors, we collectively draw on our local and international experiences and, as co-editors we recognize that we do not offer a complete history of this field. For example, we only report on events and initiatives that can be shared through the English language and we recognize that our perspectives are framed by our lives as academics from the wealthiest nations, both East and West. As researchers, we are limited, therefore, by our own lenses, experiences and capacities to understand the entire global picture of ECEfS. We do not report, for example, on what is happening in nations and regions where early childhood education as a formal societal structure may not exist, or where simply staying alive is the most pressing sustainability issue for many children. We envisage, however, that our contributions may prompt other researchers and authors to widen the scope of research and reporting, so that truly international and global insights are presented in future works.

In the early 1990s, several practitioner publications (Elliott and Emmett 1991, Gordon Community Children's Centre 1993, Targowska 1991, Wilson 1993, 1994) and emerging early childhood environmental education practitioner networks, particularly in Australia, laid the foundations for what has become the field of ECEfS. The chronology offered in Appendix 2 (p. 316) documents these tentative beginnings. However, examination of appendix entries up to 2003 illustrates early childhood environmental education's slow initial uptake. This is a common experience illustrated by several chapter authors who draw on their own political, cultural and social histories across a number of countries.

Since 2003, especially through the international work of UNESCO, the World

Organization for Early Childhood (OMEP) and a small number of key advocates, the profile of early childhood education for sustainability (renamed from early childhood environmental education) is now rapidly expanding. For example, in 2007 the first international UNESCO meeting focusing specifically on early childhood education for sustainability was held in Sweden with participants from around 30 countries. Derived from this initial meeting was the first international publication *The Contribution of Early Childhood Education to a Sustainable Society* (UNESCO 2008a) that documented the responses of 16 countries to matters at the intersection of early childhood education and education for sustainability. It is important to note, however, that most papers were aspirational, rather than based on local research or practice in education for sustainability.

A subsequent UNESCO meeting in 2008 produced the *Gothenburg Recommendations on Education for Sustainable Development* that included specific early childhood education recommendations (UNESCO 2008b), and noted that early childhood is the logical starting point for education for sustainable development. These Recommendations were later ratified by the UNESCO World Conference on Education for Sustainable Development in Bonn, Germany and fully adopted by UNESCO in 2009. In the same period, the 2010 OMEP World Congress in Gothenburg, Sweden, for the first time, promoted early childhood education for sustainability as a key theme at its international conference, which was followed by an OMEP document (Siraj-Blatchford *et al.* 2010) that highlighted the links between early childhood education and sustainability. At the 2013 OMEP World Congress in Shanghai, China, sustainability was again profiled, this time as a cornerstone of high quality early childhood services. Pramling Samuelsson, as outgoing OMEP World President and former holder of the UNESCO Chair in Early Childhood Education and Sustainable Development has been a key advocate in moving the international early childhood education field towards understanding and accepting that early childhood education can make powerful contributions to sustainability (Siraj-Blatchford *et al.* 2010). This broadening of international uptake of ECEfS is evident in Appendix 1, with the researchers represented in this text building on the rising interest in and uptake by practitioners.

Davis (2009) has previously argued the tardiness of research in ECEfS. Her literature search of 14 internationally prominent early childhood and environmental education/education for sustainability peer-reviewed journals over the 12-year period 1996–2007 revealed that fewer than 5 per cent of articles focused on this area. Further, Davis categorized those that were published according to content around the concepts of *in* the environment, *about* the environment or *for* the environment. Most commonly, articles described young children *in* the environment, experientially-engaged with gardening or playing in/observing nature. A few papers described children acquiring knowledge *about* the environment. Almost no research articles described young children as acting *for* the environment, thus failing to reflect current images of young children as capable and competent participants in the world and as change agents for sustainability. Only in more recent years has this latter line of research been explored, mostly by

Australasian-based authors (Davis 2010, Davis *et al.* 2005, Duhn with Bachmann and Harris 2010, Elliott and Davis 2009, Mackey and Vaealiki 2011, Phillips 2010, Ritchie 2010, Vaealiki and Mackey 2008) with the trend only now becoming more prevalent on a broader international scale (Ang 2010, Ärlemalm-Hagsér and Sandberg 2011, Hägglund and Pramling Samuelsson 2009, Johansson 2009, Sandberg and Ärlemalm-Hagsér 2011). The *International Journal of Early Childhood* celebrated this trend with a special edition dedicated to education for sustainability in 2009, as did the *Journal of Action Research Today in Early Childhood* in 2010. In 2012, a new journal, *The International Journal of Early Childhood Environmental Education* was launched in the United States of America to specifically capture this growing research focus. This newer body of research makes more explicit the philosophical and pedagogical links between early childhood education and education for sustainability, often advocating for an embedded and enacted culture of education for sustainability within early childhood education, rather than focusing mainly on investigating children's knowledge *about* the environment or their engagement *in* the environment.

Nevertheless, it must be noted that even in the most recent research compendium *The International Handbook of Research on Environmental Education* (Stevenson *et al.* 2013), consultation of the index locates only one item referencing early childhood education. Furthermore, this reference is in the context of young children and environmental justice and equity (Haluza-DeLay 2013), rather than early childhood education per se. Other early childhood references in the text are scant, though we do recognize Barratt-Hacking *et al.*'s (2013) research chapter focusing on primary school-aged children that is informed by early childhood philosophies and pedagogies. Reid and Payne's (2013) chapter, too, acknowledges that early childhood education is 'making inroads into environmental education research' (p. 531) and suggests that this may promote genuine innovation in how enquiries in the broader environmental education field are conceived, designed and conducted. We believe this will be shown to be so.

In this same handbook, Stevenson *et al.* (2013) remark that 'environmental education as a field of inquiry is conceptualized from a range of vantage points, including historical, theoretical, ethical perspectives; discourses, policy, curriculum, learning, and assessment are examined from an EE-perspective and key issues are raised of framing, doing, and assessing the missing voices in environmental education research' (p. 1). We acknowledge the 'missing voices' in this text, too, and as mentioned earlier, aspire in the future to encompass multiple global perspectives. As Gough (2013: 41) comments more generally, we see this book as 'a process of constructing "transcultural spaces" in which scholars from different localities collaborate in reframing and decentering their own knowledge traditions and negotiate trust in each other's contributions to their collective work'. A deepening critique and critical reflection within 'transcultural spaces' is timely, given the global imperative for urgent change in the ways human populations live, learn and 'do business'.

Identifying global imperatives for sustainability

There is no denying global concerns around sustainability matters. We live in challenging and changing times; calls to act locally and globally for sustainable futures are increasing internationally (Commonwealth of Australia Department of Climate Change and Energy Efficiency (DCCEE) 2011, Flannery 2008, 2010, Suzuki 2010, United Nations Environment Program (UNEP) 2012, World Wide Fund for Nature 2011). Advocates for broad societal change, vigorous public and political debate, and almost daily global media coverage of the impacts and challenges of climate change, water, energy and food security, pollution and biodiversity threats, heighten such calls. Many commentators see the global financial crises that have gripped international economies since 2008 as symptomatic of unsustainable economic systems based on economic growth, limited natural resources, and the exploitation of human capital. For example, the rise of China from a predominantly rural economy to a powerhouse in the last 20 years, driven largely by the production of goods for consumption is seen as exacerbating global issues in all three dimensions of sustainability – social, economic and environmental. Laszlo (2010) states that we are poised at *The Chaos Point*, a global point of critical instability, driven by inequitable wealth distribution, affluent consumption, the global financial system, population growth, the breakdown of social structures and overuse of natural resources. He states 'the decider is not new technology, but the rise of new thinking – new values, perceptions, and priorities – in a critical mass of the people who make up the bulk of society' (Laszlo 2010: 19).

We believe that new ways of thinking – and those of older, Indigenous cultures that offer new old ways of thinking – are pivotal to living sustainably and educating for sustainability. Authors Ritchie (Chapter 3) and Miller (Chapter 4) expand on this latter theme and as Indigenous authors Morgan *et al.* (2008) offer:

> If we are to solve the multitude of environmental problems that we face, then we must begin with our connection to country. We must repair and regrow relationships between peoples and peoples, and people and country that have been damaged by dispossession. Despite the environmental devastation that has been wreaked on Australia, this ancient continent continues to nourish and sustain all who live here. It gives us our water and food and it protects us in ways we do not often imagine. We cannot survive here without a loving land that cares for us, and all Australians, Aboriginal and non-Aboriginal alike are bound to its rise and fall.
>
> (p. 19)

As early as 1962, American scientist and environmentalist Rachel Carson pre-empted our current global predicament warning that 'we are dealing with dangerous things and it may be too late to wait for positive evidence of danger' (p. 16). Numerous international reports (Stern 2006, United Nations Environment Program (UNEP) 2012, World Watch Institute 2010), intergovernmental meetings

(United Nations Climate Change Conferences in Copenhagen, Denmark 2009 and Cancún, Mexico 2010, and the Rio plus 20 United Nations Conference on Sustainable Development, Rio de Janeiro, Brazil 2012), and published literature by eminent long-term advocates (Flannery 2010, Shiva 2012, Suzuki 2010) all apprise us of current dangers and immanent threats. Further, parts of the world media regularly call for urgent changes in the ways we live even though, at times, the messages seem to lose topicality stifled by 'debates' about, say, the role of human activity as a cause for climate change, controversies about carbon taxes, or the need for renewable energy sources. Our position is that the issues are omnipresent. It is 'now or never' that we actively seek sustainability and, according to Bonnett (2002: 19), 'for authentic human being the attitude of sustainability is not a bolt on option but a necessity'. Without fundamental change, the future appears perilous to many, with the biggest concerns resonating for children and future generations.

Critically, education is identified as a key platform for facilitating societal change and progressing sustainably in both formal and non-formal education sectors (Bonnett 2002, Huckle 2006, Sterling 2001, Stibbe 2009, Stone 2009). A key global initiative promoting education as a driving force for sustainability has been the UNESCO Decade of Education for Sustainable Development 2005–2014 (DESD) (UNESCO 2005). In broad terms, formal education, particularly the school sector, has responded with a range of international initiatives cited in UNESCO's most recent review (UNESCO 2012). In Australia, the DESD was enacted through iterations of a national curriculum framework for environmental education (Commonwealth of Australia Department of Environment and Heritage (DEH) 2005, 2007, Commonwealth of Australia Department of Environment Water Heritage and the Arts (DEWHA) 2009) and the establishment of the Australian Research Institute for Education for Sustainability (ARIES) (Tilbury et al. 2005).

Education for sustainability is widely promoted nationally and internationally as the vehicle for transformative change for living sustainably and is described as life-long learning. Yet, as we have written elsewhere (Elliott and Davis 2009), the purposeful engagement of the early childhood field with education for sustainability has been slow. Our discussions in the aforementioned paper were reaffirmed by the UNESCO mid-term review of the Decade of Education for Sustainable Development (DESD) 2005–2014 (2009: 49) which stated that 'in many parts of the world the role of early childhood education in developing and implementing ESD is not always clear and therefore hardly emphasized'. This situation, as we have noted, is rapidly changing with recent initiatives provoking greater uptake. We see this text as an outcome of the shift in energy within the early childhood education field as interest and action coalesce.

In the section above, the origins and orientation of this international research publication, the practitioner advocacy base history, and global imperatives driving our work set the scene for the chapters that follow. Given the complexities and differences in terminology in this arena, however, it is pertinent to provide an introductory guide to relevant key concepts.

Clarifying key concepts

A range of concepts that include early childhood, environmental education, sustainability, education for sustainability and education for sustainable development are highlighted here. We readily acknowledge that in exploring these concepts we are articulating our own particular perspectives as individual researchers, and that these are minority world perspectives; others may prefer different interpretations. Internationally, majority world perspectives are an acknowledged silence in researched understandings of the complexities of sustainability, as they are in so many areas of research endeavour. Thus, we see that what is presented here is simply a platform for future ECEfS research, rather than an incontestable volume. We trust that future researchers will recognize it as a starting point, a beginning that opens doors to alternative frameworks, and new and challenging possibilities. Here, however, the reader is alerted to some of the complexities related to key concepts, prior to fully engaging with this text.

For readers not familiar with the early childhood field, *early childhood* is commonly defined as the period of human life from birth to eight years (Bredekamp and Copple 1997) and most chapter authors refer to research related to children in this age grouping. Young children across this age span may be participating in a range of education and care programs variously referred to as kindergarten, preschool, long day care, nursery, early primary school years, or preparatory class. Such settings may be led by educators with varying qualifications including bachelors degrees offered by universities, and diplomas or certificates offered by vocational colleges. Often, too, there are volunteers working directly with children in these settings. The philosophies, pedagogies and curriculum frameworks informing teaching and learning across the range of programs and settings vary significantly on an international scale, reflecting the impacts of histories, cultures and politics as well as the shifting early childhood education paradigms and theories that have played a part in shaping how educators work with children. There is no one philosophy or theory of early childhood education to which to refer the reader. For further investigation, Dahlberg *et al.* (1999), James *et al.* (1998), MacNaughton (2003) and Woodhead (2006) provide informative insights into these shifts and changes.

Environmental education, too, can be viewed historically. It was originally framed and promoted as the antidote to growing concerns about a range of environmental issues through the 1960s and 1970s (Gough 1997) and was promoted in many parts of the world through pivotal international meetings instigated by UNESCO, mainly in industrialized nations, including in Europe, the United States, Japan, Australia and New Zealand. For example, environmental education was enshrined in *The Belgrade Charter* (UNESCO UNEP 1975) and *The Tbilisi Declaration* (UNESCO UNEP 1977) as a means of building awareness and knowledge of human interdependencies with the environment and to promote the resolution of environmental issues. Environmental education was the term readily applied internationally throughout the 1980s; even so, there are robust ongoing debates about environmental education and its history (we refer readers to Sauve (2005) and McKeown and Hopkins (2003)).

In the 1980s and beyond, *The Brundtland Report* (WCED 1987) and *Agenda 21* (UNCED 1992) signalled a shift to *sustainability* as a more encompassing term that recognized the dynamic interplay of social, political, cultural, economic, and environmental realms. Note that sustainability also encompasses an overriding temporal dimension; it is not only about humanity here and now, but promotes longer-term thinking and action-taking for the intergenerational equity of all species on the planet. As Inoue argues in Chapter 5, however, the potential overuse and misuse of the term sustainability across a range of often contradictory spheres may reduce its potency.

Education for sustainability has mostly supplanted environmental education as the term of choice in Australia and New Zealand, although at times these terms are used together or interchangeably (Commonwealth of Australia Department of Environment and Heritage (DEH) 2005, Stevenson, Brody *et al.* 2013). The term environmental education is more commonly employed in the United States and across Asia, while *education for sustainable development* is applied in European countries (UNESCO 2005). Each chapter author here aligns with their particular term of preference drawing on local historical, cultural and political contexts; interchangeability of terms is sometimes evident. Again, Inoue (Chapter 5) reminds us that 'researchers and practitioners alike should be cognisant of the ambiguities and politics embedded in the concepts of environmental education/education for sustainable development/education for sustainability'. As Australian co-editors, our preference is for education for sustainability; however, we have not sought to change chapter authors' preferences, but simply ensure consistency within each chapter.

Education for sustainability and its various iterations are most often characterized by a list of principles (Commonwealth of Australia Department of Environment Water Heritage and the Arts (DEWHA) 2009, Sterling 2001) such as holistic, experiential, critically-reflective, collaborative, problem-based, systemic and participatory. There is no one right way to engage in education for sustainability, particularly in a dynamic global context where change is the only constant (Stibbe and Luna 2009). However, drawing on the aims of the *United Nations Decade of Education for Sustainable Development* (UN DESD 2005–2014) (UNESCO, 2005), Davis (2010) and others (Huckle 2006, Sterling 2001), we have previously argued that it is the transformative agenda of education for sustainability that must take precedence for global sustainable futures. We believe that learners should be empowered to act and change their ways of being in the world. This transformative agenda is reflected by the chapter authors published here, though as Miller (Chapter 4) comments, we must ensure that action does not supplant deep thinking, especially around complex notions of race and self-identity.

Recognizing multiplicities in EfS research

While it is acknowledged that there is a 'small research base upon which to grow' (Davis 2010: 38), research itself has frequently been cited as a key element in moving forward in ECEfS (UNESCO 2008a), with this publication indicative that ECEfS research is now clearly emerging internationally. The researchers represented here embrace diverse theoretical frames that include: social constructionism, communitarianism, post colonialism, eco psychology, conflict theory, systems theory, identity theory and critical theory, thus creating a 'multiplicity platform' (Brooker and Edwards 2010). Additionally, a range of methodological approaches including ethnography, action research, discourse analysis, longitudinal research projects and case study extend the reader further in multiple directions. Capturing these multiplicities at this particular juncture, as previously identified by Elliott *et al.* (2013), sets the scene for exploring further ways forward. These might include, for example, Deleuzian rhizomatic methodologies (Deleuze and Guattari 1987) or post-human perspectives (Taylor *et al.* 2012). We invite readers to question where the gaps and silences in ECEfS research lie, and to explore, and add to, these evolving multiplicities.

Reflecting on key themes

As co-editors, we have shared a unique opportunity to review and edit, many times over, the chapters contained in this text, each time seeing new perspectives and thoughts, and identifying common themes amongst the chapters. Three thematic clusters became apparent in our analysis: Cluster 1, a small, but thematically-significant group, identifies core values and ethics as offering opportunities for deeper reflection on ECEfS; Cluster 2, reflects the impacts of diverse historical and sociocultural contexts; and, Cluster 3 the largest, offers broad coverage of ideas around curriculum and pedagogy. An overview of each cluster is now presented. However, in describing these we readily acknowledge that some chapters align with themes from two or more clusters.

Cluster 1: A theme of core values and ethics is evident in the small number of chapters comprising Cluster 1 of this publication. Three theoretically-focused chapters by Davis (Chapter 1), Johansson and Hägglund (Chapter 2) and Ritchie (Chapter 3) are strategically placed to the fore to alert the reader to the depth of critical reflection now occurring in ECEfS in relation to children's rights, values, democracy and learning through Indigenous perspectives and knowledges. Two later chapter authors in Cluster 3, Mackey (Chapter 11), and Phillips (Chapter 12), also discuss these issues in the context of their research. All of these authors place values and ethics around children's rights, democracy, social justice, Indigeneity, civic participation and citizenship at the core of thinking and rethinking how early childhood educators and researchers might engage with ECEfS.

Cluster 2: While we are most familiar with the historical and sociocultural contexts relevant to the, somewhat, *ad hoc* evolution of ECEfS in Australia, a review of the chapters from authors in other parts of the world provide stories of the unique impacts of their own local contexts in enabling or deterring paradigm shifts in the field. A number of authors clustered here are long-term ECEfS advocates who articulate the necessity of overcoming the apparent political marginalization of ECEfS, for example, Chua (Chapter 6), Inoue (Chapter 5) and Miller (Chapter 4). In some countries, the contrast between historically and socioculturally assumed positions about the environment and children, and the researched realities uncovered in the early childhood field are compelling. Sageidet (Chapter 7) discusses tensions between Norwegian traditions and current lifestyles and environmental responsibilities that require further research, while Ärlemalm-Hagsér and Engdahl (Chapter 13) in Cluster 3 also identify discrepancies between the cultural values of democracy and children's participatory rights and their enactment in early childhood education in Sweden. The chapters by Miller (Chapter 4) and Ritchie (Chapter 3) (Cluster 1) argue strongly for Indigenous cultural perspectives as integral to conceptions of ECEfS. Miller (Chapter 4) offers a thought-provoking discussion focusing on whiteness, racism, and the historical, and ongoing, marginalization of Australian Indigenous peoples, as issues for in-depth consideration while Ritchie's chapter (Chapter 3) explores relationships with Indigenous Maori in education for sustainability and the ways that the *Te Whāriki* bicultural early childhood curriculum (New Zealand Ministry of Education 1996) supports such work.

In summary, while advocating for the urgent international uptake of ECEfS, the overriding message is that 'one size does not fit all'; the research documented here identifies the diversity of historical and sociocultural contexts that have impacted, and will continue to impact, on ECEfS implementation in the field. We restate our mindfulness that the authors represented in this volume offer primarily majority world perspectives and that ECEfS is envisaged and enacted differently across the globe. We welcome future reports from a wider international community to further develop ideas and perspectives in both ECEfS practice and in research.

Cluster 3: As already noted, it is perhaps not surprising, given the historical practitioner base of ECEfS and the number of novice researchers whose work is published here, that much of the research reported in this text is clustered around curriculum and pedagogy. All chapters in this cluster highlight research aligned with the transformative agenda as per our original publication intention, and clearly align with the urgent necessity for change towards sustainable living. We argue that transformative approaches to curriculum design and teaching and learning offer a vehicle for building on early childhood philosophical and pedagogical traditions. Pramling Samuelsson and Kaga (UNESCO 2008a: 13) acknowledge 'it is not necessary to invent "new" pedagogies in order to "do" education for sustainability in the early years – one can build on its pedagogical traditions to do so'. Previously, we have proposed the pedagogical advantage of early childhood education in the uptake of education for sustainability (Elliott and Davis 2009). The key research message here is about critically reflecting on curriculum and pedagogy and actively seeking different ways of thinking, acting and relating (Kemmis 2009).

Authors Ärlemalm-Hagsér and Engdahl (Chapter 13), Elliott (Chapter 8), Ji and Stuchmke (Chapter 10), Mackey (Chapter 11), Phillips (Chapter 12) and Young and Cutter-Mackenzie (Chapter 9) variously document how in-service teachers and young children have participated in potentially transformative experiences. In particular, Ärlemalm-Hagsér and Engdahl (Chapter 13) and Ji and Stuchmke (Chapter 10) explore project approaches to curriculum, Phillips (Chapter 12) explores storytelling as a pedagogical tool in ECEfS, while Elliott (Chapter 8) and Young and Cutter-Mackenzie (Chapter 9) focus on in-service teachers' participation in professionally critical reflection about sustainability and their roles as leaders in centre transformation. We assert the underlying imperative that changes towards sustainability in the early childhood field are not only informed by research, but are facilitated by research.

A sub-theme embedded within the chapters in this cluster is outdoor nature-based studies highlighted by Barratt et al. (Chapter 14), Chawla and Rivkin (Chapter 15), Elliott (Chapter 8) and Sundberg and Ottander (Chapter 17). Their research reinforces the importance of connections with nature, oft-cited as foundational to understandings and enactment of sustainability, but alerts readers to questions about whether nature experiences, alone, are enough to promote sustainability. Aligned with the above nature orientation is discussion about place-based education supported by Mackey (Chapter 11), but also Ritchie (Chapter 3) (Cluster 1 and Miller (Chapter 4) (Cluster 2), who draw on New Zealand Maori and Australian Indigenous perspectives to inform their arguments. More broadly, the relevance of community experiences and partnerships in early childhood education is evident in the chapters by Ärlemalm-Hagsér and Engdahl (Chapter 13), Barratt et al. (Chapter 14), Chawla and Rivkin (Chapter 15), Ji and Stuhmcke (Chapter 10), Mackey (Chapter 11), Phillips (Chapter 12) and Young and Cutter-Mackenzie (Chapter 9). Throughout these chapters, children are viewed as active, visible and engaged participants and decision-makers in their communities, a core tenet of ECEfS from our perspective. Another sub-theme suggests integrated or interdisciplinary pedagogical approaches as relevant and effective in both early childhood teacher education and in early childhood settings (O'Gorman (Chapter 16), Phillips (Chapter 12), Sundberg and Ottander (Chapter 17)).

For chapter authors Gilbert et al. (Chapter 18), O'Gorman (Chapter 16) and Sundberg and Ottander (Chapter 17), critical reflection begins with pre-service teacher education. These authors offer insights into the challenges of, and potential approaches for, promoting pre-service teachers deeper engagement with EfS. In other longitudinal case studies of early career primary teachers, Kennelly (2011) identified a number of factors impacting on school-based implementation of education for sustainability; most importantly, she cites that pre-service teacher education plays a pivotal role. We suspect the same is true for early childhood teacher education and the chapters offered here provide avenues for further exploration. Overall, we question what aspects of curriculum and pedagogy have yet to be examined through a lens of sustainability, and which of the evolving research theories and methodologies might be relevant for future scrutiny.

To reiterate, our analysis of key chapter themes identified three thematic clusters: core values and ethics; historical, cultural and political contexts; and, curriculum and pedagogy. We currently view the relationship between these clusters as a funnelling of ECEfS research – from a strongly-evident curriculum and pedagogy research base, then to the impacts of contexts, then to the smaller, but critically-reflective theorizing around core values and ethics. The challenge now is to reverse this funnelling through ongoing and deepening reflection and opening up to alternative possibilities. Thus, in presenting these chapters we have deliberately placed Cluster 1 chapters as preceding Clusters 2 and 3. Opening upwards and outwards through critical reflection around core values and ethics (Cluster 1) and investigation of theoretical and methodological multiplicities will both inform and inspire future ECEfS research and practice. The depth of reflection demanded of researchers and practitioners, alike, is evident in Bonnett's (2002: 14) description of education for sustainability as a 'frame of mind' that:

> represents a perspective on that set of the most fundamental ethical, epistemological, and metaphysical considerations which describe human being; a perspective which is both theoretical and practical in that it is essentially concerned with human practices and the conceptions and values that are embedded in them.

In our frame of mind, education for sustainability is viewed as a co-evolution of social and biophysical systems played out in responsive and responsible relationships. The challenge is to translate these ideals into early childhood educational praxis, and we firmly believe that research is essential to meeting this challenge. As a group of researchers originally drawn together through the Transnational Dialogues, we seek the paradoxes, holes, barriers, silences and gaps for moving forward in what we consider to be the most compelling cause of our time. We acknowledge that there are large gaps in this text and that a wider research agenda might include, for example: links between early childhood education and young children's citizenship, wellbeing and sustainability; children's impacts on others' (particularly adult) sustainable practices; leadership for sustainability in early childhood settings; the impacts and potential of popular culture and wired technologies on children's sustainability thinking and activism; rethinking of ethical relationships/interactions between children and nature, in particular with animals; and, many more topics and themes too numerous to mention that we know are missing in this volume. To reiterate, the silence of majority world perspectives where sustainability has even more immediate dire consequences for children, is a chasm that needs addressing.

As the early childhood field increasingly engages internationally with ECEfS, it is vital that the research base continues to grow to help shape and move the field forward. Reid and Scott (2006) note in relation to environmental education research more generally, that we want nothing less than a 'healthy field of inquiry, brimming with ideas and perspectives on its past, present and future' (p. 1). It will not be in anyone's interests for the field to expand without strong, underpinning theoretical frameworks and an evidence-base. Good research adds legitimacy to what early childhood practitioners do. It informs critique and improvement of programs and projects, enhances prospects for funding to support further development of the field, minimizes the replication of mistakes and, through exposure to theorizing and review, ensures that ECEfS will no longer be marginalized and will take its legitimate place as an important contributor to global sustainability.

References

Ang, L. (2010) 'Editorial. From caring, responsible children to a sustainable future: Education for sustainability in Asia and the Pacific', *Journal of Action Research Today in Early Childhood, Special Issue*, pp. 3–4.

Ärlemalm-Hagsér, E. and Sandberg, A. (2011) 'Sustainable development in early childhood education: in-service students' comprehension of the concept', *Environmental Education Research*, 17(2): 187–200.

Barratt-Hacking, E. B., Cutter-Mackenzie, A. and Barratt, R. (2013) 'Children as active researchers' in R. B. Stevenson, M. Brody, J. Dillon, and A. E. J. Wals (eds) (2013) *International handbook of research on environmental education.* New York: Routledge, pp. 438–48.

Bonnett, M. (2002) 'Education for sustainability as a frame of mind', *Environmental Education Research*, 8(1), 9–20.

Bredekamp, S. and Copple, C. (eds) (1997) *Developmentally Appropriate Practice in Early Childhood Programs,* revised edition, Washington, DC: National Association for the Education of Young Children.

Brooker, L. and Edwards, S. (eds) (2010) *Engaging Play,* Maidenhead: Open University Press.

Commonwealth of Australia Department of Climate Change and Energy Efficiency (DCCEE) (2011) *Australian Climate Commission Report: The Critical Decade,* Canberra: Department of Climate Change and Energy Efficiency.

Commonwealth of Australia Department of Environment and Heritage (DEH) (2005) *Education for a Sustainable Future: A National Environmental Education Statement for Schools,* Carlton: Curriculum Corporation.

Commonwealth of Australia Department of Environment and Heritage (DEH) (2007) *Caring for Our Future,* Canberra: Commonwealth Department of Environment and Heritage.

Commonwealth of Australia Department of Environment Water Heritage and the Arts (DEWHA) (2009) *Living Sustainably: National Action Plan,* Canberra: Commonwealth Department of Environment Water Heritage and the Arts.

Corsaro, W. A. (1997) *The Sociology of Childhood,* Thousand Oaks, CA: Pine Forge Press.

Dahlberg, G., Moss, P. and Pence, A. (1999) *Beyond Quality in Early Childhood Education and Care: Postmodern Perspectives,* London: Falmer Press.

Davis, J. (2009) 'Revealing the research "hole" of early childhood education for sustainability: A preliminary survey of the literature', *Environmental Education Research*, 15(2): 227–41.

Davis J. (ed.) (2010) *Young Children and the Environment: Early Education for Sustainability,* Melbourne: Cambridge Press.

Davis, J. M. (2010) 'Early childhood education for sustainability: Why it matters, what it is, and how whole centre action research and systems thinking can help', *Journal of Action Research Today in Early Childhood, Special Issue,* pp. 35–44.

Davis, J., Gibson, M., Pratt, R., Eglington, A. and Rowntree, N. (2005) 'Creating a culture of sustainability: From project to integrated education for sustainability at Campus Kindergarten' in W. L. Filho (ed.), *The International Handbook of Sustainability Research,* Paris: UNESCO, pp. 563–94.

Deleuze, G. and Guattari, F. (1987) *A Thousand Plateaus: Capitalism and Schizophrenia,* trans. B. Massumi. Minneapolis, MN: University of Minnesota Press.

Duhn, I., Bachmann, M. and Harris, K. (2010) 'Becoming ecologically sustainable in early childhood education', *NZCER, Early Childhood Folio,* 14(1): 2–6.

Elliott, S. and Emmett, S. (1991) *Snails Live in Houses Too: Environmental Education for the Early Years,* Sydney: Martin Educational.

Elliott, S. and Davis, J. (2009) 'Exploring the resistance: An Australian perspective on educating for sustainability in early childhood', *International Journal of Early Childhood,* 41(2): 65–77.

Elliott, S., Edwards, S., Davis, J. and Cutter-Mackenzie, A. (2013) *ECA Best of Sustainability: Research, Theory and Practice,* Deakin West, ACT: Early Childhood Australia.

Flannery, T. (2008) *Now or Never: A Sustainable Future for Australia,* Melbourne: Black Inc.

Flannery, T. (2010) *Here on Earth: An Argument for Hope,* Melbourne: Text Publishing.

Gordon Community Children's Centre (1993), *Playing for Keeps,* Geelong, Victoria: Gordon Technical College.

Gough, A. (1997) *Education and the Environment,* Melbourne: Australian Council for Educational Research.

Gough, N. (2013) 'Thinking globally in environmental education: A critical history' in R. B. Stevenson, M. Brody, J. Dillon and A. E. J. Wals (eds) (2013) *International handbook of research on environmental education.* New York: Routledge, pp. 33–44.

Hägglund, S. and Pramling Samuelsson, I. (2009) 'Early childhood education and learning for sustainable development and citizenship', *International Journal of Early Childhood,* 41(2): 49–63.

Haluza-DeLay, R. (2013) 'Educating for environmental justice' in Stevenson, R. B. Stevenson, M. Brody, J. Dillon and A. E. J. Wals (eds) (2013) *International Handbook of Research on Environmental Education.* New York: Routledge, pp. 394–403.

Hart, P. (2002) 'Narrative, knowing, and emerging methodologies in environmental education research: Issues of quality', *Canadian Journal of Environmental Education,* 7(2): 140–65.

Huckle, J. (2006) *Education for Sustainable Development: A Briefing Paper for the Training and Development of Agency in Schools.* Online. Available: http://john.huckle.org.uk/publications_downloads.jsp (accessed 20 November 2008).

James, A., Jenks, C. and Prout, A. (1998) *Theorizing Childhood,* Cambridge: Polity Press.

Johansson, E. (2009) 'The preschool child of today – The world-citizen of tomorrow?', *International Journal of Early Childhood,* 41(2): 79–85.

Kemmis, S. (2009) 'Action research as a practice-based practice', *Educational Action Research,* 17(3): 463–74.

Kennelly, J. (2011) *Education for Sustainability and Pre-service Teacher Education.* Doctoral thesis, Armidale, NSW: University of New England.

Laszlo, E. (2010) *The Chaos Point,* London: Piatkus Books.

Mackey, G. and Vaealiki, S. (2011) 'Thinking of children: Democratic approaches with young children in research', *Australasian Journal of Early Childhood,* 36(2), 82–6.

McKeown, R. and Hopkins, C. (2003) 'EE ESD: Defusing the worry'. *Environmental Education Researcher*, 9(1): 117–28.

MacNaughton, G. (2003) *Shaping Early Childhood*. Maidenhead: Open University Press.

Morgan, S., Mia, T. and Kwaymullina, B. (2008) *Heartsick for Country*, Fremantle, WA: Fremantle Press.

New Zealand Ministry of Education (1996) *Te Whāriki. He whāriki mātauranga mō ngā mokopuna o Aotearoa: Early Childhood Curriculum*, Wellington: Learning Media.

Palmer, J. (1995) 'How research is informing practice in environmental education', *Environmental Education*, Autumn: 33–34.

Phillips, L. (2010) 'Social justice storytelling and young children's active citizenship', *Discourse: Studies in the Cultural Politics of Education*, 31(3): 363–76.

Reid, A. D. and Scott, W. A. H. (2006) 'Researching Education and the Environment: retrospect and prospect', *Environmental Education Research*, 12(3–4): 571–88.

Reid, A. and Payne, P. (2013) 'Handbooks of EE research: For further reading and writing', in R. B. Stevenson, M. Brody, J. Dillon and A. E. J. Wals (eds) (2013) *International Handbook of Research on Environmental Education*. New York: Routledge, pp. 529–41.

Ritchie, J. (2010) 'Fostering communities: Ecological sustainability within early childhood education', *Early Education*, 47(Autumn/Winter): 10–14.

Sandberg, A. and Ärlemalm-Hagsér, E. (2011) 'Play and learning with fundamental values in focus', *Australasian Journal of Early Childhood*, 36(1): 44–50.

Sauve, L. (2005) 'Currents in environmental education: Mapping a complex and evolving pedagogical field', *Canadian Journal of Environmental Education*, 10(Spring): 11–37.

Shiva, V. (2012) *Making Peace with the Earth: Beyond Resource, Land and Food Wars,* Cambridge, MA: South End Press.

Siraj-Blatchford, J., Smith, K. C. and Pramling Samuelsson, I. (2010) *Education for Sustainable Development in the Early Years,* Gothenburg, Sweden: OMEP.

Sobel, D. (1996) *Beyond Ecophobia,* Great Barrington, MA: The Orion Society.

Sterling, S. (2001) *Sustainable Education: Re-Visioning Learning and Change*, Cambridge: Green Books.

Stern, N. (2006) *Stern Review on the Economics of Climate Change,* London: The Stationery Office.

Stibbe, A. (ed.) (2009) *The Handbook of Sustainability Literacy: Skills for a Changing World*, Foxhole, United Kingdom: Green Books Ltd.

Stibbe, A. and Luna, H. (2009) 'Introduction', in A. Stibbe (ed.) *The Handbook of Sustainability Literacy: Skills for a Changing World*. Cambridge: Green, pp. 9–16.

Stevenson, R. B., Brody, M., Dillon, J., and Wals, A. E. J. (eds) (2013) *International Handbook of Research on Environmental Education,* New York: Routledge.

Stevenson, R. B., Wals, A. E. J., Dillon, J. and Brody, M. (2013) 'Introduction: An orientation to environmental education and the handbook' in R. B. Stevenson, M. Brody, J. Dillon and A. E. J. Wals (eds) *International Handbook of Research on Environmental Education*. New York: Routledge, pp. 1–6.

Stone, M. (2009) *Smart by Nature: Schooling for sustainability,* Berkeley, CA: Watershed Media/University of California Press.

Suzuki, D. (2010) *The Legacy: An Elder's Vision for a Sustainable Future,* Crow's Nest, NSW: Allen and Unwin.

Targowska, A. (1991) *An Environmental Curriculum for Preschool Children,* Karawara, WA: Lady Gowrie Child and Neighbourhood Centre.

Taylor, A., Pacini-Ketchabaw, V. and Blaise, M. (2012) 'Children's relations to the more-than-human world', *Contemporary Issues in Early Childhood*, 13(2): 81–5.

Tilbury, D. (1994) 'The critical learning years for environmental education', in R. Wilson (ed.) *Environmental Education at the Early Childhood Level*. Troy, OH: North American Association for Environmental Education, pp.11–13.

Tilbury, D., Coleman, V. and Garlick, D. (2005) *A National Review of Environmental Education and its Contribution to Sustainability in Australia: School Education,* Canberra: Australian Government Department of the Environment and Heritage and Australian Research Institute in Education for Sustainability.

UNCED (1992) *Promoting Education and Awareness and Public Training, Agenda 21, United Nations Conference on Environment and Development,* Conches, Brazil: UNCED.

UNESCO (2005) *Decade of Education for Sustainable Development 2005–2014: Draft International Implementation Scheme*, Paris: UNESCO.

UNESCO (2008a) *Early Childhood and its Contribution to a Sustainable Society,* Paris: UNESCO.

UNESCO (2008b) *The Gothenburg Recommendations on Education for Sustainable Development.* Online. Available: omep.vrserver2.cl/cgi-bin/procesa.pl?plantilla=/archivo.htmlandbri= omepandtab=art_6andcampo=c_fileandid=270 (accessed 30 January 2009).

UNESCO (2012) *Shaping the Education of Tomorrow,* Paris: UNESCO.

UNESCO UNEP (1975) *The Belgrade Charter: A Framework for Environmental Education.* Online. Available: http://unesdoc.unesco.org/images/0001/000177/017772eb.pdf (accessed 20 December 2010).

UNESCO UNEP (1977) Intergovernmental conference on environmental education: Tbilisi (USSR), 14–26 October 1997, Final Report. Paris: UNESCO.

UNICEF (1989) *United Nations Convention on the Rights of the Child.* Online. Available: www.unicef.org/crc/ (accessed 14 February 2014).

United Nations Environment Program (UNEP) (2012) *The Emissions Gap Report 2012*, Nairobi: UNEP.

Vaealiki, S. and Mackey, G. (2008) 'Ripples of action: Strengthening environmental competency in an early childhood centre', *NZCER Early Childhood Folio 12*, 7–11.

Wilson, R. (1993) *Fostering a Sense of Wonder During the Early Childhood Years,* Columbus, OH: Greyden Press.

Wilson, R. (ed.) (1994) *Environmental Education at the Early Childhood Level,* Troy, OH: North American Association for Environmental Education.

Woodhead, M. (2006) 'Changing perspectives on early childhood: Theory, research and policy', Paper commissioned for the Education for All Global Monitoring Report 2007, Strong foundations: Early childhood care and education.

World Commission on Environment and Development (WCED) (1987) *The Brundtland Report: Our Common Future,* Oxford: Oxford University Press.

World Watch Institute (2010) Environment and Climate. *Vital signs: Global trends that Shape Our Future.* Online. Available: http://vitalsigns.worldwatch.org/trends/environment-climate (accessed 1 February 2014).

World Wide Fund for Nature (WWF) (2011) *WWF Annual Review 2010,* Gland, Switzerland: WWF.

Cluster 1

Ethics and values

Examining early childhood education through the lens of education for sustainability

Revisioning rights

Julie Davis

Abstract

This chapter calls for rethinking of the rights base of early childhood education. The United Nations Convention on the Rights of the Child (UNCRC) (UNICEF 1989) has been seen as an important foundation internationally for early childhood education practice. In this chapter, I argue that while the UNCRC (1989) still serves its aspirational purpose, it is an inadequate vehicle for enacting early childhood education in the twenty-first century given the pressing challenges of sustainability. The UNCRC emerged from an individual rights perspective, and despite attempts to broaden the rights agenda towards greater child participation and engagement, these approaches offer an inadequate response to global sustainability concerns. In this chapter, I propose a five dimensional approach to rights that acknowledges the fundamental rights of children as espoused in the UNCRC and the call for agentic rights as advocated more recently by early childhood academics and practitioners. Additionally, however, discussion of collective rights, intergenerational rights and bio/ecocentic rights are forwarded, offering an *expanded* way to think about rights with implications for how early childhood education is practised and researched.

Introduction

We live in times of uncertainty and insecurity where there are increasingly urgent calls for the world's peoples to live more socially, economically and environmentally sustainable lives. UNICEF (2013) states, 'it is increasingly recognized that a sustainable world will require a shift in values, awareness and practices in order to change our currently unsustainable patterns of consumption and production' (p. 16). Education holds the key to the necessary shifts in thinking, values and practice required for these transitions (Sterling 2001, UNESCO 2005). Like all education sectors – indeed, all sectors of society – early education has a role to play in societies' transitions to sustainability. This calls for a shift from 'business as usual' in early childhood education. Here, I propose a starting point for this shift is revisioning children's rights, human rights and justice and how these concepts can be rethought for the challenges confronting humanity in the twenty-first century and beyond. At the core of my argument is that in early childhood education we currently conceptualize rights – as exemplified by the United Nations Convention on the Rights of the Child (UNCRC) (1989) with its origins in the social practices of liberal democracies post-World War 2 – far too narrowly.

While the ambitious, but aspirational goals of the UNCRC are as important now as ever before, societies of the twenty-first century are vastly different from those that framed the Universal Declaration on Human Rights (UDHR) and the UNCRC in the twentieth century. Socio-political, economic, and environmental dynamics have shifted dramatically. We live in a connected world with global movements of people and goods – made easier with the vibrancy, speed and ease of the Internet and social media. At the same time, the world appears to have become more fragmented and vulnerable with weakened economies, rising social tensions, uncontrolled human migrations, and fears about global pandemics and food security (Centre for Strategic and International Studies 2013). Such complex social, economic and environmental changes demand new responses from all sectors of society.

There has already been some reworking of the way children's rights were originally constituted in the UNCRC; however, the UNCRC, like the UDHR (1948) from which it is derived, is largely constituted as *individual* child rights (UN Regional Information Centre for Western Europe 2012). While I acknowledge that there are other early childhood scholars and practitioners who have been working at reframing children's rights, and discussing and problematizing participation rights for example, I propose a far wider conceptualization of rights, one that better meets the challenges of sustainable living now and for the future.

Why revise rights in early childhood education?

Education for sustainability is about creating changes in how we think, teach and learn; early childhood education has much to contribute to society's transformations towards sustainability. The starting point is our fundamental values, focusing in on children's rights, human rights and justice. My argument is not for any diminution of children's rights or any lessening of the universalization of human rights across the globe; what I do argue for is augmentation of thinking about children's/human rights if early childhood education is to make a lasting contribution for sustainability. Indeed, this chapter and the book, more broadly, is about elevating the rights of children as active citizens for sustainability (Johansson and Hagglund, Chapter 2). Consequently, just as there has been an evolution of children's rights from 'protection' rights to children as 'rights' holders', I argue for children as 'rights' partakers' to become the new norm, and for rights to be radically extended to include collective rights, intergenerational rights and rights beyond those held by humans.

By implication, an augmented view of children's rights asks that early childhood education be enacted differently. I contend that this challenges the current theories and pedagogies that prevail internationally in early childhood education – principally socio-cultural-historical approaches (e.g. Fleer 2010). I argue, instead, for eco-socio-cultural-historical and transformative theories and pedagogies to take early childhood education into the new territory that sustainability demands – similar to the proposal by Jickling (2013) who discusses a socio-construc-tivist/transformative education as a potential basis for Education for Sustainability (EfS). In so doing, I offer provocations and some possibilities for exploring how early childhood education might be enacted with an expanded rights framework.

What might an expanded rights framework look like?

Prompted by the challenges of sustainability, I propose a revisioning of rights in early childhood education that brings new dimensions into play. These are outlined below and illustrated in Figure 1.1, as:

- foundational rights as promulgated by the UNCRC
- agentic participation rights
- collective rights
- intergenerational rights, and
- bio/ecocentric rights

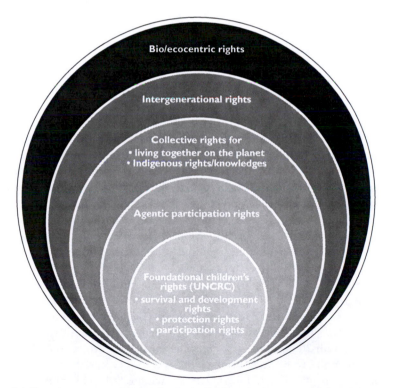

Figure 1.1 Five dimensions of rights for early childhood education in light of the challenges of sustainability

Explaining the dimensions

Here, I elaborate on each of the dimensions illustrated above. The starting point, as already noted, is the foundational and aspirational view of children's rights drawn from the UNCRC. The second dimension expands on child participation rights, but calls for active/agentic participation to be the norm. The third dimension explores collective rights as an addition to thinking about children's/human rights. The fourth dimension considers intergenerational rights, while the fifth expands beyond human rights to give consideration to the rights of all living beings and the non-living attributes of nature/natural environments. It is important at the outset, however, to acknowledge that these dimensions are not mutually exclusive; they overlap and seep into each other. Boundaries can be envisaged more as permeable membranes rather than impermeable barriers. I contend, though, that all dimensions must be considered if sustainably is ever to be realized. While it is logical that educators will focus on what they see as the best for the individual children they work with here and now, I propose that one cannot choose to ignore their collective rights, the rights of marginalized groups, future children, or non-human species when thinking about children's rights. There is no hierarchy or option associated with these dimensions, however, for elaboration purposes each dimension is addressed separately.

Dimension 1: supporting children's rights as foundational

One response to the tragedies of World War 2 were international efforts to entrench peace, rights and freedoms which led to the Universal Declaration on Human Rights (UDHR) adopted by the United Nations General Assembly in 1948. The UDHR (1948) universally recognizes that basic rights and fundamental freedoms are inherent to all humans, apply equally to everyone, and that every person is born free and equal in dignity and rights. Recognized as the foundation of international human rights law, it led to a range of more focused international human rights treaties, covenants and conventions.

One elaboration was the United Nations Declaration of the Rights of the Child (UNDRC), proclaimed in 1959, when world leaders determined that children and young people under 18 years of age required a special convention to protect them because of their perceived immaturity and potential vulnerability. This was later followed by the UNCRC (1989), the world's most ratified human rights treaty that became the first legally-binding international instrument to incorporate a wide range of human rights for children – civil, cultural, economic, political and social rights. In so doing, the Convention went beyond protective rights (MacNaughton, Hughes and Smith 2008) in recognizing children as human rights holders and not simply having rights to protection. The UNCRC has become the basis for discussion and implementation of children's rights within early childhood education around the globe (Bennett 2009, Sheridan and Pramling Samuelsson 2001).

The guiding principles of the Convention are encapsulated in 40 'articles' that revolve around rights to life, survival and development; non-discrimination and protection; and participation rights (UNICEF 2005). These are summarized below.

> *Survival and development rights:* These comprise rights to the resources, skills and contributions necessary for survival and full development, including rights to adequate food, shelter, clean water, formal education, primary health care, leisure, recreation and play, cultural activities and rights information.
>
> *Protection rights:* These rights include protection from child abuse, neglect, exploitation and cruelty, including the right to special protection in times of war, and protection from abuse in the criminal justice system.
>
> *Participation rights:* Participation rights include the right to express opinions, to have a say and to be heard in matters affecting their social, economic, religious, cultural and political life, the right to information, and freedom of association. Engaging in participation rights helps bring about the realization of all their rights and prepares children for an active role in society.
>
> (UNICEF 2005)

To summarize, like many academics and practitioners in early childhood education, I identify the Convention as foundational to our work. I acknowledge, too, ongoing discussions (Bennett 2009, Coady 2008) that enable early childhood educators to rethink different meanings of the Convention and to engage reflexively. Continuing this tradition of rethinking, and in light of the challenges of sustainability, I now offer some new thoughts about children's rights.

Dimension 2: recognizing children's agentic participation rights

Participation rights as readiness/preparation for children's active role in society is my starting point for discussion about Dimension 2. As noted above, having a voice, being heard/listened to, accessing information, and freedom of expression are fundamental rights constituted in the UNCRC. There are, however, two points for critique with this aspect of the Convention – one concerns images of children; the other relates to conceptualizations of active participation.

Regarding the first point, it is true that participation rights have been examined and rearticulated post-UNCRC (1989), to encompass issues of identity, autonomy, freedom of choice, expression of thoughts and views, and involvement in decision-making (Sheridan and Pramling Samuelsson 2001, Tomanovic 2000). Further, as MacNaughton, Hughes and Smith (2008) observe, contemporary research is now generating images of young children who:

- can construct and communicate valid meanings about the world and their place in it

- are capable social actors with a right to participate in our social, cultural and political worlds and to contribute valid and useful ideas
- know the world in alternative (not inferior) ways to adults
- have perspectives and insights that help adults better understand children's experiences.

Such images are of children as visible, social, active players in their various contexts. Nevertheless, changing the imagery of children is not enough to ensure agentic participation, which brings me to my second point of critique. I argue that the UNCRC is not explicit enough about the types of active participation that are possible for young children. As Coady (2008) states, children may be 'active' in the psycho-social sense without being demonstrably expressive 'social actors', and they may be both psycho-socially active and social actors without necessarily being 'agentic' in the more political sense of significantly influencing their situation, or being listened to.

I argue that images of children's participation – as well as images of children – also require reformulation as current conceptualizations and their attendant practices are outmoded for the dynamic, complex and challenging times in which we live. An Australian study about young peoples' participation in climate change responses, for example, identified that many participatory attempts are top-down, more concerned with process than product, and tended to replicate existing patterns of power and privilege. Overall, children remain largely invisible through tokenistic and poorly executed approaches to their participation (Strazdinis and Skeat 2011). Further, it is in professions such as paediatrics and public health (Meucci and Schwab 1997, Sheffield and Landrigan 2011), rather than in education, that calls for children's agentic participation, especially in light of climate change and other environmental threats, are being made. Early childhood educators, too, need to see active participation as offering agency to young children so that they can make contributions that create better conditions for both present and future childhoods (Daniels-Simmonds 2009, UNICEF 2013).

Dimension 3: recognizing collective rights

According to the UN Regional Information Centre for Western Europe (2012), existing human rights treaties including the UNCRC (1989) are poor vehicles for maintaining and supporting collective rights such as those aimed at creating the conditions necessary for a common sustainable existence, or for recognizing the rights of marginalized groups such as children, women, Indigenous peoples and the poor (Boyd 2010) who should be an integral part of sustainable communities. This is because most treaties reflect an individualistic concept of rights and rights-holders. Collective rights differ from individual rights. Rather than focusing on the individual independent of social groupings, the focus of collective human rights is on the rights of social groups. In contrast to the liberal proposition of the isolated human being, the idea of collective human rights begins with the view of humans as they really are, that is as social beings (Felice 1996).

While there may be public campaigns and educational programs that promulgate that individuals can 'fix the planet', the reality is that the issues confronting the globe are collective in origin, for example global financial crises, climate disruptions, human migrations, food and water security, overuse of non-renewable energy supplies, biodiversity and species losses. The problems and their solutions are complex, national, international and global in scale, requiring collective responses. Focusing on individual rights in the era of large-scale, global challenges indicates that our collective heads are deeply buried in the sand.

There is already strong evidence that individuals have poor responses to issues requiring collective answers. The tragedy of the commons, for example, refers to the depletion of a common pasture shared amongst herdsmen who act independently and rationally according to individual self-interest, despite understanding that depleting the common resource is against the group's best long-term interests (Hardin 1968). In this cautionary tale, a tragedy arises when individual consumers of an otherwise sustainable resource bring about its collapse as they seek to maximize individual benefit, rather than serving the collective interest. While no single act of consumption contributes much to the overall problem, the result of all individual actions is a collectively-inferior outcome in which the commons can no longer sustain ongoing consumption (Hickman and Bartlett 2001). The concept of 'the tragedy of the commons' has dire implications for any commonly-held resource and for resource overuse, when the cost of degrading it is lower than the cost of conserving and protecting it. The lasting legacy of the 'tragedy of the commons' comes from its persistent, ongoing and increasing relevance in the ways the environment is interacted with and utilized. In many ways, it is averting a common tragedy on a global scale that sustainability seeks to address.

Another aspect relevant to discussions about individual versus collective rights concerns how groups such as children, women, Indigenous and poor and destitute groups are represented within human rights frameworks and perspectives. Here, I confine discussion to Indigenous people's rights and representation because of acknowledged links between Indigenous peoples' perspectives and environmental and sustainability issues in many places across the globe.

Indigenous peoples' rights made their international debut in 1957 with the adoption of the Indigenous and Tribal Populations Convention by the International Labour Organization (ILO), later strengthened in 1966 when the UN General Assembly adopted the International Covenant on Civil and Political Rights (Shava 2013). The 1980s saw some UN agencies and international environmental organizations advocate for recognition of the value of Indigenous/traditional knowledges, particularly in bioconservation management, for example the World Conservation Strategy 1980). In 1982, a UN Working Group with the main mandate to prepare a draft Declaration on the Rights of Indigenous Peoples was established, approved only in 2007. This Declaration recognizes that 'respect for Indigenous knowledge, cultures and traditional practices contributes to sustainable and equitable development and proper management of the environment' (2008: 2).

Other initiatives connecting environment, sustainability and Indigenous rights and knowledges, all proclaimed in 1992, include the Earth Summit, the Earth Charter, Agenda 21, the Convention on Biological Diversity, and the Treaty on Environmental Education for Sustainable Development and Global Responsibility. While superficially these treaties and conventions give the appearance of inclusive and committed attention to Indigenous perspectives, a common critique is that in most conventions, Indigenous/traditional knowledges are viewed instrumentally and technically, perceived mainly as utilitarian in value and a resource to be extracted, documented, codified, decontextualized, universalized and widely applied (Shava 2013). Despite such criticism, however, there has been revitalization of Aboriginal languages, epistemologies, and pedagogies that recognize the importance of the land, privilege Indigenous voices, involve elders in Indigenous education, and that are seen as important factors in decolonization (Lowan-Trudeau 2013). Such revival and sharing also strengthens connections to what many Western scholars refer to as 'sense of place', a strong feeling of connectedness to a particular geographical area with deep feelings of relatedness leading to shared responsibility for both the non-human world as well as for the humans who co-habit these common spaces. For these reasons, Indigenous scholars such as Lowan-Trudeau (2013) and Shava (2013) and the non-Indigenous chapter authors in this text (Miller, Chapter 4 and Ritchie, Chapter 3), make robust claims for the inclusion of Indigenous voices within contemporary environmental and sustainability scholarship. As Lowan-Trudeau comments, an increasing number of Indigenous and non-Indigenous scholars support the perspective 'that the future success of our society rests on the combined wisdom of Aboriginal and non-aboriginal cultures' (2013: 405).

In summary, this discussion asks for a redefinition of rights towards a collective rights view aimed at bringing people together for the common, shared purpose of long-term survival. This has implications for early childhood educators, asking them to emphasize, not only individual child development and learning, but also learning opportunities within settings where the common good prevails. It also asks educators to think seriously about ways to embed Indigenous rights and perspectives – and those of other groups often marginalized – into daily practices.

Dimension 4: recognizing intergenerational rights

An extension of collective rights is intergenerational rights. Sustainability is much more than about the rights of current generations to strive for happy, healthy and secure lives. At the heart of the concept of sustainability is fairness and justice for all, including future generations. The injustice of one generation taking and using the resources and capital of the next, leaving the planet less equipped to meet the needs of future generations, is a matter of ethics and moral values. *Our Common Future* (also known as the Brundtland Report 1987), defines 'sustainable development' (sustainability) as 'development that meets the needs of the present without compromising the ability of future generations to meet their own needs' (WCED: 8). Ethical sustainability lies at the core of the challenges of environment and human development. Unless substantial change occurs, present generations are unlikely to pass on a healthy and diverse environment to future generations. As Beder (2011: 309) observes,

> Although future generations do not yet exist, it is reasonably certain that they will exist and they will require clean air and water and other basic physical requirements for life. And although it is not known who the individuals of the future will be – they are not individually identifiable – they have rights as a group or class of people, rather than individually, and we can have obligations and duties towards them.

An interesting extension of intergenerational justice is the concept of the 'chain of obligation'. Howarth (1992) argues that a chain of obligation stretches from the present into the indefinite future, and unless we ensure conditions favourable to the welfare of future generations, 'we wrong our existing children in the sense that they will be unable to fulfil their obligation to their children while enjoying a favourable way of live themselves' (p. 133). Thus, we should seek to leave a sustainable world for our children not only because it is actually beneficial to their future wellbeing, but because it qualitatively strengthens the moral and ethical position of our children towards their children. As Howarth identifies 'to the extent that principles of justice require equal treatment for contemporaries, they require equal treatment for future generations as well' (p. 135).

Hansen *et al.* (2011) note with disquiet that young people have not yet become very involved in the issue of the planet's future and need to be more insistent on intergenerational justice – after all, it is their futures that are being diminished. Mostly, these authors note, advocacy and actions to deal with issues such as climate change have been the efforts of adults on behalf of young people. In the case of the very young their inactivity is understandable, they observe. My response to Hansen *et al.*'s comment regarding young children's participation is that even the very young *can* become involved in issues that directly enhance their own futures and that contribute to intergenerational justice. As the UNCRC (General Comment No. 7 2005) notes, 'early childhood is a critical period for the realization of children's rights' (p. 1). It is through early childhood education that the processes of addressing intergenerational justice and equity can begin.

Dimension 5: recognizing biocentric/ecocentric rights

The final dimension in this augmented framework of rights for early childhood education centres on biocentric/ecocentric rights. I begin by introducing the concept of the Anthropocene, recently adopted by some leading scientists, scholars, commentators and organizations (e.g. The Geological Society of London). While the term is not a part of the official nomenclature of geology, it serves to mark the extent to which human activities have had a significant global impact on land use, ecosystems and biodiversity. The Anthropocene was coined in the early 1980s by ecologist Eugene F. Stoermer and popularized by Nobel Prize-winning atmospheric chemist, Paul Crutzen, who regards the influence of human behaviour on the Earth's atmosphere as so significant as to constitute a new geological epoch.

In denoting the Anthropocene, the most significant causal factor is anthropocentricism – literally, it means 'human-centred' – a perspective that regards humans as the most important entity on the planet. Rowe (2011) comments that anthropocentricism translates into a belief that human wellbeing is the central consideration of our concerns. Biocentrism, on the other hand, regards humans as just one of many biological species, and assigns inherent value to non-human organisms. Biocentrism holds that all living beings are equally valuable.

Ecocentrism goes one step further, also assigning value to Earth's non-living systems and processes, thus stressing that humans are reliant on the Earth's entire ecosystem, including elements (such as carbon, air and water and their interdependent cycles), landscapes, and environments such as river catchments. To some extent, ecocentrism equates with James Lovelock's (2003) 'Gaia Hypothesis'. In this theory, the Earth is considered a living organism in which its biological and physical parts are inextricably linked into a self-regulating system. While controversial, nevertheless, the Gaia hypothesis draws attention to the interconnections of biological and geological processes on a planetary scale (Vedwan 2011). Whether or not one accepts the idea of Gaia, an advantage of adopting a biocentric or ecocentric approach is that the value judgments underlying the discourse of human and environmental questions become framed differently. As Rowe (2011) notes 'when humans stop being the only measure of value, the scope of the debate is expanded' (p.31). Taken together, biocentrism and ecocentrism offer another dimension for revisioning rights in early childhood education.

While there are pros and cons on both sides of the anthropocentric versus bio/ecocentric debate, these positions do not necessarily need to be polarized, with recent debate moving towards recognition of the interconnectedness of the two positions (Rowe 2011). It is increasingly recognized that human survival and wellbeing demand a healthy Earth and, if the overall objective of a bio/ecocentric position is to protect biodiversity and the environment for its own sake, humans must also be protected as an integral component of that diversity. Such blurring between anthropocentrism and bio/ecocentricism has become evident in several recent national and international developments. Two of these are discussed here – the adoption of the 'Rights of Nature' in Ecuador's Constitution, and the codification of ecocide as a crime in the International Criminal Court (ICC).

Rights of Nature: Rights of Nature is a legal-political scholarship position that advocates for legal standing for the natural environment. This rights approach breaks from conventional environmental regulatory systems that regard nature as property, and that legalize and manage environmental degradation rather than preventing it. With the enactment of its 2008 Constitution, Ecuador – with some of the world's richest and most diverse natural ecosystems, high geographic diversity including the Galapagos Islands and the Amazon rainforests, severest impacts from logging and oil production, strong Indigenous communities, and high ecotourism potential – became the first country in the world to codify the Rights of Nature. The Constitution recognizes the inalienable rights of ecosystems to exist and flourish, gives people the authority to petition on the behalf of ecosystems, and requires the government to remedy violations of these rights.

Inclusion of the Rights of Nature also makes the Constitution more democratic and socially-inclusive reflecting Indigenous ideas of nature, *Pachamama*, as a mother that must be respected and celebrated. Incorporation of Indigenous concepts also has significance for the recognition of Indigenous groups and their right to preserve their lands and cultures. The combination of including human rights with the rights of nature in the same chapter of the Constitution is seen as offering more effective protection for Indigenous communities and is an example of bio/ecocentrism at work, 'effectively putting them on a par' (Rowe 2011). The Constitution also includes the concept of 'buen vivir' (good living), an alternative social development concept focusing on the attainment of a 'good life', akin to the concept of sustainable living, only realizable within a community, and in a community that includes nature. Perhaps this example signals a new, enacted possibility for human-environment relationships.

Ecocide, the fifth crime against peace: While codification of the Rights of Nature in the Ecuadorean Constitution focuses on nature's inherent rights, there have also been international developments to elevate environmental degradation to the level of criminality. Polly Higgins, international barrister and award-winning author, has proposed that the United Nations recognize 'ecocide' as the fifth crime against peace. (The others are war crimes, crimes against humanity, genocide, and the crime of aggression.) Ecocide is described as extensive damage to, or destruction of, ecosystems by humans, directly or indirectly, that drastically reduces enjoyment and livelihoods by local populations (Higgins 2012). The aim of establishing the crime of ecocide is to prevent war, loss and injury to life, dangerous industrial activity, pollution to all beings, and loss of traditional cultures, hunting grounds and foods. This movement places the rights of the environment and of all beings – not just humans – as central to living on the planet. While there are no mechanisms such as courts or other adjudicating bodies to enforce environmental rights, the advantage of identifying ecocide as a crime under the ICC may eventually lead to such a forum.

Historically, anthropocentrism has dominated human versus environment debates for decades. However, there does now appear to be a movement across a range of disciplines led, arguably, by law and philosophy, towards defining a bio/ecocentric approach to environment and sustainability matters. What might be the implications for early childhood education of reimagining relationships between humans and nature?

Implications of a reframed rights base for early childhood education

Above, I have outlined an expanded way of thinking about rights in early childhood education that emphasizes a shift from rights (and their associated responsibilities) viewed mainly as belonging to the individual towards collective rights. This shift facilitates thinking more deeply about the interconnected rights of children, of social groups and sub-groups within society, those of future generations, and the rights of non-human species and environments. Rethinking rights through these five dimensions also has implications for how early childhood education might be enacted. Here I offer some thoughts to advance this work.

1   As a starting point, *a focus/refocus on rights and values as central to our work* is demanded, but must acknowledge the limitations of the UNCRC. We need to be more expansive in how we think of rights. With respect to sustainability, we should discuss and debate how the UNCRC links to education for sustainability and identify relationships between enactment of rights and the responsibilities that ensue. For example, children have rights to ready access clean water and healthy food, but with these rights come responsibilities to conserve and equitably share resources, and to recognize the potential local and global environmental impacts of not doing so. Additionally, children's expressions of opinions and ideas about sustainability must be responsively listened to, and they must be supported to act on their ideas.

2   Given the troubled state of the planet and its implications for children, we need to rethink philosophies and approaches to *connect with the natural world as core business*, thus aiming to incorporate bio/ecocentric rights into early childhood practice. Early childhood education is well placed to do this with its long history of supporting children's interactions with/in nature, tracing back to Froebel's original conception of the kindergarten, a 'garden for children' where children were educated in close harmony with nature. The rise of the international *Children and Nature Network* (www.childrenandnature.org) in recent decades and the *Forest Kindergarten* movement (Europe, United Kingdom, Japan, New Zealand and now in Australia) are other education efforts that demonstrate growing re-interest in children connecting with the natural world. In a similar vein, the rise of gardening projects in schools and kindergartens, whether focusing on food and health (e.g. Stephanie Alexander's Kitchen Garden Foundation (www.kitchengardenfoundation.org.au) or for gardening experiences more broadly (e.g. The UK's Royal Horticultural Society's gardening initiatives (www.rhs.org.uk/children), indicate concerns about children's disengagement from nature coupled with efforts to remedy this. Building on Malaguzzi's idea of the environment as the 'third educator' (Gandini 1998: 177), Jane Bone also asks for a focus on 'the animal' (Bone 2013) in early childhood education, proposing animals as the 'fourth educator'.

3   *Consider the Earth Charter* as a starting point for integrating a reconceptualized rights framework into early childhood education programs and pedagogies. The Earth Charter (www.earthcharterinaction.org) is an expression of bio/ecocentrism that recognizes the interdependence of Humanity and Nature. The Charter has four principles: respect and care for the community of life; ecological integrity; social and economic justice; and democracy,

nonviolence, and peace. A children's version of the Charter (www.littleearthcharter.org) is already in use by educators in early childhood settings and schools who find it a useful guide for their work with children (see Pratt 2010). In this version, the four principles are reframed as:

- Be kind to each other and to plants and animals
- Take good care of the environment
- We are all equal
- Say yes to peace and no to violence.

4 *Take a holistic, 'common worlds' standpoint* where, as Taylor and Giugni (2012) comment, the ethics and politics of living together offers a centralizing framework for early childhood education in the age of sustainability. Such thinking has the power to promote ideas about collective rights and understandings that, for example, support explicit foci on Indigenous peoples, knowledges and perspectives, gender equity, learning for water or energy conservation, or playing outdoors in nature, not as separate elements of the early childhood curriculum, but as integral, connected parts of a systemic approach.

5 Finally, and perhaps most importantly, the field needs to *rethink the socio-constructivist frameworks that underpin early childhood education internationally*. Rethinking rights in early childhood education in light of the transformations necessary to address humanity's unsustainable, unjust and unhealthy living patterns necessitates a shift to critical, transformative early education – perhaps an eco-socio-cultural approach (see Elliott, 2014, for a fuller discussion of such a perspective). The field of education for sustainability (EfS) offers a lead here, as I explain in the following two paragraphs.

At the broadest level, EfS is about creating change, focused on rethinking and remaking educational programmes and pedagogies to support sustainable societies. EfS and its precursor, environmental education, have their origins in critical theory (Habermas 1971) and, while critical education has been taken up in early childhood education to examine gender, class and race (e.g. Ryan and Grieshaber 2004), this approach has not been all that dominant in early environmental education/education for sustainability.

EfS, however, is more than being about social critique; it focuses on creating change that integrates the social, environmental, and economic dimensions of societies. Hence, it also draws on transformative education approaches (German Advisory Council on Global Change 2012, Mezirow 2003) that require transformative teaching and learning practices where educators support children as agents of change around sustainability issues. Critical and transformative pedagogies encourage problem-solving, participating, making decisions and having choices, that is, they give children the power to do things (MacNaughton and Williams, 2009) and offer participatory, action-based pedagogies, focused on real-life issues of relevance and importance to children. Studies show that when educators promote children's success in 'making a difference', foundations are built for future resilience, agency and social participation (Stewart *et al.* 2004). Several past studies in early childhood EfS offer insights into how this can happen in early childhood settings (Davis *et al.* 2005, Elliott 2012). More recent examples and discussion of agentic, transformative approaches to early childhood education are at the core of this book.

Conclusion

Sustainability is a global issue that urgently needs addressing and for whom the most serious consequences are for children and future generations. It seems logical that early childhood educators who strive to have children's best interests at heart should be morally and ethically leading the way in educating for healthy, just and sustainable futures. Yet, historically, this has not been the case. Until recently, early childhood education has been a missing link in EfS efforts nationally and internationally. Fortunately, this is changing (see Chapter 1).

Early childhood education as an education field has embraced the UNCRC. In Australia, *Belonging, Being and Becoming: The Early Years Learning Framework for Australia (EYLF)* (DEEWR 2009: 5) upholds that early childhood educators 'reinforce in their daily practices the principles laid out in the UNCRC'. This is as it should be. The *National Curriculum for the Swedish Pre-school*, Lpfö-98 (The Swedish National Agency for Education 2010) has also been inspired by the principles of the UNCRC although, even in this national context where adherence to democratic principles is emphasized, its application in practice has been critiqued (Sandberg and Ärlemalm-Hagsér 2011; Sheridan and Pramling Samuelsson 2001). Nevertheless, my position is that relying on the 1989 UNCRC as the foundation for our rights work is too narrow for dealing with sustainability issues. With its World War 2 origins emphasizing the rights of the individual and child protection, and even with updates that include participation rights, the UNCRC cannot be anything but silent on collective rights, intergenerational rights and the rights of non-humans to live and thrive on the planet. Responding to the challenges of sustainability will not be achieved unless we all think more deeply and broadly about rights and justice. I suggest that the rights revisioning as outlined in this chapter offers a starting point. A consequence, of course, is that educators' practices, too, must change, and these changes must support children and adults working together for sustainability, with children as agentic participants at the heart of the changes.

This opening out of the rights framework for early childhood education also has implications for researchers. Thus, I finish this chapter by extending a provocation to early childhood education academics and researchers.

- How might an expanded rights framework alter the work of teacher educators?
- What ethical outcomes should we demand of teachers when sustainability is introduced into early childhood settings?

- What opportunities open up for cross-disciplinary research and dialogue for early childhood educators for example, with colleagues in law, philosophy, public health?
- How can we teach, more broadly, about rights within early childhood teacher education when sustainability is introduced?
- What theoretical approaches, paradigms and methodologies might better suit rethinking of rights in early childhood education?

While I do not have answers to such questions, I do hope this chapter sparks new ideas and thinking to guide early childhood education as we confront the sustainability challenges that lie before us.

References

Beder, S. (2011) 'Intergenerational justice', in H. S. Schiffman and P. Robbins (eds), *Green Issues and Debates: An A-to-Z Guide*, The Sage Reference Series in Green Society towards a Sustainable Future. Thousand Oaks, CA: Sage, pp. 309–14.

Bennett, J. (2009) 'A comparative analysis of provision made in national curricula to strengthen children's democratic participation in early childhood centres', in G. MacNaughton, P. Hughes and K. Smith (eds), *Young Children as Active Citizens: Principles, Policies and Pedagogies*. Newcastle-upon-Tyne: Cambridge Scholars Publishing, pp. 120–47.

Bone, J. (2013) 'The animal as fourth educator: a literature review of animals and young children in pedagogical relationships', *Australasian Journal of Early Childhood*, 38(2): 57–64:

Boyd, J. K. (2010) *2048: Humanity's Agreement to Live Together*. San Francisco, CA: Berrett-Koehler Publishers Inc.

Centre for Strategic and International Studies (CSIS) (2013) *Critical Questions for 2013: Global Challenges*. Online. Available: from www.cscs.org (accessed 26 January 2014).

Coady, M. (2008) 'Beings and becomings: Historical and philosophical considerations of the child as citizen' in G. MacNaughton, P. Hughes and K. Smith (eds), *Young Children as Active Citizens: Principles, Policies and Pedagogies*. Newcastle-upon-Tyne: Cambridge Scholars Publishing, pp. 2–14.

Daniels-Simmonds, L. (2009) *Early Childhood Professions' Beliefs and Practices Regarding the Rights of Young Children to Express Views and to be Heard*. Dissertation, Texas Women's University, Denton, Texas.

Davis, J. M., Gibson, M., Rowntree, N., Pratt, R., and Eglington, A. (2005) 'Creating a culture of sustainability: From project to integrated education for sustainability at Campus Kindergarten', in Walter L. Fihlo (ed.), *Handbook of Sustainability Research*, Frankfurt: Peter Lang, pp. 563-94.

Department of Education, Employment and Workplace Relations (DEEWR) (2009) *Belonging, Being and Becoming: The Early Years Learning Framework for Australia*. Online. Available: www.apo.org.au/node/18428 (accessed 26 January 2014).

Elliott, S. (2012) *Sustainable Outdoor Playspaces in Early Childhood Centres: Investigating Perceptions, Facilitating Change and Generating Theory*. Unpublished doctoral thesis, University of New England, Armidale, NSW.

Elliott, S. (2014) *Sustainability and the Early Years Learning Framework*. Mt Victoria, NSW: Pademelon.

Felice, W. F. (1996) *Taking Suffering Seriously: The Importance of Collective Human Rights*. Albany, NY: State University of New York Press. Online. Available: www.sunypress.edu/pdf/53499.pdf (accessed 26 January 2014).

Fleer, M. (2010) *Early Learning and Development: Cultural-historical Concepts in Play*, Melbourne: Cambridge University Press.

Gandini, L. (1998) 'Education and caring spaces', in C. Edwards, L. Gandini and G. Forman (eds), *The Hundred Languages of Children*. Greenwich, CT: Ablex.

German Advisory Council on Global Change (WBGU) (2012) *Factsheet 5: Research and Education: Drivers of Transformation*. Berlin: WBGU and German Government.

Habermas, J. (1971) *Knowledge and Human Interests*. Boston, MA: Beacon.

Hansen, J. et al. (2011) *Scientific Case for Avoiding Dangerous Climate Change to Protect Young People and Nature*. Online. Available: http://arxiv.org/ftp/arxiv/papers/1110/1110.1365.pdf (accessed 26 January 2014).

Hardin, G. (1968) 'The tragedy of the commons'. *Science*, 162(3859): 1243–8.

Hickman, J. and Bartlett, S. (2001) 'Global tragedy of the commons'. *Synthesis/Regeneration: A Magazine of Green Social Thought*, 24(Winter). Online. Available: www.greens.org/s-r/24/24-26.html (accessed 26 January 2014).

Higgins, P. (2012) *Eradicating Ecocide Global Initiative*. Online. Available: http://eradicatingecocide.com (accessed 26 January 2014).

Howarth, R. (1992) 'Intergenerational justice and the chain of obligation'. *Environmental Values*, 1: 133–40.

Jickling, B. (2013) 'Probing normative research in environmental education', in R. B. Stevenson, M. Brody, M. J. Dillon and A. E. J. Wals (eds), *International Handbook of Research on Environmental Education*. New York: Routledge, pp. 74–86.

Lovelock, J. (2003) 'Gaia: The living Earth', *Nature*, 426: 769–70.

Lowan-Trudeau, G. (2013) 'Indigenous environmental education research in North America', in R. B. Stevenson, M. Brody M., J. Dillon, and A. E. J. Wals (eds), *International Handbook of Research on Environmental Education*. New York: Routledge, pp. 404–8.

MacNaughton, G., Hughes, P. and Smith, K. (eds) (2008) *Young Children as Active Citizens: Principles, Polices and Pedagogies*. Newcastle-upon-Tyne: Cambridge Scholars Publishing.

MacNaughton, G. and Williams, G. (2009) *Techniques for Teaching Young Children: Choices in Theory and Practice*, 3rd edn, Frenchs Forest, NSW: Pearson Education Australia.

Meucci, S. and Schwab, M. (1997) 'Children and the environment: Young people's participation in social change'. *Social Justice*, 24(3): 1–10.

Mezirow, J. (2003) 'Transformative learning as discourse'. *Journal of Transformative Education (1541–3446)*, 1(1): 58–63.

Pratt, R. (2010) 'Practical possibilities and pedagogical approaches for early childhood educating for sustainability', in J. Davis (ed.), *Young Children and the Environment: Early Learning for Sustainability*. Melbourne: Cambridge University Press, pp. 104–53.

Rowe, B. M. (2011) 'Anthropocentrism versus biocentrism', in H. S. Schiffman and P. Robbins (eds), *Green Issues and Debates: An A-to-Z Guide*, 12. Sage Reference Series on Green Society towards a Sustainable Future. Thousand Oaks, CA: Sage.

Ryan, S. and Grieshaber, S. (2004) 'It's more than child development: Critical theories, research, and teaching young children'. *Young Children*, 59(6): 44–52.

Sandberg, A. and Ärlemalm-Hagsér, E. (2011a) 'Play and learning with fundamental values in focus'. *Australasian Journal of Early Childhood*, 36(1): 44–50.

Sandberg, A. and Ärlemalm-Hagsér, E. (2011b) 'Sustainable development in early childhood education: in-service students' comprehension of the concept'. *Environmental Education*

Research, 17(2): 187–200.

Shava, S. (2013) 'The representation of indigenous knowledges', in R. B. Stevenson, M. Brody, M. J. Dillon, and A. E. J. Wals (eds), *International Handbook of Research on Environmental Education*. New York: Routledge, pp. 384–93.

Sheridan, S. and Pramling Samuelsson, I. (2001) 'Children's conceptions of participation and influence in pre-school: A perspective on pedagogical quality', *Contemporary Issues in Early Childhood*, 2(2): 169–94.

Sheffield, P. and Landrigan, P. (2011) 'Global climate change and children's health: Threats and strategies for prevention'. *Environmental Health Perspectives*, 119(3): 291–8.

Sterling, S. (2001) *Sustainable Education: Revisioning Learning and Change*. Devon: Green Books.

Stewart, D., Sun, J., Patterson, C., Lemerle, K. and Hardie, M. (2004) 'Promoting and building resilience in primary school communities'. *International Journal of Mental Health Promotion*, 6(3): 26–33.

Strazdinis, L. and Skeat, H. (2011) *Weathering the future: Climate Change, Children and Young People and Decision-making*. Canberra: Australian Research Alliance for Children and Youth.

Taylor, A. and Giugni, M. (2012) 'Common worlds: Reconceptualizing inclusion in early childhood communities'. *Contemporary Issues in Early Childhood*, 13(2): 108–19.

The Swedish National Agency for Education. (2010) *Curriculum for the pre-school, Lpfö 98*. Stockholm: The Swedish National Agency for Education.

Tomanovic, S. (2004) 'Family habitus as the cultural context for childhood', *Childhood: A Global Journal of Child Research*, 11(3): 339–60.

United Nations Declaration on the Rights of Indigenous Peoples (2008) *Resolution adopted by the General Assembly*. Online. Available: ww.un.org/esa/socdev/unpfii/documents/DRIPS_en.pdf (accessed 26 January 2014).

UNESCO (2005) *UN Decade of Education for Sustainable Development (2005–2014)*. Online. Available: www.unesco.org/education/tlsf/extras/img/DESDbrief.pdf (accessed 26 January 2014).

UNICEF (1989) *United Nations Convention on the Rights of the Child (UNCRC)*. Online. Available: www.unicef.org/crc/ (accessed 14 February 2014).

UNICEF (2005) *United Nations Convention on the Rights of the Child (UNCRC)*. Online. Available: www.unicef.org/crc/index_30177.html (accessed 25 March 2014).

UNICEF (2013) *Sustainable Development Starts and Ends with Safe, Healthy and Well-educated Children*. Online. Available: www.unicef.org/socialpolicy/files/Sustainable_Development_post_2015.pdf (accessed 26 January 2014).

United Nations Regional Information Centre for Western Europe (UNRIC) (2012) Online. Available: www.unric.org/en/indigenous-people/27309-individual-vs-collective-rights (accessed 26 January 2014).

United Nations Universal Declaration on Human Rights (UDHR) (1948) Online. Available: www.ohchr.org/EN/UDHR/Documents/UDHR_Translations/eng.pdf, www2.ohchr.org/english/law/pdf/crc.pdf (accessed 26 January 2014).

Vedwan, N. (2011) 'Social learning'. in H. S. Schiffman and P. Robbins (eds), *Green Issues and Debates: An A-to-Z Guide*, 12: 310–12. Sage Reference Series on Green Society towards a Sustainable Future. Thousand Oaks, CA: Sage.

World Commission on Environment and Development (WCED) (1987) *Our Common Future*. Oxford; Oxford University Press.

Chapter 2

Belonging, value conflicts and children's rights in learning for sustainability in early childhood

Solveig Hägglund and Eva M. Johansson

Abstract

This chapter elaborates a view of learning for sustainability as a human right, where children's rights are regarded as a particular case. It draws on theoretical concepts and models developed within the tradition of childhood sociology, in particular its conceptualization of how societal and generational aspects of childhood restrict and limit children's possibilities to participate in society. Inspiration from conflict theory as developed by Chantal Mouffe (1989, 2000, 2005) will also be used in order to open up a perspective that involves value conflicts as inevitable when approaching sustainability as a democratic human right. Value conflicts will be discussed in relation to early education learning contexts with particular emphasis on power issues and democratic values regarded as closely linked with aspects of belonging, namely justice and solidarity. References will be made to research, particularly in the Nordic context, then drawing on results and questions, specific challenges will be outlined when learning for sustainability is to be enacted within early childhood education. 'Belonging' and 'value conflicts' will be suggested as dynamic 'working concepts' in the search for theoretical clarity of issues related to learning for sustainability in early education as a human right.

Introduction

Sustainable development raises questions about justice, rights, responsibility and caring for human beings and the world. Although the role of education for sustainability has expanded during the last decades, little attention has been directed to early education as a context for this (Ärlemalm-Hagser 2013, Davis 2009, Hägglund and Pramling Samuelsson 2009, Johansson 2009). In the Nordic context, national curricula (Kunnskapsdepartementet 2011, Skolverket 2011) and other documents assign early education significant responsibility to ensure that children develop knowledge about the environment and sustainability, and have opportunities to participate in and influence life in the preschool. In our view, both knowledge learning and being responded to as a person who genuinely contributes to the common daily life in preschool, go hand in hand with learning for sustainability. Both aspects, knowledge learning and learning to become a democratic world citizen, are integral to learning for sustainability.

Research reveals both tasks – supporting participation and learning to work with issues of sustainability as content – as problematic. Studies in the Nordic countries have pointed out that learning for sustainability is related to issues of rights and democracy (Bae 2010, Hägglund 2011, Johansson 2009, Kjørholt 2011) and therefore needs to be integrated into cultures of everyday practice. When developing such strategies within early childhood education, some issues have been identified as important for consideration. One line of reasoning highlights that early childhood institutions in the Nordic countries have historically been used as political arenas for societal change in the development of the Nordic welfare states (Dahlbeck and Tallberg Broman 2011). In such contexts, learning for sustainability is embedded in institutional traditions and cultures related to current political discourses. What implications this may have for the development of sustainability as a dimension in educational practice is not possible to fully predict, but the close relationship between policy and practice is notable.

Other studies stress the importance of the dynamics involved in ongoing collective interpretations of values related to sustainability that take place in peer-cultures. Some studies have shown that children's social representations of belonging, justice, and trust mediate their shared meanings and understanding of power and participation (Hägglund and Löfdahl 2010, Johansson 2007). Other studies, where observations were conducted on the ethical aspects of sustainability as practiced in younger children's peer-groups, reported insights about ongoing learning with relevance to justice and caring for others (Johansson 2009). In this way, research from inside peer-cultures and peer-groups has revealed ongoing learning around aspects of sustainability that concern values in relation to other human beings.

Finally, research linked with issues of sustainability in Nordic preschool contexts has been reported from institutions where the Nordic tradition of relating to nature with respect and familiarity has guided the practice. Here, we find early childhood settings that literally place their pedagogy in nature, and where sustainability is regarded as an important educational issue. Some of these studies argue that programs aspiring to develop children's learning for sustainable development are often based on an idea about what is 'right' for the individual child to learn and how to behave as a good protector of nature (Ärlemalm-Hagser 2013, Pearson and Degotardi 2009, Siraj-Blatchford 2009). While there is an emerging awareness of the complexity of sustainability and its relation to democracy education, educational practice seems far from these ways of thinking about children and learning for sustainability. It could be argued that a normative approach appears to be the main way of dealing with learning for sustainability in the preschool context.

This very brief overview of research summarizes recent insights into what the assignment to educate for sustainability in early childhood institutions in Nordic countries must consider. We have pointed at historical roots where the question of sustainability is necessarily linked with political and professional traditions, and where interests and values are not always in harmony. We have also mentioned a few studies that highlight the presence of active peer-cultures and peer-groups where children act as interpreters and doers of democratic values and where sustainability is anchored in children's ongoing learning of what it means to belong to a social and cultural context. Finally, we pointed to the presence of a normative view of sustainability as a specific content to be learned, as a challenge to educate for less restricted meanings of sustainability.

These aspects illustrate a collection of views with diverse theoretical and conceptual foundations. We will not discuss this further but, by introducing two 'working concepts', *belonging* and *conflicts*, our ambition in this chapter is to contribute to a conceptual elaboration of some critical issues involved in learning for sustainability in early childhood education. We argue for a view of the young child as a holder of rights to learn and to act in ways that support the sustainability project at large. We also put forward a position where sustainability is not only perceived as something normative for children to learn about, but is also part of our common existence and, as such, is intertwined with belongings, value conflicts, hegemonies and struggles. We base our discussion on the two interrelated concepts, *belonging* and *conflicts* since we regard these as important and dialectical dimensions in sustainability.

Learning for sustainability

A core dimension of sustainability is that it concerns conditions for life and survival related to economical, ecological, moral and social matters, stretching into the future of humankind and the Earth (Kemp 2005). The idea of sustainability is anchored in democratic values such as equality, justice and solidarity, and is inevitably connected with issues of human relations and ethics. Learning for sustainability thus encompasses these issues and, in this chapter, takes place in preschool settings with children and teachers as actors.

According to the United Nations Convention on the Right of the Child (UNICEF 1989) the young child is a holder of political, civil and social rights. These rights include a right to express views on matters of the child's concern and to do so in ways decided upon by the child (ibid., Articles 12 and 13). When human rights are specified as young children's human rights, and when young rights holders are regarded as agents for change in far-reaching work for sustainability (Davis and Elliott 2009), questions and dilemmas are likely to emerge. In the literature, it has been argued that there is resistance from the adult society to putting young children in the position of holding rights (Freeman 2009). When working with the child as a learner for sustainability, their position as a rights holder may be questioned for reasons linked to deeply rooted views on generational relationships (Alanen 2001, 2009). The child by definition, due to age and experience, is regarded as less competent than the adult to handle difficult issues such as the survival of humankind. Resistance to accepting the child as a holder of rights and to inviting children into a partnership for sustainability is considered a challenge in the task of creating arenas that support learning for sustainability. In the context of sustainability, this means seriously inviting children and their life experiences into partnerships towards a future of world citizenship that involves both responsibilities and rights for national and international societies (Kemp 2005). Taken together and based on the view of the child as a fully worthy human rights holder, we refer our comments in this section as being linked with connectedness or belonging. Although often positively loaded, we argue that belonging may also have negative connotations. We elaborate on this later.

Apart from raising the issue of children's potentially excluded position in sustainability learning some comments also need to be made in relation to the concept 'sustainability' itself, as this is not an unambiguous concept. Although documents are being signed and represent agreements on sustainability as a goal for political, economic, social and environmental strategies, contradictory interpretations and interests are still at hand. At the heart of these ambiguities lie challenges to power relations and a loss of privileges. The United Nations climate conference in Doha (November–December 2012), and its difficulties to come to a final protocol from the meeting is a recent illustration of this.

While value conflicts have been interpreted as a concept with a negative dimension, often in contrast to ideals of harmony and consensus, we suggest it also carries positive connotations and possibilities. Since conflicts are dynamic and open to change, they carry important implications for sustainability. We come back to this issue later.

There is an emerging awareness in early childhood education of the complexity of sustainability, at least on a rhetorical level. As briefly mentioned above, however, education for sustainable development, in practice, appears to be more rooted in normativity (the 'right' things for children to learn) and harmony between human beings and the environment, rather than illuminating value conflicts, power relations and loss of privileges (Ärlemalm-Hagser 2013, Björneloo 2007, Chan et al. 2009). Research has revealed that educational programs aspiring to develop children's learning for sustainable development are often based on the idea of sustainability as normative content for children to learn. This content most often concerns issues about caring for nature. From our perspective, this is problematic as it restricts the complexities and ambiguities of sustainability, including aspects of values and connectedness that may be fundamental to identify and challenge, when learning for sustainability.

Belonging

In this section, we elaborate three layers of meaning of the concept of belonging in relation to sustainability: belonging as a dimension of world citizenship; belonging as a dimension of time; and belonging as a right to be seriously involved in the sustainability project.

Belonging as a dimension of world citizenship and as a dimension of time

Here, we discuss, together, the first two ways of belonging. The concept *belonging* accentuates the idea of connectedness as a human being living in a world shared with others. According to the Danish philosopher Peter Kemp (2005), a central idea in sustainable development is the idea of the 'world citizen'. Kemp discusses the meaning of being brought up as a world citizen as a part of sustainability. The idea of the world citizen, writes Kemp, is about belonging and identity. The world citizen identifies her- or himself as part of at least two communities. One kind of belonging refers to the national and local communities in which we are born and/or live our lives. Another kind of belonging concerns our existence as human beings in a shared world. Kemp also refers to Levinas' ethics (Levinas 1961/1966) where 'the Other' is considered as someone radically different and unique. The other refers not only to the other as living here and now, but also to ancestors and descendants. According to Kemp we take it for granted that our descendants will be like us, just as we experience ourselves as similar to our ancestors.

This connectedness forces us to be concerned about and consider also *future others*, a thought that reveals an idea where time can be seen as a context for belonging. This is interesting as the sustainability problem, as such, involves time in its definition. Actions of today are regarded as having consequences for tomorrow and our responsibility is to limit the negative impacts of today's activities into the future. In literature, the challenge to be responsible for the life of future generations has been referred to as a 'distance moral' (avståndsmoral) (Almers 2009), a concept that also covers responsibilities for human beings in distant parts of the globe in a geographical sense. As learning for sustainability is not directed only towards life here and now, but also to life conditions for tomorrow, we regard our concept of belonging as also covering a time dimension.

Further, the concept of 'the Other' does not only refer to human beings; it can also refer to the living world in general asserts Kemp (2005). Neither nature nor the other human beings are raw material for us to control and exploit. Rather we have to relate to the other as unique, irretrievable and irreplaceable. These thoughts accentuate that senses of belonging are important issues in education for sustainable development. If children are to develop such belongings and identities, they need to be part of a community that puts these issues at the forefront (Johansson 2009).

Belonging as the right to be involved

The concept *belonging* is used here as a way to accentuate the idea of connectedness as a human being living in a world shared with others, but also to underpin the meaning of a child's right to be involved in sustainability. When we see the young child as a subject with rights to be involved in and contribute to sustainability, this demands a context where the child is not only invited to learn, but to actively participate in a partnership with her/his experiences, thoughts and visions in a sustainable space for dialogue. In turn, this calls for conceptualizations of processes, obstacles, power and mutual relationships. When invited to participate and contribute in actions for sustainability, a relationship between the child and the society (via the early childhood education-context and the adults) is established. Once involved in such partnerships, a link to the future is created for the child to be a part of and to belong to.

However, belonging to a partnership in learning for sustainability that may offer not only, and probably not primarily, harmony and good feelings, means that dark, difficult and threatening aspects need to be let in as well. We know from peer-culture research that children create shared worlds and belongings. They negotiate, settle and change the ethics of their communities and defend their shared worlds, where power as a collective dimension, embedded in the peer-cultures, becomes visible in relation to others (Corsaro 2005, Hägglund and Löfdahl 2010, Johansson 2011a,b, 2007). Children use their collective strength towards friends outside their play-world; it seems essential for them to build, protect and safeguard their play-worlds (Johansson 2007, see also Corsaro 1997). Other studies report that children´s collectively-formed social knowledges reframe rules for social inclusion. While the general norm was that everyone should be included in activities in an investigated preschool group, the children collectively resisted this by using age or gender as a legitimate reason to exclude other children (Löfdahl and Hägglund 2007).

To conclude this section then, several layers of meanings are attached to the concept of belonging as dimensions of sustainability. Belonging in the sense of a child being invited as a world citizen to participate in communities for change is significant. Other meanings of belonging with bearing on educational practice is for teachers to identify and challenge the belongings created by children in their peer-cultures. In these contexts, rules and premises for inclusion and justice that are collectively agreed and acted upon, are not always aligned with norms and values expressed and defended by their teachers.

The concept of belonging, as we suggest, is complex and open for negotiation. It offers positions for human beings with competence and legitimacy to act for a sustainable future. It carries dimensions of preparedness for fairly sharp, political opposition and resistance, based on knowledge about sustainability and conditions for justice and democracy. From such a perspective, issues of power and conflict inevitably demand attention. In the section below we do so by looking more closely at the concept of value conflict.

Values and value conflicts

The idea of sustainable development as comprising multiple identities and having multiple belongings is a moral issue and justice is the base (Kemp 2005). But, what is justice in this context? And what kind of prioritizing of values is implied by an ethics for sustainability? If we look at existing research and educational programs for sustainability in early childhood settings, they often imply an ideal of consensus and harmony (Chan *et al.* 2009). On the one hand, it is indeed difficult to object to these ideas. But, what kind of harmony is presupposed, and can sustainability ever be reached as a result of consensus? In this text, we discuss the role of value conflicts and tensions in education for sustainability. Our view is that the presence of conflicting values is inevitable when learning to understand conditions for sustainability. This means that value conflicts are both important and necessary for ethical consideration and for provoking change through learning for sustainability. Such conflicts however, are inevitably built on agonism and friendly opposition with a mutual interest among the actors to find a solution, rather than antagonism and fighting each other (Mouffe 2005).

Conflicts – prerequisites in learning for sustainability

Educational practice that seeks to create preschool belongings and a sense of community, to a large extent, relate to children's and teachers' concerns for rights, justice and others' wellbeing (Johansson 2009: 90ff.). Such values are linked with issues of sustainability and are also intertwined with power and value conflicts as embedded in contexts of early childhood education. In this light, learning for sustainability means, per se, that issues of (in)justice need to be confronted, implying that someone sometimes will lose her/his priorities (Johansson 2009). Tensions and (dis)agreements are based on various interests, positions and value priorities (Johansson 2009, Löfdahl and Hägglund 2012). As an alternative to an understanding of values anchored in a kind of values harmony, we suggest a concept of values where conflicts are necessarily embedded in teaching as well as learning for sustainability, a condition that we anticipate is inevitably present in the concept of belonging introduced above. According to Chantal Mouffe (1989, 2000, 2005), conflicts and (political) struggles are prerequisites for democracy and, in line with our reasoning, should also be prerequisites in relation to sustainability. Democracy, states Mouffe, is conditional on confrontations of various, and often, conflicting ideas; passion and affects are also involved in such democratic processes.

Learning for sustainability is a complex issue constituted of belongings and collective identities as well as value conflicts and power issues. This inevitable tension is often neglected in educational debates about learning for sustainability. When institutions hinder or restrict value conflicts and confrontations, and when different ideas and positions are silenced, democracy is in danger (Mouffe 2005). Conflicts allow for negotiations and open up possibilities for change. It is important to state, however, that the kind of conflicts described by Mouffe, are agonistic rather than antagonistic, namely they involve friendly opposition with a mutual interest among the actors to find a solution rather than to fight each other.

Such conflicts allow for new perspectives to merge and provoke possibilities for change. However, disagreements must be expressed and dealt with in a friendly and respectful way. This means that the ways teachers and children approach value conflicts in everyday practice are important in emergent learning for sustainability, democracy and justice.

Studies in early childhood settings have reported that children create shared worlds and belongings and that they negotiate, settle and change the ethics of their communities (Hägglund and Löfdahl 2010, Johansson 2007). Value conflicts are often the starting point for such ethical considerations and also for creating change. Children argue for, share and distribute rights collectively and individually, and they create (dis)agreements for how to share resources and the content of their play scenarios. They expect from each other respect for their shared worlds. Justice is given both a collective and democratic dimension and the distribution of rights is based on certain principles where equal power and belongings are involved (Johansson 2007).

Childhood today, as we have already shown, is to a large extent tied to educational institutions based on a diversity of values and different belongings. If children are to develop at least the two identities suggested by Kemp (2005), one being part of a local community, and the other being part of and responsible for a common world, then they need to be part of a community where issues of belongings are placed at the forefront. Everyday interactions in early childhood settings concern the kinds of understandings of self, of others and the world that children are given opportunities to develop (Johansson 2009). We take Kemp's identity concept one step further, by arguing that it also holds a dimension of belonging, a concrete and necessary connectedness to other people, to all of humankind (past, present and future), and to non-humans. Sharing a wish to survive means in its deepest, philosophical sense, a wish to belong. Such belongings may not necessarily be built on harmony and agreement; they may also be built on tensions, disagreements and value conflicts. Belonging and conflicts are interrelated. Belonging is a prerequisite for dialogues where conflicting views on values are discussed. In turn, such dialogues create arenas for belonging. This perspective on learning for sustainability in the context of early childhood education includes children's knowledges and experiences. It allows, and even demands, the dark, difficult and negative aspects of sustainability to enter into these dialogues. We think that it also opens up possibilities for illumination and analysis of those aspects.

Belonging and value conflicts in learning for sustainability concluding comments

In this chapter, children's learning for sustainability is referred to as a human right stretching into the future. It embraces values such as justice, rights, responsibility and caring for human beings and the world at large. We suggest that children's knowledge about sustainability and its conditions is framed by the idea that a major challenge for the survival of humanity and the planet is to find ways to communicate, challenge and question inequalities and power distributions. Learning for sustainability in the context of early childhood education is suggested as a pedagogic assignment characterized by opposition, negotiation and conflict.

We have introduced the concepts of belonging and value conflicts as a way of grasping some of the complexities that are revealed as education for sustainability becomes embedded in early childhood settings. As we see it, belonging is related to connectedness in time and place here and now, but also stretches into the future and to faraway places. Therefore, it is linked with an identity as a world citizen. We have also suggested the concept of value conflicts as interrelated with belonging in the sense that the presence of conflicting values is inevitable when learning to understand conditions for sustainability. Value conflicts connected with belongings open up spaces for change and learning. By illuminating both tensions and inter-relationships between belongings and value conflicts, new ways of understanding and relating to education for sustainability are offered. Inspiration from sociological, philosophical and political theories can help teachers develop new perspectives and gain new tools for analysing tensions in teaching and learning for sustainability in the early years.

When the Polish paediatrician Janusz Korzak, referred to as advocate for and one of the initiators of the *UN Convention on the Rights of the Child*, writes about respect for children and their rights, he emphasizes it in this way, the necessity of not concealing the dark side of life from children:

> What kind of preparation for life is it to tell children that everything is just, fair, sensible, well-motivated and unchangeable? In our agenda for upbringing we have forgotten to insert the idea that the child needs to learn not only to love the truth, but also to recognize a lie, not only to love but also to hate, not only to respect but also to reject, not only to overlook, but also to be indignant, not only to adapt but also to revolt.
>
> (Our translation from Janusz Korczak 2002: 97)

References

Alanen, L. (2001) 'Childhood as a generational condition. Children's daily life in a central Finland town', in L. Alanen and B. Mayall (eds), *Conceptualizing Child-adult Relations*. London: Falmer Press, pp. 129–43.

Alanen, L. (2009) 'Generational order', in J. Qvortrup, W. A. Corsaro and M-S. Honig (eds), *The Palgrave Handbook of Childhood Studies*. Basingstoke: Palgrave Macmillan, pp. 157–74.

Ärlemalm-Hagser, E. (2013) *Engagerade i världens bästa? Lärande för hållbarhet i förskolan* (Engaged in the world's best. Learning for sustainability in preschool, in Swedish). Gothenburg: Acta Universitatis Gothoburgensis, No. 335.

Almers, E. (2009) *Handlingskompetens för hållbar utveckling. Tre berättelser om vägen dit* (Action competence for sustainable development. Three narratives). Jönköping University, School of Education and Communication, Dissertation No 6.

Bae, B. (2010) 'Realizing children's right to participation in early childhood settings: Some critical issues in a Norwegian context'. *Early Years*, (30)3: 205–218.

Björneloo, I. (2007) 'Innebörder av hållbar utveckling. En studie av lärares utsagor om under-visning (Meanings of sustainable development. A study of teachers' statements on their education)'. Gothenburg: Acta Universitatis Gothoburgensis.

Chan, B., Choy, B. and Lee, A. (2009) 'Harmony as the basis for education or sustainable development: A case example of Yew Chung International Schools'. *International Journal of Early Childhood*, 4(2): 35–48.

Corsaro, W. A. (1997) *The Sociology of Childhood*. Thousand Oaks, CA: Pine Forge Press.

Corsaro, W. A. (2005) *The Sociology of Childhood*, 2nd edn. Thousand Oaks, CA: Pine Forge Press.

Dahlbeck, J. and Tallberg Broman, I. (2011) 'Ett bättre samhälle genom pedagogik: om högre värden och barnet som budbärare (A better society through education: On higher values and the child as a messenger)", in P. Williams and S. Sheridan S. (eds), *Barns lärande i ett livslångt perspektiv* (Children's learning in a lifelong perspective). Stockholm: Liber, pp. 202–15.

Davis, J. (2009) 'Revealing the research "hole" of early childhood education for sustainability. A preliminary survey of the literature'. *Environmental Education Research*, 15(2): 227–41.

Davis, J. and Elliott, S. (2009) 'Exploring the resistance: An Australian perspective on educating for sustainability in early childhood'. *International Journal of Early Childhood*, 41(2): 65–77.

Freeman, M. (2009) 'Children's rights as human rights: Reading the UNCRC', in J. Qvortrup, W. A. Corsaro and M-S. Honig (eds), *The Palgrave Handbook of Childhood Studies*. Basingstoke: Palgrave Macmillan, pp. 377–93.

Hägglund, S. (2011) 'Förskolebarnet och rätten till lärande för hållbar utveckling – några tankar om förutsättningar, möjligheter och utmaningar (The preschool child's right to learn for sustainability: Some thoughts on premises, possibilities and challenges)', in P. Williams and S. Sheridan (eds), *Barns lärande i ett livslångt perspektiv* (*Children's Learning in a Life Long Perspective*). Stockholm: Liber, pp. 245–55.

Hägglund, S. and Löfdahl, A. (2010) 'Social representations of belonging in preschool children's peer-cultures', in M. Chai, B. Danermark and S. Selander (eds), *Education, Professionalization and Social Representations*. New York: Routledge, pp. 171–84.

Hägglund, S. and Pramling Samuelsson, I. (2009) 'Early childhood education and learning for sustainable development and citizenship'. *International Journal of Early Childhood*, 41(2): 49–63.

Johansson, E. (2007) *Etiska överenskommelser i förskolebarns världar* (Moral agreements in preschool-children's worlds, in Swedish). Gothenburg: Acta Universitatis Gothoburgensis, No. 251.

Johansson, E. (2009) 'The preschool child of today – the world citizen of tomorrow'. *International Journal of Early Childhood*, 2(41): 79–96.

Johansson, E. (2011a) 'Investigating morality in toddler's worlds', in E. Johansson and J. E. White (eds), *Educational Research with Our Youngest: Voices of Infants and Toddlers*. New York: Springer, pp. 127–40.

Johansson, E. (2011b) 'Moral discoveries and learning in preschool', in N. Pramling and I. Pramling Samuelsson (eds), *Educational Encounters: Nordic Studies in Early Childhood Didactics*. New York: Springer, pp. 127–39.

Kemp, P. (2005) *Världsmedborgaren. Politisk och pedagogisk filosofi för det 21 århundradet* (The world citizen. Political and educational philosophy in the 21st decade, in Swedish). Gothenburg: Daidalos.

Kjørholt, A-T. (2011) 'Rethinking young children's rights for participation in diverse cultural contexts', in M. Kernan and E. Singer (eds), *Peer-relationships in Early Childhood Education and Care*. Abingdon: Routledge, pp. 38–48.

Korczak, J. (2002) 'Hur man älskar ett barn (How to love a child)', del 1: 98, In *Barnets rätt till respekt* (The child's right to respect), 3rd edn. Stockholm: Natur & Kultur.

Kunnskapsdepartementet (2011) *Rammeplan for barnehhagens innhold og oppgaver*. Revidert utgave. Bergen: Fagbokforlaget. Online. Available: www.publikasjoner.dep.no (accessed 26 January 2014).

Levinas, E. (1961/1996) *Totalitet og underlighed* (Totality and infinity). Copenhagen: Hans Reitzels forlag.

Löfdahl, A. and Hägglund, S. (2007) 'Spaces of participation in preschool. Arenas for establishing power orders'. *Children and Society*, 231: 328–38.

Löfdahl, A. and Hägglund, S. (2012) Diversity in preschool: Defusing and maintaining differences. *Australasian Journal of Early Childhood (AJEC)*, 37(1): 119–26.

Mouffe, C. (1989) 'Radical democracy: Modern or postmodern?' *Social Text*, 21: 31–45.

Mouffe. C. (2000) 'Politics and passions: The stakes of democracy'. *Ethical Perspectives*, 7(2–3): 146–50.

Mouffe, C. (2005) *On the Political*. New York: Routledge.

Pearson, E. and Degotardi, S. (2009) 'Education for sustainable development in early childhood education: A global solution to local concerns?' *International Journal of Early Childhood*, 2(41): 97–112.

Siraj-Blatchford, J. (2009) 'Editorial: Education for sustainable development in early childhood'. *International Journal of Early Childhood*, 2(41): 9–22.

Skolverket (2011) *Läroplan för förskolan, Lpfö 98 Reviderad 2010*. Stockholm: Fritzes. Online. Available: www.skolverket.se/publikationer?id=2442 (accessed 26 January 2014).

UNICEF (1989) *United Nations Convention on the Rights of the Child*. Online. Available: www.unicef.org/crc/ (accessed 14 February 2014)

Chapter 3

Learning from the wisdom of elders

Jenny Ritchie

Abstract

This chapter offers a series of provocations coming from a critical, place-based orientation, regarding the ways in which early childhood educators, might develop relationships with local Indigenous peoples, in order to strengthen the Indigenous understandings that they incorporate within their programs. Dialogical interaction with both Indigenous peoples and the local place itself, is seen as a source for interpreting ways of caring deeply for our planet, positioning we humans alongside local ecologies as 'co-habitors' of the earth. The chapter then provides examples from recent research to illustrate some of the ways these notions have been applied within early childhood care and education programs in Aotearoa New Zealand.

Introduction

Attitudes and behaviours attached to the exploitation of the environment are associated with pervasive globalized discourses of Western colonialism, capitalism and profit-orientated consumption, all of which contribute to a distancing from engagement with particular places and their local ecologies. As the climate crisis deepens into an imminent emergency, educators can play a pivotal role in generating pedagogies of place (Penetito 2009: 196–197) that reflect a sense of localized place consciousness (Gruenewald 2003). Indigenous peoples of each locality have, over many years of living closely with the land and as cohabitants of that place, garnered specific, intimate understandings of their local ecologies, and the ways in which humans can respectfully and sustainably coexist within these places and ecologies (Rose 2002, 2005). Through working to build relationships with Indigenous colleagues and elders, non-Indigenous educators may gain considerable understanding and insight into practices that sustain local ecologies. This chapter draws on recent research in Aotearoa New Zealand (Ritchie *et al.* 2010) to illustrate ways in which educators have been learning from Indigenous sources and are applying this knowledge within their early childhood programs.

Provocations

This chapter raises provocations for consideration by early childhood care and education practitioners and scholars. Prioritizing 'care' in our work acknowledges children's emotional, spiritual and physical wellbeing as pre-conditions for learning. First, how might we transcend the distancing from experiences of the daily imperatives of natural cycles and ecologies that are generated through our technologized, industrialized, and predominantly urban life-styles? Secondly, how can we foster pedagogies which are specific and responsive to the particular localized ecologies in which we are situated? Third, how might we strengthen our relationships with local Indigenous children, families and elders, to the point that they become willing to share their histories, stories, and ecological/sustainability knowledge of that particular place? Lastly, how might we consider the potential of early childhood care and education programs informed by local Indigenous knowledges, to provide opportunities for restorative reconnection with the land, insects, birds, and other creatures, 'nature's' cycles and seasons, fostering a sense of commitment to sustainable ways of knowing, being and doing?

From distance to interconnectedness

Concern has been expressed regarding the increasing distance between children and natural, wild spaces, such as forest, bush, wetland, grasslands, streams, rivers and seashores (Davis 2010, Elliott 2010, Louv 2010). For Val Plumwood, the Western project of colonization has utilized hyper-separation as a justification for the exploitation of the 'Other', resulting in 'othering' of both Indigenous peoples and the environment. The hierarchical mode of understanding the world that positions (white, male) humans at the top of the evolutionary 'tree', has not only resulted in the colonization and disempowerment of both Indigenous people and the environment, but has led to a commensurate lessening of empathy and care for them (Plumwood 1999a, 1999b). This anthropocentric frame 'distort[s] our sensitivity to and knowledge of nature, blocking humility, wonder and openness in approaching the more-than-human, and producing narrow types of understanding and classifications that reduce nature to raw materials for human projects' (Plumwood 1999a: 196–197). The term 'more-than-human' is used to deliberately de-centre our anthropocentric worldview and reminds us of our sensory, storied entanglement within the inter-relational agency of other animals, plants, insects and the rest of the nonhuman world around us (Abram 1996).

While the majority of urban settlers may have become distanced from a sense of 'kinship with nature' (Rose 2005: 303), many rural settlers, such as farmers, have developed over generations, a deep connectivity with their lands expressing their own 'language of kinship' (Rose 2002: 313). Deborah Bird Rose describes this as 'a language of emplacement: of keeping your body in the place, and putting your labour into the place, of learning to know the place, and of being available to the place' (Rose 2002: 313). She suggests that over time lived closely on the land, settlers can begin to acknowledge our connections with indigenous people: the same soil gets into our blood, the same waters quench our thirst, the sweat of us all resides in the ground. We and other living things are co-participants in earthly reciprocities of being, becoming, and dying.

(Rose 2002: 322)

Rose proposes a restorative process of 'dialogical interpenetration' (Rose 2002: 322), a restorative, decolonizing conversation between people and their places. Instead of perpetuating a stance of historical amnesia and denial regarding the impact of our Western civilizations on both Indigenous peoples and the environment, we need to engage in a transformative shift to a positioning that acknowledges our intimate, physical, emotional and spiritual relationship within both our immediate and wider spheres. This alternative view requires sensitivity toward our ecosystems which allows us to be invited by 'nature' into reciprocal interaction within our ecological systems, as is practised by Indigenous peoples. Intrinsic to this process is feeling and demonstrating respect for the more-than-human realm (Abram 1996, Plumwood 1999a), which requires us to both acknowledge, confront and transform our anthropocentrism (Russell 2008, as cited in Kahn and Humes 2009: 186).

Critical pedagogies of place

Critical pedagogies of place acknowledge histories of Indigenous and environmental colonization (Greenwood 2008, Greenwood et al. 2009, Gruenewald 2003). David Gruenewald has highlighted for us the challenge of adopting pedagogical approaches that enable scholars/educators/students/children to unlearn much of what we have learnt from dominant culture and schooling practices, in order that we become receptive towards, and committed to, alternative, 'socially just and ecologically sustainable ways of being in the world' (Gruenewald 2003: 9). This involves a process of decolonizing our thinking and behaviours, while 'recovering and renewing traditional, non-commodified cultural patterns' (p. 9).

Critical pedagogies of place are historically, culturally, and ecologically specific, recognizing the 'uniqueness of cultural and geographical experience, [and] the varied interactions between mindscape, cultural group, and landscape' (Greenwood 2008: 339). These understandings regarding 'the particularities of places' need to be accessed via the knowledges and ethics of 'the people who know them best', that is, local Indigenous peoples (Greenwood 2008: 339). Such an approach is intersectional, inviting educators with a sociocultural background to widen their considerations to include responsiveness to the environment, while similarly encouraging those with an environmental education focus to reflect more on issues of colonization and Indigeneity. Greenwood/Gruenewald highlight the importance of critical place-based pedagogies in providing a countering approach to the current narrowing of curriculum through the imposition of neo-liberal education policy priorities (Greenwood 2008, Gruenewald 2003).

According to Māori education scholar Wally Penetito (2009), place-based education is inherent within both historical and contemporary models of Māori education. Penetito views place-based education as a corrective to the distancing syndrome critiqued above. Penetito points out that for Indigenous peoples, a sense of place is a fundamental human need, and that Indigenous peoples see themselves as 'co-habitors' with and within their environments. For Māori, pedagogies need to be underpinned with a consciousness of spiritual interconnectedness, or *wairua* (Penetito 2009: 20).

Indigenous wisdoms

Indigenous people have traditionally been responsive, resilient, and intra-active within their environments, and are well-positioned to continue their role as guardians (in Māori, *kaitiaki*) of their locales (Kanawa 2010). Māori scholar Mason Durie explains an Indigenous view of the relationality and unity of humans and their environment:

> Relationships between people and the natural environment, between tangible and intangible dimensions, between organic and inorganic material, and between past and future constitute the foundations upon which indigenous populations understand the world. An energy flow that spirals outwards connects the multiple threads so that even very small objects become part of a wider context that gives them shape and meaning.
>
> (Durie 2010: 239)

This close relationship with the land is expressed through traditional practices involving stories and songs, food-gathering and healing. Language and knowledge systems reflect a deep respect for and intimate connection with the land, rivers, mountains, seas, wetlands and forests. Everything has its own *mauri* or life force – this includes both living and inanimate objects such as mountains and rocks, and spiritual rituals are important to protect and maintain the spiritual balance, recognizing the existence of *wairuatanga* (spiritual interconnectedness). People are obligated to care for others (*manaakitanga*) and to be guardians of their environment (*kaitiakitanga*). The *whakatauki* (a Māori proverb) 'Kakari kaihiku, kia haere kai upoko' can be translated as 'Unity comes with a fair sharing of resources' (Halba et al. 2011: 69).

There is an expectation of reciprocity in the existence of a 'mutual entanglement of benefits' (Rose 2005: 299). An example provided by Rose is that of Australian Indigenous people leaving behind some precious fruit on trees for other creatures to eat. Rose was told by one of her Indigenous teachers: 'It's not waste … this food is for everyone' (p. 297). Another of Rose's teachers, April Bright, explained the importance of 'listening to country' in order to be guided in the practice of 'firestick burning':

The country tells you when and where to burn. To carry out this task you must know your country. You wouldn't, you just would not attempt to burn someone else's country. One of the reasons for burning is saving country. If we don't burn our country every year, we are not looking after our country.

(Rose 2002: 78–82)

Such an Indigenous worldview is not hierarchical with people positioned as the dominant, authoritarian species. Instead, it is one of entangled, interdependent relationships, whereby Indigenous practices are aimed towards 'sustaining life through the twin processes of life for itself and life for others' (Rose 2005: 297) in an ongoing recursive cycle of regenerating the environment. This is underpinned by recognition that 'Care of country means caring for others as well as self' (Rose 2005: 300) and requires a deep, responsive hearing, reading, recognition, and participation within the cyclical patterns and codes of intra-action of local ecosystems.

Twenty years ago Paula Gunn Allen of the Laguna Pueblo and Sioux North American Indigenous peoples, wrote that:

If American society judiciously modelled the traditions of the various Native Nations, the place of women in society would be central, the distribution of goods and power would be egalitarian, the elderly would be respected, honoured and protected as a primary social and cultural resource, the ideals of physical beauty would be considerably enlarged … the destruction of the biota, the life sphere, and the natural resources of the planet would be curtailed, and the spiritual nature of human and nonhuman life would become a primary organizing force of human society.

(Allen 1992: 211, as cited in Cannella and Manuelito, 2008: 52)

In order to confront and remedy the challenges facing our planet from anthropogenic climate change, the repositioning of Western notions of relationality as being in relation with the Earth can be modelled on the wisdom of Indigenous peoples garnered over many centuries (Kincheloe and Steinberg 2008). It is vital, however, that such change be led by Indigenous people, and conducted within their traditional spiritual practices, supported by non-Indigenous allies, rather than appropriated by well-meaning Westerners (Korteweg and Russell 2013).

In the following section, examples are provided from three recent research projects conducted with early childhood care and education communities located in Aotearoa New Zealand. All participating teachers had a strong commitment to cultural sustainability, in relation to the local Indigenous (Māori) cultures. In the following examples, from 'mainstream' early childhood care and education settings, teachers were conscious of working with local Indigenous people and knowledges, proactively using these to inform the sustainability practices of these centres' curriculum.

Examples from recent research

In all three of our studies, we utilized emergent, narrative, responsive qualitative methodologies, informed by kaupapa Māori values, and with an overt commitment to counter-colonial consciousness (Bishop 2005, Denzin Lincoln and Smith 2008, Otterstad 2007, Ritchie and Rau 2012, Smith 1999/2006). Prior to and during our three recent two-year studies (Ritchie *et al.*, 2010, Ritchie and Rau 2006, Ritchie and Rau 2008) funded by the New Zealand Teaching and Learning Research Initiative, my colleague Cheryl Rau and I had, and have, sustained longstanding relationships with Māori elders, in particular, with our *kuia* (female elder), Rahera Barrett-Douglas, and our kaumatua (male elder) Huata Holmes. Their wisdom and support was a source of strength and guidance for our work, and for that of our co-researcher teachers. The research in all three projects was grounded in the New Zealand early childhood curriculum: *Te Whāriki. He whāriki mātauranga mō ngā mokopuna o Aotearoa: Early childhood curriculum* (New Zealand Ministry of Education 1996). This curriculum recognizes as foundational *Te Tiriti o Waitangi*, the 1840 treaty in which Māori chiefs allowed British settlement in exchange for protection of their self-determination, lands, villages and resources. *Te Whāriki* has been acclaimed internationally, commended for being progressive, non-prescriptive, inclusive (both of infants and toddlers and of (bi)cultural specificities), and for its focus on learning processes (Hedges 2013).

Through our relationship with a Southern Māori elder, Huata Holmes, we learnt of the way his dialect honours the specificities of different birds and trees which, for example, have different names at different cycles of the seasons. During our most recent study (Ritchie *et al.* 2010), Huata was able to share with the children of Richard Hudson Kindergarten in Dunedin, in the South Island of New Zealand, some Southern Māori versions of traditional cosmologies, legends and songs. These had significant appeal to the children, enabling them to feel a deep sense of connection to, and compassion for, Papatūānuku (the Earth Mother) and Ranginui (Sky Father) (Ellwood 2010, Ritchie 2011). Three examples from this study are now provided to illustrate ways in which teachers in 'mainstream' early childhood settings worked to open up spaces for Indigenous understandings within their early childhood programs.

Example 1: teachers' proactivity in initiating relationships with local Indigenous people

Te Whāriki, the New Zealand early childhood curriculum, states under Strand Two, 'Belonging' that 'Liaison with local tangata whenua [people of that land] and a respect for papatūānuku [Earth Mother] should be promoted' (1996: 54). The teachers in our studies realized that it was their responsibility to initiate relationships with local *iwi* (tribes). The teachers at Meadowbank Kindergarten, located within the large urban metropolis of Auckland, in the North Island, for example, arranged participation – along with kindergarten children and families – in a tree-planting ritual honouring the Atua (spiritual guardian) Tāne Māhuta at the local

Orākei *marae* (Māori village meeting place). This was so successful that they intend making this an annual commitment (Ritchie *et al.* 2010).

Example 2: teachers seeking in-depth, local Indigenous knowledges

The teachers involved in our study were sensitive to the need to consult with local *iwi* (tribes) in order to gain in-depth understandings, rather than to superficially appropriate Māori constructs. The Head Teacher of Galbraith Kindergarten in the small rural, predominantly Māori town of Ngāruawahia, a small township in the North Island, described their consultative approach:

> Papatūānuku is another real strength [in our] philosophy. That at the moment is in draft and we're discussing it because what does the wider concept of Papatūānuku [mean]? We could say 'Mother Earth' but there's a wider concept to it and we need to work with all whānau [families] and with our local iwi about what does that mean to them?
>
> (as cited in Ritchie et al. 2010: 19)

Teachers not only consulted Māori elders and Māori family members of children attending their centres; they also conducted their own research and wider reading by accessing material from public libraries and websites in order to become more familiar with Māori philosophies and practices. Teachers also checked the relevance of material that they had read with local Māori advisors, since they recognized the importance of regional specificities and tribal differences. As Māori scholar Hirini Mead states, 'There is always a need to refer to the tikanga [beliefs and practices] of the local people' (2003: 8).

Example 3: teachers applying Indigenous philosophies

The teachers demonstrated the depth of their understanding of Māori philosophies by applying these approaches within their educational practice and to their work in the research project, as illustrated by this example from a teacher at Papamoa Kindergarten, near the city of Tauranga in New Zealand's North Island:

> The research is about Māori ecological principles, how they're informing and enhancing a *kaupapa* [philosophy] of ecological sustainability ... The Māori worldview is holistic and cyclic, one in which every person is linked to every living thing and to the *Atua*, which is the Gods. Māori customary concepts are interconnected through our *whakapapa*, which is your genealogy that links to *te taha wairua*, which is your spiritual element, and *te taha kikokiko*, which is your intellect or your body and your whole spirit.
>
> (as cited in Ritchie et al. 2010: 13)

Teachers also applied Māori philosophies and practices within the everyday routines and rituals of the early childhood care and education centre, as described in this example from Hawera Kindergarten, in a small rural North Island town:

> Our little pot plants had finished flowering so we recycled them by trans-planting succulents in the pots. First we had *karakia* [spiritual incantation] to acknowledge Tāne Mahuta, then broke off pieces of the succulent plants, sat them in the pots and watered them. The children carried river stones from the gravel pit and poured them into the planter boxes. We talked about gardening, looking after the plants, where the stones came from and experienced the *mauri* [life force] in the plants and stones. It was a good team effort. When we had finished, the children admired their work. When one works with Papatūānuku, one can find it relaxing and peaceful. It teaches patience and nurtures the soul.
>
> (as cited in Ritchie *et al.* 2010: 33)

These examples provide a glimpse of ways in which teachers have consciously and respectfully incorporated Indigenous ways of being, knowing and doing within their daily programs.

Final thoughts on possibilities for critical, place-based, Indigenous-informed pedagogies

In addition to accessing the wisdom of Indigenous peoples, we are also fortunate to have many wise elders with backgrounds in Western science, who continue to share their wisdom with us. The world renowned Canadian environmental scientist David Suzuki wrote recently, that

> As an elder, I am impelled by a sense of urgency that comes from the recognition that my generation has induced change and created problems that we bequeath to my children and grandchildren and all generations to come. That is not right, but I believe that it is not too late to take another path.
>
> (Suzuki 2011: 3)

Suzuki quotes anthropologist Bernard Campbell, who recognizes – as do many Indigenous peoples – that both human and planetary survival clearly depends on the recognition of human interdependence within the web of our living planet:

> There is no escape from our interdependence of with nature; we are woven into the closest relationship with the Earth, the sea, the air, the seasons, the animals and all the fruits of the Earth. What affects one affects us all – we are part of a greater whole – the body of the planet. We must respect, preserve and love its manifold expression if we hope to survive.
>
> (Campbell, as cited in Suzuki 2011: 32–33)

Suzuki points out that recent science is now confirming the 'ancient understanding' that anthropogenic effects on the planet directly rebound to impact on us (p. 71). Professor Tim Flannery (2010), the Australian scientist, conservationist and climate change expert who was Chief Commissioner of the Australian Climate Commission, explains that, with advancing technology, humans have moved out of our historic co-evolutionary relationship within the natural world. He emphasizes that a return to a condition of cultural and biological 'co-evolution' 'is critical to our hopes for sustainability' (p. 68). Like Suzuki, Flannery sees the value in ancient practices of Indigenous peoples that have enabled, after admittedly some periods of trial and error, protection of natural ecosystems throughout the ages. He sees such knowledges as useful in that they demonstrate how people have learnt interactively, over time, to live sustainably, founded in a deep respect for other human beings and for nature. He points out that a lack of economic egalitarianism means that people in impoverished, marginalized situations are being forced into destroying wilderness, thus contributing further to the loss of biodiversity. Flannery advocates a conscious, deliberate process of 're-wilding' of our planet, enabling its biodiversity to be re-established and to flourish, in recognition that 'our fate and that of the Earth are inextricably interwoven' (Flannery 2010: 276).

It is intended that the arguments and examples in this chapter demonstrate ways in which early childhood care and education programs, through a critical, place-based pedagogy informed by local Indigenous knowledges, can enable children and their families to access a philosophy and practice of caring for one another and our planet. Rather than directly being taught 'about' sustainability, which has the potential to alarm young children about the urgency and severity of climate disruption (Sobel 2007), children are supported to be receptive to understandings and daily practices which position them as 'kaitiaki', as guardians, caregivers of the natural world. In this way, early childhood care and education services can become 'communities of care' (Sobel 2008: 18), that is, sites of respectful shared optimism and endeavour.

The central challenge for educators in this era of frightening climate disruption and depletion of wilderness and biodiversity is to recognize the need to address these challenging issues while, at the same time, recognizing that we are part of the Western technicist worldview that contributes to these issues. We all, then, need to take on the hard work of 'un-learning' our comfortable ways of practising education, through critical reflexivity that enables openness to alternative, Indigenous framings of ways of being, knowing and doing. An essential aspect of this change is re-learning our 'place' and helping young children make new meanings. Building relationships with local Indigenous advisors and drawing on materials and knowledges, particularly those pertaining to local Indigenous histories and traditions, are essential for such a process.

Glossary

Atua – spiritual guardian/compartmental God
iwi – tribe(s)
kaitiaki – guardian
kaitiakitanga – guardianship/stewardship of their environment
kaumatua – elder, male elder
kaupapa – philosophy
kuia – female elder
manaakitanga – a person who cares, generosity
marae – village meeting place
mauri – life force
Papatūānuku – Earth Mother
Ranginui – Sky Father
Tāne Māhuta – *Atua* of the forests, birds and insects
te taha kikokiko – physical aspects
te taha wairua – spiritual dimension
tikanga – beliefs and practices that are correct for Māori
wairuatanga – spiritual interconnectedness
whakapapa – genealogy
whakatauki – proverb
whānau – families, extended families

Acknowledgements

I offer appreciation and gratitude for the funding support of the New Zealand Teaching and Learning Research Initiative; to Cheryl Rau who has been research-ing and writing with me or the past ten years; and to Janita Craw and Iris Duhn who joined us as co-directors of the study *Titiro Whakamuri, Hoki Whakamua. We are the future, the present and the past: caring for self, others and the environment in early years' teaching and learning.*

References

Abram, D. (1996) *The Spell of the Sensuous. Perception and Language in a More-than-human World,* New York: Vintage Books.

Bishop, R. (2005) 'Freeing ourselves from neocolonial domination in research: A Kaupapa Māori approach to creating knowledge', in N. K. Denzin and Y. S. Lincoln (eds), *The Sage Handbook of Qualitative Research,* 3rd edn, Thousand Oaks, CA: Sage, pp. 109–64.

Cannella, G. S. and Manuelito, K. D. (2008) 'Feminisms from unthought locations. Indigenous worldviews, marginalized feminisms, and revisioning an anticolonial social science', in N. K. Denzin, Y. S. Lincoln, and L. T. Smith (eds), *Handbook of Critical and Indigenous Methodologies.* Thousand Oaks, CA: Sage, pp. 45–59.

Davis, J. (2010) 'What is early chidhood education for sustainability?', in J. Davis (ed.), *Young Children and the Environment. Early Education for Sustainability,* Cambridge: Cambridge University Press, pp. 21–42.

Denzin, N. K., Lincoln, Y. S. and Smith, L. T. (2008) *Handbook of Critical and Indigenous Methodologies,* Thousand Oaks, CA: Sage.

Durie, M. (2010) 'Outstanding universal value: How relevant is Indigeneity?', in R. Selby, P. Moore and M. Mulholland (eds), *Outstanding Universal Value: How Relevant is Indigeneity?* Wellington: Huia, pp. 239–251.

Elliott, S. (2010) 'Children in the natural world', in J. Davis (ed.), *Young Children and the Environment: Early Education for Sustainability,* Cambridge: Cambridge University Press, pp. 43–75.

Ellwood, A. (2010) 'Caring for Papatūānuku. Yesterday, today and tomorrow', *Early Education,* 47: 19–22.

Flannery, T. (2010) *Here on Earth. A Natural History of the Planet,* Toronto: HarperCollins.

Greenwood, D. A. (2008) 'A critical pedagogy of place: From gridlock to parallax', *Environmental Education Research,* 14: 336–48.

Greenwood, D. A., Manteaw, B. O. and Smith, G. A. (2009) 'Environmental education: From international resolve to local experience and inquiry', in J. Andrzejewski, M.P. Baltodano and L. Symcox (eds), *Social Justice, Peace, and Environmental Education. Transformative Standards.* New York: Routledge, pp. 80–98.

Gruenewald, D. (2003) 'The best of both worlds: A critical pedagogy of place', *Educational Researcher,* 32: 3–12.

Halba, H., McCallum, R. and Holmes, H. (2011) 'Tū taha, tū kaha: Transcultural dialogues'. *Australasian Drama Studies,* 59: 69–87.

Hedges, H. (2013) 'The future of Te Whāriki: Political, pedagogical and professional concerns', in J. Nuttall (ed.), *Weaving Te Whāriki. Aotearoa New Zealand's Early Childhood Curriculum Document in Theory and Practice.* Wellington: NZCER Press, pp. 277–98.

Kahn, R. and Humes, B. (2009) 'Marching out from ultima thule: Critical counterstories of emancipatory educators working at the intersection of human rights, animal rights, and planetary sustainability', *Canadian Journal of Environmental Education,* 14: 179–95.

Kanawa, L. (2010) 'Climate change implications for Māori', in R. Selby, P. Moore and D. M. Mulhollan (eds), *Māori and the environment: Kaitiaki.* Wellington: Huia.

Kincheloe, J. L. and Steinberg, S. L. (2008) 'Indigenous knowledges in education. Complexities, dangers, and profound benefits', in N. K. Denzin, Y. S. Lincoln and L. T. Smith (eds), *Handbook of Critical and Indigenous Methodologies.* Thousand Oaks, CA: Sage, pp. 135–56.

Korteweg, L. and Russell, C. (2013) 'Editorial. Decolonizing + Indigenizing = Moving environmental education towards reconciliation', *Canadian Journal of Environmental Education,* 17: 5–14.

Louv, R. (2010) *Last Child in the Woods. Saving Our Children from Nature-Deficit Disorder,* London: Atlantic Books.

Mead, H. M. (2003) *Tikanga Māori. Living by Māori values,* Wellington: Huia.

New Zealand Ministry Of Education (1996) *Te Whāriki. He whāriki mātauranga mō ngā mokopuna o Aotearoa: Early Childhood Curriculum,* Wellington: Learning Media.

Otterstad, A. M. (2007) 'Doing and unpacking de-colonizing methodologies: Who is at risk?' *Contemporary Issues in Early Childhood,* 8: 170–4.

Penetito, W. (2009) 'Place-based education: Catering for curriculum, culture and community', *New Zealand Annual Review of Education,* 18: 5–29.

Plumwood, V. (1999a) 'Ecological ethics from rights to recognition', in N. Low (ed.) *Global Ethics and Environment,* New York: Routledge, pp. 188–212.

Plumwood, V. (1999b) *Environmental Culture. The Ecological Crisis of Reason,* London, Routledge.

Ritchie, J. (2011) 'Caring for ourselves, others, and the environment: Applying an indigenous paradigm in early childhood education in Aotearoa, New Zealand', in J. Lin and R. Oxford (eds), *Transformative Eco-education for Human and Planetary Survival*, Charlotte, NC: Information Age Publishing, pp. 239–53.

Ritchie, J. and Rau, C. (2006) '*Whakawhanaungatanga. Partnerships in Bicultural Development in Early Childhood Education*', Final Report to the Teaching and Learning Research Initiative Project. Wellington: Teaching Learning Research Institute.

Ritchie, J. and Rau, C. (2008) '*Te Puawaitanga – partnerships with tamariki and whānau in bicultural early childhood care and education*', Final Report to the Teaching Learning Research Initiative, Wellington: Teaching Learning Research Institute.

Ritchie, J. and Rau, C. (2012) 'Exploring possibilities for critical relational de/colonizing methodologies in early childhood education contexts in Aotearoa', in G. S. Cannella and S. R. Steinberg (eds), *Critical Qualitative Research (CQR) Reader*, New York: Peter Lang, pp. 536–47.

Ritchie, J., Duhn, I., Rau, C. and Craw, J. (2010) *Titiro Whakamuri, Hoki Whakamua. We are the Future, the Present and the Past: Caring for Self, Others and the Environment in Early Years' Teaching and Learning*, Final Report for the Teaching and Learning Research Initiative. Wellington: Teaching and Learning Research Initiative.

Rose, D. B. (2002) 'Dialogue with place: Toward an ecological body', *Journal of Narrative Theory*, 32: 311–25.

Rose, D. B. (2005) 'An indigenous philosophical ecology: Situating the human', *The Australian Journal of Anthropology*, 16: 294–305.

Smith, L. T. (1999/2006) *Decolonizing Methodologies. Research and Indigenous Peoples*, London and Dunedin: Zed Books Ltd and University of Otago Press.

Sobel, D. (2007) 'Climate change meets ecophobia'. *Connect* 21, 14–21. Online. Available: http://cf.synergylearning.org/displayarticle.cfm?selectedarticle=683 (accessed 24 May 2013).

Sobel, D. (2008) *Childhood and Nature: Design Principles for Educators*, Portland, ME: Stenhouse Publishers.

Suzuki, D. (2011) *The Legacy. An Elder's Vision for Our Sustainable Future*, Vancouver: Greystone Books/David Suzuki Foundation.

Historical and sociocultural contexts

Chapter 4

Intercultural dialogues in early childhood education for sustainability

Embedding Indigenous perspectives

Melinda G. Miller

Abstract

Embedding Indigenous perspectives in early childhood education for sustainability (ECEfS) upholds social and political action goals that support a holistic approach to promoting sustainability in educational contexts. Such goals should be responsive to particular contexts and their histories to ensure local issues are a focus of sustainability alongside global areas of concern. This chapter explores how intercultural dialogues and priorities foreground broader themes of sustainability that attend to local issues around culture and diversity and equity in relations between groups of people. Attending to such themes in educational practice unsettles a standard environmental narrative and broadens the scope and potential for ECEfS in early years settings. Strengthening intercultural priorities in ECEfS requires a commitment to reflective practices that attend to the influence of one's cultural background on teaching and learning processes. Educators committed to reflective practices provide even greater capacity for children to act as change agents (Davis 2008, 2010) around multiple dimensions of sustainability.

Introduction

This chapter explores how early childhood education for sustainability (ECEfS) can be underscored by social and political action goals, along with environmental issues. In a broad sense, sustainability has interrelated dimensions that are social, cultural, political, economic and environmental (UNESCO 2006a). In recent years, the environmental dimension of sustainability has received due attention in early childhood education in Australia, but often with much less consideration of how social, political and economic dimensions always underpin environmental concerns and initiatives (Hickling-Hudson and Ferreira 2004, Miller 2010). To provide a current example, the recently introduced National Quality Framework for early childhood education in Australia positions sustainability and related practices under the quality area 'physical environment', with a focus on children 'becoming environmentally responsible and show[ing] respect for the environment' (Australian Children's Education and Care Quality Authority (ACECQA) 2013). Children have great capacity to be 'active agents of change' (Davis 2008: 2) around environmental responsibilities, but they also have a right to engage with broader sustainability themes that introduce them to concepts of culture, diversity and equity between groups of people in the places in which they live. In Australia, this includes a right for *all* children to engage with the histories and cultures of Aboriginal and Torres Strait Islander peoples and to be supported by educators and others to think critically about the shared history of Indigenous and non-Indigenous groups (Craven 1999, Dodson 2010). To broaden the scope and potential of the promising ECEfS movement in Australia, it is timely to explore ways to unsettle the common framing of ECEfS practice within an environmental paradigm, and consider how social and political action goals can strengthen responses to sustainability in educational contexts.

I begin this chapter with a discussion about the call for intercultural dialogues (Gorski 2008, Gundara and Portera 2011) in ECEfS and how this translates to the Australian context. This provides a basis for exploring how environmental and intercultural dimensions of sustainability interrelate and impact on each other. Specifically, I draw on data from a recent doctoral study (Miller 2013a) to explore and trouble what intercultural dialogues might look like in ECEfS underscored by social and political action goals. The study invited early childhood educators in two urban childcare centres to participate in action research focused around broad themes of culture and diversity, with the aim of effecting change in thinking and practices. Rather than reporting examples of 'good practice', the study identified how racism and whiteness continued to operate in the educators' work around culture and diversity even when their practices were seen to be outwardly productive and inclusive. Analysis was supported by the use of whiteness theories and related critiques to locate how hidden racisms are present in diversity-related work despite the best of intentions. The study was limited in scope given action research is a localized methodology, although the data provide useful examples for exploring aspects of intercultural work that focuses specifically on embedding Indigenous perspectives. In the Australian context, embedding Indigenous perspectives should be central to ECEfS (Miller 2010) and form part of intercultural dialogues that attend to localized historical, social and political circumstances. Later in this chapter I explain embedding processes as a range of practices that encompass personal and professional accountabilities, as well as ways of working with Indigenous peoples and Indigenous perspectives and frameworks in educational contexts (Department of Education and Training 2011, Dreise 2007). Such practices align with the international *Guidelines on Intercultural Education* developed by UNESCO in 2006. Along with the rights of learners, these guidelines encompass critical awareness of the role of education in general, in reducing ongoing effects of racism and discrimination (UNESCO 2006b). This resonates with increasing acknowledgement about the critical role of early childhood education in supporting awareness and action around sustainability.

Intercultural dialogues in ECEfS

A clearer focus on intercultural dialogues in ECEfS presents an opportunity to explore connections between environmental issues and intersections of culture, 'race' and ethnicity. This is both in terms of an inward look at one's own ethnicity (including whiteness) and related cultural positioning, and an outward look at the standpoints and perspectives of individuals and various cultural groups. Intercultural dialogues extend beyond celebration of differences and the co-existence of different groups in societies (Gundara and Portera 2011). The key premise is to engage people in challenging stereotypes and ongoing effects of racism and discrimination in order to develop more inclusive attitudes and behaviours in their personal and professional lives (Gorski 2008). Intercultural dialogues promote strategies for thinking critically about relations between different groups. This includes how power and the distribution of resources between different groups are bound by historical circumstances which influence the present. Conley and Bryan (2009) discuss this as embracing 'different paradigms and often uncomfortable truths' (p. 22). For people in mainstream cultures, it is particularly vital to actively question what informs their worldview and what is silenced in the stories and histories they attend to in the present. Self-awareness and understanding form a critical part of intercultural dialogues.

In recent years, numerous authors have commented on the need for a clearer focus on how environmental and cultural dimensions of sustainability interrelate and impact each other. For example, Nordström (2008) questions whether environmental education and multicultural education are too close to be separate and states that 'strategies of environmental education need to be tailored to the cultural context' (p. 134). In defining similarities in objectives, values and content, Nordström (2008) outlines shared characteristics of environmental education and multicultural education including respect, belonging, and goals for individual, institutional and social reform. Burnett and McArdle (2011) view education for sustainability (EfS) as offering 'new discursive nodes around which educators can regain pedagogical traction for many of the original tenets of multiculturalism' (p. 51). This statement is drawn from the authors' recognition that educators' understandings about sustainability often marginalizes goals of multicultural education and broader sustainability themes including cultural diversity, peace, human security and gender equity. The prevailing focus on ecological or 'greening' initiatives and concerns limits broader potential around educators' conceptualizations of EfS and its uptake in educational contexts (Burnett and McArdle 2011).

In mapping the relationship between EfS and cultural diversity, the UNESCO *Guidelines on Intercultural Education* (2006b) identify education as a key site for communication about intercultural goals, but also as a social institution that has contributed to silencing and marginalizing local Indigenous knowledge systems in the past and present. In order for intercultural dialogues to flourish in educational contexts, the guidelines point to the need for new approaches to intercultural competencies that support individuals, early childhood centres and schools to accept that there are multiple legitimate ways of seeing the world and that shared understandings between different groups is critical to sustainable outcomes (UNESCO 2006b). Key themes in the guidelines around pedagogy and building relationships between cultural groups include strategies for educational practice, such as:

- Learning to understand the significance of the past for a sustainable future, using a critical lens and exploring multiple versions of history.
- Viewing learning as a journey for inner growth to enhance the capacities of learners for self-reflexivity.
- Engaging stakeholders from diverse socio-cultural groups, including Indigenous groups, in a *dual challenge* to explore different worldviews and knowledge systems and negotiate pathways for productive futures.

Such strategies place responsibility on individuals, early childhood centres and schools to work holistically toward intercultural goals – from developing strategies for inward-facing self-analysis to forming reciprocal relationships with stakeholders and local communities. Although critically important, this work is complex and challenging and requires long-term commitment to achieve even small gains, both at an individual and institutional level (Tilbury and Henderson 2003).

The contribution of early childhood education to achieving intercultural goals should not be understated, particularly given the introduction of national policies and statements that address intercultural education more explicitly, including *Belonging Being Becoming; The Early Years Learning Framework for Australia* (Department of Education, Employment and Workplace Relations (DEEWR) 2009) for children from birth to five years and the *Australian Curriculum* (Australian Curriculum Assessment and Reporting Authority 2011) for formal schooling contexts. Both documents foreground intercultural priorities, with particular reference to recognizing and engaging with Aboriginal and Torres Strait Islanders' histories and cultures. Despite positive reforms, Miller and Petriwskyj (2013) caution that greater emphasis on professional education, tools for reflective practice, and deeper engagement with the goals of intercultural education is needed to support the translation of policies to reforms in Australian early childhood education practice. Later in this chapter, I present examples of practice from an Australian urban childcare centre to acknowledge and trouble small, but important, gains toward achieving intercultural goals.

Intercultural dialogues in the Australian context

In Australia, intercultural dialogues are central to relations between Indigenous and non-Indigenous peoples because Aboriginal and Torres Strait Islander peoples are recognized as the First Peoples of Australian lands and territories. Indigenous and non-Indigenous people have a shared history, although the experiences of each group have been re-told differently since European contact (Phillips 2005, 2012).

As Phillips (2005) explains, 'the experiences of Indigenous peoples become known as "black history" and the experiences of non-Indigenous people as "Australian history"' (p. 12). Stories of the arrival of the British First Fleet in 1788, early settler pioneers, and the Federation of Australia in 1901, have informed much of what non-Indigenous people understand about Australian history and these stories continue to shape misrepresentations and assumptions about Indigenous peoples (Elder 2007). To engage in intercultural dialogues, non-Indigenous people require knowledge, understanding and acceptance about truths in Australian history which have remained largely silent in mainstream realms. This work is both inward- and outward-facing, incorporating self-analysis of one's ethnicity and related positioning in society *in relation to* Indigenous peoples, as well as learning about Indigenous histories and cultures. In previous publications (Miller 2010, 2013b) I aligned this work with reconciliation and stated that reconciliatory goals must form part of any discussion about sustainability and EfS in Australia. I reiterate this point here in terms of alignment with creating intercultural dialogues, and understandings about issues and concerns that are relevant and pressing in the Australian context.

Critical self-analysis and learning about Indigenous histories and cultures form part of a broad range of practices related to embedding Indigenous perspectives in educational contexts. In the section following, I outline embedding processes and relate these specifically to intercultural priorities in ECEfS.

Embedding Indigenous perspectives as central to intercultural dialogues

Developing capacity to understand and work with multiple perspectives in relation to Aboriginal and Torres Strait Islander peoples is multifaceted. Embedding Indigenous perspectives involves a broad range of practices that align with the goals of intercultural education listed above. As outlined by Dreise (2007) and the Department of Education and Training (2011), these include, but are not limited to:

- Demonstrating professional and personal accountabilities (e.g. critical awareness of one's attitudes and perceptions and that of colleagues, parents, community and children).
- Understanding Indigenous perspectives and processes (e.g. gaining appreciation of the diversity of Indigenous peoples and the ways unique knowledge systems are embedded in community practices, relationships, rituals and institutions).
- Understanding Indigenous protocols (e.g. awareness and use of appropriate local protocols to make introductions, establish open communication and build positive relationships).
- Planning appropriate curriculum materials (e.g. taking responsibility for educating oneself, appropriate inclusion of content and procedural knowledge); and
- Developing community partnerships (e.g. seeking partnerships with a diverse range of people, attending Aboriginal and Torres Strait Islander events).

Embedding the broad range of practices listed above involves a committed whole-centre or whole-school approach. A holistic approach to embedding processes aligns with recommendations for whole-school approaches to sustainability that are more likely to achieve systemic change within an educational site; from classroom teaching to operational procedures and connections with local communities and organizations (Ferreira *et al.* 2006). While the term 'embedding' is sometimes over-used and has therefore lost currency (Burnett and McArdle 2011), it does describe processes whereby educators' decision-making and actions become less conscious and deliberate and more automatic. Embedding processes move away from distinct studies and selective inclusion (Department of Education and Training 2011) that would likely translate as a theme or project approach to Indigenous perspectives, or as a specific focus during a recognized calendar event such as NAIDOC (National Aborigines and Islanders Day Observance Committee) week.

As Indigenous perspectives are not limited to one particular way of viewing or experiencing the world, it is essential for educational institutions, including early childhood settings, to form partnerships with members of local Indigenous communities (Grace and Trudgett 2012, Townsend-Cross 2004). This is not always possible, but as Nakata (2007) explains, engagement with Indigenous people is essential to enable talk of Indigenous knowledge systems rather than talk *about* Indigenous cultures. Nakata's (2007) point takes in several key issues related to misrepresentations of Indigenous perspectives in mainstream educational contexts including childcare centres and schools. First, in mainstream institutions, there is a tendency to endorse Indigenous 'content' (e.g. knowledge *about* Indigenous peoples and Indigenous technologies) in place of Indigenous pedagogies or processes (e.g. connections with place, community links, communal learning, peer-to-peer teaching, learning through meaningful stories and symbols) (Abayao 2006, Ninnes 2000, Yunkaporta 2009). Indigenous 'content' is often packaged and segmented for use in various parts of the curriculum (Conley and Bryan 2009, Ninnes 2000). For example, an art activity may focus on Aboriginal dot paintings, but without consideration of differences in techniques, understanding about representation, or knowledge of artists, their collective works, and their connections to land. When such elements are absent, there is no recourse to disrupt non-Indigenous knowledge and pedagogy structures. Second, presenting Indigenous 'content' as a universally applied blueprint is contradictory to 'the very concept of Indigenous knowledge as situated knowledge rooted in a particular place' (Abayao 2006: 183). While intercultural competencies endorse awareness of multiple legitimate ways of seeing the world, it is important to recognize diversity within and across cultural groups and their practices, and to attend to local perspectives.

Of key importance to intercultural goals is an educator's capacity to locate the relevance of embedding Indigenous perspectives in mainstream curricula, separate from policy requirements. There is perhaps greater facility in the early years to align practices with localized Indigenous pedagogies or processes because relationship-based pedagogy is the foundation of contemporary early childhood education curriculum design (Sims and Hutchins 2011). However, there is no guarantee that non-Indigenous educators, who represent the primary demographic for the teaching profession in Australia, will engage in critical self-analysis given the ways many were socialized. As Moreton-Robinson (1999) explains, self-analysis is rarely undertaken autonomously by non-Indigenous (white) people because there is no measure of accountability to question one's racial identity in their everyday lives.

Here, I draw on an excerpt from the previously mentioned doctoral study (Miller 2013a) to show an important gain for an early childhood educator committed to exploring ways to embed Indigenous perspectives in practice. This example aligns with personal and professional accountabilities that form part of embedding processes, and also shows commitment to inner growth and self-reflexivity in line with intercultural goals. In this excerpt, the educator, Jenny (a group leader), is responding to my question about whether her understandings about her ethnicity had changed during the study.

> Well, I just remember you saying about whiteness as a culture and I've never thought about it like that. For me, that was one thing that sort of stood out. It's like, 'Yeah, I do have my own culture', and before it was like, sort of, because I am White, that I don't consider that because I am in the majority that I don't think about it like that, and I think for me, that's what I've sort of worked out ... We don't even think about that, all the tiny things we take for granted. And in that conversation with [Vicky], like, that, it has to be 'non-Indigenous'.
>
> (Jenny: 2.10.08)

Jenny's comment suggests she had come to understand whiteness as a racial identity. She identified that whiteness is attached to particular values and privileges – 'all the tiny things we take for granted' – and to her positioning in society. Jenny showed understanding of how individuals in the majority have difficulty locating their position because being white is posited as the human norm (Dyer 1997, Moreton-Robinson 1999). Of particular interest is Jenny's capacity to think about whiteness *in relation to* Indigenous peoples, a critical component of intercultural work in terms of understanding the significance of historical circumstances in local contexts and related circumstances for particular groups. Her comment that 'it has to be non-Indigenous' suggests a willingness to ideologically position Indigenous peoples in the centre rather than on the periphery of mainstream society. Jenny's shift in understanding is an example of an inward journey and developing capacity for self-reflexivity in relation to one's own identity and the identities of others; goals that are outlined in the UNESCO *Guidelines on Intercultural Education* (2006b).

Of the available examples of approaches to embedding Indigenous perspectives employed by non-Indigenous early years settings, few are yet to attend to learning through, as well as 'about', Indigenous perspectives, and the formation of non-hierarchical partnerships with Indigenous people. One notable exception is the work of educators in non-Indigenous centres in the *Walking Respectfully* project (Fisher *et al.* 2008) commissioned by the Victorian State Branch of Early Childhood Australia (the peak professional body in Australia). Examples of early childhood educators' practices within the project highlight attempts to centralize Indigenous pedagogies and processes, form non-hierarchical partnerships with Indigenous people (at least as part of curriculum initiatives), and develop a personal rationale for locating the relevance of embedding Indigenous perspectives in non-Indigenous childcare centres. Alongside positive outcomes, researchers in the study also reported the educators' fears about implementing inappropriate practice and causing offence. The issue of fear is reported widely in non-Indigenous educators' efforts to embed Indigenous perspectives in curricula (for examples see Miller 2013a, Mundine 2010, Yunkaporta 2009). For this reason, I expand on issues about fear and associated notions of 'risk' in the section following.

Issues with fear

Fear plays a role in the ways practitioners construct and calculate risk when making changes to their practices (Stoll and Temperley 2009). With the prevailing focus on environmental approaches to ECEfS, notions of fear relate largely to physical safety in natural and outdoor environments, rather than in relation to social and cultural dimensions of sustainability. Change that involves the introduction of content seen to be too political or socially 'risky' can create anxiety for educators, particularly in terms of the potential reactions of key stakeholders. In reporting on early childhood educators' experiences in the *Walking Respectfully* project, Newman (2008) identified that assumptions about parental response became a key issue in the educators' decision-making about embedding Indigenous perspectives in practice. Fear of adverse parental reaction was common for the educators involved, particularly when they enacted pedagogies considered overtly political, such as the display of an Aboriginal flag and the introduction of Indigenous protocols including acknowledging Aboriginal and Torres Strait Islander peoples as the traditional owners of the land (now known as Australia) prior to commencing meetings and key events (Newman 2008). Educators may distance themselves from potential 'risk' by stating that others, including colleagues and children, could face consequences from their pedagogical actions. Resulting distillation or silence around 'risky' topics becomes a form of institutional racism because children are denied knowledge and understanding about the true histories of peoples in the context in which they live (Butler-Bowdon and Nowland 2003, Newman 2008). This issue resonates with early responses to sustainability education for and with young children that was seen to be too political (i.e. too 'green') and too risky in terms of invoking fear and uncertainty about issues and events that impact the Earth (Elliott and Davis 2009). In both instances, there is an underlying belief that children are separate from and oblivious to complex real-world issues that are a part of and, that impact their everyday lives (Davis 2010).

Finding ways forward from fear and constructions of risk is difficult, but necessary. As Mundine (2010) comments, 'good intentions of non-Aboriginal people trying to make a difference in early childhood education are important, so finding ways forward from the fear of 'doing it wrong' needs to be the focus of our ongoing work together' (p. 20). Here, Mundine (2010) emphasizes partnerships between Indigenous and non-Indigenous people and the importance of joint responsibility (or a *dual challenge*) for finding ways forward in the work of embedding Indigenous perspectives (see also Ritchie in this volume). Such notions align with primary goals of sustainability, particularly in terms of social sustainability and ways to build reciprocity in relations between different groups. Partnerships with Indigenous colleagues, centres and local community members are ideal, although it is important for non-Indigenous educators to develop a philosophical and theoretical rationale for embedding Indigenous perspectives of their own accord (Lampert 2012, Smith 2010).

Limitations on non-Indigenous educators' practices

Despite the necessity for educators to embed Indigenous perspectives, it is vital to acknowledge associated difficulties, particularly in non-Indigenous educational contexts. For example, there are real concerns with non-Indigenous representations of Indigenous peoples, the pedagogies employed, risks associated with appropriation, and expectations around Indigenous authority and involvement (Craven 1999, Kitson and Bowes 2010, Perey and Pike 2010, Santoro and Reid 2006). In point form, such risks translate as:

- Trivializing the richness and diversity of Indigenous peoples through simplistic talk, images and resources.
- Romanticizing aspects of Indigenous cultures and relying on overt cultural symbols (e.g. art, dance, music and food) that objectify Indigenous peoples and practices.
- Accessing support and engagement as a reactive step, including educators making contact only when gaps in their own knowledge become apparent or in response to new policy directions; and
- Failing to demonstrate preparedness (e.g. listening, learning, unlearning, self-analysis) in partnerships with Indigenous people to support reciprocity and long-term engagement.

In educational practice, risks such as these are evident in educators' talk and actions despite good intentions. In effect, such risks marginalize Indigenous peoples and Indigenous perspectives, outcomes that conflict with ideals of sustainability and goals of intercultural education. Here, I draw on another excerpt from the aforementioned doctoral study to demonstrate this point in relation to a whole-centre approach to embedding Indigenous perspectives. At one of the participating centres, the educators considered inviting local Indigenous people to participate as members of the centre management committee. This committee was the employing body and responsible for decisions made about the everyday operation of the centre. Leslie, the director, raised the idea as a long-term goal and included it in her action plan during a conversation with both Jenny and me early in the study.

> It's an interesting issue because there is scope within our constitution to have [Indigenous] community people on our management committee, not just parents, but we haven't used that, but there is potential around that. It's also quite tricky because the management committee is involved in a lot of very detailed personal stuff around all sorts of things about managing the centre. But it doesn't mean that you can't deal with that. We're reviewing the constitution at the moment so even looking at some potential for how you could perhaps build in some other structure which was like associate members or advisory members or something like that.
>
> (Leslie: 12.09.08)

On first reading, there is intention here to invite the participation of Indigenous people in whole-centre activities, in line with recommended embedding processes and strategies for achieving intercultural goals. However, a critical lens can be applied to Leslie's comments to identify how risks around embedding processes manifest in practice, often in subtle forms. For example, Leslie made a subtle differentiation between two very different forms of participation. The afterthought that 'community people' could be 'associate' or 'advisory' members does position Indigenous individuals on the periphery of the management structure and affords a position of ongoing control to the non-Indigenous (white, middle class) management group. This is reflective of contemporary forms of colonialism that reveal how dominant roles are still expected by whites in relation to Indigenous people (Kessaris 2006). Leslie's suggestion that Indigenous people could be 'advisory members' raises questions about what they would be invited to advise on, particularly given her comment that participation is 'quite tricky' because of 'very detailed personal stuff' to do with 'managing the centre'. As the committee is responsible for decisions about the everyday running of the centre, associate or advisory membership could become tokenistic, with Indigenous members excluded from having direct ownership over centre matters. Such a model situates Indigenous people outside key institutional structures under the guise of participation. It also constructs Indigenous participation along racialized lines (Colbung et al. 2007, Dei 2008, Fredericks 2009).

Alongside critical awareness of how risk manifests in approaches to embedding Indigenous perspectives, it is important to acknowledge and celebrate shifts in thinking and practice that translate to small, but important, gains. While I have presented a critique on an early childhood educator's statement about the potential for Indigenous peoples' engagement above, here I draw attention to the introduction of Indigenous protocols – a practice that is central to embedding processes and goals of intercultural dialogues. Protocols should not wholly replace the presence of Indigenous peoples in educational contexts, but they should be introduced to show respect and recognition for Indigenous peoples as the First

Australians and Traditional Owners of Australian lands and territories. In a communal journal used to record the thinking and actions of the educators and myself as
researcher throughout the study, Leslie (the director), recorded the following entry.

> Another outcome of our explorations of Indigenous issues has been to include
> an acknowledgement of traditional owners of the land at AGM and GM. I
> included this as a recommendation in a Director's Report late last year and the
> committee was happy to pass this recommendation that this happen at our
> future large formal parent meetings. The secretary followed up with me to
> ensure the correct wording was used. I think translating a value into the
> established practices of the centre is an important part of structural change.
>
> (Leslie: Journal entry: 03.04.09)

This outcome was positive given that this form of Indigenous protocol had not
occurred previously at the centre. Leslie's reference to translating intercultural
values into established centre practices aligns clearly with goals of sustainability and
intercultural education, and characteristics of systemic institutional reform.

It is important to acknowledge that non-Indigenous educators cannot be
experts on Indigenous Australia (Lampert 2012), but they do have responsibility for
contributing to broad reconciliation agendas and shaping intercultural dialogues
that benefit key stakeholders and local communities. As Newman (2008) argues:

> Children certainly need to hear from Aboriginal people, but they also need to
> hear from non-Indigenous people talking about Aboriginal and Torres Strait
> Islander cultures and history. This can help children understand that this is part
> of Australia's shared (hi)story, rather than just about 'other' people. It is also a
> part of non-Indigenous people taking responsibility for addressing past
> injustices and their impact on the present – reconciliation in action.
>
> (p. 19)

While intercultural dialogues present a *dual challenge* (UNESCO 2006b) for non-
Indigenous and Indigenous people, it is always necessary to be mindful of how the
lived experiences of Indigenous persons and their access to and responsibilities
with knowledge can be overshadowed by the 'needs' of non-Indigenous educators.
As Jones (1999) explains, just because white educators wish to include Indigenous
perspectives may not mean that the Indigenous people they invite to help them are
in a position to share their experiences. Invited guests may also not wish to act in
ways that benefit the 'needs' and desires of the dominant group only. Some forms
of knowledge are not spoken and others are not suitable for certain audiences
(Irving 2003, Jones 1999). Placing culturally-laden expectations and boundaries
around how Indigenous people contribute in educational contexts is inappropriate
and can inhibit rather than encourage participation.

Conclusion

This chapter may prompt more questions than answers in relation to embedding Indigenous perspectives and has outlined cautions around early childhood educators' work that may appear discouraging to their commitment and effort. While embedding processes present challenges at times, they still ought to be actioned if intercultural dialogues are to be responsive to relevant and pressing issues in the Australian context. In relation to developing intercultural dialogues in ECEfS, I am interested in Mang's (2005) proposal about rethinking what education is for – to the point of slowing down the impetus to action to consider, more thoughtfully, the landscape in which action occurs. This comment is highly relevant to embedding Indigenous perspectives in ECEfS, both in terms of personal and professional accountabilities and the pragmatics of embedding processes. Here, I return to concerns about the prevailing environmental paradigm in ECEfS, borrowing the words of Selby (2012) to question how mainstream approaches reinforce a dominant western view of sustainability in terms of motivations to 'go green' at the expense of broader sustainability themes. As Selby (2012: 4) asks, 'are we missing an understanding of the importance of cultural diversity and democratic processes in our mission to achieve global sustainability?' I encourage early childhood educators to be reflective about why they might see and recount issues of water wastage, pollution, inefficient use of energy and other unsustainable practices (see McKeown 2002), but have difficulty articulating the why and how of developing intercultural dialogues, particularly in relation to self-analysis and appropriate forms of engagement with Indigenous histories, cultures and peoples.

In ECEfS, there are clear gaps in what is researched and how it is reported. The current focus on environmental or 'greening' practices raises questions about how early childhood educators conceptualize sustainability and how the policies that guide their work influence approaches to sustainability education. Research around the critical place of intercultural priorities in ECEfS requires ongoing attention and this should occur alongside consideration about how educators can be supported to develop a strong reflective approach to intercultural dialogues, in conjunction with ongoing concerns about environmental issues. Recognition of researcher positionality should also carefully inform research design, as well as the processes involved in conducting and reporting the research. In terms of the study reported in this chapter (Miller 2013a), as co-researcher I came to understand how a sense of belonging in the two mainstream childcare centres over the course of the research was attributed not only to my authority as researcher, but also to my whiteness. While the research focused on broad themes of culture and diversity, and embedding Indigenous perspectives more specifically, this occurred in research sites that were historically built on white terms. Recognition of the history of the land where the two centres were located required more conscious application *during* the research. Thinking about the relevance of location and my position as co-researcher, mainly in a retrospective sense, disengaged me from more effective attempts to reduce the impact of racism individually and with others *at the point of conducting the research.*

Embedding Indigenous perspectives in ECEfS can be simultaneously practical, ideological and theoretical. At a practical level, educators can work to effect change in centre practices and pedagogies, and connect with local Indigenous peoples to develop shared goals and priorities. Demonstrating preparedness to listen to and follow the lead of Indigenous peoples and organizations in ECEfS initiatives is critical to building reciprocity (see Ritchie, Chapter 3) and intercultural dialogues that benefit all parties. Ideological work is more difficult, meaning many educators will require sustained support and tools to shift long-held ideas and understandings. *Belonging Being Becoming: The Early Years Learning Framework for Australia* (DEEWR 2009) recommends that early childhood educators draw on a range of theories in their work in order to 'investigate why they act in the ways they do', 'consider the consequences of their actions' and 'find new ways of working fairly and justly' (p. 11). When put into practice, such actions provide useful starting points that can open up richer understandings and dialogues around ECEfS. New ways of thinking and working are critical to practical and ideological change that attends more carefully to intercultural priorities in sustainability education for and with young children.

Author note

In this chapter, the term 'Indigenous' is used as an encompassing term for both Aboriginal and Torres Strait Islander peoples who are recognized as the First Peoples of Australian lands and territories. While it is now more common to use 'Aboriginal and Torres Strait Islanders' rather than the term 'Indigenous', the use of 'Indigenous' is accepted in most of the literature in Australia.

References

Abayao, L. E. (2006) 'Articulating Indigenous people's culture in education', in I. Abu-Saad and D. Champagne (eds), *Indigenous Education and Empowerment: International Perspectives*, Lanham, MD: AltaMira Press.

Australian Children's Education and Care Quality Authority (ACECQA) (2013) *Quality Area 3: Physical Environment*. Online. Available: www.acecqa.gov.au/Physical-environment (accessed 10 May 2013).

Australian Curriculum Assessment and Reporting Authority (ACARA) (2011) *The shape of the Australian Curriculum Version 3.0*. Online. Available: www.acara.edu.au/verve/_resources/The_Shape_of_the_Australian_Curriculum_V3.pdf (accessed 29 March 2012).

Burnett, B. and McArdle, F. A. (2011) 'Multiculturalism, education for sustainable development (ESD) and the shifting discursive landscape of social inclusion', *Discourse: Studies in the Cultural Politics of Education*, 32(1): 43–56.

Butler-Bowdon, T. and Nowland, S. (2003) *Aboriginal Cultural Awareness in Children's Services*, South Australia: ARMSU Network Resource, Advisory and Management Services Inc.

Colbung, M., Glover, A., Rau, C. and Ritchie, J. (2007) 'Indigenous peoples and perspectives in early childhood education', in L. Keesing-Styles and H. Hedges (eds), *Theorising Early Childhood Practice: Emerging Dialogues*, Castle Hill, NSW: Pademelon Press.

Conley, E. and Bryan, V. C. (2009) 'Elements needed to support social, ecological, and economic sustainability on a global basis by educational practitioners for Native American Indigenous people', *International Forum of Teaching and Studies*, 5(2): 22–6.

Craven, R. (ed.) (1999) *Teaching Aboriginal Studies,* New South Wales: Allen & Unwin.

Davis, J. M. (2008) 'What might education for sustainability look like in early childhood? A case for participatory, whole-of-settings approaches, *The Contribution of Early Childhood Education to a Sustainable Society*, New York: UNESCO Publications.

Davis, J. M. (2010) 'What is early childhood education for sustainability?', in J. M. Davis (ed.), *Young Children and the Environment: Early Education for Sustainability*, Melbourne: Cambridge University Press.

Dei, G. J. S. (2008) 'Indigenous knowledge studies and the next generation: Pedagogical possibilities for anti-colonial education', *The Australian Journal of Indigenous Education*, 37: 5–13.

Department of Education and Training. (2011) *Embedding Aboriginal and Torres Strait Islander Perspectives in Schools: A Guide for School Learning Communities*. Online. Available: http://deta.qld.gov.au/indigenous/pdfs/eatsips_2011.pdf (accessed 12 October 2011).

Department of Education, Employment and Workplace Relations (DEEWR) (2009) *Belonging, Being and Becoming: The Early Years Learning Framework for Australia*, Canberra: Commonwealth of Australia.

Dodson, M. (2010) 'Challenges and opportunities in Australian Indigenous education', in I. Snyder and J. Nieuwenhuysen (eds), *Closing the Gap in Education? Improving Outcomes in Southern World Societies*, Clayton, Victoria: Monash University Publishing.

Dreise, M. (2007) *My Country, My Mob: Embedding Indigenous Perspectives in Schools, An Arts Framework*, Canberra: Department of Education, Training and the Arts.

Dyer, R. (1997) *White*, London: Routledge.

Elder, C. (2007) *Being Australian: Narratives of National Identity*, Crows Nest, NSW: Allen & Unwin.

Elliott, S. and Davis, J. (2009) 'Exploring the resistance: An Australian perspective on educating for sustainability in early childhood', *International Journal of Early Childhood*, 41(2): 65–77.

Ferreira, J., Ryan, L. and Tilbury, D. (2006) *Whole-school Approaches to Sustainability: A Review of Models for Professional Development in Pre-service Teacher Education,* Canberra: Australian Government Department of the Environment and Heritage and the Australian Research Institute in Education for Sustainability (ARIES).

Fisher, B., Hydon, C., Jewell, P. and Nyland, B. (eds) (2008) *Walking Respectfully: Exploring Indigenous Culture and Reconciliation in Early Childhood Practice*, Melbourne: Early Childhood Australia, Victoria Branch.

Fredericks, B. (2009) 'The epistemology that maintains white race privilege, power and control of Indigenous studies and Indigenous peoples' participation in universities', *Australian Critical Race and Whiteness Studies Association ejournal*, 5(1): 1–12.

Gorski, P. (2008) 'Good intentions are not enough: A decolonizing intercultural education', *Intercultural Education*, 19(6): 515–25.

Grace, R. and Trudgett, M. (2012) 'It's not rocket science: The perspectives of Indigenous early childhood workers on supporting the engagement of Indigenous families in early childhood settings', *Australasian Journal of Early Childhood*, 37(2): 10–18.

Gundara, J. and Portera, A. (2011) 'Theoretical reflections on intercultural education', *Intercultural Education*, 19(6): 463–8.

Hickling-Hudson, A. and Ferreira, J. (2004) 'Changing schools of a changing world?', in B.

Burnett, D. Meadmore and G. Tait (eds), *New Questions for contemporary Teachers: Taking a Socio-cultural Approach to Education*, Sydney: Pearson.

Irving, F. (2003) 'Learning to listen to Indigenous voice: Dialogue and dilemmas', Paper presented at the *International Education Research Conference AARE*, November 30–December 3, Auckland, New Zealand.

Jones, A. (1999) 'The limits of cross-cultural dialogue: Pedagogy, desire and the absolutions in the classroom', *Educational Theory*, 49(3): 299–316.

Kessaris, T. (2006) 'About being Mununga (Whitefella). Making covert group racism visible', *Journal of Community and Applied Social Psychology*, 16(5): 347–62.

Kitson, R. and Bowes, J. (2010) 'Incorporating Indigenous ways of knowing in early childhood education for Indigenous children', *Australasian Journal of Early Childhood*, 35(4): 81–9.

Lampert, J. (2012) 'Becoming a socially just teacher: Walking the talk', in J. Phillips and J. Lampert (eds), *Introductory Indigenous Studies in Education: Reflection and the Importance of Knowing*, 2nd edn. Frenchs Forest, NSW: Pearson.

Mang, P. (2005) 'What is education for? Connecting learning with sustainable living', *Independent School*, 64(3): 14–18.

McKeown, R. (2002) *Education for Sustainable Development Toolkits: Tools to Orient Education to Address Sustainability*. Online. Available: www.esdtoolkit.org/esd_toolkit_v2.pdf (accessed 12 February 2013).

Miller, M. G. (2010) 'Repositioning and ethic of sustainability in early childhood education, with reconciliation as central', In J. M. Davis (ed.), *Young Children and the Environment: Early Education for Sustainability*, Melbourne: Cambridge University Press.

Miller, M. G. (2013a) *Action for Change? Embedding Aboriginal and Torres Strait Islander Perspectives in Early Childhood Education Curricula*. Unpublished PhD Thesis, Queensland University of Technology, Brisbane, Australia. Online. Available: http://eprints.qut.edu.au/60905/ (accessed 10 July 2013).

Miller, M. G. (2013b) 'Connecting sustainability work with reconciliation', *In the Loop Magazine*, Winter 2013, Health and Community Services Workforce Council, Australia, 4–5.

Miller, M. G. and Petriwskyj, A. (2013) 'New directions for early intercultural education in Australia', *International Journal of Early Childhood*, 45(2): 251–66.

Moreton-Robinson, A. (1999) 'Unmasking whiteness: A Goori Jondal's look at some Duggai business', in B. McKay (ed.), *Unmasking Whiteness: Race Relations and Reconciliation*, Nathan, Queensland: Queensland Studies Centre, School of Humanities, Griffith University.

Mundine, K. (2010) 'Flower girl', in M. Giugni and K. Mundine (eds), *Talkin' Up and Speakin' Out: Aboriginal and Multicultural Voices in Early Childhood*, Castle Hill, NSW: Pademelon Press.

Nakata, M. (2007) 'The cultural interface', *The Australian Journal of Indigenous Education*, 36: 7–14.

Newman, B. (2008) 'Involving children in real issues – children connecting with real issues', in B. Fisher, C. Hydon, P. Jewell and B. Nyland (eds), *Walking Respectfully: Exploring Indigenous Culture and Reconciliation in Early Childhood Practice*, Melbourne: Early Childhood Australia, Victoria Branch.

Ninnes, P. (2000) 'Representations of Indigenous knowledges in secondary school science textbooks in Australia and Canada', *International Journal of Science Education*, 22(6): 603–17.

Nordström, H. K. (2008) 'Environmental education and multicultural education – too close to be separate?', *International Research in Geographical and Environmental Education*, 17(2): 131–45.

Perey, R. and Pike, T. (2010) *Country and Sustainability: Applied Holistic Thinking from an Aboriginal Perspective.* Online. Available: www.aries.mq.edu.au/projects/deewr_indigenous_concepts/index.php (accessed 21 August 2011).

Phillips, J. (2005) 'Indigenous knowledge: Making space in the Australian centre', in J. Phillips and J. Lampert (eds), *Introductory Indigenous Studies in Education: The Importance of Knowing*, Frenchs Forest, NSW: Pearson.

Phillips, J. (2012) 'Indigenous knowledge perspectives: Making space in the Australian centre', in J. Phillips and J. Lampert (eds), *Introductory Indigenous Studies in Education: Reflection and the Importance of Knowing*, 2nd edn. Frenchs Forest, NSW: Pearson.

Santoro, N. and Reid, J. (2006) '"All things to all people": Indigenous teachers in the Australian teaching profession', *European Journal of Teacher Education*, 29(3): 287–303.

Selby, C. (2012) Integrating culture as a cornerstone of success in sustainability education. *Journal of Sustainability Education: 2012, The Geography of Sustainability*. Online. Available: www.jsedimensions.org/wordpress/2012-the-geography-of-sustainabilty/ (accessed 1 March 2013).

Sims, M. and Hutchins, T. (2011) *Program Planning for Infants and Toddlers: In Search of Relationships*, 2nd edn. New South Wales: Pademelon Press.

Smith, J. (2010) 'Teaching about Indigenous forms of knowledge: Insights from non-Indigenous teachers of visual arts education in New Zealand', in O. Kwo (ed.), *Teachers as Learners: Critical Discourse on Challenges and Opportunities*, Hong Kong: Springer.

Stoll, L. and Temperley, J. (2009) 'Creative leadership: A challenge of our times', *School Leadership and Management*, 29(1): 65–78.

Tilbury, D. and Henderson, K. (2003) 'Education for intercultural understanding in Australian schools: A review of its contribution to education for sustainable development', *Australian Journal of Environmental Education*, 19: 81–95.

Townsend-Cross, M. (2004) 'Indigenous Australian perspectives in early childhood education', *Australian Journal of Early Childhood*, 29(4): 1–6.

UNESCO (2006a) *Four Dimensions of Sustainable Development*. Online. Available: www.unesco.org/education/tlsf/TLSF/theme_a/mod02/uncom02t02.htm (accessed 30 January 2009).

UNESCO (2006b) *Guidelines on Intercultural Education*. Online. Available: http://unesdoc.unesco.org/images/0014/001478/147878e.pdf (accessed 30 January, 2013).

Yunkaporta, T. (2009) *Aboriginal Pedagogies at the Cultural Interface. Draft Report for the Department of Education and Training, Western Australia*. Online. Available: http://eprints.jcu.edu.au/10974/ (accessed 20 January 2010).

Chapter 5

Perspectives on early childhood environmental education in Japan

Rethinking for a sustainable society

Michiko Inoue

Abstract

Japan has a long history of early childhood education which began in the nine-teenth century. Environmental education was first introduced into government environmental policy during the 1980s and later, in 1989, into the national curriculum. However both streams, early childhood education and environmental education, have never been combined. First, in this chapter, I describe early child-hood education and environmental education in Japan, and then I outline my analyses of official guidelines and the work of academics and educators that demonstrate limited concern for environmental education in early childhood education. Finally, I discuss the necessity for rethinking early childhood education in Japan and suggest four key concepts for moving forward in early childhood environmental education to contribute to the transition necessary to build a sustainable society. These concepts are critical thinking, children's active participation, an ecological worldview, and empathy with nature. I finish by discussing the need to consider the diverse cultural contexts into which education for sustain-ability must fit if an international movement is to become effective.

Introduction

Education is one of the most important strategies for transitioning to a sustainable society. Environmental issues are complex and difficult to understand, let alone resolve, requiring environmental, social and economic considerations. It is neces-sary, therefore, to develop effective methods for dealing with complexity when educating for sustainability. Although environmental education commenced in the 1970s, research focusing on environmental education in early childhood was limited before the 1990s (Davis 2009, New South Wales Environment Protection Authority 2003). Then, in the early 1990s, Wilson in the United States published many papers on early childhood environmental education (e.g. Wilson 1993, 1994). Since the late 1990s, Australia has been the most prolific country in this field in terms of scholarly research outputs. A recent initiative to build research in early childhood education for sustainability has been an international research network instigated by Australian academic, Davis, in 2010 (refer to introductory chapter). Currently, early childhood environmental education/education for sustainability research is entering a new phase. However, when we progress our research transnationally, it is important to know something of the historical, political and cultural contexts of each country so that we can learn effectively from each other. This chapter explains the historical context of early childhood environmental education in Japan and proposes a way forward for rethinking existing early childhood education programs in order to contribute to the transition to a sustainable society.

Early childhood education in Japan

Japan has a long history of early childhood education from the middle of the nineteenth century (see National Institute for Educational Policy Research 2009). Currently, there is a dual early childhood education system with two types of authorized services, kindergartens and nursery centres. The target demographic groups, length of care time, legal foundations, governing bodies, and regulatory standards are different for each of these. The oldest kindergarten was founded in 1876 for educating the children of upper-middle class families, while the oldest nursery centre was founded in 1890 to care for the children of working-class families. Thus, from the start, the dichotomy of kindergartens focusing on education and nursery centres on care was established.

Successive governments in Japan have developed national standards for early childhood education beginning in the nineteenth century (see Table 5.1). At present, there are two sets of guidelines for early childhood education. One is a *Course of Study for Kindergarten* first published in 1956, and the other is a *Guideline for Care and Education in Nursery Centres*, first published in 1964. Although these two guideline documents were developed and managed under different governing ministries, the educational aims for children aged three to five years have been aligned for 20 years. In 2006, the government founded a new type of early childhood education service referred to as *Centres for Early Childhood Education and Care* in order to enhance unification of kindergartens and nursery centres. However, the numbers of children enrolled in this new service type has not increased since 2006; only 2.2 per cent of children (aged three to five years) were enrolled in 2012 (Ministry of Education, Culture, Sports, Science and Technology 2012a).

In terms of qualifications, the certificate for a kindergarten educator is a 'Teacher's Licence' issued by the Ministry of Education, Culture, Sports, Science and Technology. The certificate for a nursery centre worker is a 'Qualification as a Nursery Teacher' given by the Ministry of Health, Labour and Welfare. Usually, a student graduating from a registered early childhood teacher education school/faculty is awarded both these certificates and most educators do have both. The awarding professional education institutions include technical schools, junior colleges (two-year teacher preparation) and universities (four-year teacher preparation). Teacher education curricula for both qualifications are strictly regulated by

Table 5.1 A chronology of national Japanese early childhood education policies and
curriculum guidelines 1899–2008

Year	Guidelines for kindergartens	Guidelines for nursery centres
1899	Regulation on Kindergarten Contents and Facilities	
1926	Kindergarten Order	
1946	Basic Act on Education	
1947	School Education Act	Child Welfare Act
1948	Nursing Guideline	
1956	Course of study for Kindergarten (National Curriculum Standards for Kindergartens)	
1964	Course of study for Kindergarten (1st revision)	
1965		Guideline for Care and Education in Nursery Centres
1989	Course of study for Kindergarten (2nd revision)	
1990		Guideline for Care and Education in Nursery Centres (1st revision)
1998	Course of study for Kindergarten (3rd revision)	
1999		Guideline for Care and Education in Nursery Centres (2nd revision)
2006	Basic Act on Education (1st revision)	
2006	Act on Advancement of Comprehensive Service Related to Education and Care for Preschool Children	
2007	School Education Act (1st revision)	
2008	Course of study for Kindergarten (4th revision)	Guideline for Care and Education in Nursery Centres (3rd revision)

the Japanese government. For kindergartens, the percentage of early childhood educators who finished four or more years of education in universities or graduate schools was 23.9 per cent in 2012 (Ministry of Education, Culture, Sports, Science and Technology 2012b). In a report published by the Organization for Economic Co-operation and Development (OECD), Taguma et al. (2012) stated that early childhood education and care (ECEC) in Japan had 'a well-established practice regarding the provision and encouragement of professional development' and 'highly qualified ECEC staff – especially with regard to nursery workers compared with most other OECD countries'. While Japan's enrolment rate for children under the age of three years in formal nursery centres (24.5 per cent) was below the OECD average in 2008, the enrolment rates for three-year-olds (79.8 per cent) and five-year-olds (97.8 per cent) were above the OECD average. Overall, well-established early childhood education in Japan with well-qualified staff and high enrolment rates are reasonably comparable to many similarly-developed nations. This suggests that early childhood education in Japan has a large potential to develop education for sustainability when educators recognize its significance and if supported by well-developed national guidelines.

Environmental education in Japan

In Japan, education about pollution and nature conservation has been practised in schools and communities since the 1960s (e.g. Asaoka 2005, Kawashima *et al.* 2002). The term 'environmental education' was later imported from Western countries after the United Nations Conference on the Human Environment, held in Stockholm in 1972. The Japanese government introduced environmental education into its environmental policy and established several official research committees for environmental education in the 1980s. Environmental education was officially introduced into the national curriculum for schools later in 1989. The then Ministry of Education published official teachers' handbooks for environmental education (for secondary school teachers in 1991 and for primary school teachers in 1992, later revised in 2007), thus firmly locating environmental education as a part of the nation's environmental policies.

In the new millennium, a new movement for environmental education began. The government enacted the Law for Enhancing Motivation on Environmental Conservation and Promoting of Environmental Education in 2003. Then the government revised the Basic Act on Education in 2006, which was the first revision to the Act since its enactment in 1946, adding a new aim for education. This was: 'To foster an attitude to respect life, care for nature, and contribute to the protection of the environment' (Articles 2–4). The government also revised the Law for Enhancing Motivation on Environmental Conservation and Promoting of Environmental Education in 2011 to promote the steady progress of environmental education throughout Japan, and formulated a basic policy for the promotion of environmental education in 2012. It is noted here that the government sectors of both environment and education in Japan mostly use the term 'environmental education' in their official discourses when referring to laws, education policy, environmental policy and other associated areas.

In relation to the broader concept of sustainability, the terms 'sustainable society' and 'sustainable development (SD)' have appeared in documents from the Ministry of the Environment since 1993. Indeed, it was the Japanese government that initiated the Decade of Education for Sustainable Development (DESD) at the World Summit on Sustainable Development held in Johannesburg in 2002. DESD was launched and the Japanese government established an inter-ministerial meeting that included 11 government ministries and agencies in 2005. The Ministry of the Environment took the key initiative to promote education for sustainable development (ESD) and started '+ESD project' to unite various existing social movements around education for sustainable development (e.g. community-based nature conservation activities, city planning projects, environmental education in schools). In addition, non-governmental organizations such as the Japan Council on the United Nations Decade of Education for Sustainable Development and the Asia/Pacific Cultural Centre for the United Nations Educational, Scientific and Cultural Organization (UNESCO) also worked to promote ESD. Consequently, some schools and non-profit groups have started to revise their existing practices related to environment and community towards ESD practices which combine environmental with social and economic dimensions (National Institute for Educational Policy Research 2012).

However, neither the terms 'education for sustainable development (ESD)' nor 'education for sustainability (EfS)' have been adopted in law, environmental policies, or educational guidelines; environmental education is still the most strongly entrenched term used in official discourses. For example, the primary school teacher's handbook for environmental education (first revision by National Institute for Educational Policy Research in 2007) briefly refers to ESD and its relationship to environmental education, but continues to refer to environmental education throughout the text. Recently in Japan, the words 'sustainability' and 'sustainable' have become more popular and are now used more frequently in the discourses of politics and economics, but make no reference to environmental matters. From the viewpoint of environmental education, the more holistic concepts of 'sustainability' and 'sustainable' may become weakened by this misuse and may lose their original power and impact.

Environmental education in early childhood

The status of official guidelines/policies in Japan

As mentioned above, environmental education was first imported into Japan in the 1970s and was embedded into all subjects in primary and secondary schools when the national guidelines were revised in 1989. Nevertheless, even though the *Course of Study for Kindergarten* was revised in the same year, environmental education was not included in the revision. Even when environmental conservation was described in 2006 for the first time in the Basic Act on Education which overarches other educational policies and guidelines, this change did not influence the early childhood education guidelines revision in 2008; environmental education was still not explicitly included in early childhood education.

A major reason for this absence is the ambiguity about the definition of early childhood environmental education. In the Law for Enhancing Motivation on Environmental Conservation and Promoting of Environmental Education, environmental education is officially defined as 'education and learning conducted to deepen understanding of environmental conservation' (2003: Articles 2–3). In the primary teacher's handbook for environmental education published in 2007, environmental education is described as 'fostering concerns and knowledge on

environment and environmental issues, skills and abilities to think and judge logi-
cally to promote environmental conservation based on comprehensive
understanding of relationship between human activity and environment, attitudes
to independently participate in activities to improve the environment, and to
behave in environmentally-responsible ways for a sustainable society' (National
Institute for Educational Policy Research: 6). From these very broad definitions, it
is difficult to determine the actual practices for early childhood environmental
education in Japan.

In a similar generalist vein, there is one paragraph that references early childhood education in the primary teacher's handbook for environmental education
(National Institute for Educational Policy Research 2007: 20). This paragraph states
that early childhood environmental education comprises nature-based activities
and learning about resource savings. However, such activities have previously been
described in early childhood education guidelines stemming from long-held beliefs
that nature-based activities are important for child development and that resource
savings is a traditional Japanese way of thinking. Consequently, environmental
education has not been recognized as a new educational issue for most early childhood educators in Japan.

Professional associations and early childhood environmental education in Japan

The Japanese Society of Environmental Education was founded in 1990 and has
almost 1,700 members. Although this academic/professional society has always
indicated that environmental education/education for sustainable development
should start from early childhood, the society merely notes this and has not
demonstrated any clear commitment. Further, researchers in environmental education often specialize in environmental science, biology, agricultural science, or
social science and have little concern with and/or knowledge of early childhood
education. The number of early childhood educators or researchers who focus on
early childhood pedagogy or psychology has not expanded within this society over
many years. However, in 2013, a new research group for early childhood environmental education was established in the society, illustrating an emerging focus for
some members.

In terms of the early childhood field, the largest academic society for early
childhood education, the Japan Society of Research on Early Childhood Care and
Education, founded in 1948, has approximately 4,000 members. Most are practitioners or researchers specializing in early childhood pedagogy or child psychology
and appear to be more interested in issues concerned with child development and
early childhood pedagogy, such as special needs education and family support,
rather than with environmental or sustainability issues.

While many papers on environmental education were found in a database of
research articles (CiNii) held by the National Institute of Informatics in 2013 (see
Table 5.2), there are far fewer papers referring to 'education for sustainable

Table 5.2 Results of CiNii Japanese academic database search for key words in whole publications and titles conducted in 2013

Publication category	Keyword 1 / Keyword 2	Young children		Early childhood education and care		No keyword	
		Whole publication	Title only	Whole publication	Title only	Whole publication	Title only
Journal articles and conference papers	Environmental education	103	61	97	59	8,373	5,670
	Education for sustainable development	4	2	2	0	288	189
	Education for sustainability	0	0	0	0	11	9
Books and reports	Environmental education	18	5	9	2	929	712
	Education for sustainable development	0	0	0	0	62	37
	Education for sustainability	0	0	0	0	0	0

development' or 'education for sustainability'. Although 103 papers were found by searching online for the terms 'environmental education (kankyo kyoiku)' with 'early childhood children (youji)' and 97 papers with 'early childhood education and care (hoiku)', they account for no more than 1 per cent of the total number of papers about environmental education. Japanese researchers in environmental education and early childhood education, then, do not appear to demonstrate much concern for or interest in early childhood environmental education. Reflecting similar international trends (Davis 2009), these papers have been published mainly since the early 1990s. Of these, almost 60 per cent explicitly include the keywords noted above in their titles. However, most authors appear to have only temporarily engaged with early childhood environmental education and have not continued to research in this area. As I am one of a few researchers who has continuously explored early childhood environmental education since 1992, around one-quarter of the papers located were self-authored (Inoue 2009, 2012). This demonstrates the fragility of the research base in early childhood environmental education in Japan, and the need for it to be nurtured.

Early childhood educators/practitioners engagement with environmental education in Japan

As mentioned earlier, the Japanese early childhood education guidelines describe the importance of nature-based activities and resource savings. In 2003, Muto and I conducted a survey of 417 early childhood services (226 kindergartens and 201 nursery centres) in two prefectures (Hyogo and Tokyo) based on ideas and theoretical underpinnings of early childhood environmental education as espoused by Wilson (1993, 1994). Wilson made a distinction between science education and environmental education, highlighting ecological understandings, based on interconnections, rather than simply plant and animal biology, and placed an emphasis on environmental justice as important themes for environmental education at the early childhood level.

Our survey explored teacher's understandings of the concepts of 'nature' and 'environment' arising from the different histories of environmental education and early childhood education in Japan (Inoue 1995, 1996, 2000). Since kindergartens are legally required to have outdoor playgrounds, all kindergartens, as expected, did have these on-site. Although there is no similar legal obligation for nursery centres, 98.5 per cent also had their own outdoor playgrounds. Educators who responded to the survey described how there were several kinds of insects and small creatures, even in centres located in densely built city areas (Inoue and Muto 2006). Half of the surveyed services had garden beds, spaces for wild grasses, fruit trees, and plants that children could freely use in their play. Children were able to play in the playgrounds on average for two hours per day, which is about one-third of the time a child spends each day in a kindergarten, and approximately one-quarter of the child's day for a nursery centre. Animals were cared for in 88 per cent of services and each centre cared for four different kinds of animals on average, such as crayfish, goldfish, rabbits, and butterfly larvae (Inoue and Muto 2009). Most services took children outside their centres (e.g. to parks, shrines, rice fields, community gardens and other green spaces) to experience various types of environments, around once or twice a month (Inoue and Muto 2010).

In relation to resource conservation, early childhood educators included water, food, and energy savings in their daily activities and used waste materials for art activities as part of their regular program. Sometimes children participated in community-based rubbish clean-ups or recycling activities. As it is now over ten years since this survey was conducted, I have recently updated the survey, which includes a stronger focus on sustainability concepts and practices. New data will enable some comparisons with the earlier data to identify any changes over the years, and will also generate some transnational practice comparisons as the survey has now been distributed to practitioners in Australia and Sweden.

From my ongoing research, I speculate that there are two issues that have led to the slow uptake of early childhood environmental education in Japan. First, when early childhood environmental education is defined as nature-based activities and environmentally-responsible lifestyle learning, many early childhood educators who already incorporate these aspects into their practice, do not recognize environmental education as a new educational issue with broader meanings encompassing sustainability. The second problem relates to the prioritizing of competing issues within early childhood education. Recently, Japanese early childhood educators have encountered a range of other contemporary issues also in need of addressing such as family support, child abuse, and special needs education. They struggle with these difficult issues every day and, hence, do not recognize early childhood environmental education as an equally important and urgent issue.

Rethinking early childhood environmental education for a sustainable society

Environmental Education and Education for Sustainability: clarifying meanings

It is difficult to judge whether early childhood education practice in Japan functions as environmental education/education for sustainable development/education for sustainability without clarifying their meanings. I define education for sustainability as 'education for building a sustainable society', and I see environmental education as 'a part of education for sustainability and education for fostering an ecological/environmental view towards sustainability' (Inoue 2012). I do not use the term education for sustainable development because it is possible that this concept – with its multiple meanings and potential for misuse – will lead to unwise decisions, as discussed by others in various fields such as philosophy, economics and environmentalism (Bonnet 2007, Brown et al. 1987, Jacob 1988, Latouche 2004, 2007, Rist 1996, Shiva 1992).

Here, Figures 5.1 a and b offer a conceptual diagram to further clarify meanings. Figure 5.1a represents the current context where new educational issues, such as environmental education, citizenship education, special needs education, and human rights education, have been successively added on to existing education curricula. As education for sustainable development and education for sustainability are regarded as new educational issues by many educators, and as a replacement for environmental education, they too are bolted on to the existing education system in Japan. In this figure, mainstream education always takes precedence over any additional new educational issues. Such an approach is not likely to lead to structural change in education and works to continue the marginalization of environmental education/education for sustainability.

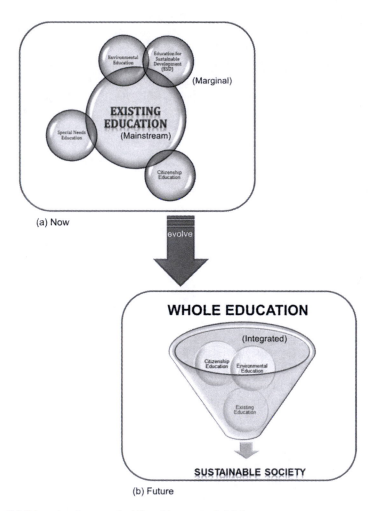

Figure 5.1 Education for sustainability: (a) now and (b) future

The significance of environmental education was recognized globally in the 1970s and practices related to environment, environmental issues and nature protection were added to the existing education paradigm as environmental education. Now, though, educators and the public have greater knowledge of environmental issues and the necessity for nature conservation. However, when new educational issues are merely added to the existing education framework with little critical reflection of how or why social change is necessary, the existing education system remains essentially unchanged, and new educational issues are often superficially or only tentatively explored. As a result, mainstream education has not succeeded in helping to build sustainable societies to date. Therefore, we need to reflect and rethink whether the existing education paradigm can build sustainable societies.

In my view, environmental education should not be regarded as a way of adding additional topics to education, but must fundamentally transform the educational paradigm in order to promote sustainability (see Figure 5.1b). In the future, the whole of education should equate to education for sustainability. This is not a new idea because 'reorientation of existing education' has already been described in various documents on education for sustainable development such as *Agenda 21* (United Nations 1992, Chapter 36) and *United Nations Decade of Education for Sustainable Development (2005–2014): International Implementation Scheme* (UNESCO 2005). However, it seems that 'reorientation' under the concept 'development' would be a precarious approach for transforming the educational paradigm. The traditional concept of 'development' is deeply and strongly embedded into existing education, and it is difficult to discard this traditional concept which has built unsustainable societies (Rist 1996). A more radical theoretical framework is necessary to transform the whole of education to education for sustainability.

Key concepts for rethinking existing early childhood education for sustainability

As a consequence, we should rethink the whole of the existing early childhood education paradigm and reconstruct all practices, not only for enhancing individual children's learning and development, but also for the broader concept of sustainability. There is no simple way to do this; it is a complex matter.

Drawing on my academic research and lengthy engagement with early childhood environmental education, I propose the following four broad concepts as useful for re-imagining education: critical thinking, children's active participation, an ecological worldview, and empathy with nature. Recently, the first two concepts have come to the fore as important, and especially in discussions about early childhood education for sustainability (Davis 2008, Mackey 2012), although there is not yet much evidence of these concepts being applied in practice. The latter two concepts, however, still appear to be somewhat ignored in early childhood education because of the belief that they are being fostered through nature-based learning experiences.

As previously mentioned, there is a long tradition of nature-based activities in Japan; children have been learning about the natural world as required by national curriculum guidelines since the end of the nineteenth century. In the past, there were more undeveloped natural areas in Japan and few alternatives to compete with nature-based outdoor play in children's daily lives. Nevertheless, in spite of such past rich opportunities for nature-based experiences, previous generations have failed to prevent the destruction of natural areas and the depletion of natural resources caused by rapid economic development. Hence, current and future generations are now facing unsustainable futures. This situation indicates that simply conducting the same kinds of nature-based activities that children have engaged in in the past will not facilitate the development of attitudes, knowledge and skills necessary for building a sustainable society. It is necessary, therefore, to reflect upon and evaluate existing educational thinking. Embedding the four concepts mentioned earlier offer a way to rethink current early childhood environmental education in Japan.

How might the key concepts work in practice?

To enhance children's learning and development, early childhood educators usually develop learning objectives to inform planning and pedagogical practice. The official guidelines for early childhood education in Japan traditionally describe the objectives for nature-based activities as being about fostering emotions, thinking, curiosity, expressiveness, a sense of attachment to and awe for nature, respect for life, and social responsibility. In general, Japanese children regularly engage in nature-based activities and appear to enjoy them. There are, however, no objectives in the existing early childhood education guidelines to match with the four sustainability-oriented concepts previously outlined. If educators intentionally seek to include these suggested underpinning concepts into their learning objectives for children, this may change the way they create the educational environment, how they support children's learning and engagement, and how they reflect on and evaluate their practices. Such changes could potentially transform their pedagogical practices. For example, Japanese educators' learning objectives for nature-based activities are usually described as 'children enjoy the natural environment in autumn' or 'children are aware of the various colours and shapes of natural materials'. If educators rewrite these objectives so that they foster an ecological worldview where interconnections between elements are paramount, then nature-based activities could be broadened to include concepts such as biodiversity, ecosystems, bio-capacity, and human-nature relationships. For example, objectives such as 'children are aware of life and the role of decomposers such as fungi or mini-bugs' or 'children are aware of the relationships between animals and plants' may encourage educators to revitalize children's playgrounds into places where children can encounter decomposers and bugs, grow vegetables that are easy to care for, and cook produce such as sweet potatoes, display ecology-related books, posters and factsheets, and intentionally teach children about ecological concepts. These sites also offer possibilities for children and their teachers to engage actively in caring for, problem-solving, and repairing their local environment. To facilitate children's understandings about how interdependencies with nature/natural environment are important to human existence, educators should explicitly connect these with children's daily lives.

Learning from diverse cultures

Recently, early childhood researchers have become more interested in early childhood education for sustainability and an international network for early childhood education for sustainability is beginning to emerge. It must not be forgotten, however, that each nation has its own education system and pedagogical approaches that are informed by its own histories and cultures. When early childhood education for sustainability is discussed in international forums, it is important that participants recognize and acknowledge this diversity. As already noted, even basic concepts such as environmental education/education for sustainable development/education for sustainability are recognized and understood differently in different countries. For example, in official environmental policies and educational guidelines which influence educational practices, the term 'environmental education' is mainly used in both Japan and the United States. 'Education for sustainable development' is mainly used in European Union countries, while 'education for sustainability' is more common in Australia and New Zealand. In addition, definitions for each of the terms environmental education/education for sustainable development/education for sustainability are not commonly understood, not only in public policy, but also in academia. Researchers and practitioners alike need to be cognisant of the ambiguities and politics embedded in the concepts of environmental education/education for sustainable development/education for sustainability.

Giving consideration to cultural differences is also indispensable for rethinking the existing education paradigm using the four key concepts discussed previously. For example, critical thinking is a concept that has developed in Western cultures and is based on a long tradition of Western philosophy since the ancient Greeks (around 3000 years ago). It was adopted by education theorists such as Dewey, and become more widespread within Western education in the 1980s (e.g. Cederblom and Paulsen 1982). Active child participation is another concept that has developed in recent times aimed at promoting and protecting children's rights (Convention on the Rights of the Child, United Nations Children's Fund 1989). These two concepts are important for changing current education towards sustainability. However, non-critical importation of these concepts into pedagogical practice may not work so well in non-Western cultures such as Japan because people from different cultures have different communication styles and different family models (Fitzgerald 2002, Lun et al. 2010, McGuire 2007, Smith et al. 2006). For example, Tian and Low (2011) reviewed research papers about the lack of critical thinking skills amongst Chinese and other Asian students and discussed the necessity of multi-dimensional understandings of cultural backgrounds to promote critical thinking in Asian education. For active participation, offering opinions and asking questions are important. However, Murata (2011) reported Japanese students were unwilling to offer their own opinions and questions in educational settings and suggested that Japanese specific cultural backgrounds were a factor. Cross-cultural psychology also reveals differences in attention, perception, cognition and social-psychological phenomena, such as the concept of self, between different cultural groups. Even within relatively homogenous culture groups such as Japanese, Korean and Chinese we can find differences (Nisbett 2004, Shiraev and Levy 2009). Such differences are likely to influence educational approaches, with several studies also revealing differences in care and education practices of parents and early childhood educators among different cultures (Clarke-Stewart *et al.* 2006, Hoffman 2000, Johnston and Wong 2002, Minami 1994; Tobin 2005). Therefore, educators should not adopt educational methods superficially from other cultures, but aim to find appropriate approaches to practise, based on their own cultural backgrounds.

With regard to the other two sustainability concepts – taking an ecological world-view and fostering empathy with nature – these have been recognized as being embedded into many Indigenous cultures around the world. Indigenous cultures did not have formal education systems until colonization forced this upon them; previously, an ecological worldview and empathy with nature had been handed down from generation to generation through informal education (Cajete 1993, 1999, Reagan 1996). For example, Ross *et al.* (2003) found that Native American children tended to have stronger 'ecological reasoning' and described the possibility that not only nature-based experiences, but culture played an important role in the development of folk-biological knowledge. It is acknowledged that Indigenous peoples' learning was/is strongly connected with their daily lives and economic circumstances, although many Indigenous societies have struggled to maintain their traditional ways of life in the modernized world (Blaser *et al.* 2004, Grim 2001). Their ecological worldview would have been transmitted in informal/familial relationships, rather than through schooling or textbooks. It may be possible to learn something about sustainable living by exploring this informal education mode.

Recommendations for further practice and research in early childhood education for sustainability in Japan

Examining the history and current circumstances of environmental education and early childhood education in Japan reveals that early childhood environmental education is mainly about nature-based activities, and that this narrow thinking has prevented the development of more effective practices to support environmental education/education for sustainability. We need to rethink our existing practices, such as nature-based activities and the learning of environmentally-responsible ways of living, and seek to transform the whole of education towards education for sustainability. For this to occur, the concepts of critical thinking, children's active participation, an ecological worldview, and empathy with nature are useful tools.

For educators, it is important to explicitly introduce these concepts into the learn-ing objectives that guide daily teaching because children's learning can be significantly reorientated towards sustainability through such measures, even if the practices superficially appear to be similar. If educators think only of child devel-opment objectives for teaching and learning, they are less able to critically reflect on, and evaluate their existing practices, from the viewpoint of sustainability. Reflection and evaluation in co-operation with early childhood education for sustainability researchers will be helpful for embedding these concepts into early childhood programs.

For researchers and theorists in education for sustainability, it is important that they take account of the socio-historical contexts of fundamental concepts such as environmental education/education for sustainable development/education for sustainability, and of early childhood education, and strive for the most appropriate fit within their own cultures. Research in cross-cultural psychology may be help-ful when thinking about the place of critical thinking and children's active participation in different cultural contexts. In addition, it is important to under-stand the informal education practices of Indigenous/traditional cultures in order to learn how they have taught, learnt and shared their ecological worldviews and empathy with nature over successive generations. Such investigations are likely to reveal that early childhood was, and remains, a significant and critical stage for fostering ecological worldviews and empathy with the nature world.

Japan has a long tradition of early childhood education and has promoted many positive outcomes for children and their families with highly qualified educators working with well-developed national guidelines. However, early childhood education has not been concerned with sustainability issues. Rethinking early childhood education, by considering the above four key concepts within Japanese cultural contexts, has the potential to change everyday practices and make rich contributions towards building a sustainable society in Japan.

References

Asaoka, Y. (ed.) (2005) *Practices of New Environmental Education* (in Japanese), Tokyo: Kobundo Publishing.

Blaser, M., Feit, H. A. and McRae, G. (2004) *In the Way of Development: Indigenous Peoples, Life Projects and Globalization*, London: Zed Books.

Bonnet, M. (2007) 'Environmental education and the issue of nature', *Journal of Curriculum Studies*, 39(6): 707–21.

Brown, J. B., Hanson, M. E., Liverman, D. M. and Merideth, Jr. R. W. (1987) 'Global Sustainability: toward Definition', *Environmental Management*, 11(6): 713–19.

Cajete, G. (1993) *Look to the Mountain: An Ecology of Indigenous Education*, Durango, CO: Kivaki Press.

Cajete, G. (1999) *Native Science: Natural Laws of Interdependence*, New Mexico: Clear Light Publishers.

Cederblom, J. and Paulsen, D. W. (1982) *Critical Reasoning: Understanding and Criticizing Arguments and Theories,* Belmont, CA: Wadsworth Publishing.

Clarke-Stewart, K. A., Lee, Y., Allhusen, V. D., Kimb, M. S. and McDowe, D. J. (2006) 'Observed differences between early childhood programs in the US and Korea: Reflections of "developmentally appropriate practices" in two cultural contexts', *Journal of Applied Developmental Psychology*, 27: 427–43.

Davis, J. (2008) 'What might education for sustainability look like in early childhood education: A case for participatory, whole-of-settings approaches', in I. Pramling Samuelsson and Y. Kaga (eds) *The Contribution of early Childhood Education to a Sustainable Society*, Paris: UNESCO, pp. 18–24.

Davis, J. (2009) 'Revealing the research "hole" of early childhood education for sustainability: a preliminary survey of the literature', *Environmental Education Research*, 15(2): 227–41.

Fitzgerald, H. (2002) *How Different Are We? Spoken Discourse in Intercultural Communication: The Significance of the Situational Context*, Bristol: Multilingual Matters.

Grim, J. A. (ed.) (2001) *Indigenous Traditions and Ecology*, Cambridge, MA: Harvard University Center for the Study of World Religions.

Hoffman, D. M. (2000) 'Pedagogies of self in American and Japanese early childhood education: A critical conceptual analysis', *The Elementary School Journal*, 101(2): 193–208.

Inoue, M. (1995) 'Difference in the meaning of "environment" between early childhood care and education and environmental education' (in Japanese), *Environmental Education*, 4(2): 25–33.

Inoue, M. (1996) 'On the two-dimension aspects of environmental education in early childhood' (in Japanese), *Environmental Education*, 5(2): 2–12.

Inoue, M. (2000) 'A historical study on the significance of "nature" in early childhood education in Japan – from a viewpoint of environmental education' (in Japanese), *Environmental Education*, 9(2): 2–11.

Inoue, M. (2009) 'Review of the research on environmental education during early childhood in the past 20 years' (in Japanese), *Environmental Education*, 19(1): 95–108.

Inoue, M. (2012) *Environmental Education at Early Childhood Level – Fostering an Environmental View to Build a Sustainable Society* (in Japanese), Kyoto: Showado.

Inoue, M. and Muto, T. (2006) 'A survey of the natural environment of playgrounds in kindergartens and nursery schools' (in Japanese), *The Japanese Journal for the Education of Young Children*, 15: 1–11.

Inoue, M. and Muto, T. (2009) A survey on nature activities in kindergartens and nursery schools (2) (in Japanese), *The Bulletin of Education and Social Welfare*, 35: 1–7.

Inoue, M. and Muto, T. (2010) 'A survey on nature activities in kindergartens and nursery schools (3)' (in Japanese), *Bulletin of Osaka Ohtani University*, 44: 117–32.

Jacob, N. (1988) 'Sustainable development: A view of limitless growth?', *Trumpeter*, 5(4): 131–2.

Johnston, J. R. and Wong, A. (2002) 'Cultural differences in beliefs and practices concerning talk to children', *Journal of Speech, Language, and Hearing Research*, 45(5): 916–26.

Kawashima, M., Ichikawa S. and Imamura, M. (eds) (2002) *Introduction to Environmental Education* (in Japanese), Kyoto: Minelva Shobo.

Latouche, S. (2004) *Survivre au développement : De la décolonisation de l'imaginaire économique à la construction d'une société alternative*, Paris: Mille et une nuits.

Latouche, S. (2007) *Petit traité de la décroissance sereine*, Paris: Mille et une nuits.

Lun, V. M., Fischer, R. and Ward, C. (2010) 'Exploring cultural differences in critical thinking: Is it about my thinking style or the language I speak?', *Learning and Individual Differences*, 20: 604–16.

Mackey, G. (2012) 'To know, to decide, to act: the young child's right to participate in action for the environment', *Environmental Education Research*, 18(4): 1–12.

McGuire, J. M. (2007) 'Why has the Critical Thinking Movement not come to Korea?', *Asia Pacific Education Review*, 8(2): 224–32.

Minami, M. (1994) 'English and Japanese: A cross-cultural comparison of parental styles of narrative elicitation', *Issues in Applied Linguistics*, 5(2): 383–407.

Ministry of Education, Culture, Sports, Science and Technology (2012a) *International Comparison of Education Indexes* (in Japanese), Online. Available: www.mext.go.jp/b_menu/toukei/data/kokusai/__icsFiles/afieldfile/2013/02/05/1318687_3_1.pdf (accessed 1 March 2013).

Ministry of Education, Culture, Sports, Science and Technology (2012b) *Survey of School Teachers* (in Japanese), Online. Available: www.e-stat.go.jp/SG1/estat/List.do?bid=000001038370&cycode=0 (accessed 1 March 2013).

Murata, K. (2011) 'Voices from the unvoiced: A comparative study of hidden values and attitudes in opinion-giving', *Language and Intercultural Communication*, 11(1): 6–25.

National Institute for Educational Policy Research (2007) *Teacher's Handbook for Environmental Education* (in Japanese), Online. Available: www.nier.go.jp/RSL_User_seika/RSL_OM_GetFile?LIT_CODE=SEIKADB1&LIT_NUM=443&TAG=TXT&BR=NOT (accessed 1 March 2013).

National Institute for Educational Policy Research (2009) *Preschool Education and Care in Japan*, Online. Available: www.nier.go.jp/English/EducationInJapan/Education_in_Japan/Education_in_Japan_files/201109ECEC.pdf (accessed 23 March 2013).

National Institute for Educational Policy Research (2012) *Research Report on Education for Sustainable Development in Schools* (in Japanese), Online. Available: www.nier.go.jp/kaihatsu/pdf/esd_saishuu.pdf (accessed 23 March 2013).

New South Wales Environment Protection Authority (2003) *Patches of Green A Review of Early Childhood Environmental Education*, Sydney, NSW: New South Wales Environment Protection Authority.

Nisbett, R. (2004) *The Geography of Thought: How Asians and Westerners Think Differently … and Why*, New York: Free Press.

Reagan, T. G. (1996; 3rd edn 2010) *Non-Western Educational Traditions: Alternative Approaches to Educational Thought and Practice*, London: Routledge.

Rist, G. (1996 in French; 3rd edn 2009) *The History of Development: From Western Origins to Global Faith*, London: Zed Books.

Ross, N., Medin, D., Coley, J. D. and Atran, S. (2003) 'Cultural and experiential differences in the development of folk-biological induction', *Cognitive Development*, 18: 25–47.

Shiraev, E. B. and Levy, D. A. (2001; 4th edn 2010) *Cross-Cultural Psychology: Critical Thinking and Contemporary Applications*, Boston, MA: Pearson.

Shiva, V. (1992) 'Recovering the real meaning of sustainability', in D. E. Cooper and J. A. Palmer (eds) *The Environment in Question*, London: Routledge, pp. 187–93.

Smith, P. B., Bond, M. H. and Kagitcibasi, C. (2006) *Understanding Social Psychology Across Cultures: Living and Working in a Changing World*, London: Sage Publications.

Taguma, M., Litjens, I. and Makowiecki, K. (2012) *Quality Matters in Early Childhood Education and Care: Japan*, OECD publications, Online. Available: www.oecd-ilibrary.org/education/quality-matters-in-early-childhood-education-and-care-japan-2012_9789264176621-en (accessed 23 March 2013).

Tian, J. and Low, G. D. (2011) 'Critical thinking and Chinese university students: A review of the evidence', *Language, Culture and Curriculum*, 24(1): 61–76.

Tobin, J. (2005) 'Quality in early childhood education: An anthropologist's perspective', *Early Education and Development*, 16(4): 421–34.

United Nations (1992) *Agenda 21*, Online. Available: http://sustainabledevelopment.un.org/content/documents/Agenda21.pdf (accessed 25 July 2013).

United Nations Educational, Scientific and Cultural Organization (UNESCO) (2005) *United Nations Decade of Education for Sustainable Development (2005–2014): International Implementation Scheme*, UNESCO publications, Online. Available: http://unesdoc.unesco.org/images/0014/001486/148654E.pdf#search=%27United+Nations+Decade+of+Education+for+Sustainable+Development+%282005 2014%29%3A+International+Implementation+Scheme%27 (accessed 25 July 2013).

Wilson, R. A. (1993) *Fostering a Sense of Wonder During the Early Childhood Years,* Columbus, OH: Greyden Press.

Wilson, R. A. (ed.) (1994) *Environmental Education at the Early Childhood Level,* Washington, DC: North American Association for Environmental Education.

Chapter 6

The role of early childhood education in building Singapore as a sustainable nation

Hui-Ling Chua

Abstract

Singapore has recently recognized the necessity of a National Green Plan (Ministry of the Environment and Water Resources (MEWR) 2012) for the long-term survival and the wellbeing of its people. The Plan includes active development in many different areas, community partnerships and the delivery of environmental education. Although not widespread, environmental education programs include a few at the early childhood level. The motive for this chapter is consideration of how the early childhood community may emerge as a strong and likely partner in the building of Singapore as a sustainable nation. The chapter includes a description of the National Green Plan, and establishes the premise for a response from early childhood educators drawing on current literature. Challenges and issues within early childhood education in Singapore may make the implementation of early childhood education for sustainability (ECEfS) problematic. However, a critical reading of current policies and curriculum guidelines, together with findings from the author's research indicate the possible and timely participation of the early childhood community in Singapore's plans for sustainability. The chapter concludes with a summary of pertinent ideas for action and a call to the early childhood community to acknowledge ECEfS in professional practice.

Introduction

Singapore recognizes the urgency of a National Green Plan for the long-term survival and the enduring wellbeing of its people (MEWR 2012). The Plan includes active development in the areas of waste management, air quality, a sufficient water supply, good public health, and the conservation of nature, through innovation and collaborative international and community partnerships. Community partnerships aim to strengthen private and public sector ownership of environmental concerns and deliver a range of environmental education events and programs at various levels. Although not yet widespread, environmental education programs currently include just a few for preschool-aged children. Given the serious appeal by Singapore's government to its people that 'sustainability cannot be a mere fad ... our very survival depends on it' (MEWR 2012: 2), this chapter outlines and discusses a rationale as to how the early childhood education community can emerge as a robust and likely partner in the nation's efforts to build a sustainable nation. Although the Green Plan largely addresses environmental sustainability rather than the broader conceptualization of sustainability as having social, economic as well as environmental dimensions, this plan provides a good start for Singapore's road to sustainability.

Small city-state with a national green plan

Singapore is a small city-state, with over 5 million people spread across 7,100 square kilometres. This multi-racial country is one of the most densely populated in the world with about 6,500 people per square kilometre; for comparison, the United States of America (USA) has a population density of only 32 people per square kilometre. Since independence 47 years ago, Singapore has changed the natural environment from a tropical jungle to a concrete jungle. However, because the first Prime Minister, Lee Kuan Yew, initiated visionary plans for greening Singapore in the 1960s, it also boasts urban landscapes of lush, managed greenery with many parks and green spaces. Singapore is popularly known as a 'Garden City'. The greening plan was two-fold: first, to improve the population's health by providing a more ecologically-friendly environment; and second, to promote the country's commitment towards sustainable development among the wider international community (Han *et al.* 1998). It was recognized at the time that economic success alone was not enough to ensure Singaporeans' health and wellbeing. Green surrounds were seen as offering restorative environments for its citizens in a city where space is scarce. Today, Singapore's green network spans over 300 kilometres across the whole island, making it easy for people to move from park to park (National Parks 2008–2009). Singapore is also seeking to shape itself as a 'City of Waterways'. To this end, the Public Utilities Board (PUB) is working alongside the Urban Redevelopment Authority (URA) on the Parks and Waterbodies Plan that includes several coastal park connectors. These connectors will provide for a range of outdoor experiences through mangroves and waterfronts, a boardwalk, and along foot/cycle paths (Feng 2010). The Green Plan also included provision for study and preservation of Singapore's tropical biodiversity. With more than 2,900 species of plants, and over 1,300 species of animals (National Parks Board 2010), biodiversity research is on-going. The 'greening' of Singapore has been so successful that the term 'Garden City' has now been changed to a 'City in a Garden' (National Parks Board 2009, Sia 2009).

Another intention for greening Singapore was to build a sustainable Singapore so that it would remain attractive to investors (Han *et al.* 1998). To this end, Singapore also has a plan for its longer-term sustainability. Its vision statement 'Towards an enduring Singapore' (MEWR 2012: II) calls for 'judicious stewardship of resources to optimize the balance between Man and Nature', and for innovation and strategic partnerships to overcome Singapore's limitations in order to build a sustainable Singapore.

To move the plan for sustainability forward, Singapore has also begun to develop environmental education programs for the children and youth of Singapore. Preschoolers, for example, can be involved in a 'Thumbs up for Earth' program developed in 2001 (Wee 2001), and the 'Singapore Clean and Green Schools Carnival' (National Environment Agency (NEA) 2008). Schools, in particular, have been singled out as important in developing and maintaining Singapore's environmental health. For example, in its conclusion, the Green Plan places strong emphasis on educating Singaporeans, stating that 'the best technologies in the world …will mean nothing if there is no human drive to extract the most benefit from them' (MEWR 2012: 52).

It is vital for the early childhood community to consider how they, too, can participate and contribute towards Singapore's national sustainability efforts. While, to date, sustainability has focused on the natural environment and less on sociocultural and economic sustainability, it is a significant step in the right direction. The time is ripe for the early childhood education community to play its part. As education for sustainability has its roots in environmental education, a rational first step for this Singaporean professional community is to advance environmental education in preschools, and thereafter, develop and implement a framework for early childhood education for sustainability[1] (ECEfS).

Significance of early childhood environmental education and the Singaporean child

The World Watch Institute and the United Nations have warned that the world's population has grown more in the past 30 years than it has in the 100,000 years before the mid-twentieth century, and that forest cover and cropland loss have accelerated beyond expectations (United Nations Environment Program 2012, World Watch Institute 2000, 2010). They also warn about the impacts of climate change and the effects of synthetic chemicals that are regularly introduced into the air, water systems, and, their effects on many species, including humans.

An American study examining the effects of rapid urban growth on nature and people further asserts that urbanization is likely to bring about permanent loss of some animals, plants and natural resources (The Nature Conservancy 2008). Further, Kahn (2002: 113) draws attention to the fact that if the natural environment continues to be impoverished through human actions and interventions that degrade the environment, it will affect the richness and diversity of children's interactions with the natural world, and, consequently, will 'destroy the wellsprings of their psychological constructions'. He argues this may lead to 'environmental generational amnesia' (Kahn 2002: 105), where the natural environment encountered in childhood is the norm from which environmental degradation is measured later in life: 'as we lose daily, intimate positive affiliations with nature and accept negative experiences (such as pollution) as the norm, we suffer physically and psychologically and hardly know it' (Kahn 2002: 113).

Indications are that the natural environment needs urgent and active custodians.

Such custodians include young children who engage regularly with the natural world, establish vital relationships with Nature, who learn to love it and, consequently, care for it (Sobel 1999). As an urban city-state with few natural resources, Singapore is seeking to protect and enhance its natural environment. Thus, it is highly appropriate for the nation to call upon all its citizens, including the youngest, to be actively involved.

A strong rationale for environmental education is that children must receive appropriate stimulation during certain sensitive periods (Mustard 2010) or their potential to develop dispositions that support understandings of the natural environment and to take a role in caring for the Earth might be jeopardized. Current literature on environmental education presents much evidence that the early childhood years are critical years for the development of environmental attitudes (Chawla and Derr 2012, Kellert 2012).

A second rationale for environmental education is that positive interactions with the natural world are important for children's healthy development (Faber Taylor and Kuo 2006, Kellert 2002). There are significant benefits pertinent to the development of Singaporean children. For example, researchers have established a link between children's play and exploration in green spaces and higher cognitive functioning (Crain 2001, Louv 2008, Pyle 2002, Wells 2000). Confronted with Nature's unpredictable and continuous changes, children are challenged to respond with creative, adaptive skills (Faber Taylor et al. 1998, Fjørtoft 2001, Kellert 2002), increasing their capacities to concentrate and pay attention (Faber Taylor et al. 2001, Faber Taylor and Kuo 2006). As intellectual development is a major concern for many Singaporean parents (Ebbeck and Gokhale 2004, Raban and Ure 1999, Tan-Niam 2000), creating preschools with a strong focus on environmental education should be a priority, given the benefits for learning when engaging with nature.

Another consideration is that of physical health. When playing outdoors, children develop better coordination, balance, agility, and stamina and are unwell less often (Dyment and Bell 2008, Faber Taylor and Kuo 2006, Fjørtoft 2001). With a diverse range of stimuli, free play in the natural world can also be therapeutic for children, buffering stress and minimizing anxiety and feelings of depression (Burdette and Whitaker 2005, Van Den Berg et al. 2007, Wells and Evans 2003). In a local play study (Chia 2009), it was suggested that Singaporean children have hurried, highly-scheduled lifestyles that offer little time for play. Parents feel compelled to fill children's lives with 'gainful' activities, often comprising academic and enrichment classes that are mostly sedentary. Chia (2009) further asserts that the physical play frequently offered virtually through 'cyber sports' – for example 'Wii tennis' – appears to be more attractive than actual physical outdoor sports. This is not surprising given that Singapore is one of the world's most wired nations with computers and electronic media highly accessible to most (Nielsen 2009, Urban Redevelopment Authority (URA) 2005). In Nielson's study (2009), Singapore was second behind the Philippines, as one of the most avid owners and consumers of global entertainment technology. The later 2009 URA Lifestyle

Survey also concluded that increasingly Singaporean youth and adults spend their time indoors engaged in sedentary activities, leaving young children with fewer role models to promote outdoor experiences. A sedentary lifestyle can also contribute to obesity; trend studies in Singapore have shown that the weights of children from 6 to 18 years are increasing (Loke *et al.* 2008).

With the high usage of technology, Singaporean children may also be experiencing high levels of electronically-mediated learning (Cohen 1994, Louv 2008, Moore 1997). Information technology makes information easily accessible, but largely through the senses of sight and sound. Growing up in a wired society, Singaporean children may, therefore, be missing out on multi-sensorial experiences that bring a sense of wonder and inquisitiveness regarded as important in creating positive, lifelong dispositions for learning. It is timely, therefore, for environmental education to emerge, to support many developmental benefits for Singaporean children, not necessarily as a replacement, but at least as a complement to 'wired' leisure and learning activities.

Singapore's educational policies in support of early childhood environmental education

A critical reading and analysis of policy documents, speeches about national agendas for Singapore, and national and international research articles yield sizeable support for the implementation of environmental education in early childhood education in Singapore. In the late 1990s, there were efforts to align Singapore's education system with global trends – deliberate efforts to move from a traditional emphasis on efficiency-driven learning, standardized education and a prescriptive curriculum, towards inquiry-based, child-centred education, and teachers as reflective thinkers (Ng 2011, Tzuo 2010). These changes filtered into early childhood education (Tan 2007), beginning with a policy framework to raise the quality of preschool education.[2] The *Framework for a Kindergarten Curriculum*,[3] was founded on six principles: holistic development and learning, integrated learning, active learning, supporting learning, learning through interactions, and learning through play (Singapore Ministry of Education (MOE) 2003). Six critical learning areas were identified to support these principles: aesthetics and creative expression, environmental awareness, language and literacy, motor skills development, numeracy and self and social awareness.

The Framework also incorporated the 'Teach Less, Learn More' initiative where teachers were expected to be more reflective in their teaching approaches, and encouraged to facilitate children's learning through engaging and active methods, interactive approaches, and through play. In 2008, the MOE produced the *Kindergarten Curriculum Guide* (MOE 2008) to help teachers translate the Framework principles into practice. Most recently, the MOE has produced a revised curriculum Framework (MOE 2012a). In a local press release (MOE 2012b) the MOE asserted that the revised Framework was to emphasize the importance of holistic development, the need to build confidence and social skills during the preschool years and for children to develop lifelong dispositions for learning. On closer examination, the revised Framework was largely based on the earlier Framework's learning principles albeit with a clearer and expanded explanation of these. The other significant change was in the learning area of 'Environmental Awareness', which is now termed 'Discovery of the World' (MOE 2012a); however, the concepts and ideas surrounding this area remain largely unchanged.

On this basis it can be asserted that Singapore's recent policies for early childhood education provide strong support for early childhood environmental education. In particular, both the old and revised Frameworks include environmental awareness or 'discovery of the world' as it is now known, as a key learning area, and encourage pedagogies that support meaningful engagement with the natural environment.

Environmental awareness in Singapore's early education policy

The Curriculum Guide (MOE 2008: 65) outlines the following principles for preschoolers' awareness of the environment:

- Children will develop an understanding of the world around them, providing the foundations for learning in science, history and geography.
- Teachers will guide children to extend their natural curiosity, discover things for themselves, build on what they already know and understand, come up with their own solutions and reasons for explanations, and cultivate a sense of care and appreciation of the environment.

The revised Framework similarly calls on preschoolers to be aware of the importance of responsibility, care and respect for living things and the environment (MOE 2012a: 77). It further asserts that they should be aware of the impacts of human actions on themselves, others and the Earth.

These suggest the importance of children learning about both the physical and the sociocultural world around them, promoting a deeper knowledge of who they are, their place in nature, and what sustains their community. It sets the scene for 'place-based education' as a means of inspiring children towards stewardship of the Earth, thus contributing to sustainability (Sobel 2004). Place-based education also supports integrated learning. As Sobel asserts, place-based education is an effective way to integrate curriculum areas around the study of a place, using 'the local community and environment as the starting point for learning concepts in language, arts, mathematics, social studies, science, and other subjects in the curriculum' (Sobel 2004: 7).

Pedagogies that support engagement with the environment

Pedagogical principles in the new Framework call for teachers to provide 'ample opportunities for children to explore their environment and interact with their peers, teachers and other adults in a variety of contexts' (MOE 2012a: 54). When such play-based opportunities extend to the natural environment where it is considered an inherently engaging space for children to play and learn, children will develop a sense of mastery and control while interacting with their surroundings (Elliott 2008, Pyle 2002, White 2008, Wilson 2008).

Teachers are also asked to provide the necessary support for new learning to take place by observing the children as they explore, formulating questions to arouse and sustain children's interests, motivating them to think and acquire inquiry attitudes (MOE 2012b: 54). At the same time, the Framework recognizes children as co-constructors of knowledge that is relevant to the real world, and if supported by quality interactions with their teachers, the children can investigate topics, solve problems and clarify concepts (MOE 2012a: 36).

These principles support children's encounters and experiences with the environment and suggest that, in the hands of observant and reflective teachers, valuable learning experiences will ensue (Howes 2008). Thus, the intention for children to learn about the world around them, and supportive pedagogical principles in the Framework open the doors for meaningful engagement with the environment in Singaporean preschool programs. However, implementation is not without challenges.

Challenges in implementing early childhood environmental education in Singapore

First, the Framework competes with expectations of parents who perceive preschool[4] as a place for their children to secure academic skills in preparation for entry into Singapore's competitive education system (Ang 2008, Ng 2009). This often translates into a structured curriculum with regular worksheets and repetitive exercises (Ang 2006, Tan-Niam 2000). As preschools in Singapore are private enterprises dependent on a market-led economy, and structured curricula are highly popular with parents, they tend to focus on preparing children for achievement in academic skills (Ang 2008, Ng 2009), despite the stated principles for preschools outlined in the Framework.

Another challenge is that provision for outdoor learning in preschool programs is not clearly defined in the Framework. As merely a set of guidelines, the proportion of time that children might spend daily outdoors with nature is left largely to the individual practices of preschools and the initiative, or otherwise, of early childhood practitioners. The hot climate, with constant high humidity and temperatures of 30 degrees Celsius or more, is another mitigating factor. Additionally, land is scarce in Singapore and so it is difficult for preschools to acquire large playgrounds or outdoor spaces as part of their land holdings even though they are strongly encouraged by the regulating authorities to allocate areas for developing children's large motor skills (MOE 2010, Ministry of Community Development for Youth and Sports (MCYS) 2009). Such factors, along with the concerns for safety outdoors, impact on teachers' choices (Davies 1996, Kong 1999, Rivkin 2000), even if green spaces are available near a preschool.

Furthermore, there is the question of how gross motor-skill development is presented in policy. While the Curriculum Guide (MOE 2008: 72) suggests that children must have opportunities for 'unrestricted movement' to develop their physical skills 'naturally' during 'gross motor play time', the revised Framework suggests that teachers plan a variety of games and activities to facilitate children's motor-skill development (MOE 2012b: 88). Common observations support the latter, where outdoor play appears to occur mainly in a highly structured manner, often with hoops, balls and other equipment, regardless of whether it is outdoors or indoors. There is little 'on the ground' acknowledgement in Singaporean preschools of the benefits for children of unrestricted movement in open spaces, where the many inherent physical affordances are stimulants and catalysts for a range of developmentally important motor skills (Fjørtoft 2001, Faber Taylor and Kuo 2006).

Another challenge is that the recent policy initiatives discussed here require early childhood practitioners to step away from the comfort of traditional, teacher-centred approaches, into a newer, more child-centred paradigm. Ang (2006) suggests that Confucian ideology underpins much of Singapore's education system and that this reinforces a more teacher-centred approach to children's learning. Teachers, accustomed to these ideals, may find it a challenge to use more child-centred approaches. Furthermore, in a study of teachers' responses to the earlier Framework (MOE 2003), Ang (2008) found that many teachers felt there was a lack of resources available to help them change, and that they needed more guidance and professional development. In a similar study, Ng (2009) identified that while teachers believed in the principles of reflective teaching, they also felt it was too time-consuming and overwhelming to implement. Overall, it requires considerably more effort from teachers who are accustomed to didactic approaches.

Overcoming these challenges

Nevertheless, there are some signs of change within the preschool system in Singapore. I conducted a case study in a preschool with a particular focus on children's engagement with the natural world. The aim of the study was to identify the conditions and contexts that promoted children's successful engagement with nature in the preschool setting (Chua 2013). Analysis of the preschool documents demonstrated that, first, there was a clear focus on children's regular engagement with nature as reflected in the preschool's promotional brochures, policy documents and website. Second, the program supported the children's regular time for learning and playing outdoors, adopting the pedagogical principles from the earlier more child-centred Framework (MOE 2003: 20 and 25). The teachers also had autonomy to deviate from planned activities in favour of a child-directed emergent curriculum whenever they perceived the need.

Third, although the teachers were locally trained and therefore had been exposed to more structured curricula, they had relevant dispositions and professional competencies to facilitate child-led outdoor learning in nature. They were enthusiastic about the changed focus of the centre, and recognized that spontaneity and some 'disorder' in teaching can make positive contributions to children's learning. Furthermore, they became increasingly adept at identifying and developing opportunities for children to direct their own learning. In explaining these particular teacher characteristics and behaviours, further study findings revealed that the teachers underwent intensive interviews to identify such dispositions and competencies before they were employed. Also, critically, the centre principal was inspiring with her passion for children's involvement with nature, and provided the necessary support and development for the teachers for whom she was responsible.

Similarly, in her (1996) study of schools with 'more-than-sporadic' early childhood environmental education programs, Wilson identified that these schools had several elements that resonate with aspects of the Singaporean preschool discussed here. Most notably, Wilson described that effective environmental education programs focused on, both, the overall development of the child and on fostering understandings of the natural environment. The latter included developing empathy and a sense of wonder rather than learning 'facts' about the natural environment, and offered time outdoors on a daily basis for the exploration of the natural environment.

On examining the limitations of this study, however, several factors emerged for consideration. First, the parents were an eclectic group: only about 25 per cent were Singaporeans, the majority coming from Australia, the USA, China and Europe. Both the Singaporean centre manager and the founding principal had been partially educated in Australia and the USA, respectively. Another important element of this preschool was that it had a physical setting surrounded by large open spaces that provided easy access for the children to engage with the local environment, uncommon for a Singaporean preschool. All these factors are likely to have contributed to support for a more holistic, child-led, outdoor-oriented program. In-depth interviews with the Singaporean parents confirmed support for such programs, which suggests that this could be an emerging trend in Singapore. The limitations noted, however, provoke opportunities for further research.

Untapped partnerships for early childhood environmental education

In order to advance environmental education, early childhood practitioners can draw support from the many untapped resources within the 'green' community in Singapore. The following points highlight potential partnerships that could be developed to enrich preschool environmental education:

- The existing 'Learning Journeys' program offered by National Parks (National Parks Board 2012), currently designed for primary and secondary students to promote understandings of the balance between nature and the built environment, and to support the values of caring for nature and conserving the natural heritage, could be easily revised for preschoolers.

- Collaboration between National Parks and early childhood practitioners could see existing green spaces redesigned to become accessible, stimulating play spaces for nearby preschools.
- In collaboration with agencies such as the Botanic Gardens, National Parks, and the Raffles Museum of Biodiversity, pre-service and in-service professional development modules for early childhood practitioners could be developed on topics such as place-based education, the Greening of Singapore, and the appreciation of local biodiversity. These would enable teachers to become better informed and more skilled in providing meaningful experiences for children in Singapore's natural environment.
- Inter-ministerial collaboration could be developed to include preschoolers and their families. For example, the observance of Earth Day or World Environment Day could be conducted nationwide. All preschools could be invited to participate through planting trees, or participating in a national bird count. More importantly, such collaboration would demonstrate that early childhood education is recognized as an important part of the nation's sustainability efforts.

Early childhood education's contribution to Singapore's sustainability: a step forward

Discussions in the preceding sections have argued for the inclusion of environmental education as a stepping-stone towards ECEfS programs in Singapore, despite existing challenges. I have also called for collaboration between various community and government agencies to leverage the nation's 'green' Singapore and sustainability vision to be inclusive of preschool education. These discussions suggest that a new framework for quality early childhood education, where environmental education has an important place, may become feasible. However, there are three important additional points that need to be considered.

First, early childhood practitioners must acknowledge the importance of environmental education in the early childhood years as critical to the construction of environmental attitudes and need to understand the benefits of environmental education for children's wellbeing and development.

Second, early childhood practitioners need to acknowledge that they, too, are part of the 'human drive' and 'strategic partnership' that is required to attain the goals of the Green Plan for Singapore. Collaboration between government agencies and community groups can be forged to create integrated, outdoor-oriented, environmental curricula for children and for early childhood teacher education. Singapore's network of greenery and natural corridors has yet to be tapped.

Third, and the final point, while current education policies advocate for pedagogies that facilitate learning experiences integral to environmental education, the early childhood community must itself make efforts to surmount the implementation challenges such as parents not seeing the value of child-led learning. To effect significant change, courage is needed and, in this case, the stakes are high. Children and their futures are at risk.

Concluding call

While the Singaporean government is investing much in preserving the country's natural biodiversity and in its National Green Plan for sustainability, it will be a missed opportunity if Singapore's youngest citizens were not encouraged to participate. The impacts will be even more serious should these young citizens succumb to 'environmental generational amnesia' (Kahn 2002). Alternatively, the collective efforts of Singaporean citizens could lead to new perspectives for high quality early childhood education where the goals for Singapore's children include not only academic development, but also socio-emotional goals such as sensitivity to the environment, empathy for all living things, and the courage to participate and act for sustainability.

While this chapter has not elaborated on the details of what environmental education might look like in Singapore, ideas have been provided for the first steps that the nation might take in redefining the role of early childhood education in contributing to the nation's sustainability. As Davis (2010) has powerfully asserted, children need not be vulnerable to the impacts of unsustainable living. Early childhood education has an important role in building children's resilience and capabilities. Early childhood practitioners, working in partnership with the wider community must respond swiftly in order to secure the long-term wellbeing and sustainability of this city-state and its current and future citizens.

Notes

1   ECEfS is the abbreviated term used by practitioners in Australasia for early childhood education for sustainability and, hereafter, this abbreviation will be used.
2   Preschool education is the term used by the Ministry of Education in Singapore to describe early childhood education programs for children three to six years old.
3   Thereafter referred to as the Framework.
4   Preschool denotes both child care centres for children 18 months to 6 year olds, and kindergartens for 4 to 6 year olds.

References

Ang, L. (2006) 'Steering debate and initiating dialogue: A review of the Singapore preschool curriculum'. *Contemporary Issues in Early Childhood,* 7(3): 203–12.

Ang, L. (2008) 'Singapore preschool teachers' responses to the Introduction of a framework for a kindergarten curriculum in the context of three preschool settings'. *Asia-Pacific Journal of Research in Early Childhood Education,* 2(1): 55–81.

Burdette, H. L. and Whitaker, R. C. (2005) 'Resurrecting free play in young children: Looking beyond fitness and fatness to attention, affiliation, and affect'. *Archives of Pediatrics and Adolescent Medicine,* 159(1): 46–50.

Chawla, L. and Derr, V. (2012) 'The development of conservation behaviours in childhood and youth', in Clayton, S. D. (ed.), *The Oxford Handbook of Environmental and Conservation Psychology.* New York: Oxford University Press, pp. 527–55.

Chia, M. (2009) 'Play reconsidered, resurrected and repositioned in children: case study results from Singapore'. *Sport Science.* Online. Available: www.sposci.com/PDFS/

BR0201/SVEE/04 CL 06 MC.pdf (accessed 9 November 2012).

Chua, H. L. (2013) 'The study of children's engagement with nature in early childhood'. Thesis to be submitted in fulfilment of the requirements for the degree of Doctor of Education, University of South Australia.

Cohen, S. (1994) 'Children and the environment: Aesthetic learning'. *Childhood Education,* 70(5), pp. 302–5.

Crain, W. (2001) 'How nature helps children develop'. *Montessori LIFE,* pp. 22–4.

Davis, J. M. (2010) 'Early childhood education for sustainability: Why it matters, what it is, and how whole centre action research and systems thinking can help'. *Journal of Action Research Today in Early Childhood (ARTEC),* Special Issue, pp. 35–44.

Davies, M. M. (1996) 'Outdoors: An important context for young children's development'. *Early Child Development and Care,* 115(1): 37–9.

Dyment, J. E. and Bell, A. C. (2008) 'Grounds for movement: Green school grounds as sites for promoting physical activity'. *Health Education Research,* 23(6): 952–62.

Ebbeck, M. and Gokhale, N. (2004) 'Child-rearing practices in a selected sample of parents with children in childcare in Singapore'. *Contemporary Issues in Early Childhood,* 5(2): 194–204.

Elliott, S. (ed.) (2008) *The Outdoor Playspace Naturally: For Children Birth to Five Years.* Sydney: Pademelon Press.

Faber Taylor, A. and Kuo, F. E. (2006) 'Is contact with nature important for healthy child development? State of the evidence', in C. Spencer and M. Blades (eds), *Children and Their Environments.* Cambridge: Cambridge University Press, pp. 124–40.

Faber Taylor, A., Kuo, F. E. and Sullivan, W. C. (2001) 'Coping with ADD: The surprising connection to green play settings'. *Environment and Behaviour,* 33(1): 54–77.

Faber Taylor, A., Wiley, A., Kuo, F. and Sullivan, W. (1998) 'Growing up in the inner city: Green spaces as places to grow'. *Environment and Behaviour,* 30(1): 3–27.

Feng, Z. (2010) 'From green to sea'. *The Straits Times,* July 28.

Fjørtoft, I. (2001) 'The natural environment as a playground for children: The impact of outdoor play activities in pre-primary school children'. *Early Childhood Education Journal,* 29(2): 111–17.

Han, F. K., Fernandez, W. and Tan, S. (1998) *Lee Kuan Yew: The Man and His Ideas,* Singapore, Times Editions.

Howes, E. V. (2008) 'Educative experiences and early childhood science education: A Deweyan perspective on learning to observe'. *Teaching and Teacher Education,* 24(3): 536–49.

Kahn, P. H., Jr. (2002) 'Children's affiliation with nature: Structure, development, and the problem of environmental generational amnesia', in P. H. Kahn Jr. and S. R. Kellert (eds) *Children and Nature: Psychological, Sociocultural, and Evolutionary Investigations.* Cambridge, MA: MIT Press, pp. 93–116.

Kellert, S. R. (2002) 'Experiencing nature: Affective, cognitive, and evaluative development in children', in P. H. Kahn Jr. and S. R. Kellert (eds) *Children and Nature: Psychological, sociocultural, and evolutionary investigations.* Cambridge, MA: MIT Press, pp. 117–51.

Kellert, S. R. (2012) *Birthright: People and Nature in the Modern World,* New Haven, CT and London: Yale University Press.

Kong, L. (1999) *Nature's Dangers, Nature's Pleasures: Urban Children and the Natural World* (Online). Singapore. Online. Available: http://profile.nus.edu.sg/fass/geokong/children.pdf (accessed 21 August 2007).

Loke, K. Y., Lin, J. B. Y. and Deurenberg-Yap, M. (2008) 'Third College of Paediatrics and child health lecture – the past, present and the future shape of things to come'. *Annals Academy of Medicine*, 37. Online. Available: www.cfps.org.sg/sfp/35/354/354_unit1.pdf (accessed 9 November 2012).

Louv, R. (2008) *Last Child in the Woods: Saving Our Children from Nature-Deficit Disorder.* Chapel Hill, NC: Algonquin Books.

Ministry of Community Development for Youth and Sports (MCYS) (2009) *Guide to Setting Up a Child Care Centre* (Online). Singapore: Child Care Division. Ministry of Community Development, Youth and Sports. Online. Available: www.childcarelink.gov.sg/ccls/uploads/CCC_Guide.pdf (accessed 12 December 2011).

Ministry of Education (MOE) (2003) 'Nurturing early learners: A framework for a kindergarten curriculum in Singapore', in P.-S. E. UNIT (ed.). Singapore: Ministry of Education – Preschool Education Unit.

Ministry of Education (MOE) (2008) *Kindergarten Curriculum Guide,* Singapore: Ministry of Education – Preschool Education Branch.

Ministry of Education (MOE) (2010) *Registration of New Kindergartens* (Online). Singapore: Ministry of Education. Online. Available: www.moe.gov.sg/education/preschool/files/ preschool-registration-general-information.pdf (accessed 18 January 2011).

Ministry of Education (MOE) (2012a) *Nurturing Early Learners: A Curriculum Framework for Kindergartens in Singapore*. Singapore: Ministry of Education. Online. Available: www.moe.gov.sg/education/preschool/files/kindergarten-curriculum-framework.pdf (accessed 12 May 2013).

Ministry of Education (MOE) (2012b) *Refreshed Kindergarten Curriculum Framework Spells Out Clearer Learning Outcomes, Emphasizes Holistic Development: Press Release* (Online). Singapore, Ministry of Education. Online. Available: www.moe.gov.sg/media/press/ 2013/02/refreshed-kindergarten-curricu.php (accessed 12 May 2013).

Ministry of the Environment and Water Reources (MEWR) (2012) *The Singapore Green Plan 2012: Beyond Clean and Green Towards Environmental Sustainability* (Online). Singapore: The Singapore Government. Online. Available: http://app.mewr.gov.sg/data/ ImgCont/1342/sgp2012.pdf (accessed 22 February 2012).

Moore, R. C. (1997) 'The need for nature: A childhood right'. *Social Justice,* 24(3): 203–20.

Mustard, J. F. (2010) 'Early brain development and human development', in R. E. Tremblay, R. G. Barr, R. Dev Peters, and M. Boivin (eds) *Encyclopedia on Early Childhood Development*. Montreal, Quebec: Centre of Excellence for Early Childhood Education. pp. 1–5.

National Environment Agency (NEA) (2008) *News Release. Clean and Green Singapore Schools' Carnival launches first Preschool Environmental Education Kit (PEEK) developed by students* (Online). Singapore. Online. Available: http://app2.nea.gov.sg/news_detail_ 2008.aspx?news_sid=20081105720854432196 (accessed 20 May 2009).

National Parks (2008–2009) *A Park for Everyone: Annual Report 2008–2009.* Singapore: National Parks Singapore.

National Parks Board (2009) *Singapore: A City in a Garden.* Singapore: National Parks. Online. Available: www.nparks.gov.sg/cms/index.php?option=com_content&view= article&id=78&Itemid=66 (accessed 1 June 2011).

National Parks Board (2010) *Biodiversity 2010.* Singapore: National Parks. Online. Available: www.nparks.gov.sg/cms/index.php?option=com_content&view=article&id=186& Itemid=165 (accessed 10 January 2011).

National Parks Board (2012) *Do Your Own Guided Walk* (Online). Singapore: National Parks. Online. Available: www.nparks.gov.sg/cms/index.php?option=com_content&view= article&id= 192&Itemid=173 (accessed 12 November 2012).

Ng, J. (2009) 'Exploring the perceptions of stakeholders in a Singapore kindergarten during a period of curriculum reform'. Online. Available: www.aare.edu.au/09pap/ng091323.pdf (accessed 12 January 2011).

Ng, J. (2011) 'Preschool curriculum and policy changes in Singapore'. *Asia-Pacific Journal of Research in Early Childhood Education,* 5(1): 91–122.

Nielsen (2009) 'Singapore ranks second in the world as the country with the highest ownership and usage of media technology: Nielsen survey finds East West divide in media habits'. Online. Available: http://sg.nielsen.com/site/20090106.htm (accessed 18 February 2011).

Pyle, R. M. (2002) 'Eden in a vacant lot: Special places, species and kids in Community of Life', in P. H. Kahn Jr. and S. R. Kellert (eds), *Children and Nature: Psychological, Sociocultural, and Evolutionary Investigations.* Cambridge, MA: MIT Press, pp. 307–27.

Raban, B. and Ure, C. (1999) 'Literacy in three languages: A challenge for Singapore preschool'. *International Journal of Early Childhood,* 31(2): 45–54.

Rivkin, M. (2000) 'Outdoor experiences for young children'. Online. Available: http://openlearn.open.ac.uk/file.php/1641/!via/oucontent/course/132/prim_ey1_12t_3.pdf (accessed 2 June 2011).

Sia, A. (2009) *Singapore: Garden Goals.* Singapore: Wild Singapore. Online. Available: http://wildsingaporenews.blogspot.com/2009/08/singapore-garden-goals.html (accessed 1 June 2011).

Sobel, D. (1999) 'Beyond ecophobia'. *Yes! Magazine.* Online. Available: www.yesmagazine.org/other/pop_print_article.asp?ID=803 (accessed 11 August 2007).

Sobel, D. (2004) *Place-based Education: Connecting Classrooms and Communities,* Great Barrington, MA: The Orion Society.

Tan, C. T. (2007) 'Policy developments in preschool education in Singapore: A focus on the key Reforms of kindergarten education'. *International Journal of Child Care and Education Policy,* 1(1): 35–43.

Tan-Niam, C. (2000) 'Facilitating fantasy play in the early years', in C. Tan-Niam and M. L. Quam (eds) *Investing in Our Furture: The Early Years.* Singapore: McGraw-Hill, pp. 140–50.

The Nature Conservancy (2008) 'Global Impact Of Urbanization Threatening World's Biodiversity and Natural Resources.' *Science Daily.* Online. Available: www.sciencedaily.com/releases/2008/06/080610182856.htm (accessed 12 July 2012).

Tilbury, D. (1994) 'The critical years for environmental education', in R. A. Wilson (ed.), *Environmental Education at the Early Childhood Level.* Washington, DC: North American Association for Environmental Education, pp. 11–13.

Tzuo, P. W. (2010) 'The ECE landscape in Singapore: Analysis of current trends, issues, and prospect for a cosmopolitan outlook'. *Asia-Pacific Journal of Research in Early Childhood Education,* 4(2), pp. 77–98.

United Nations Environment Programme (UNEP) (2012) *The Emissions Gap Report 2012.* Nairobi. Online. Available: www.unep.org/pdf/2012gapreport.pdf (accessed 21 January 2013).

Urban Redevelopment Authority (URA) (2005) *URA Lifestyle Survey 2002–2004* Singapore: Urban Redevelopment Authority. Online. Available: www.ura.gov.sg (accessed 22 March 2008).

Van Den Berg, A. E., Hartig, T. and Staats, H. S. (2007) 'Preference for nature in urbanized societies: Stress, restoration, and the pursuit of sustainability'. *Journal of Social Issues,* 63(1): 79–96.

Wee, C. S. B. (2001) *Thumbs up for Earth: Activities for Ages 4–8,* Singapore, Singapore Environmental Council.

Wells, N. M. (2000) 'At home with nature: Effects of greenness on children's cognitive functioning'. *Environment and Behaviour*, 32(6): 775–95.

Wells, N. M. and Evans, G. W. (2003) 'Nearby nature: A buffer of life stress among rural children'. *Environment and Behaviour*, 35(3): 311–30.

White, J. (2008) *Playing and Learning Outdoors: Making Provision for High Quality Experiences in the Outdoor Environment*, Abingdon: Routledge.

Wilson, R. A. (1996) *Starting Early: Environmental Education in the Early Childhood Years*. Columbus OH: ERIC Digest. Online. Available: www.ericdigests.org/1998–1/ early.htm (accessed 27 August 2007).

Wilson, R. (2008) *Nature and Young Children: Encouraging Creative Play and Learning in Natural Environments*, New York: Routledge.

World Watch Institute (2000) 'Earth Day 2000: A 30-year report card'. *World Watch Magazine*. World Watch Institute.

World Watch Institute (2010) 'Environment and climate'. *Vital Signs: Global Trends That Shape Our Future*. Online. Available: http://vitalsigns.worldwatch.org/trends/environment-climate (accessed 5 April 2013).

Chapter 7

Norwegian perspectives on ECEfS

What has developed since the Brundtland Report?

Barbara Maria Sageidet

Abstract

Ideas about sustainability have been part of Norwegian public thinking long before the Brundtland Report (World Commission on Environment and Development (WCED) 1987) that was eventually implemented through Norwegian national and local regulations. Norway has a long tradition of outdoor education and sustainable practices such as recycling in early childhood services. Within the *National Framework Plan for the Content and Tasks of Kindergartens* (Ministry of Education and Research 2006), education for sustainability (EfS) is part of the subject 'Nature, Environment and the Techniques', but little is known about the actual role of education for sustainability in the everyday life of kindergartens. However, we do know that some kindergartens are inspired by Arne Næss' deep ecological philosophy (Næss 1973, 1989, 2005), and an annual environmental project to attain the international 'green flag' certification will soon become compulsory in every Norwegian municipality.

This chapter offers insights into Early Childhood Education for Sustainability (ECEfS) in Norway, and discusses challenges and possibilities related to ECEfS, based on literature studies and an interview with an experienced environmentalist in Norway. Both Norwegian children's and adult's interests and motivations for addressing sustainability issues are influenced by complex interrelationships between traditions, a demand for environmental responsibility, personal identity development, relatedness, materialism and self-realism, competence and autonomy in post-modern society. The kindergarten is a vital arena for exploring these interrelationships. Therefore, more research is necessary about what can further promote ECEfS in kindergartens in Norway.

Introduction

Ideas about sustainability have been part of Norwegian public thinking since the middle of the twentieth century with earlier conceptions about environmental matters being strongly connected to the preservation of natural areas, especially those of the Norwegian Indigenous people, the Sami. The Brundtland Report

(WCED 1987) suggests that equity, growth and environmental maintenance are simultaneously possible by means of gradual technological and social change. The concept of sustainability has been gradually implemented in Norwegian national and local regulations and enacted through Agenda 21. At the 1992 United Nations Conference on Environment and Development in Rio de Janeiro, Brazil, many of the world's governments agreed to Agenda 21, the program for sustainability at local and regional levels internationally (UNEP 1992).

In the Nordic countries (Iceland, Finland, Denmark, Sweden, Norway) strategies for sustainable development focus on climate change, the preservation of nature, sustainable production and consumption, and the Nordic welfare model which is based on the core values of equal opportunity, social solidarity, security for all, and equal access to social and health services, education and culture. These strategies extend to knowledge of sustainable development in curricula and guidelines for elementary schools, youth education, adult education and higher education (Nordic Council of Ministers 2009). The Norwegian government's current strategy for education (Ministry for Education and Research 2012a) recognizes preschools in particular, showing that there is increasing consciousness about the importance of starting education for sustainable development early in life (Davis 2010, Norddahl 2008). (Note: Education for sustainable development is commonly used in Europe and is abbreviated as ESD; in Australia, Education for Sustainability is more commonly used and is abbreviated as EfS. In this chapter, the latter term will be used.)

Specifically, the Norwegian *National Framework Plan for the Content and Tasks of Kindergartens* (Ministry of Education and Research 2006, 2011) refers to the *Kindergarten Act, Section 2, Content for Kindergartens*, which describes the fundamental values of kindergartens. These are based on fundamental values in the Christian and humanist heritage and tradition, such as respect for human dignity and nature, intellectual freedom, charity, forgiveness, equality and solidarity – values that also appear in other religions and beliefs and originated from human rights (Kindergarten Act 2005: 1). The National Framework Plan further underlines the importance of fostering a sense of responsibility for the natural environment and states that an understanding of sustainable development is to be promoted in the kindergarten's everyday life, that respect for life, charity and solidarity are fundamental, and that these dispositions also relate to a global perspective. Kindergartens are also expected to lay the foundations for lifelong learning and active participation in a democratic society.

One of the aims for children within the preschool subject 'Nature, environment and technology' is to begin to understand the significance of sustainable development. This includes developing a love of nature, and understandings of interactions within nature, and between humans and nature. In order to work towards these goals, preschool teachers are expected to promote understandings of sustainable development through words and actions, and to select literature and activities that promote such understandings and the development of an interest in the environment amongst the children (Ministry of Education and Research 2006). These regulations open up potential opportunities for a wide range of individual inter-pretations and diverse practices within kindergartens throughout Norway. When the new Framework Plan for Preschool Teacher Education was implemented, there was a greater focus on interdisciplinary ways of working, on inquiry-based learn-ing and on education for sustainability (Ministry for Education and Research 2012b). Here, then, there are possibilities to further strengthen ECEfS in Norwegian preschools.

Within this contextual backdrop, this chapter offers insights into ECEfS in Norway, and discusses some of the challenges and possibilities related to its imple-mentation. These insights are based on a review of current literature, the author's experience as an early childhood teacher educator in science, and an interview with a locally well-known and experienced Norwegian environmentalist with an interest in ECEfS.

Provocations for the early childhood education field

A set of questions, that can act as provocations for the early childhood education field in Norway in relation to education for sustainability, guide the structure and discussion for the rest of this chapter. These questions are:

- What traditions, lifestyle practices and philosophies impact on EfS in Norway?
- What has developed within ECEfS in Norway since the Brundtland Report (WCED 1987) and particularly since the inclusion of EfS in the National Framework Plan for the Content and Tasks of Kindergartens (Ministry of Education and Research 2006, 2011)?
- What are the challenges for ECEfS in Norway?
- How do Norwegian kindergartens work with EfS?
- Does EfS play a role in the everyday life of Norwegian kindergartens and, if so, how extensive is EfS within their learning cultures?
- What can further promote ECEfS in Norwegian kindergartens?

Norwegian traditions and way of life

In Norway, use of phrases like 'responsibility for the management of nature' and having an attitude of respect for nature and environment, were familiar long before the Brundtland Report (WCED 1987). Indeed, the first national preschool teacher education frameworks included the following goal within the sciences in preschool: 'to promote the will to actively protect the nature and environment' (Ministry of Children and Family 1995: 50). Norwegian culture and traditions may explain this relatively early recognition of EfS within the kindergarten regulations. Norway, together with the other Nordic countries, has a long tradition of close contact with nature and outdoor life. In many Norwegian kindergartens, recycling, reusing and composting are inspired by both a traditional spirit of community and a deep tradition of fostering positive attitudes towards nature (Fjørtoft 2001). This latter tradition is strengthened by the practice of outdoor education in kinder-gartens. Braute and Bang (1994), building on a typical Norwegian attitude, point out that being in nature is the best start for children, building a foundation for love of nature, knowledge of nature, caring for nature, and ultimately speaking for nature in society.

As most Norwegian people still live quite close to nature, and are part of a culture that supports positive relationships with nature, they typically would evaluate them-selves as living sustainably and having sound nature-related traditions. Many do not realize, however, that attaining a high living standard even if living close to nature, promotes a large ecological footprint. According to Ewing *et al.* (2010), the global ecological footprint of an average Norwegian citizen was 5.56 global hectares per capita in 2007 (for Sweden 5.88; Denmark 8.26; Finland 6.16; Australia 6.84; United States of America 8.00; the world average is 2.70 global hectares per capita). Thus, the ecological footprint left by the average Nordic citizen is far larger than in many other places in the world (Ewing *et al.* 2010). Perhaps, then, while Norwegians show a deep regard to nature, most Norwegians are presumably not fully aware of the determinants of sustainable behaviour. According to Steg and Vlek (2009), only a real understanding of these determinants will enable people to develop and evaluate interventions to bring about positive behaviour change towards living sustainably.

With his philosophy and strong engagement in society, Arne Næss has chal-lenged the Norwegian people's thinking about such matters and became Norway's most known and influential philosopher and environmentalist, since the twentieth century. He has inspired non-philosophers and people of all ages to think more deeply about how they live.

Arne Næss and the deep ecology philosophy

Since the increasing consciousness of global ecological problems that arose in the late 1960s, Arne Næss's deep ecology philosophy has had an important influence on contemporary environmental philosophy (Barnhill *et al.* 2006, Næss 1973). Deep ecology represents a fundamental rethinking that aspires to deep questioning about environmental issues. It investigates the causes of environmental problems and the underlying worldviews of those who frame environmental policies (Barnhill *et al.* 2006). In 1984, Næss formulated eight principles, known as the deep ecological platform, with which to evaluate environmental concerns. At the heart of this platform is the emphasis on the inherent and intrinsic value of all human and nonhuman life on Earth and its diversity, independent of its usefulness to human purposes. Current human interference with the nonhuman world is seen as excessive, and policies for the environment are needed which go to the core of the economic, technological and ideological structures of society. An increasingly higher standard of living, for example, should be replaced with a deeper apprecia-tion of life quality (Barnhill *et al.* 2006, Næss 2005). The views and values of the ecological platform are intended to address a wide range of approaches to environmental thinking across the globe.

The philosophy of deep ecology includes the principle of wholism – seeing the organic wholeness of nature, with humans as fully part of it. In other words, each individual – human or nonhuman – is a distinct node in the web of nature, not an 'other'. Identification with nature, then, yields an intuitive tendency to avoid harm to the wholeness, and wanting nature to flourish. Contemporary deep ecologists are also significantly concerned about the social dimensions of environmental problems, about social injustice and issues of fairness and equity (Barnhill *et al.* 2006). Arne Næss described the ideal society as a 'green society'. This is a society that is decentralized and characterized by grassroots democracy, social responsibility, mutual aid, non-violence, public transportation, absence of social hierarchy and male domination, and ecological/organic agriculture. Put succinctly, people should live in voluntary simplicity with a feeling of community (Næss 2005: 14).

Some kindergartens in Norway have been inspired by this philosophy. An example is the Randineborg kindergarten in Tjøme municipality, about 50km south of the capital, Oslo. This kindergarten has an eco-philosophical logo and seeks to convey through its curriculum and pedagogy that each individual's acting, thinking and feeling is interrelated with nature, society, and other individuals (http://randineborg.barnehage.no/Innhold/Side/2881). Kindergarten staff aim to build positive attitudes for sustainability by focusing on good relationships between children, staff, and parents, and towards nature. The kindergarten focuses on being in nature, building knowledge of nature through philosophical conversations with children, while sustainable practices are simply normal.

Children and preschool teachers – Norwegians of today

Another, perhaps more important theoretical perspective for understanding contemporary Norwegians and their ideas about sustainability – adults, youth and children – is present-day late modernity (see Fornäs 1995, Giddens 1991; Schreiner 2006). A post-modern society is described as highly pluralistic and diverse, with no universal principles and no common ideas that can direct social development (Giddens 1991). According to Schreiner (2006) the way people understand themselves and their surroundings is related to cultural, political and economic characteristics of the society. Globalization connects people and societies through time and space and leads to universal standardization. Both modernization and globalization are leading to individualization and liberation of people, in the sense that people can choose their life and who they want to be. Media, the Internet and travel are opening up potential for meetings and exchanges between cultures as never before, and also for the diffusion of cultural traditions, perceptions and belief systems. Services and goods are not only for utility and use, but also for symbolizing status and identity (Frønes 1998, 2007, Schreiner 2006). Theories about identity construction in a post-modern world commonly focus on children and young people, but multiple perspectives also apply to other age groups (Schreiner 2006), and may be important for both young children and their preschool teachers' personal motivations and value orientations towards sustainable development.

As citizens of one of the world's richest countries, Norwegians appear as, more or less, materialistically orientated. This is reflected in surveys contained in the ROSE (The Relevance of Science Education) project (Sjøberg and Schreiner 2006) which mapped interest in and attitudes towards, the natural sciences, technology and environmental challenges among 15-year-old youths in many countries. Choices related to everyday matters like clothing, leisure activities, and beliefs, all carry a message about one's identity (Frønes 2007, Giddens 1991). According to ROSE (Sjøberg and Schreiner 2006), many Norwegian girls do not like the natural sciences, preferring to work in social services roles. It may be assumed, as a consequence, that some of this group will be found among Norwegian preschool teachers. In light of new knowledge and new experiences, humans are continuously reconsidering and redeveloping themselves (Giddens 1991).

According to self-determination theory (Deci and Ryan 2000), the psychological needs of every human-being are relatedness, competence and autonomy (Cooke and Fielding 2009). Relatedness is the need and desire to be connected to others, to love and care for, and to be loved and cared for by others (Baumeister and Leary 1995, Deci and Ryan 2000, Johansson 2001). This includes the desire to belong to groups, and to be respected, appreciated, and supported by group members (Frønes 2007, Schreiner 2006). Competence describes the desire to be effective within an environment and to derive valued outcomes. The need for autonomy is characterized by the desire to have a choice and to act voluntarily (Cooke and Fielding 2009, Deci and Ryan 2000, cf. Maslow 1970). Taking these ideas into account, the key to sustainable attitudes and behaviour may be their integration into personal feelings of identity, relatedness, and being appreciated.

Although there is enough information available on environmental issues, people may 'lack the desire to assimilate the relevant information' (Pelletier et al. 1999). From my personal experiences as a preschool teacher educator, the younger generation, especially, barely knows about Agenda 21 (UNEP 1992). Further, Pelletier et al. (1999) and Cooke and Fielding (2009) acknowledge that many people seem to have joined a global 'helplessness belief' that prevents them from engaging with environmental and sustainability issues. There may also be a general loss of interest in political, social and science questions among Norwegian youth (Sjøberg and Schreiner 2006), as well as among others in the wealthier parts of the world (Johansson et al. 2009, Pelletier et al. 1999). Preschool teachers are recruited from these groups, as are the parents of kindergarten children.

Norwegians – children, preschool teachers, parents and other citizens – live in the tension, then, between Norwegian traditions, demands for environmental responsibility, and their individual orientation within late modernity, all of which shape their motivational tendencies and personal value orientations. Rasmussen (2001) also acknowledges that children's lives may be fragmented into various areas, giving them vastly different experiences and values. There is no 'normal' for today's twenty-first-century children.

Overall, it is difficult to say whether people have become less engaged with sustainability than in the period of the Brundtland Report (WCED 1987). In each time period, attitudes and behaviours reflect the contemporary spirit. Today, there is a much wider range of choices for Norwegians than even 20 years ago. While enthusiastic people may have engaged in environmental issues in the 1980s, today they may become engaged in a sports club or an Internet-based group, for example. Such diversity of options and experiences, and their impact on engagement in current sustainability questions, are reported by Gabriele Brennhaugen, Project Manager at the Department of the Environment, Stavanger Municipality, an experienced environmentalist with a long history of roles related to sustainable development, especially those focused on children.

The quality of learning activities and the quality of sustainable development pedagogy with young children will, in some ways, be an extension of each preschool teacher's own motivations and background. The learning culture in a kindergarten is influenced by the preschool teacher's own understandings of the relationships between culture, society, sustainable development and the kindergarten practices, and his/her own conceptualizations of learning (Alvestad and Løvberg 2005: 352, Davis 2010, Hollins 2008: 7, Sageidet in preparation, Thulin 2006). This learning culture is essential for children, as their early ideas, skills and attitudes emerge and support later development and learning, and provide interest, motivation and practical experience (Ausubel 1968, Johnston 2005). There is, presumably, a connection between early experiences related to EfS and the development of interest for, and skills related to, this issue that significantly influence later life (Braute and Bang 1994).

Implementation of EfS in Norwegian kindergartens, inside and out

The Norwegian government sponsors and cooperates with many non-governmental organizations. One example is the independent children's organization Eco-Agents ('Miljøagentene', formerly 'Blekkulfs Miljødetektiver' (Octopus environmental detectives), which supplies information and practical activities related to sustainable development and group identity (Frønes 2007, cf. Schreiner 2006) to kindergartens. Following the government's 'green' city concept (established in 1996), Eco-Agents has introduced 'Green Children's Cities'. Oslo was the first such city in 2001; Stavanger was the second, in 2002. Within green cities, kindergartens can become 'green kindergartens', when they work on a project focused on sustainable development and environmental protection as part of everyday life. In practice, this means that these kindergartens can achieve the international environmental 'green flag' certification for early childhood services and schools, associated with the international eco-school movement founded by the Foundation for Environmental Education (FEE). Kindergartens in Norway can also become Eco-lighthouses, another program that offers environmental certification for private and public enterprises or they can join 'Clean City' projects. Such projects in kindergartens and schools often include a link to issues of fairness by supporting projects for children in developing countries, in harmony with Næss's ecological platform.

In 2006, Stavanger (which was awarded the newly established Nordic Sustainability prize in 2011) was one of the first municipalities in Norway to make 'green flag' participation compulsory for kindergartens; other municipalities have now followed this lead. Brennhaugen (personal communication, 24 January 2013) from the Stavanger Municipality comments that the aim of the 'green flag' is to integrate sustainable activities into the everyday life of the kindergartens. While most kindergarten staff members are positive and supportive, about one-third of the kindergartens require the stimulus of a compulsory program and need guidance; in other words, they are not intrinsically driven to engage in sustainability. Some settings, for example, do not maintain even the minimum requirement of engaging in annual sustainability project tasks. In order to overcome such barriers, Brennhaugen and her team organize information meetings about how to realize sustainable projects, with each kindergarten being allocated their own contact person. Presentations of tasks by experienced 'green kindergarten' staff were seen as very useful aspects of the professional development for newcomers to the program.

Brennhaugen reports that parents are fascinated by the 'green flag' projects, and often ask kindergarten staff to further develop the environmental focus. Upon interview, she cited the case of kindergarten staff who were initially sceptical and unmotivated to attain the 'green flag', but finally achieved real change in their daily routines through a focus on sustainable meal preparation using organic ingredients. Brennhaugen states that often 'just doing things' can be the start for changing minds. When people begin to feel a part of something interesting and successful, they become engaged (Deci and Ryan 2000, cf. Giddens 1991). In this case, the adults and children discussed sustainability in relation to meal preparation and considered the use of local raw food, use of simple, non-electrical kitchen equipment, recycling, and the final 'product' of the sustainability learning, a healthy meal. Such an experience became a positive and illustrative example of both inquiry-based learning and EfS in kindergartens (Sageidet 2012).

While kindergartens can freely choose their sustainability project, it is anticipated that they will choose from 'green flag' focus projects. These are diverse, but include waste management, reusing and recycling, composting and kitchen garden, biodiversity, energy conservation and environmentally-friendly transport. Brennhaugen estimates that about 90 per cent of kindergartens start with a project on waste and recycling, perhaps because this task is familiar from the regular routines of private households in the municipality, and therefore requires limited new knowledge. Sageidet (in preparation) has identified that many preschool teachers consider the implementation of EfS and natural science related activities as difficult because their personal knowledge is limited and request further knowledge of EfS and the sciences. To support them during the 'green flag' process, kindergartens can obtain such information from 'Green Living', a professional network of sustainability officers that advises about sustainable everyday practices.

This network is distributed across Norway with eight local offices. 'Green Living' offers a range of informative courses on topics such as composting and recycling.

Examples of successful kindergartens that promote ECEfS include Lassamyra kindergarten in Stavanger that has established an environmental council including five year olds, who suggest rules such as 'nobody is allowed to throw away banana skins'. Additionally, children from Stavanger's Buøy kindergarten held a staged revue about life in the compost, using mops for millipede costumes (Reilstad 2009). The experience of being respected as an equal and being heard, values children's moral dimensions, and has the potential to strengthen their feelings of caring about the environment (cf. Johansson 2001, 2009). Brennhaugen also commented that kindergartens with environmental profiles will eventually attract environmentally engaged preschool teachers; thus, they may become increasingly sustainable and more popular with environmentally conscious parents. This is one way a kindergarten becomes a sustainable community (cf. Davis 2010: 273), in turn, potentially inspiring other kindergartens and the local community to also embrace EfS.

Strengthening ECEfS in Norway

More research is required about the complex interrelationships between the above-mentioned factors that influence both adults/preschool teachers and children in their lifelong learning processes. The kindergarten is a vital part of Norwegian society, and has the potential to play an important role both for the personal development of children and adults, and for the environment. This potential has been poorly investigated and should be the subject of further research.

Some possible research questions follow. What are young children's imaginings around environment and sustainability, and their role in children's lives? What do we mean by sustainable attitudes and behaviours in relation to the kindergarten? What might be the attitudes towards environmental issues of children at various ages who have attended a kindergarten focused on sustainability? What happens with respect to children's early motivations and engagement around environmental and sustainability issues as they mature and move into schools? What can be done to maintain sustainability as a vital part of children's and adults' lives? Searching for answers to such questions may be helpful in developing meaningful and authentic learning experiences for young children in kindergarten.

Further questions also arise, for example, what competencies related to sustainability are significant for young children? What competencies do preschool teachers request that are related to sustainability matters? How can the kindergarten contribute to the development of such competencies, and to children's active participation in nature and society? The Ministry for Education and Research (2012a) attempts to give guidelines, but more knowledge is needed from the various perspectives of the kindergarten's role in sustainability and research is needed to find ways to develop and maximize this role. To date, examples like the Randineborg, Lassamyra and Buøy kindergartens show that EfS in kindergartens seems to be highly dependent on individual enthusiastic preschool teachers, a finding common to other educational contexts and in other countries (NSW EPA 2003).

A key to developing ECEfS in Norwegian kindergartens might be to strengthen the feelings of relatedness, competence and autonomy of both adults and children. Another key may be to address the kindergarten as a community of learners (Davis 2010, cf. Johansson 2001). For preschool teachers, one possibility is to enhance EfS in preschool teacher education, through extending scientific and social knowledge about environmental issues, as well as deepening understandings of successful kindergarten pedagogies that support EfS. Preschool teachers require comprehensive and relevant knowledge about environmental issues, and need to be familiar with international and national documents concerning education for sustainability (Ekborg 2002). Additionally, understanding relationships between culture, society, sustainable development and kindergarten practices and how learning is conceptualized with such understandings should be a subject for research. Participatory action research including research engagement with staff, parents and children in kindergartens would be informative for all and locally promote understandings.

Conclusions

The interests and motivations of both children and adults in Norway, for addressing sustainability issues are influenced by complex interrelationships between traditions, a demand for environmental responsibility, personal identity development, relatedness, materialism and self-realism, competence and autonomy in the post-modern society. The kindergarten is a vital arena for these interrelationships and has the potential to play an important role for both the personal development of children and adults, and for local and national sustainable development. To date, this potential has been poorly investigated and should be the subject of research. Children and preschool teachers should be asked about their sustainability attitudes and behaviours, and their needs for various competencies and skills.

An area for longitudinal research study is the impact of early learning about sustainability in the kindergarten on later attitudes. Additionally, international comparative research may reveal global similarities and local variations that can help to advance ECEfS uptake and enhance practices. National, Nordic and international research cooperation should be strengthened and developed. Through ongoing research and support for existing successful practices in kindergartens such as those highlighted in Stavanger, children's participation in decision-making for a sustainable society will be strengthened.

Acknowledgement

Many thanks to Gabriele Brennhaugen for a useful interview. Also, many thanks to Eva M. Johansson and the research group 'Transnational dialogues in research in early childhood education for sustainability', for inspiration.

References

Alvestad, M. (2005) 'Årsplanar i barnehagen – intensjonar og realitetar i praksis?' *Norsk pedagogisk tidskrift,* 1: 90–102.

Alvestad, T. and Løvberg, R. (2005) 'Barnehagen i endring hva tenker førskolelærere om det?' *Norsk Pedagogisk tidskrift,* 5: 345–54.

Ausubel, D. (1968) *Educational Psychology: A Cognitive View.* New York: Holt, Rinehart & Winston.

Barnhill, D., Sarkar, S. and Kalof, L. (2006) 'Deep ecology', in C.J. Cleveland, (ed.) *Encyclopedia of Earth.* Washington, DC: Environmental Information Coalition, National Council for Science and the Environment. (First published in *Encyclopedia of Earth,* 12 October 2006; last revised 30 April 2012; Online. Available: www.eoearth.org/article/ Deep_ecology (accessed 24 October 2012).

Baumeister, R.F. and Leary, M.R. (1995) 'The need to belong: desire for interpersonal attachments as a fundamental human motivation'. *Psychological Bulletin,* 117(3): 497–529.

Braute, J. and Bang, C. (1994) *Bli med ut. Barn i naturen.* Oslo: Universitetsforlaget.

Cooke, A. and Fielding, K. (2009) 'Fun environmentalism! Potential contributions of autonomy supportive psychology to sustainable lifestyles'. *Management of Environmental Quality: An International Journal,* 21(2): 155–64.

Davis, J.M. (2010) *Young Children and the Environment – Early Education for Sustainability.* Cambridge: Cambridge University Press.

Deci, E.L. and Ryan, R.M. (2000) 'The "what" and "why" of goal pursuits: human needs and the self-determination of behaviour'. *Psychological Inquiry,* 11(4): 227–68.

Ewing, B., Moore, D., Goldfinger, S., Oursler, A., Read, A. and Wackernagel, M. (2010) *Ecological Footprint Atlas 2010.* Oakland: Global Footprint Network. Online. Available: www.footprintnetwork.org (accessed 28 January 2014).

Ekborg, M. (2002) 'Naturvetenskapelig utbildning för hållbar utveckling'. Göteborg studies in educational sciences 188, *Acta Universitatis Gothoburgensis,* 1–303.

Fjørtoft, I. (2001) 'The natural environment as a playground for children: The impact of outdoor play activities in pre-primary school children'. *Early Childhood Education Journal,* 29(2): 111–17.

Flavell, J.H., Miller, P.H. and Miller, S.A. (2002) *Cognitive development,* 4th edn. Upper Saddle River, NJ: Prentice Hall.

Fornäs, J. (1995) *Cultural Theory and Late Modernity.* London: Sage.

Frønes, I. (1998) *De likeverdige. Om sosialisering og de jevnaldrendes betydning* (On equal level. About socialization and the significance of the age peers). Oslo: Universitetsforlaget.

Frønes, I. (2007) *Moderne barndom.* 2. Utgave, Oslo: Cappelen, p. 166.

Giddens, A. (1991) *Modernity and Self-Identity. Self and Society in the Late Modern Age.* Cambridge: Polity Press.

Hollins, E. A. (2008) *Culture in School learning,* 2nd edn. First published in 1996. New York: Routledge.

Johansson, E. (2001) 'Morality in children's worlds – rationality of thought or values emanating from relations?' *Studies in Philosophy and Education. An International Quarterly,* 20(4): 345–58.

Johansson, E. (2009) 'The preschool child of today – the world-citizen of tomorrow?' in E. Johansson, D. Berthelsen, A. Klerfelt and P. Nykänen (eds) Sustainable development in early childhood. Special Issue. *International Journal of Early Childhood,* 41, 79–95.

Johansson, E., Berthelsen, D. Klerfelt, A and Nykänen P. (eds) (2009) 'Sustainable development in early childhood'. Special Issue. *International Journal of Early Childhood*, 41: 2.

Johnston, J. (2005) *Early Explorations in Science. Exploring Primary Science and Technology*.
Buckingham: Open University Press.

Kindergarten Act (2005) 'Act no. 64 of June 2005 relating to Kindergartens (the
Kindergarten Act)'. Norwegian Ministry of Education and Research. Online. Available:
www.regjeringen.no/upload/KD/Vedlegg/Barnehager/engelsk/Act_no._64_of_
June_2005_web.pdf (accessed 27 October 2012).

Maslow, A.H. (1970) *Motivation and Personaliy*, 2nd edn. London: Harper and Row.

Ministry of Church and Education (1980) *Førskolelærerutdanning – studieplan*. Oslo:
Universitetsforlaget.

Ministry of Children and Family (1995) *Rammeplan for barnehagen*. Q-0903 B. Oslo:
Akademika As.

Ministry of Education and Research (2006) *Rammeplan for barnehagens innhold og oppgaver*
(Framework plan for the content and tasks of kindergartens). Online. Available:
www.regjeringen.no/upload/kilde/kd/reg/2006/0001/ddd/pdfv/282023-
rammeplanen.pdf (accessed 28 January 2014).

Ministry of Education and Research (2011) *Rammeplan for barnehagens innhold og oppgaver*
(Framework plan for the content and tasks of lindergartens). Revised edition. Online.
Available: www.regjeringen.no/upload/KD/Vedlegg/Barnehager/Rammeplan_2011/
KD_bokmal_Rammeplan_2011_web.pdf (accessed 28 January 2014).

Ministry of Education and Research (2012a) *Kunnskap for en felles fremtid*. Revidert strategi
for utdanning for bærekraftig utvikling (2012–2015), Utdanningsdirektoratet 2012.
Online. Available: www.regjeringen.no/upload/KD/Vedlegg/UH/Rapporter_og_
planer/Strategi_for_UBU.pdf (accessed 28 January 2014).

Ministry of Education and Research (2012b) 'Nasjonal forskrift om rammeplan for barne-
hagelærerutdanning'. Fastsatt av Kunnskapsdepartementet 04.06.2012 med hjemmel i
lov om universiteter og høyskoler av 1 April 2005 nr. 15 § 3–2 annet ledd. Online.
Available: www.regjeringen.no/upload/KD/Vedlegg/UH/Rammeplaner/
Barnehagelaerer/BLU_rammeplan.pdf (accessed 28 January 2014).

Næss, A. (1973) 'The shallow and the deep, long-range ecology movement. A summary'.
Inquiry, 16(1): 95–100.

Næss, A. (1989) 'Ecology, community and lifestyle: Outline of an ecosophy'. *Inquiry*, p. 223.

Næss, A. (2005) 'Deep ecology of wisdom', in Glasser, G. and Drengson, A. (eds) *The Selected
Works of Arne Næss*. Volume 10, Dordrecht: Springer, p. 688.

Norddahl, K. (2008) 'What might Early Childhood Education for Sustainability look like?'
in I. Pramling Samuelsson and Y. Kaga (eds) *The Contribution of Early Childhood Education
to a Sustainable Society*. Paris: UNESCO, p. 136.

Nordic Council of Ministers (ed.) (2009) *Sustainable Development – New Bearings for the
Nordic Region*. Revised edition with goals and priorities 2009–2012. Copenhagen:
Nordic Council of Ministers.

NSW EPA (2003) *Patches of Green: Early Childhood Environmental Education in Australia –
Scope, Status and Direction*. Sydney: NSW Environment Protection Authority EPA Social
Research Series 2003/35.

Pelletier, L.G., Dion, S., Tuson, K. and Green-Demers, I. (1999) 'Why do people fail to adopt
environmental protective behaviours? Towards a taxonomy of environmental amotiva-
tion'. *Journal of Applied Social Psychology*, 29(12): 2481–504.

Rasmussen, K. (2001) 'Børnekulturbegrebet – set i lys af aktuelle barndomstendenser og teoretiske problemstillinger', in B. Tufte, J. Kampmann and B. Juncker(eds) *Børnekultur. Hvilke børn? Og hvis kultur?* Copenhagen: Academisk forlag.

Reilstad, K. (2009) 'Spiller larver og skrukketroll – Buøy barnehage tar sin grønne profil helt ut og lager revy om livet i komposten'. *Rogalands Avis* 17.03.2009, Stavanger.

Sageidet, B.M. (2012) 'Inquirybaserte naturfagaktiviteter i barnehagen', in T. Vist and A. Alvestad (eds) *Læringskulturer i barnehagen.* Stavanger, Norway: Cappelen Damm Academisk, pp. 115–39.

Sageidet, B.M. (in preparation) *Are Natural Sciences Related Activities a Part of the Daily Learning Culture in Norwegian Kindergartens? A Study Based on Preschool Teacher's Daily Choices and Attitudes.*

Schreiner, C. (2006) *Exploring a ROSE-garden: Norwegian youth's orientations towards science – seen as signs of late modern identities.* Doctoral thesis, University of Oslo, Faculty of Education, Department of Teacher Education and School Development, Oslo.

Sjøberg, S. and Schreiner, C. (2006) *Holdninger til og forestillinger om vitenskap og teknologi i Norge – En fremstilling basert på data fra Eurobarometer og ROSE.* Norges Forskningsråd NFR, nettpublikasjon, 136 s. internettside: Online. Available: www.forskningsradet.no/ no/Nyhet/Ja+til+vitenskap+men+ikke+som+karriere/1153831952342 (accessed 28 January 2014).

Steg, L. and Vlek, C. (2009) 'Encouraging pro-environmental behaviour: An integrative review and research agenda'. *Journal of Environmental Psychology,* 29: 309–17.

Thulin, S. (2006) *Vad händer med lärandets objekt?* En studie av hur lärare och barn i förskolan kommunicerar naturvitenskapeliga fenomen. *Acta Wexionensia* 102/2006, Växjö: Växjö University Press, p. 134.

UNEP (1992) 'Agenda 21. United Nations Environment Programme'. Online. Available: www.unep.org/Documents.Multilingual/Default.asp?documentid=52 (accessed 28 January 2014).

WCED (1987) *Our Common Future.* A report from the United Nations World Commission on Environment and Development. Oxford: Oxford University Press.

Cluster 3

Curriculum and pedagogy

Early childhood education for sustainability and natural outdoor playspaces

Researching change and theorizing about interfaces

Sue Elliott

Abstract

The implementation of early childhood education for sustainability (ECEfS) is often explicitly linked with natural playspaces in early childhood settings. In this chapter, I question how natural playspaces offer contexts for ECEfS and how early childhood services might engage in transformative change for sustainability. The research project on which this chapter is based involved Critical Participatory Action Research (CPAR) with two case study early childhood centres in Victoria, Australia. These were Acacia Kindergarten and Banksia Childcare Centre, and the study was conducted over a one-year period. The interfaces, or points of interaction, between the natural outdoor playspace context and educators' socially-constructed understandings of sustainability and education for sustainability were explored, and analyses of these centres' transformative changes invited theorizing about the interfaces. In an attempt to better understand the natural outdoor playspace as a context for ECEfS, a theoretical framework emerged as the study progressed, depicted here as three nested triangles informed by Sterling's (2001) nested systems theory. This chapter offers insights into transformative research approaches in early childhood settings and the complexities of using natural outdoor playspaces as contexts for ECEfS. I conclude that in some settings a few sustainable practices may provoke early childhood educators to think and act differently not only about sustainability, but also about early childhood pedagogy and philosophy.

Introduction

In Australia and internationally, the early childhood sector has been relatively slow to embrace education for sustainability when compared with other education sectors (Davis, 2009, Tilbury *et al.* 2005). Elliott and Davis (2009) have postulated reasons why early childhood education has been tardy and have noted that children playing in nature – a common practice in many early childhood settings – may be perceived by many practitioners as a sufficient response to addressing sustainability issues. I question, however, whether this is really sufficient. Increasingly, a range of practitioner publications offer support for the development of natural outdoor playspaces in early childhood settings (Elliott 2008, Gamson Danks 2010, White 2008, Wilson 2008), and the benefits of play in natural settings for children's health, well-being and learning are well-documented (Lester and Maudsley 2006, Moore and Cooper-Marcus 2008, Munoz 2009). Indeed, there is an increasing sense of urgency around the promotion of natural outdoor play opportunities for busy urbanized children (Louv 2008). This trend towards play in nature has not gone unnoticed by early childhood accreditation and regulatory authorities in Australia. Natural outdoor playspaces for children to experience and explore are now required as part of the provision of quality early childhood services (Australian Children's Education and Care Quality Authority (ACECQA) 2013) and natural playspaces are well-supported by the first national early childhood curriculum *Belonging Being Becoming: The Early Childhood Learning Framework for Australia* (DEEWR 2009).

In light of such broad advocacy for play in nature, the research project outlined here questions the connections between the natural outdoor playspace context and early childhood educators' socially-constructed meanings of sustainability and education for sustainability (EfS) in early childhood settings. These connections are envisaged as interfaces where the physical context and the socio-culturally derived meanings and relationships offer an interactive and dynamic space for investigation. This Critical Participatory Action Research (CPAR) was centred on asking 'What lies at the interfaces between natural playspaces, sustainability and education for sustainability? For example, is the presence of items such as rocks and logs in natural outdoor playspaces sufficient to address the issues of sustainability?' Here, I briefly outline the CPAR methodology that was employed (Kemmis and McTaggart 2005) and identify the early childhood centre case study contexts. I then offer two vignettes to illustrate the somewhat divergent transformations that occurred in these two centres. Systems theory (Bateson 1979, Capra 1997, 2002) and, specifically, nested systems theory (Sterling 2001) offer a basis for theorizing about the interfaces and inform the theoretical framework that was developed as a result of the study. The potential of CPAR in early childhood settings coupled with the complexities inherent in using natural outdoor playspaces as contexts for ECEfS are evident. I conclude that much more than the provision of natural elements such as rocks and logs is required to fully address sustainability in early childhood settings.

Methodology

The methodology, CPAR (Kemmis and McTaggart 2005), in addition to its principles of inclusion, collective action, emancipation and critical reflection, was also underpinned by a biocentric rather than an anthropocentric stance and this researcher's personal, ethical commitment to sustainability. Thus, it was my clear intention as a co-researcher with the educators and parents to engage in a potentially empowering and collaborative research journey for sustainability with the participants at both centres. Informed by critical theories (Fay 1987, Friere 1976, 1999), CPAR offers the possibility of transformative journeys for all research participants, including the co-researcher, through the potential for all participants to engage with the world in new and different ways as a result of direct experiences/actions, critical reflection and rational discourse within the research process (Mezirow 1997). As Comstock (1982: 389) states, critical research 'is aimed at not merely understanding the world, but changing it' and the intent, through evolving socially constructive processes, was facilitation of different ways of thinking, acting and relating for sustainability (Kemmis 2009).

The two participating case study centres were Banksia Childcare Centre, a long daycare centre providing full-time or part-time education and care for children from six weeks to five years of age and Acacia Kindergarten, a sessional kindergarten offering several half-day sessions per week for children aged three to five years. Case study data were created over a one-year research period through participant observations, interviews with educators and parents, focus groups, photographs of the outdoor playspaces and the collation of centre documentation including program plans, parent newsletters and centre policies. A pivotal strategy with each case study centre community was to invite participants to discuss a potential action priority for their outdoor playspace. The action priority was negotiated during an initial staff and parent focus group and confirmed by participants as they implemented the action priority over several months. Banksia Childcare Centre community chose to install a worm farm during a centre working-bee where parents, staff and children worked together to undertake various maintenance tasks. At Acacia Kindergarten, a bird nesting box was constructed at home then installed in a tree in the kindergarten grounds by a parent. Overall, the research approach invited participants' perceptions about sustainability, education for sustainability and their centres' outdoor playspaces, and supported the documentation of their actions, discourses and reflections as transformative changes evolved within each centre community.

Case study contexts

Both centres were owned by a local council, but were managed by elected parent and staff Committees of Management. Banksia Childcare Centre was a 50-place centre with the children accommodated in four age-based groupings. This study focused on the three- to five-year-old group outdoor playspace that was registered for 23 children, however due to part-time attendance, some 50 children participated overall each week. A teacher and two certificate-qualified assistants worked with this group. Acacia Kindergarten offered two sessional programs for four year olds and one for three-year-old children. Three educators including a teacher/director, a certificate-qualified assistant and an intervention aide (who worked with children with additional needs) supported 70 children who attended the centre each week. Only one of the four-year-old groups, comprising 23 children, was the focus for this study.

Both Banksia Childcare Centre and Acacia Kindergarten had large, above-regulation, sized (520 and 314 square metres respectively) relatively natural outdoor playspaces that included areas of tanbark, sandpits, and mature trees and bushes (see Figures 8.1 and 8.2). At Banksia Childcare Centre the planting density was greater, but this centre lacked the grassed areas that were present at Acacia Kindergarten. These vegetation differences, alone, created a visual sense of openness and sparseness at the kindergarten when compared to the childcare centre. The kindergarten also had fixed outdoor structures comprising a small multi-functional timber fort and a purpose-built cubby house, while the childcare centre had a timber-edged vegetable garden and two areas of low wooden bench seating. The Banksia Childcare Centre playspace included two small areas of synthetic surfacing, a rubber tricycle track, and an artificial grass carpet around the sandpit. Essentially, both centres evidenced natural outdoor playspaces as described by outdoor playspace design guides (Elliott 2008, Gamson Danks 2010). A further commonality between the centres was that both had experienced significant physical changes in the outdoor playspace that required remediation. Both had lost bushes or trees through time and/or drought and the educators stated a preference for replanting with more drought-tolerant native bushes and trees as a remedy.

Also, in both centres, educators and parents, alike, valued the naturalness and the relatively large sizes of the playspaces; yet, almost no explicit evidence of education for sustainability was identified in centre documentation or interviews. Opportunities for playful exploration of natural elements, caring for and

Figure 8.1 Banksia Childcare Centre outdoor playspace

Figure 8.2 Acacia Kindergarten outdoor playspace

knowledge of the environment and a proactive approach to water conservation were feasible, but not apparently enacted. The observed physical similarities of natural playspaces, yet the apparent lack of education for sustainability suggested to me as researcher that an investigation of the interfaces between the natural outdoor playspace context and the educators' and parents' socially-constructed meanings of sustainability and education for sustainability was warranted.

Vignettes from transformative journeys

During the year-long data collection period and later after analysis of the case study data, it became clear that two, somewhat divergent, ECEfS journeys were emerging. Banksia Childcare Centre educators not only had enacted their negotiated action priority, but increasingly embraced sustainability as foundational to their centre practices. They began to put into place the principles of education for sustainability identified in significant national and international documents, including holistic approaches, critical thinking, participatory decision-making, partnerships for change and systems thinking (DEWHA 2009, UNESCO 2005). Sustainability became an overarching 'frame of mind' (Bonnett 2002: 14) or an embedded culture (Davis *et al.* 2005). Substantial signs of multiple transformative journeys for the research participants and for the centre as a whole were recorded; drawn from interviews, focus groups and a review of centre documentation at the conclusion of the research period. In contrast, Acacia Kindergarten educators made minimal change towards sustainable practices. Although there was some evidence of rethinking of linkages between elements akin to some engagement with systems thinking, the transformative journey was only just beginning at this site. The following vignettes (Elliott 2012: 147) from data collected during the study illustrate the differences between the two centres and their respective journeys and provoke questions as to why the transformative journeys were so different for the two case study centres.

Acacia Kindergarten vignette

The educators placed a water bucket in the sandpit to limit water usage for play by the children; the limit set by educators was one bucket per day. Educators varied in how they experienced this change, the Director/teacher described how water conservation was discussed with the children and she acknowledged the children were now using water more wisely and doing different things with the water. The intervention aide indicated there was no discussion occurring with children and her own lack of awareness suggested there had been no educator communication about why the physical change had been made or how it might create learning opportunities for children about sustainability. Fewer reminders from educators about flushing the toilets reinforced water conservation, but further water conservation practices typical in early childhood centres could have been implemented.

While there was some changed thinking emerging at Acacia Kindergarten in relation to water conservation practices with these becoming everyday practices in the sandpit, there was potential for so much more. Only one illustrative vignette is offered here, but it typifies many observations at Acacia Kindergarten and suggests some initial practically-orientated beginnings of change. Later analysis of the data and my critical reflections as a researcher revealed that several factors impeded change in this case study site. A key factor was the Director's overarching early childhood philosophy and pedagogical approaches that – from her interview and from field observations – appeared to be drawn from developmentally-deficit images of children. This was evident when the children were often directed or informed about what to do, rather than being viewed as capable and active co-participants in their curriculum and learning with opportunities to exercise agency.

For example, when the parent made and installed the bird box in the outdoor play-space, children's involvement was limited to encouragement by the educators to look for birds after the event. This example reflects an earlier era of early child-hood education philosophy and pedagogy – still quite common – when psychology-based, developmental paradigms predominated (Bredekamp 1987, Woodhead 2006) that pre-date the United Nations Convention on the Rights of the Child (UNCRC) (UNICEF 1989) which enshrines children's rights as partic-ipants and decision-makers. As a researcher, I questioned how different the outcomes might have been for the children, if contemporary images of children and curriculum had informed the experiences. Would children themselves have researched, designed and built the bird box, then problem-solved the most appro-priate location and documented the observed birds?

Banksia Childcare Centre vignette

The dead or dying non-native plants were physically evident in the outdoor playspace and a priority for the centre working-bee was to remove and/or prune them back. Parents at the working-bee undertook this action and invited assistance from some children present to measure the bushy playspaces against their heights. Following the working-bee, the new bushy playspaces were creatively used by educators and children for play experiences. In recog-nition of the physical changes and to support enhanced play affordances, the limits previously in place about not playing in the garden bed were removed. Such was the positive impact for both educators and children that this revi-sion of play limits was to be extended through formal staff discussion to all outdoor playspaces in the centre.

In contrast, at Banksia Childcare Centre, both educators and parents appeared to hold more contemporary, reconceptualized images of children as competent, capable and active participants in the world (Cannella 1997, MacNaughton 2003). The pruning of vegetation at the centre working-bee could have occurred as a simple ground main-tenance task. However, the engagement of educators, parents and children informed by evolving understandings of education for sustainability, prompted a different outcome and importantly, an outcome in which children were active participants. Also, the vignette illustrates critical reflection about playspace limits, participatory decision-making, and responsiveness to the children's play needs. More contemporary approaches to early childhood pedagogy and philosophy, including embedding of, and applying, the principles of education for sustainability were enacted in the Banksia Childcare Centre. In particular, children were active participants. Collaborative and responsive relationships between children, educators and parents were integral to the task undertaken. Elliott and Davis (2009) have previously noted alignment between contemporary early childhood pedagogy and philosophy and the principles of educa-tion for sustainability and here this alignment was well-illustrated.

The transformative journeys briefly highlighted in these vignettes suggest that multiple elements were at play in the interfaces between the natural outdoor play-space context and the socially-constructed understandings of sustainability and education for sustainability. In the following section, I draw further on the journeys of Banksia Childcare Centre and Acacia Kindergarten, described in full elsewhere (Elliott 2012), to outline the interconnections between the themes that I drew from the data analysis. In doing so, I also present a theoretical framework that explains relationships between the interfaces.

Nested systems and a theoretical framework

Before presenting this theoretical framework, systems theory (Bateson 1979, Capra 1997, Maturana and Varela 1987) and the notion of nested systems (Sterling 2001) are briefly described as these were integral to how this study was conceived and implemented. Systems theory prioritizes relationships over objects or entities (Capra 1997), and describes the evolving nature of relationships in dynamic contexts (Maturana and Varela 1987). The various themes drawn from the data throughout this study highlighted that, irrespective of the entities involved (Council, children, educators, parents), proactive, responsive and collaborative relationships were vitally important in promoting change for sustainability within the dynamic context of the early childhood outdoor playspace.

Nested systems described by Sterling (2001) draws on Koestler's (1976) earlier holarchy work about the nesting of holons or systems in a hierarchical manner that evolve and change with the dynamics of the environment. Each system is a self-regulating whole, but its location in a nested hierarchy requires ongoing interaction and integration such that a suprasystem 'shapes, limits and gives meaning to' each subsystem (Sterling 2001: 31). In other words, like nested Russian Babushka dolls, each doll is entire, but through positioning defines the next smaller doll in the hierarchical relationship. In particular, Sterling (2001: 32) locates educational change for sustainability within multiple hierarchical systems to call for 'continuous co-evolution where both education and society are engaged in a relationship of mutual transformation – one that can explore, develop and manifest sustainability values'. Possibly more familiar to early childhood educators is the application of nested systems in *Bronfenbrenner's Ecological System Theory* (Bronfenbrenner 1979) that described child development in terms of multiple nested systems of relationships evolving over time. The application of nested systems cited here reinforces the importance of relationships and offers a basis for theoretically-framing the interfaces and transformative processes described within a nested systems approach.

The framework developed from this study comprises a hierarchical nesting of two systems with the physical context depicted by three seriated over-lapping Triangles, 1, 2 and 3 respectively (see Figure 8.3). Triangle 1 (the largest) represents the socially-constructed system of understandings around sustainability; Triangle 2 illustrates the socially-constructed system of understandings around early childhood education for sustainability. Triangle 3 (the smallest) represents the outdoor

playspace physical context. Shades of grey in the figure convey a sense of difference, but overall cohesiveness of the whole system. The selection of dotted outlines
illustrates the potential for fluid interactions between the three hierarchical levels.
The triangle shape is a metaphor, in that a triangle is multi-faceted and the
strongest geometric shape in engineering terms, with each apex being integral to
the strength of the whole system. Differences between the centres and their
changes over time are illustrated by comparing the initial figure for both centres at
the start of the study (see Figure 8.3) with the figures that illustrate the different
endpoints (see Figures 8.4 and 8.5). In the following paragraphs, the nested triangles are described in light of this framework.

Triangle 1: This system was exemplified by participants' shared understandings of
sustainability that included 'big picture' notions of environmental stewardship,
resource conservation and intergenerational equity; hence, sustainability is denoted
here by the largest triangle (1). At times these big picture notions were elusive and
supplanted with illustrative practices by participants, but remained a topic of collective and evolving discussion in both centres. The shared understandings reflected
the often-debated and contentious multiple meanings of sustainability (McKeown
and Hopkins 2003). Sometimes, participants' significant personal experiences were
instrumental in provoking critical reflection as illustrated by a teacher with
Zimbabwean relatives who discussed food security challenges for her family and
linked this to political contexts, sustainability and global responsibilities. The multi-
faceted triangle image illustrates the notion of multiple understandings and, for any
individual or community; there may be several mutually-supportive understandings
that inform perceptions of sustainability. In turn, these perceptions most likely

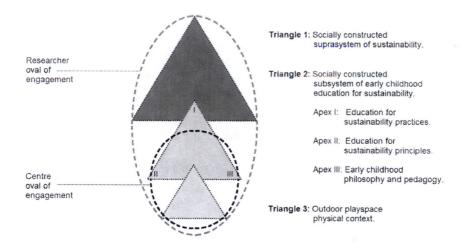

Figure 8.3 The study starting point for Banksia Childcare Centre and Acacia
Kindergarten

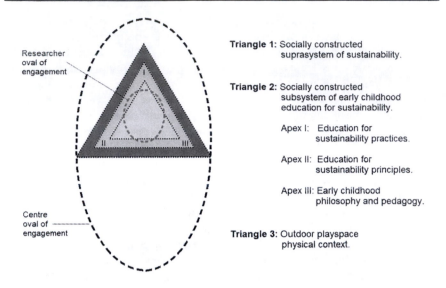

Researcher oval of engagement

Triangle 1: Socially constructed suprasystem of sustainability.

Triangle 2: Socially constructed subsystem of early childhood education for sustainability.

Apex I: Education for sustainability practices.

Apex II: Education for sustainability principles.

Apex III: Early childhood philosophy and pedagogy.

Centre oval of engagement

Triangle 3: Outdoor playspace physical context.

Figure 8.4 Study end point for Banksia Childcare Centre: nested systems

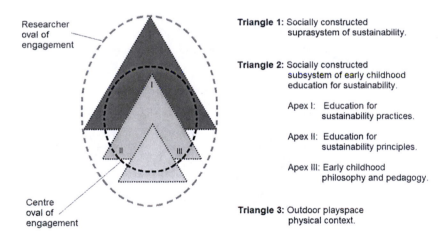

Researcher oval of engagement

Triangle 1: Socially constructed suprasystem of sustainability.

Triangle 2: Socially constructed subsystem of early childhood education for sustainability.

Apex I: Education for sustainability practices.

Apex II: Education for sustainability principles.

Apex III: Early childhood philosophy and pedagogy.

Centre oval of engagement

Triangle 3: Outdoor playspace physical context.

Figure 8.5 Study end point for Acacia Kindergarten: not yet fully nested systems

inform the construction of an overarching 'frame of mind' (Bonnett 2002: 14) of education for sustainability, denoted by the second triangle.

Triangle 2: This triangle is described as the subsystem of ECEfS and is informed by the suprasystem of sustainability (see Triangle 1 above). The three components – education for sustainability practices, education for sustainability principles, and early childhood philosophy and pedagogy – are assigned to the apices of Triangle 2. Relationships between these tips or peaks are essential to the strength of the whole early childhood education for sustainability triangle (2) or 'frame of mind' (Bonnett 2002: 14). In both centres, the existing education for sustainability practices frequently cited by research participants provided a point of overlap or commonality between the suprasystem triangle of sustainability (1) and the subsystem triangle of early childhood education for sustainability (2). In particular, the negotiated action priority for each centre provided a centralizing education for sustainability practice around and through which data was created.

While everyday practices offer tangible evidence of ECEfS in action, they must be supported by principles of education for sustainability as previously cited (DEWHA 2009, UNESCO 2005); these are located at the second apex of Triangle 2. It is a noteworthy point to make that the principles were often described by participants in terms of the role of adults, rather than referring to children's possible roles. Adults were viewed as sustainably-aware individuals: explaining or modelling sustainability, employing holistic, systemic or interdisciplinary approaches, engaging children in hands-on doing, educating for change, thinking and reflecting differently, working collectively (children, adults and community), and, normalizing the everydayness of education for sustainability within each centre. There was support for education for sustainability as part of broader societal change and it this was perceived as needing to begin in early childhood. Lastly, contemporary early childhood philosophies and pedagogies were located at the third apex of Triangle 2. To reiterate, all three apices are viewed here as essential to the strength of the ECEfS subsystem and the potential for transformative processes for sustainability. In relation to the described vignettes, the third apex was significantly different for the two case study settings and, ultimately, identified a critical point that determined the degree of centre transformation for sustainability.

Triangle 3: In contrast to the above socially-constructed triangles, the third and smallest triangle (3) represents the physical context of the outdoor playspace. Comprising both built and natural elements, the physical context was the site for early childhood education for sustainability to be enacted. The affordances (Gibson 1986) of each physical context described in this study might have impacted on the extent of enactment of sustainable practices. My later interpretation, however, is that, given that both centres' physical contexts comprised similar natural elements as previously described, it was the socially-constructed second triangle (2) of early childhood education for sustainability that most significantly determined the levels of enactment and change related to sustainability and education for sustainability. Participants at Banksia Childcare Centre, for example, perceived the natural playspaces as offering a wide variety of play opportunities for children including physical, dramatic, sensory, imaginative and social. Playspaces were also, viewed as places for connecting with nature in affective ways for the purposes of fostering of life-long values and passions for environmental stewardship. Similarly, the participants at Acacia Kindergarten focused on observing, discussing and caring for nature, while access to fresh air, freedom and physical activity, and diverse play opportunities were priorities. The notion of creating a playspace where nature was central was suggested by the teacher who recognized that some children did not have many nature experiences and lacked opportunities to play outdoors in their home lives.

The three triangles described above can be elaborated upon further in terms of the transformative processes for each case study centre. As enactment of the negotiated action priority (the worm farm at Banksia Childcare Centre and the bird nesting box at Acacia Kindergarten) occurred in each outdoor playspace, other changes became apparent. The sustainable practices that had originally illustrated participants' understandings about sustainability and education for sustainability were still present, but became more effectively supported. For both centres, the principle of employing holistic, systemic or interdisciplinary educational approaches surfaced within their programs, and it seemed that the potential for education for sustainability could now be seen infiltrating many aspects of the early childhood programs. Ultimately, this was more fully enacted at Banksia Childcare Centre, and the pedagogical roles of adults as sustainability-aware individuals, were significantly enhanced over time. Actions by educators included discussing and modelling sustainability practices with children, working collectively with children, adults and the wider community on shared projects such as a vegetable garden, and inviting children's hands-on participation. To put it simply, they were, normalizing education for sustainability into the everyday. At Acacia Kindergarten, it became apparent that alternative ways of thinking and reflecting about children and sustainability were becoming evident by the conclusion of the project. This indicated that there was ongoing potential for these educators to rethink their early childhood pedagogy and philosophy to engage in sustainability in the future.

As the centres' underpinning principles changed or were strengthened, 'ripples of action' (Vaealiki and Mackey 2008: 7) were observed as changes in practices that went beyond the originally-negotiated action priority. At Banksia Childcare Centre, changes were readily observed in situ, or described enthusiastically by the participants. Changes were diverse, ranging from aspects of program planning for the outdoor playspace such as offering choices for children to be indoors or outdoors, provision of natural materials for play, and increased documentation of outdoor play and learning, to the introduction of water conservation practices and establishment of a vegetable garden. Staff now also proactively chose to be outdoors with children, rather than preferring to be indoors. These changes were supported with educator training, centre policy review, and the acquisition of additional teaching and learning resources sourced from external organizations. Furthermore, sustainability was now described as a 'vision' that informed the redesign of the outdoor playspace and the centre's future directions. At Acacia Kindergarten, while many potential changes were discussed, only a few came to fruition during the research period: water conservation in the sandpit; energy conservation with lights and heating; and an Indigenous mural painted on an outdoor wall. While, these beginnings emerged from a very different philosophical starting point from that of the other participating centre, as noted earlier, nonetheless, they illustrated a turn towards positive sustainable practice changes.

In summary, based on this synthesis of the centres' transformative processes, the triangles depicting Banksia Childcare Centre were fully nested at the end point of the study (Figure 8.4). An embedded culture of sustainability was evident (Davis *et al.* 2005). At Banksia Childcare Centre the big picture sustainability suprasystem (Triangle 1) appeared to be informing education for sustainability principles and practices and support for children as active and capable participants was derived from the educators' contemporary early childhood philosophy and pedagogy (Triangle 2). Changes in the physical context afforded many new possibilities and plans for redevelopment fostered further possibilities. In contrast, at Acacia Kindergarten, as depicted in Figure 8.5, while some changed thinking and practices did occur, such that the three triangles overlapped more than initially, fully nested triangles were not in evidence.

Implications for research and practice

The nested triangles theoretical framework derived from the two centre case studies may inspire further research questions and other practical interpretations and applications in the field of ECEfS. The research project was undertaken with an awareness of significant gaps in early childhood education for sustainability research and theorizing (Davis 2009). The nested triangles theoretical framework offered here provides a basis for understanding the dynamics and complexities of the interfaces between natural outdoor playspaces, sustainability and education for sustainability. The interactive relationships between the physical context (Triangle 3), the socially-constructed systems of sustainability (Triangle 1) and early childhood education for sustainability (Triangle 2) were revealed. In particular, early childhood education for sustainability (Triangle 2) involved three integral elements: education for sustainability principles; education for sustainability practices; and early childhood philosophy and pedagogy. Such a framework presents a significant departure from earlier iterations of early childhood environmental education (Elliott and Emmett 1991, Wilson 1993) that focused on children's knowledge, skills and attitudes. Systems theory and socially contextualized framing also fills the void between the all-too-common and simplistic lists of sustainable practices frequently offered as ways to 'do ECEfS', and aligns with the 'big picture' notions of sustainability and education for sustainability argued for by Siraj-Blatchford *et al.* (2010) and represented diagrammatically by Pratt (2010: 108).

Further, this framework of nested systems invites critical reflection and offers multiple starting points for early childhood educators to engage in thinking, acting and relating for sustainability (Kemmis 2009), thus creating their own pathways of transformative change. For example, a starting point could be the identification of an action priority, a collective discussion about meanings of sustainability or the mapping of a centre's philosophy and pedagogy against principles of education for sustainability. Early childhood education for sustainability as praxis is envisaged and must be a reflexive process that grounds practice in theory. Significantly, it offers theory aimed directly at informing practice that has largely been absent from the discourse of early childhood education for sustainability (Davis 2009).

This framework is proposed at a time when the Australian early childhood sector, in particular, is experiencing high political visibility and major systemic change (COAG 2008). Key platforms for change include increasing educators' qualifications (COAG 2008), the first-ever national curriculum *Belonging Being and Becoming: The Early Years Learning Framework for Australia* (DEEWR 2009) and new National Quality Standards (ACECQA 2013) that are inclusive of sustainability and natural playspace standards. All these policy directions could be considered as facilitating factors in terms of promoting professional currency and enhanced alignment between early childhood philosophy and pedagogy, and the principles of education for sustainability. The question is raised, however, as to whether sustainability can become culturally embedded or a 'frame of mind' (Bonnett 2002: 14), if educators' early childhood philosophies, pedagogies and images of children do not reflect contemporary thinking, and are not aligned with the principles of education for sustainability as at Acacia Kindergarten. Perhaps a few sustainable practices can provoke some early childhood educators to think and act differently not only about sustainability, but also about early childhood pedagogy and philosophy. In fact, education for sustainability may offer an opportunity for building broader changes in ways of working with children. There are synergies to be realized in Australia and internationally between early childhood pedagogy and philosophy and education for sustainability.

Conclusion

As co-researcher with the study participants, when I withdrew from the case study centres at the conclusion of the research period, I felt confident that Banksia Childcare Centre would build on the momentum established, but was unsure that Acacia Kindergarten would continue to explore sustainability. Subsequent informal contact has borne out these predictions. The case studies described here suggest complex interfaces; enacting education for sustainability requires much more than a natural outdoor playspace with rocks and logs. The proposed framework of nested triangles indicates that the physical outdoor playspace and, specifically, a sustainability-related action priority may provide a useful entry point for enacting education for sustainability. It is only when the overarching socially-constructed triangles of sustainability and early childhood education for sustainability are fully nested however, that significant transformative change toward sustainability can occur. In early childhood centres, this theoretical framework may offer a diagnostic tool, a starting point, or an overarching frame for reflecting on centre journeys in sustainability.

Acknowledgement

The author acknowledges that this previously unpublished research was part of doctoral studies at the University of New England, Armidale, New South Wales, Australia supervised by Associate Professor Nadine McCrea and Dr Helen Edwards.

References

Australian Children's Education and Care Quality Authority (ACECQA) (2013) *Guide to the National Quality Standard*. Online. Available: http://files.acecqa.gov.au/files/National-Quality-Framework-Resources-Kit/NQF03-Guide-to-NQS-130902.pdf (accessed 10 March 2014).

Bateson, G. (1979) *Mind and Nature: A Necessary Unity*, New York: Ballantine Books.

Bonnett, M. (2002) 'Education for sustainability as a frame of mind', *Environmental Education Research*, 8(1): 9–20.

Bredekamp, S. (1987) *Developmentally Appropriate Practice in Early Childhood Programs Serving Children from Birth through Age 8*, expanded edn. Washington, DC: National Association for the Education of Young Children.

Bronfenbrenner, U. (1979) *The Ecology of Human Development*, Cambridge, MA: Harvard University Press.

Cannella, G. (1997) *Deconstructing Early Childhood Education: Social Justice and Revolution*, New York: Peter Lang.

Capra, F. (1997) *The Web of Life: A New Synthesis of Mind and Matter*, London: Harper Collins.

Capra, F. (2002) *The Hidden Connections*, London: Flamingo.

Council of Australian Governments (COAG) (2008) *A National Quality Framework for Early Childhood Education and Care: A Discussion Paper*, Canberra: COAG.

Commonwealth of Australia Department of Education, Employment and Workplace Relations (DEEWR) (2009) *Belonging, Being and Becoming: Early Years Learning Framework for Australia*, Canberra: Department of Education, Employment and Workplace Relations.

Commonwealth of Australia Department of Environment Water Heritage and the Arts (DEWHA) (2009) *Living Sustainably National Action Plan*, Canberra: DEWHA.

Comstock, D. E. (1982) 'A method for critical research', in E. Bredo and W. Feinberg (eds), *Knowledge and Values in Social and Educational Research*, Philadelphia, PA: Temple University Press, pp. 370–90.

Davis, J. (2009) 'Revealing the research 'hole' of early childhood education for sustainability: A preliminary survey of the literature,' *Environmental Education Research*, 15(2): 227–41.

Davis, J., Gibson, M., Pratt, R., Eglington, A. and Rowntree, N. (2005) 'Creating a culture of sustainability: From project to integrated education for sustainability at Campus Kindergarten', in W. L. Filho (ed.), *The International Handbook of Sustainability Research*, Paris: UNESCO, pp. 563–94.

Elliott, S. (ed.) (2008) *The Outdoor Playspace: Naturally*, Sydney: Pademelon Press.

Elliott, S. (2012) *Sustainable Outdoor Playspaces in Early Childhood Centres: Investigating Perceptions, Facilitating Change and Generating Theory*. Unpublished doctoral thesis, University of New England, Armidale, NSW.

Elliott, S. and Emmett, S. (1991) *Snails Live in Houses Too: Environmental Education for the Early Years*, Sydney: Martin Educational.

Elliott, S. and Davis, J. (2009) 'Exploring the resistance: An Australian perspective on educating for sustainability in early childhood', *International Journal of Early Childhood*, 41(2): 65–77.

Fay, B. (1987) *Critical Social Science: Liberation and its Limits*, Ithaca, NY: Cornell University Press.

Friere, P. (1976) *Education the Practice of Freedom*, London: Writers & Readers.

Friere, P. (1999 first published 1972) *Pedagogy of the Oppressed*, New York: Continuum.

Gamson Danks, S. (2010) *Asphalt to Ecosystems: Design Ideas for Schoolyard Transformation*, Oakland, CA: New Village Press.

Gibson, J. (1986) *The Ecological Approach to Visual Perception*, Mahwah, NJ: Laurence Erlbaum.

Kemmis, S. (2009) 'Action research as a practice-based practice', *Educational Action Research*, 17(3): 463–74.

Kemmis, S. and McTaggart, R. (2005) 'Participatory action research: Communicative action and the public sphere', in N. K. Denzin and Y. S. Lincoln (eds), *Handbook of Qualitative Research*, 3rd edn. Thousand Oaks, CA: Sage Publications, pp. 559–603.

Koestler, A. (1976) *The Ghost in the Machine. The Danube Edition*. London: Hutchinson.

Lester, S. and Maudsley, M. (2006) *Play, Naturally: A Review of Children's Natural Play*, London: Children's Play Council.

Louv, R. (2008) *The Last Child in the Woods: Saving Our Children from Nature Deficit Disorder*, 2nd edn. Chapel Hill, NC: Algonquin Books.

McKeown, R. and Hopkins, C. (2003) 'EE ESD: Defusing the worry', *Environmental Education Researcher*, 9(1): 117–28.

MacNaughton, G. (2003) *Shaping Early Childhood*, Maidenhead: Open University Press.

Maturana, H. and Varela, F. (1987) *The Tree of Knowledge: The Biological Roots of Human Understanding*, Boston, MA: New Science Library/Shambhala Publications.

Mezirow, J. (1997) 'Transformative learning: Theory to practice', *New Directions for Adult and Continuing Education*, 74: 5–12.

Moore, R. C. and Cooper-Marcus, C. (2008) 'Healthy planet, healthy children: Designing nature into the daily Spaces of childhood', in S. R. Kellert, J. Heerwagen and M. Mador, *Biophilic Design: The Theory, Science and Practice of Bringing Buildings to Life*. Hoboken, NJ: Wiley, pp 153–203.

Munoz, S. (2009) *Children in the Outdoors: A Literature Review*. Online. Available: www.countrysiderecreation.org.uk/Children%20Outdoors.pdf (accessed 20 December 2010).

Pratt, R. (2010) 'Practical possibilities and pedagogical approaches for early childhood education for sustainability', in J. Davis (ed.), *Young Children and the Environment: Early Education for Sustainability*. Melbourne: Cambridge University Press, pp. 104–53.

Siraj-Blatchford, J., Smith, K. C. and Pramling Samuelsson, I. (2010) *Education for Sustainable Development in the Early Years*, Gothenburg: OMEP.

Sterling, S. (2001) *Sustainable Education: Re-visioning Learning and Change*, Cambridge: Green Books.

Tilbury, D., Coleman, V. and Garlick, D. (2005) *A National Review of Environmental Education and its Contribution to Sustainability in Australia: School Education*, Canberra: Australian Government Department of the Environment and Heritage and Australian Research Institute in Education for Sustainability.

UNESCO (2005) *Decade of Education for Sustainable Development 2005–2014 Draft International Implementation Scheme*, Paris: UNESCO.

UNICEF (1989) *United Nations Convention on the Rights of the Child*. Online. Available: www2.ohchr.org/english/law/crc.htm (accessed 30 October 2009).

Vaealiki, S. and Mackey, G. (2008) 'Ripples of action: Strengthening environmental competency in an early childhood centre', *NZCER Early Childhood Folio 12*, 7–11.

White, J. (2008) *Playing and Learning Outdoors*, London: Routledge.

Wilson, R. (1993) *Fostering a Sense of Wonder During the Early Childhood Years*, Columbus, OH: Greyden Press.

Wilson, R. (2008) *Nature and Young Children: Encouraging Creative Play and Learning in Natural Environments*, New York: Routledge.

Woodhead, M. (2006) *Changing Perspectives on Early Childhood: Theory, Research and Policy*, Paper commissioned for the Education for All Global Monitoring Report 2007, Strong foundations: Early childhood care and education.

Chapter 9

An AuSSI early childhood adventure

Early childhood educators and researchers actioning change

Tracy Charlotte Young and Amy Cutter-Mackenzie

Abstract

The Australian Sustainable Schools Initiative (AuSSI) was launched through a partnership between the Australian Government and the states and territories to support teaching and learning about sustainability in primary and secondary schools. While this school-based initiative was considered monumental in 2003, to date, the early childhood education sector has been excluded from such initiatives despite the efforts of early childhood researchers, advocates and educators who affirm that sustainability in the early years is 'essential not optional' (Elliott 2010). In direct response to this omission, early childhood educators and researchers have proactively adapted and implemented AuSSI at the grassroots level. This chapter reports on findings of the Sustainable Early Childhood Project (SECP) in which four Australian children's services and an early childhood education researcher implemented an early childhood version of AuSSI. Insights are offered into what AuSSI might look like in early childhood settings with discussion centred around the theme of community engagement.

The Australian early childhood education landscape and AuSSI

The early childhood profession in Australia is experiencing significant changes in relation to government agendas that support quality reform and professionalization of the sector (Council of Australian Governments 2009, Organization for Economic Co-operation and Development 2006). This reform agenda includes the development of *National Quality Standards* (ACECQA 2011 revised 2013) and *Belonging Being Becoming: The Early Years Learning Framework for Australia* (DEEWR 2009). In many respects, environmental education (and its various iterations Education for Sustainability (EfS), Education for Sustainable Development (ESD) and Sustainable Education (SE)) has not been an overt part of this reform within early childhood education.

At the same time, the changing environmental landscape, in terms of climate change, loss of biological diversity, increased human demands on natural resources and degradation of ecosystems, has given rise to increasing social and political pressure for sustainability (Australian Climate Change Commission (ACCC) 2011) to be integrated across all education sectors. Despite mounting pressure, the early childhood education field in Australia has had difficulty responding beyond the small-scale interests of individual advocates and centres. This is partly because early childhood education (ECE) is complicated by a range of service structures for young children from birth to eight years of age which have, until very recently, operated within both local regulatory jurisdictions and/or federal accreditation requirements, may be funded by local, state or federal governments, or commercially-owned and funded. Such complicated governance has played a part in excluding early childhood education from government-sponsored environmental education and other related sustainability initiatives. This exclusion or marginalization is also evident in the field of environmental education/education for sustainability research where early childhood education is typically not a focal point (Davis 2009). As acknowledged by Davis (2008: 18) while interest is growing, there is a long way to go as 'EfS in early childhood is under-practiced, under-resourced and under-researched'.

Nevertheless, there is now a groundswell of interest and concern for the inclusion of environmental education into children's services in Australia. For example, at the time of the research study reported here (2010), a small number of children's services were already demonstrating exemplary sustainable practices. These services had identified the benefits of integrating environmental and sustainable thinking and practices into their settings through the adoption of holistic systems approaches to curriculum, community engagement and centre operations including building design or retrofitting with technologies to produce significant cost, energy and water reductions (Elliott 2010, Kinsella 2007, Young 2007). Nevertheless, as noted earlier, despite such exemplars of grassroots interest and commitment, early childhood education has not typically been included in state, territory and national environmental education and sustainability programs and initiatives. This was the case for the Australian Sustainable Schools Initiative (AuSSI), considered by many to be Australia's most significant nationally funded education program (Gough 2011: 13).

> The Australian Sustainable Schools Initiative (AuSSI) has been one of the longest lasting and most impressive actions … It was given a central role in the Australian implementation strategy for the UN Decade (DEH 2006) and in the second National Action Plan (DEWHA 2009: 11) where its effectiveness is highlighted: 'This is a successful example of how a partnership between the Australian Government, the states and territories can lead to systemic change. The initiative entails a whole-of-school, action learning approach to sustainability, which is generating measurable social, educational, financial and environmental outcomes'.

Beginning the sustainable early childhood project: getting started through conversation

In 2005, Young, whose research informs this chapter, participated in discussions with the education team at the Centre for Education and Research into Environmental Strategies (CERES) in Melbourne, Victoria. Established in 1982, CERES is an award winning, not-for-profit, environmental education centre and urban farm. It has been recognized as a leading organization in promoting sustainability through on-site educational programs conducted in the CERES sustainable park and community farm located by the Merri Creek, Brunswick East, Melbourne. Observations of the education programs at CERES identified that they were not particularly pertinent to young children, nor reflected early childhood pedagogical approaches. Conversation turned to the AuSSI programs that CERES and the Gould League (an independent environmental education resource organization) were then managing in Victoria. The inevitable question was asked by the researcher 'Why was this national government initiative not inclusive of early childhood settings?' The CERES team demonstrated the now familiar response of invisibility and misunderstanding about the marginalized early childhood field when they articulated that they had not even considered extending AuSSI into the early childhood sector, nor did they have expertise in this area. This conversation became the catalyst for the Sustainable Early Childhood Project (SECP), and the focus of Young's research.

The AuSSI is based on similar global initiatives including the European Environment and Schools Initiatives (ENSI), the Foundation for Environmental Education (FEE International) Eco-schools, Green Schools Award in Sweden, Green Schools Program in China, and Enviroschools in New Zealand (DEWHA 2008). The AuSSI is a 'whole-school' framework that offers support, professional development, mentoring and opportunities for sharing resources between participating schools. The principles of AuSSI are woven through the curriculum with environmental education and sustainability integrated into various teaching and learning areas and subject domains. Each state and territory in Australia has adapted the framework to their particular contexts, with a key component being the development of a system for measuring and monitoring progress. In Victoria, schools can be accredited through the AuSSI[1] 5-star certification requiring implementation of action plans for five modules (a core introduction to key principles of sustainability and then foci of water, waste, energy and biodiversity). Participation in the certification process involves the collection of baseline data measuring reductions in water, waste and energy consumption, or how the school has improved biodiversity. The process is identified in the following twelve-step action plan (Remenyi 2011: 12):

AuSSI Twelve-step action plan:

1 Whole-school commitment
2 Committee is established (including parents)
3 Introduction to sustainability
4 Policy development
5 Goals and targets
6 Baseline data collection

7   Assessment and audit of practices, infrastructure and operations
8   Community partnerships
9   Develop action plan
10   Develop curriculum plan
11   Implement action plan
12   Monitoring and evaluation

The AuSSI partnership statement (DEWHA 2008: 2) also emphasizes the importance of working collaboratively with children, teachers, families and communities:

> AuSSI schools … strengthen social cohesion amongst the school community.
> The aim is to equip the whole school community with the attitudes, values,
> behaviours and capacity to meaningfully engage with complex issues such as
> sustainability.

Sustainable early childhood project: describing the research contexts

Drawing on the AuSSI framework described above, the SECP was implemented in four Melbourne children's services sites, three in the inner suburbs and one located in an outer south-eastern suburb of the city. The study aim was to adapt the principles and processes of AuSSI to the contexts and pedagogies of early childhood education services, and to critique processes and outcomes. The research took place over a two-year period. During the first year (Stage 1), the children's services teaching teams worked through the AuSSI action plan process supported by site visits from the researcher – an experienced early childhood educator and environmental educator – who facilitated professional development, and coordinated team meetings and baseline data collection. During the second year (Stage 2), the teams continued to work through the process of the SECP as the qualitative research phase of data collection and analysis commenced at the sites.

Sustainable early childhood project: describing the theoretical frames and research methodology

Systems theory was employed as a framework and lens to inform this research study. According to Sterling (2003), the distinguishing characteristics of whole systems thinking in education are that it: (1) articulates an ecological, participatory epistemology; (2) recognizes a co-evolutionary ontology; and (3) Manifests a systemic methodology.[2] The term sustainable education was chosen to define and differentiate the focus of this research.

Further, ethnography, as the selected qualitative methodology, inspired an active research process. By active research we mean 'happening alongside' the actual SECP project. In effect, Young (as researcher and ethnographer) sought to formulate 'stories' about the cultural worlds of the participants built upon their own language and expressions of their participation. Werner and Schoepfle (1987) identify culture as a system of knowledge (including knowledge about knowledge) that recognizes social interrelationships and physical universes that form an integrated whole. Through the formulation of stories, there is juxtaposition between the knowledge of the researcher and that of participants so that, as Van Maanen (1988: 4) proposes, ethnographies 'pose questions at the margins between two cultures. They necessarily decode one culture while recoding it for another'. In such a scenario, it is crucial that the ethnographer 'speaks' the native language. In the case of this study, the language is that of early child-hood education on the subject of sustainable education in its various guises.

This active ethnographic research process occurred through sustained contact with the participants in their workplaces (Bogdan and Biklen 2003). This approach promoted the researcher's discoveries of understandings and meanings from the data, rather than from any preconceived notions. Empirically, there was a need to unveil meanings from the participants' knowledge, attitudes and beliefs and reflect upon how these were manifested in their environmental education practices. During the first year of the study, data gathered included participant comments and observations from meetings and workshops, photographs, and reflective journals written by educators and the researcher. In the following year, data was drawn from individual semi-structured interviews with educators and parents, plus the educa-tors' reflective journals and their documentation of the SECP's progress. Eleven participants, including eight educators, four of whom were also directors of their service, one school principal and two parents contributed.

The study was underpinned by the following objectives:

1   Examine the practice of sustainable education with a focus on educators' experiences in the development and implementation of sustainable education programs.
2   Examine whether community engagement informs and influences sustainable education and how this enables young children to participate in community life as active and informed environmental citizens.
3   Examine how sustainable education is incorporated into the curricula and how this enables young children to construct environmental world-views.
4   Identify the barriers and drivers to the emergence of sustainable education with a focus on systems thinking and ethics.

The following guiding vision for the SECP was developed in partnership between the researcher and the participants from the four early childhood services (Young 2010: 5):

To take every opportunity to conserve natural resources and consolidate environmental sustainability as an integrated, component of the operations, curriculum and community of early childhood services.

The key features of the four participating services are outlined in Table 9.1. It is important to note that these services were selected because they had previously demonstrated a commitment to environmental education and were already using a range of sustainable practices. This was purposeful sampling to 'inform an understanding of the research problem and central phenomenon in the study' (Creswell 2013: 156). Being purposefully selected, the comments and conclusions offered here are not representative of the diversity of early childhood services and educators in Melbourne, nor more broadly in Australia. Nevertheless, they do provide a window into what is happening in early childhood settings and what is possible. Another limitation of the study was that the Stage 2 reflective educator journals from services B and D were incomplete. For example, they lacked examples of children's participation in the curriculum – a key objective of the project – and these educators' critical reflection about pedagogy, community engagement, and their thinking about the research process. As a researcher, this made it difficult to fully examine educator participation in the SECP and to incorporate these journals as part of the research analysis. This was particularly evident in relation to the impact of the project for children under three years of age and how sustainability was, or was not, integrated into their curricula.

Table 9.1 Descriptions of the four participating children's services

Service	Description of service	Improvement goals	Outcome
Service A Kindergarten for children aged three and four years Registered for 55 children Parent managed Inner city location	Has operated since 1911 with rich history of implementing environmental education in past 20 years; well known for innovative practices; had many sustainable features in place including: water tanks, cloth hand towels, strategies to reduce water and consumption.	Reduce energy consumption Increase biodiversity Increase water tank capacity to support tank-to-toilet system Document greater inclusion of sustainability content into curriculum	Achieved five-star certification with the SECP-adapted AuSSI; was the first in Australia to do so
Service B Children's Centre Child care centre for children aged six months to six years Registered for 50 children Council managed and operated Inner city location	Operated since the 1940s; owned and managed by the City of Melbourne Council which has a strong commitment to sustainable education Has a natural outdoor environment with native and indigenous plantings. Educators integrate animal study and care in the curriculum, including free range chickens	Council hoping to use the centre as a model of sustainable practice Reduce waste, (particularly food waste from the industrial kitchen that supplies food to four services) Reduce water and energy consumption Include more food plantings Install underground water tank	Achieved some modules of certification; the local council installed a 100-litre water tank; the service made reductions in food waste

Table 9.1 continued

Service	Description of service	Improvement goals	Outcome
Service C Early Learning Centre Kindergarten for children aged three and four years Registered for 47 children Private school South-eastern suburbs location	Located within a primary and secondary school on 40 hectares of semi-rural land, bush and lake setting. The School opened in 1984 and has had a strong environmental education and sustainability ethos built into its philosophy Philosophy inspired by the Italian Reggio Emilia education approach. The children's connection to nature has been a consistent theme in recent years The larger school has received awards for its endeavours and leadership in this area.	Improve targets in relation to all areas Engage families in the program Greater connection and involvement of kindergarten children with the wider school through the variety of sustainable education programs offered (younger children were not always included in whole school events) Improve outside environment by creating more naturalistic areas	Did not achieve any of the formal certification for the SECP; Director found the paperwork difficult and meaningless; Although certification not achieved, staff excelled in documenting curriculum and engaging children and families in authentic and meaningful ways.
Service D Community Children's Centre Child care centre for children aged six months to six years Registered for 52 children Parent managed Inner-city location	Operating for 14 years; situated on the campus of a tertiary institution Has created a diverse and interesting outside environment with many tree and shrub plantings that have been initiated by both parents and staff Implements a vegetarian/fish menu for cultural and health reasons and is able to purchase organic fruit and vegetables with the reduction in meat costs	Aim to reduce waste, water and energy Desire to create a whole team approach to drive the changes	This service did not achieve any of the certification for the SECP and found the requirements difficult; a large staff turnaround impinged the process Has since established many sustainable practices

Sustainable early childhood project: key findings and outcomes

Analysis of the intricate layers of data collected during Stages 1 and 2 of the study revealed three key themes – community engagement, pedagogy and curriculum. The analysis drew on the participants' reflections about their experiences and, also, what these reflections revealed about how sustainable education was understood and practiced in these early childhood education settings. In doing so, the themes emerged from the data analysis, rather than merely described what the respective services 'did'. Each theme comprised three sub-themes, thus creating a thematic network as illustrated in Figure 9.1. Thematic networks are employed to system-atize the process of data analysis around global, organizational and basic hierarchical themes that 'are then presented in web-like maps depicting the salient themes at each of the three levels, and illustrating the relationships between them' (Attride-Stirling 2001: 388). In this study, the over-arching global theme was sustainable education in early childhood, the three organizational themes were community engagement, pedagogy, and curriculum, and then each of these initiated three basic themes, as illustrated in the figure below.

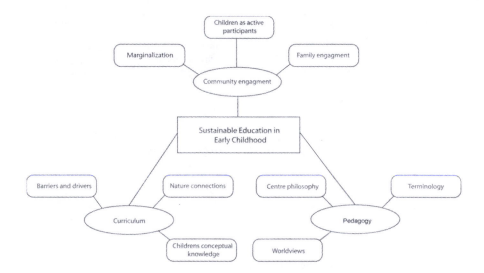

Figure 9.1 Thematic network for this study: the global theme, three organizational themes and their respective basic themes

In this chapter, just one of the organizational themes is reported on – commu-nity engagement – as this is the most pertinent to the publication brief for this chapter with its focus on young children as active citizens for sustainability. For elaboration of the other themes, the reader is referred to Young (2010).

Organizational theme: community engagement

As community engagement is a significant component of AuSSI, I sought to deter-mine how community engagement and participation were implemented by the children's services during the SECP. Rogoff (2003: 51) describes community engagement as a 'transformation of participation' in which knowledge, ideas and practices are experienced through a process of change where children contribute to shared cultural endeavours. These shared undertakings, then, have the ability to create change both with the child and from the child. Initially, there was a mixed response when interview participants were asked: *What actions have you taken, either as an individual or within your service, regarding an environmental issue?* Six educators expressed that they had never been involved as an individual in any environmental community events. While two parents were engaged in such community events, other responses were ambivalent with only one educator citing involvement in any environmental community activities.

> Jessie: I planted trees in my new estate; I made sure I planted a native garden with indigenous plants. This happens here too, there are a few of us who know a bit about plants and I have just researched companion plants for fruit trees with Sustainable Gardening Australia.

Not only was I interested in the adults' levels of engagement with environmental issues, I wanted to uncover their perceptions about young children's participation in environmental/sustainability issues. The following scenario adapted from Hydon (2007: 7) with a follow-on question, was put to participants:

> I have a friend who recently enrolled his baby at a nearby childcare centre and commented. "What's this thing about teaching children about the environment? They're only babies – surely they're too young to have to worry about recycling and all that?"
> What would be your response to a comment such as this?

Two respondents discussed the importance of role modelling sustainability practices for children and three respondents identified that the general community underestimated the skills and knowledge of young children as change agents, while four respondents noted how sustainability is part of living in the world and, therefore, children have a right to be engaged. The following responses are illustrative of their comments:

> Kim: I would think my response would be that just because children are small and can't articulate, that how they feel does not mean that they don't care.
>
> Kelly: I would be asking what is his image of the baby? A baby is very capable and they are great thinkers and the earlier the better to embed those practices … Even if it's modelling what you are doing and they are watching. It's amazing what they pick up and people underestimate all children, but babies in particular.

It was evident from the data that, although many of the respondents were not engaged in environmental issues themselves, they did feel that children and babies should be exposed to practices and sustainability content knowledge. This provokes the question: *Do educators believe that children should just be exposed to the ideas and content, or be actively engaged as citizens who have the potential and right to be agents of change?*

Basic theme: children as active participants

I became interested, then, in how the four children's services participating in the SECP were engaging the children as active participants in community events and issues. During educator interviews, the question was asked: *Are the children in your service involved in community events that link to sustainability? Why or why not?* Not surprisingly in light of the responses noted above, there were no examples of children's investigations of sustainability in the community. Seven of the interviewees focused particularly on the difficulties associated with forging community connections through excursions or participation in environmental events as illustrated below:

Jolene: I don't feel comfortable having children go on excursions. I would rather do it in-house.

Researcher: Can you tell me what the tension with excursions is?

Jolene: It is the risk factor of carrying out the excursion. They are fantastic and the information you get from them is worthwhile, but the stress on the staff and the risk of getting to and from the location and the room for error is huge. I would rather have an incursion where they come here, like the wildlife reptiles, that sort of thing. We used to walk the children up the road to the place that recycled cans, but we have stopped that at the moment as it is under review.

Such comments highlight the tensions about perceived safety, and policy and regulatory constraints. They also reveal underlying issues related to children's exclusion from engagement in community life and civic participation that has been escalating over past decades (Gill 2007, Louv 2005). Also, Nimmo (1998: 305) offers a provocation 'Do we view the young child as living only in nests composed of family and friends and hidden from public life?' In our efforts to protect children, it could be said that we are disengaging children from community life and the opportunity to develop a 'sense of place'. Establishing a sense of place has been identified as a useful pedagogy for environmental education (Sobel 2004) as it supports an emotional and cognitively engaging context for learning, and is dependent upon human engagement with local natural and cultural landscape features. Furthermore, a transformative approach to sustainable education recognizes that young children have the potential (and right) to be active agents for sustainability in their communities (Davis 2010). Active engagement, Nimmo (1998: 306) asserts, offers possibilities for authentic understandings of local issues, landmarks, how communities function on a daily basis, and how children partici-pate in their communities. 'Bringing children into the public sphere celebrates their potential to contribute and lets them feel the pulse of their future lives'.

In contrast to Jolene's stated concern above about safety during excursions, the educators from service C consistently engaged the children in community projects. Although not necessarily linked to environmental content, they regularly invited visitors with expertise to visit the service, and conducted excursions. This appeared to be reflective of the school philosophy and the Reggio Emilia project approach adopted by the centre (Edwards *et al.* 1998). The principal of the school where this service was located described, for example, how the secondary school students visited nursing homes, worked in a local charity shop, and were involved in a plant-ing group of local indigenous flora. Unlike the educators at other study services, he did not subscribe to a 'protectionist paradigm', stating that the safety risks of young children embarking on excursions were an issue that could be reconciled.

Basic theme: family engagement

As noted previously, AuSSI is built on a principle of fostering community partner-ships, particularly with families. For the children's services involved in this study, it was important to ascertain how or whether such partnerships were being imple-mented. Children's services B and D experienced considerable difficulties engaging parents in the SECP and educators in these services struggled with this aspect of the program. Responses to my enquiry: *How would you describe families' involvement with the work you have been doing around sustainability in your centre?* were exemplified by the following comments:

Rina: Zero, very little. Enthused when they see what children are learning, and shocked and surprised they are doing these things.

Jessie: Zero, we are not allowed to do anything on the weekends although we came in and worked on this new garden bed. When we did that, here is an example of bureaucracy in all its glory; parents were saying we would love to come and help but they were not allowed to come. Council have told us this but they are not allowed to, they say because of insurance.

These responses were indicative of an approach that attempted to engage families, but did not ask the families how they would like to be involved nor did they actively engage them in the process. Families from these two services were not invited to any of the SECP workshops or meetings, whereas the other two serv-ices (A and C) had significant success with family participation, and invited parents to SECP events and expected family engagement as part of their holistic pedagog-ical approach. It seems that families are more likely to engage in events that directly involve their children and where they (the families) have a defined role. As Grace, a member of the service A's parent sustainability committee articulated:

Grace: We are all time poor and we all want to do things, but we have family and work commitments … by having a simple structure you can break down the tasks and it doesn't look so daunting … and you don't have to dream up a big plan that takes ages to develop So, by having a time frame of this is something you can complete in six or twelve months.

Both services A and C developed a range of strategies to include families in the SECP, with positive results. The kindergarten had 17 parents nominated for their committee and developed a sustainability sub-committee where parent roles were allocated to manage each of the four key foci of AuSSI – water, waste, energy and biodiversity. This division of roles ensured that the committee was successful in achieving a range of SECP targets including a 26 per cent reduction in energy use over two years and a 40 per cent reduction in water consumption. It was evident that active engagement by families enriched the SECP. Furthermore, the data revealed that parent involvement in the SECP also led to sustainable practices and knowledge being transferred between the children's services and home settings.

Service C also had success in engaging families through the use of regular meetings, daily diaries and newsletters. In her interview, Kelly outlined her approach to engaging families in which she identified the need to be open to how parents wanted to contribute, even if this was not how educators originally envisioned family engagement.

Kelly: The sustainable living meeting we had at night was fantastic … There was a lot of discussion, sharing what they do at home and what they believe, questions about each other – a really good conversation. In reflection, it was a real foundation … When MAD (Make a difference) week came along, we wanted to make a difference to our school with our sustainable lens. All these things we had talked about, a lot of them popped up; they had obviously been talking and we sent out a sheet with some of the projects we had in mind, like the frog bog. I don't think if we had not had that sustainable meeting we would not have had the interest.

Community engagement is an intrinsic component of the vision for sustainability in early childhood services (Davis 2010, Nimmo 1998, 2008, Siraj-Blatchford 2008). This research revealed many examples that highlighted the benefits of engaging children, families and the wider community. The research also identified why some services were not successful in achieving their desired outcomes and did not make significant progress with the SECP. In summary, a commitment to an integrated community engagement process needs to be adopted by the service.

Concluding thoughts and provocations

The AuSSI early childhood adventure, as experienced through the SECP, has demonstrated that there are benefits to be gained from including early childhood services in broader sustainable education initiatives, particularly when community and family partnerships are deliberately built into the processes in order to share knowledge and practices. It is essential, however, that such school-based initiatives are adapted to meet the particular contexts, needs and pedagogical perspectives of early childhood education. In this chapter, we have elaborated on only one of the organizational themes of this research – community engagement. However, the themes of pedagogy and curriculum are also emerging areas for early childhood sustainable education with the findings of this research revealing gaps and tensions that have been investigated in later research (Cutter-Mackenzie and Edwards 2013, Edwards and Cutter-Mackenzie 2011). Although there are now signs of the early childhood field beginning to engage with sustainable education there is still much to be learnt from the theorizing and critique that comes with research. As chapter authors, we hope that the vision of a holistic approach to sustainable education offered by initiatives such as the AuSSI can be realized across the early childhood education sector, and that ongoing AuSSI research will offer insights for all education sectors. This chapter, we believe, makes a contribution to these ambitious goals.

To conclude, the following questions are offered as provocations for further thinking and research about issues that this SECP study has identified:

- Why is the early childhood education sector typically excluded from mainstream education initiatives and funding schemes such as the AuSSI?
- How can early childhood educators advocate for inclusion and how are early childhood activists already trying to progress this goal?
- What are the broader benefits and implications for the early childhood education sector in becoming a part of a significant education initiative such as the AuSSI?
- How do education initiatives such as AuSSI impact the identity and pedagogy of early childhood education?
- What can be learnt from the two services that did not achieve certification and how might an initiative like AuSSI strengthen participant and community engagement, and enhance capacity for early childhood sustainable education?

Notes

1 Since the completion of this research, the AuSSI framework in Victoria has undergone a change of name. The process remains similar and currently operates under Sustainability Victoria's ResourceSmart brand (Remenyi 2011: 12).
2 For a deeper understanding of the theoretical framing applied to and adapted in this research please refer to Young (2010).

References

Attride-Sterling, J. (2001) Thematic networks: an analytic tool for qualitative research, *Qualitative Research*, 1, 385–405.

Australian Children's Education and Care Quality Authority (ACECQA) (2013) *Guide to the National Quality Standard.* Online. Available: http://files.acecqa.gov.au/files/National-Quality-Framework-Resources-Kit/NQF03-Guide-to-NQS-130902.pdf (accessed 10 March 2014).

Bogdan, R. and Biklen, S. (2003) *Foundations of Qualitative Research for Education: An Introduction to Theory and Methods,* Boston, MA: Allyn & Bacon.

Council of Australian Governments (2009) National partnership agreement on the national quality agenda for early childhood education and care, Canberra, ACT: Commonwealth of Australia.

Creswell, J. W. (2013) *Qualitative Inquiry and Research Design,* Thousand Oaks, CA: Sage.

Cutter-Mackenzie, A. and Edwards, S. (2013) 'Towards a model for early childhood environmental education: Foregrounding, developing and connecting knowledge through play-based learning', *Journal of Environmental Education,* 44(3): 195–213.

Davis, J. (2008) 'What might education for sustainability look like in early childhood? A case for participatory, whole-of-settings approaches', in I. Pramling Samuelsson and Y. Kaga (eds) *The Contribution of Early Childhood Education to a Sustainable Society.* Paris: UNESCO, pp. 18–24.

Davis, J. (2009) 'Revealing the research "hole" of early childhood education for sustainability: A preliminary survey of the literature', *Environmental Education Research,* 15(2): 227–41.

Davis, J. (2010) *Young Children and the Environment: Early Education for Sustainability,* Melbourne: Cambridge University Press.

Department of Education Employment and Workplace Relations (DEEWR) (2009) *Belonging, Being and Becoming: The Early Years Learning Framework for Australia,* Canberra: Commonwealth of Australia.

Department of the Environment, Water, Heritage and the Arts (DEWHA) (2008) *AuSSI: A Partnership Statements for the Australian Government and the States and Territories,* Canberra: Commonwealth of Australia.

Edwards, C., Gandini, L. and Forman, G. (eds) (1998) *100 Languages of Children. The Reggio Emilia Approach – Advanced Reflections,* 2nd edn. Westport, CN: Ablex Publishing Corporation.

Edwards, S. and Cutter-Mackenzie, A. (2011) 'Environmentalizing early childhood curriculum through play-based pedagogies', *Australasian Journal of Early Childhood,* 36(1): 51–9.

Elliott, S. (2010) 'Essential not optional: Education for sustainability in early childhood centres', *ChildCareExchange,* March/April: 34–7.

Fleer, M. (2010) *Concepts in Play: A Cultural Historical View of Early Learning and Development,* Cambridge: Cambridge University Press.

Gill, T. (2007) *No Fear: Growing Up in a Risk-Averse Society,* London: Calouse Gulbenkian Foundation.

Gough, A. (2011) 'The Australian-ness of curriculum jigsaws: Where does environmental education fit?', *Australian Journal of Environmental Education* (Special issue – The "ness" of environmental education – Edited by Amy Cutter-Mackenzie), 27: 264–73.

Grieshaber, S. (2008) 'Interrupting stereotypes: Teaching and the education of young children', *Early Education and Development,* 19(3): 505–18.

Hydon, C. (2007) 'A way of travelling: The environment and our code of ethics', *Every Child. The Sustainability Issue,* 13(1): 7.

Kinsella, R. (2007) *Greening Services: Practical Sustainability*, Watson, ACT: Early Childhood Australia.

Kollmuss, A. and Agyeman, J. (2002) 'Mind the gap: Why do people act environmentally and what are the barriers to pro environmental behaviour?', *Environmental Education Research*, 8(3): 239–60.

Louv, R. (2005) *Last Child in the Woods. Saving Our Children from Nature-Deficit Disorder*, Chapel Hill, NC: Algonquin Books.

Nimmo, J. (1998) 'The child in the community: Constraints from the early childhood lore' in C. Edward, L. Gandini and G. Forman (eds) *100 Languages of Children. The Reggio Emilia Approach – Advanced Reflections*, 2nd edn. Westport, CN: Ablex, pp. 295–312.

Nimmo, J. (2008) 'Young children's access to real life: An examination of the growing boundaries between children in child care and adults in the community', *Contemporary Issues in Early Childhood*, 9: 3–13.

Organization for Economic Co-operation and Development (2006) *Starting Strong II: Early Childhood Education and Care*, Paris: OECD.

Prout, A. (2003) 'Children, representation and social change', European Early Childhood Research Association Conference, Glasgow.

Remenyi, C. (2011) 'The resourcesmart AuSSI Vic story: A short history of how sustainability in schools in Victoria has developed', *Eingana. The Journal of the Victorian Association for Environmental Education*, 34: 12–15.

Rogoff, B. (2003) *The Cultural Nature of Human Development*, New York: Oxford University Press.

Siraj-Blatchford, I. (1999) 'Early childhood pedagogy: Practice, principles and research', in P. Mortimore (ed.) *Understanding Pedagogy and its Impact on Learning*, London: Paul Chapman Publishing Ltd, pp. 20–45.

Siraj-Blatchford, J. (2008) 'The implications of early understandings of inequality, science and technology for the development of sustainable societies', in I. Pramling Samuelsson and Y. Kaga (eds), *The Contribution of Early Childhood Education to a Sustainable Society*, Paris: UNESCO, pp. 67–72.

Sobel, D. (1996) *Beyond Ecophobia Reclaiming the Heart in Nature Education*, Great Barrington, MA: The Orion Society.

Sobel, D. (1998) *Mapmaking with Children: Sense of Place Education for the Elementary Years*, Portsmouth, NH: Heinemann.

Sobel, D. (2004) *Place-based Education: Connecting Classrooms and Communities*, Great Barrington, MA: Orion Society.

Sterling, S. (2003) *Whole System Thinking as a Basis for Paradigm Change in Education: Explorations in the Context of Sustainability.* PhD Thesis, University of Bath.

Thepa, B. (1999) 'Environmentalism: The relation of environmental attitudes and environmentally responsible behaviours among undergraduate students', *Bulletin of Science Technology Society*, 19: 426–38.

Werner, O. and Schoepfle, G. M. (1987) *Systematic Fieldwork*, Vol. 1, Thousand Oaks, CA: Sage.

United Nations Education Scientific and Cultural Organization (2009) *Bonn Declaration. UNESCO World Conference of Education for Sustainable Development*, Bonn: UNESCO.

Van Maanen, J. (1988) *Tales of the field: On writing ethnography*, Chicago, IL: University of Chicago Press.

Young, T. (2007) 'emPower: Beyond compost and worm farms', *Every Child. The Sustainability Issue*, 13(1): 10. Watson, ACT: Early Childhood Australia.

Young, T. (2010) *'The Crack Where the Light Gets In': An Examination of Sustainable Education in Early Childhood Education.* Master of Education Thesis. Melbourne: Monash University.

Chapter 10

The Project Approach in early childhood education for sustainability

Exemplars from Korea and Australia

Okjong Ji and Sharon Stuhmcke

Abstract

This chapter presents two case studies involving young children as they participated in education for sustainability projects. One project took place in Korea and the other in Australia. Both projects are adaptations of the Project Approach, an established pedagogical approach founded in constructivism that is now quite widely employed within early childhood programs in different parts of the world (Katz and Chard 2000). The Project Approach encourages lengthy exploration of topics and themes, and supports deep learner engagement. The projects outlined in this chapter differ from more typical project approaches in early childhood, as these synthesize constructivism and co-constructivism with transformative teaching and learning, drawn from education for sustainability. The result is a transformative project approach where young children become involved in local problem-solving and show leadership within their local communities to create and implement sustainable practices.

Introduction

The world is faced with serious environmental issues including pollution, global warming, food security, the destruction of ecosystems and resource depletion. This chapter is written from the viewpoint that early childhood education has an important role, indeed a responsibility, to act for the enhancement of the natural environment and for creating sustainable futures for all citizens. As co-authors, we operate within social ecologist Bookchin's (1990) framework which identifies that the 'intellectual power' possessed by humans differs qualitatively from that of other beings, thus making humans responsible for the maintenance of ecosystems and for advancing ecological thinking. However, our focus is wider than education for the environment. We work within an education for sustainability frame that differs from earlier forms of environmental education that focused only on the environmental dimension of sustainability. We view education for sustainability as a comprehensive and holistic approach to education that considers the interconnections between four systems – environment, society, economics and politics (UNESCO 2005). Thus, education for sustainability integrates wider issues including poverty, consumption, community life, citizenship, futures education and democracy (Davis 2010, Siraj-Blatchford *et al.* 2010). We believe the projects described here are just as powerful in their contributions to building the social capabilities of children and their communities as they are in protecting the natural environment and conserving resources.

Early childhood is a critical period for all aspects of human development, including values and attitudes formation pertinent to environmental/sustainability concerns. These values are best summarized by the four ethical principles of early childhood education for sustainability suggested by Robinson and Vaealiki (2010: 159): an ethic of caring; an ethic of listening; an ethic of participation; and, an ethic of helpfulness. Further, we believe in the importance of promoting young children's thinking, participation and action around local environmental and sustainability issues (Davis and Elliott 2003, Ji 2011, Taylor *et al.* 2009). Active participation enables young children to contribute to their family life and their communities, thus engaging in citizenship in the process. We acknowledge, too, the importance of working with issues that children identify (Jensen 2002), and to facilitate problem-solving and action-taking around these.

In this chapter, two transformative projects in early childhood settings are presented. Both projects focused on children's agency and action-taking and fostered community life and citizenship as well as addressing environmental concerns. The first project described here is the Musim Stream Project, which was implemented in a childcare centre (for children aged two to five years) in Cheongju City, Korea. The second project is the Rainforest Project implemented in a kindergarten (for children aged three to five years) near Brisbane, Australia. While developed in very different locations, cultures and early childhood contexts, these projects were similar in that both utilized the Project Approach (Katz and Chard 2000) as their underpinning pedagogical framework.

The Project Approach

According to Katz and Chard (2000), the Project Approach is based on much earlier work by Kilpatrick (1919) and Dewey (1944). *The Project Method* (Kilpatrick 1919) was developed from Dewey's progressive education philosophy of child-centred approaches, although Dewey did not specifically use the term 'project method'. In later work, Katz and Chard (2000) describe a project as an in depth study of a particular topic undertaken by one or more children. The Project Approach is aligned with integrated development of knowledge, skills, dispositions and feelings.

In recent times, the Project Approach has been utilized in many countries across the globe, mainly because the goals of the Project Approach closely parallel those of twenty-first-century education. In the information age, learners require the ability to select and evaluate appropriate information from amongst the masses of data, information and messages and to develop inquiry, and problem-solving skills (Elkind 1993, Short 1991). The Project Approach is an effective educational method in that it pursues broader intellectual goals rather than narrower academic goals (Katz and Chard 2000). It is often described as offering multiple ways for teachers to inspire children to reach a high level of interest, develop intrinsic motivation, and work to high standards. Children are described as initiating project work, asking researchable questions, and undertaking individual and collaborative investigations that are structured to achieve high standards of learning (Chard 2011). Generally speaking, the Project Approach involves three phases:

Phase 1: Getting projects started
Phase 2: Projects in progress
Phase 3: Concluding projects

In Phase 1, the teacher and children share their experiences, ideas and thoughts regarding a proposed project topic. This might be directly from children's ideas as occurred in the Rainforest Project, initiated by the teacher as occurred in the Musim Stream Project, or negotiated jointly by children and teachers. During this phase, the teacher learns about children's understandings and misunderstandings, as well as their interests and specific questions about the topic. In Phase 2, the children become involved in answering child-initiated questions related to the topic. During this phase, the children might research water – as occurred in the Musim Stream Project – and explore the water cycle, read books, undertake field trips, and meet with experts in their community. Children might also represent their discoveries and new knowledge about the selected topic through discussion, painting and drawing, story-writing, model-making, sculpture, music or drama.

As the project progresses, learning from earlier stages may be expanded, reduced or integrated, and new content may be added depending on the children's interests, additional resources, the educational intentions of the teacher, participation of parents or community members, or other unexpected situations or inputs. Teachers and learners adjust accordingly; a particular strength of the Project Approach is its emergent nature. In Phase 3, the culminating phase, teachers and children finalize the project. For example, this might involve a concluding event such as a showcase for parents and community, or the children might choose to share their project documentation in a public space.

Katz and Chard (2000) elaborate on the role of the three key participants in the Project Approach: teacher, children and parents (and others in the wider community). At first, the teacher plays several roles including guide, moderator, facilitator and co-worker with children. As the project proceeds, the children play more active roles as they investigate what they want to know and co-operate with others to answer their questions about the project topic. Aligned with social constructivism perspectives (Vygotsky 1978), reflective thinking and interactions between the teacher and child, and child and child, are crucial factors in the success of a project.

Aligning with a key principle of early childhood education for sustainability, the active engagement of as many participants as possible is also sought in this socially-constructed process. Ideally, parents should take an active role in the project too.

Parental support and willingness to co-operate are important in building strong bonds between the early childhood centre and home-settings. Similarly, the local community may offer field trip sites and helpful experts related to the children's project topic. When all these participants work together on a common sustainability-related project, meaningful learning and other diverse benefits can result. As Katz and Chard (2000: 160) write, 'by definition, the Project Approach can encompass a wide range of topics that are locally suitable and culturally relevant to the participants'. We believe, however, that for children to fully engage in education for sustainability as change agents, children must be able to participate in transformative education, engage in critical thinking, be empowered and participate in democratic decision-making processes; this necessitates a shift from environmental education to education for sustainability. Early childhood education for sustainability promotes such transformative forms of early education, rather than those that replicate current practices. This is represented by Figure 10.1 (Stuhmcke 2012).

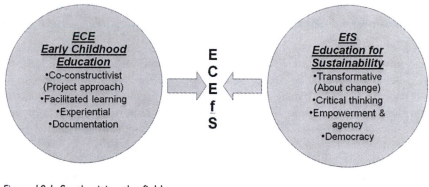

Figure 10.1 Synthesizing the fields
Source: Stuhmcke 2012

In Korea, the Musim Stream Project by five-year-old children not only focused on the environmental conservation of the stream, it also encompassed the social and political dimensions of sustainability including supporting the local culture and fostering social responsibility. As is described later in this chapter, project participants engaged in a wide range of learning activities. Not only did the children learn about the stream ecosystem and food chains, they also became active participants in the local political life of Cheongju City. They did this by sending a letter to Cheongju City Hall asking for a special map to be made of the stream, explaining key features and habitats, for the city's younger children to complement the already-existing map available for adults. The children also campaigned publicly for the protection of the stream, bringing citizens' attention to the plight of local wildlife, particularly the otter.

Similarly, the Rainforest Project in Australia was a case study involving four-year-old children who investigated environmental issues within their local area. They initiated sustainability actions within their kindergarten and also influenced their families and the wider community through sharing their learning. For example, they created a book about what they had learnt during the project, designed with the specific intention of teaching others (their families) about ways to care for the Earth. Parents, then, were inspired to build possum boxes for the kindergarten (to provide homes as 'people and animals should live together'), changed their shopping habits thus reducing the use of plastic shopping bags, and accompanied their children to the local shops where posters promoting recycling (made by children) were given to shopkeepers. Using a transformative project approach, it became evident that the children were change agents for sustainability as a result of their learning in both projects.

The Project Approach in Korea: the Musim Stream Project in Mipyung Childcare Centre

Background to ECEfS in Korea

In Korea, there are two types of formal education settings for birth to five years of age – kindergartens for three to five year olds and childcare centres from birth to five years of age. Interest in environmental education for young children began in Korea in the 1990s and, more recently, support for high quality early childhood education has been growing steadily. In particular, the importance of environmental education for young children was identified in the revised national early childhood curriculum in 2007; 'respect both Human and Nature' was emphasized (The Korean Education Ministry 2007).

In 2008, the Korean government committed to a low-carbon, green growth strategy as part of the nation's long-term development. In the education field, this national strategy has taken the form of Green Growth Education (Presidential Committee on Green Growth of Korea 2009). Within the early childhood sector, the new 'Nuri' curriculum (The Korean Education Ministry 2011), implemented in 2011 for five year olds, reflects Green Growth Education with a focus on both 'environment' and 'economy' as important characteristics (Ji, Lee, Jang and Oh 2012). In 2012, this green growth focus was further extended to include the curriculum for three to five year olds. These recent changes have provided strong motivation for incorporating environmental education/education for sustainability within early childhood education in Korea.

Context of the project

The Musim Stream is 34.5 kilometres in length, with six smaller tributaries that flow from north to south through downtown Cheongju City. The stream plays an important role as a meeting and recreation place in the daily lives of Cheongju citizens. Mipyung Childcare Centre is located in Cheongju City, and one of eight early childhood services within the Project Learning Community that was supported professionally by Professor Ji, this chapter's co-author. For the past few years these eight services, five kindergartens and three childcare centres, have engaged in early childhood education for sustainability using the Project Approach. During the study period, the teachers formed a Project Learning Community and kept daily records to reflect on their projects' progress. They gathered together (once a week for three hours) to discuss unresolved problems in the progress of their projects. In effect, these group members from both kindergartens and childcare centres were involved in multiple-case action research, with Professor Ji being their critical friend and supporter.

The teachers of Mipyung Childcare Centre decided that the Musim Stream would be a good subject for their centre's education for sustainability project, citing the following reasons: it was conveniently located nearby and familiar to the children; provided the possibility of experiencing wildlife first-hand; and, offered potential for both environmental and community learning. The Musim Stream Project took place over five weeks (about three hours per day) in 2009, and involved a teacher, teacher's aide and 23 children (aged five years) from one class in the centre.

Preparation for the Musim Stream Project

Prior to commencing the project, the teacher and children constructed a topic/curriculum web of the Musim Stream to provide a glimpse of possible learning activities, set educational goals, and to promote learning alignment with the Korean national curriculum. Specifically, the goals focused on: (1) recognizing the value of the stream as a rural water supply, and as a site for recreation and physical activities such as walking, jogging, bicycle riding and roller-skating for city-dwellers; (2) a place to observe wildlife; and, (3) a stimulus for taking action to protect the stream's fragile ecosystem. After considering the range of possible activities, the teacher then compiled a resource list for the children to access. She soon realized, however, that most of the materials about the Musim Stream were targeted towards adults. The teacher arranged the classroom with Musim Stream pictures, picture books about streams, and picture cards (made by the teacher) about plants and animals living in Musim Stream. Notices were sent out to the parents asking them to take their children to observe the animals and plants in and around Musim Stream.

Phase 1: getting the project started

In the first week of Phase 1, the teacher and children developed the topic web plan through sharing their own experiences of the Musim Stream with the teacher asking the children questions to determine their previous experiences and understandings of Musim Stream. This starting point of finding out children's prior knowledge led the teacher to realize that most of the children were quite familiar with the name of the stream as it is a key local feature. However, the children also demonstrated significant misunderstandings, for example, some thought Musim Stream was a sea 'where whales lived'. Further, the teacher identified that most of the children had only limited direct experience with the stream such as roller-skating on the paths beside the stream or visiting it just briefly. Realizing the value of children having an authentic relationship with the stream, the teacher organized a field trip to observe the wildlife and invited the children to play among the grasses and wildflowers growing on the banks.

Phase 2: the project in progress

While there were many learning activities and experiences in Phase 2, the focus in this chapter is on the children's learning about otters to demonstrate how the project integrated sustainability issues. Specifically, this account shows how the children learnt about interconnections between humans and the natural environment, and how they engaged as citizens participating in the political life of their local community. The progression of inquiry learning activities about the otters of Musim Stream is outlined below:

The prompt
A child remarked to classmates: 'My mother said there were many otters in Musim Stream before, but now they are gone'.
Children's responses and displays of curiosity: 'I have never seen an otter in Musim Stream. Are otters still living in the stream? What do they look like?'

Problem solving
1   With the teacher's guidance, the children watched video clips on the Internet about otters and reviewed pictures in a brochure about Cheongju City.
2   A visiting local expert from a community organization explained to the children that otters did still inhabit Musim Stream and showed photographs as evidence. The children expressed sympathy for the otters on hearing that the otter population had significantly decreased because of poaching and a polluted food supply.

Further questions
'Where do otters live now? How do otters build their houses? Do otters eat only fish and no cookies?'

Problem-solving through research
1   Finding information from books: the children learnt that otters only live in clean water and they excrete near water so they can escape danger quickly.
2   Watching movie clips on the Internet: they learnt more about the characteristics of otters.

3   Learning from experts in the field and demonstrating their learning: the children went on an excursion with an otter expert looking for traces of otters. They found otter footprints and excrement near a bridge. The children discovered stones covered with excrement and otter urine for detailed investigation (Figure 10.2). They demonstrated their new knowledge by creating a song, drawing pictures (Figure 10.3), and building clay models of otters.

Figure 10.2 An exciting moment: finding otter excrement

Figure 10.3 Children's drawing after finding an otter footprint

Further learning

1   The children wrote letters describing their love and concern for the otters living in Musim Stream, for example:
    'Dear otter, I hope you have many babies and live happily in clean water. I really want to see you, but don't come out of the water. Don't get caught by the hunters'.
2   They observed an actual otter: The children visited Cheongju Zoo and compared the characteristics of the otters in the zoo with those of Musim Stream.
3   The children made a book about otters illustrating otter characteristics including their appearance, diet, and natural enemies.

Children learning to be active citizens

The children submitted a proposal to Cheongju City Hall about the current Musim Stream biotope (December 2008) a map that shows the animals, plants and birds living in and around the stream, all presented in the same graphic.

1   Children's proposition:
    'There is no explanation about otters in the Musim Stream biotope map, when Cheongju City's brochures claim that otters are living in Musim Stream. Please include the otters in the biotope map. Also, the Musim Stream biotope map shows animals, plants, fish, and birds all on one page, which is difficult for young children to read and understand. Please make a separate biotope map for plants and animals'.
2   Response from Cheongju City Hall:
    'We will consider the inclusion of otters in the biotope map if the existence of otters in Musim Stream is confirmed by investigation'.
3   Resubmission to Cheongju City Hall:
    After verifying with the community research centre that had published the book *Otters of Musim Stream* (The Education Research Institute of Village Community 2006), the children resubmitted their proposal with text, related pictures, and inquiry findings attached. The Cheongju City Officer replied that they would budget to remedy the map in the future, but that they could not do this immediately.

Making a Musim Stream biotope map for the younger children's class

In addition to submitting the above proposal to Cheongju City Hall, the children decided to create their own *Musim Stream biotope map for young children*. This illustrated the wildflowers and wildlife they had found during the project, including the otters that lived in the Musim Stream. In fact, the children made two maps – one for animals and one for plants because of the difficulties they had experienced when using Cheongju City Hall's biotope with all the plants and animals depicted together in the one map. They also decided to identify the locations where the wildlife was found during their project, and to name the plants and animals on the back of each map for the younger children. To facilitate the children's map-making, the teacher provided images and artefacts collected during the project to assist the children's recall of details about the various plant and animal forms. After completing this task, the children then presented their maps to the younger children in the childcare centre to aid their learning about the Musim Stream. The following figures are of the animal map made by the children.

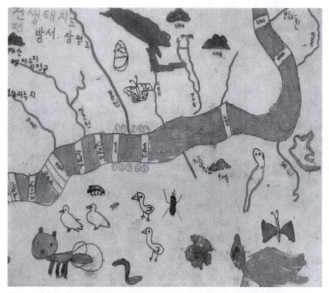

Figure 10.4 Front side of the Musim Stream animal map

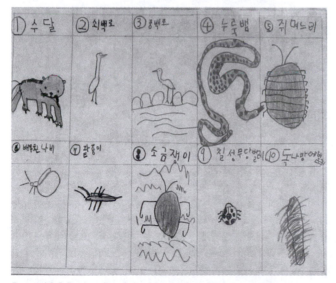

Figure 10.5 Back side of the Musim Stream animal map

Phase 3: concluding the project

For the Musim Stream Project, the culminating event was held in Sangdang Park where many Cheongju City citizens regularly gathered. The children proceeded to the park holding a sign that read 'Protect the otters in Musim Stream'. They then gave a short performance singing songs that they had written about the otters and answered questions from the residents based on their learning about otters. After the performance, the children distributed educational materials to the citizens: badges with hand-drawn pictures of otters (Figure 10.6); flyers explaining otter characteristics; and, 'The 10 Requests to Protect the Otters' (e.g. Please do not throw garbage in Musim Stream). They then chanted 'Save the Otters'. News about this event and the children's campaign for otter protection gained publicity from local newspapers and acted as a catalyst for huge interest in the local community about otter protection.

Figure 10.6 An otter badge

The project legacy/impact

Well beyond the end of the five-week project, the children – who by then were enrolled in elementary school – continued to show interest in the wellbeing of otters and endeavoured to keep 'our promises to protect the otters'. For example, teachers at the childcare centre reported that they regularly received messages from the parents of the children who had participated in the project who insisted, for example, that their families use less shampoo in order to prevent water pollution of the Musim Stream. Another outcome was that many friends and relatives of the children – including the author – continued to have discussions with Cheongju City Hall about the need for a Musim Stream biotope map for young children. These ongoing outcomes of the Project Approach for early childhood education for sustainability illustrate how these young children's participation in the project supported not only their learning, but influenced the wider community to take notice of local sustainability issues.

Using a transformative project approach in an Australian kindergarten: the Rainforest Project

Background to ECEfS in Australia

Australian early childhood services are required to work with the nationally-recognized outcomes-based curriculum, *Belonging Being Becoming: The Early Years Learning Framework for Australia* (EYLF) (Australian Government Department of Education, Employment and Workplace Relations (DEEWR) 2009). Learning Outcome 2 of this framework states that: 'Children are connected with and contribute to their world' (DEEWR 2009: 3). This is elaborated further as children's active participation and children becoming socially responsible and showing respect for the environment. The shift towards embedding education for sustainability within Australian early childhood curricula is also recognized in, and now required by National Quality Standards (Australian Children's Education and Care Quality Authority (ACECQA) 2011 revised 2013). Quality Area 3, which focuses on the physical environment of an early childhood service includes Standard 3.3 'The service takes an active role in caring for its environment and contributes to a sustainable future'. In turn, Standard 3.3 comprises the following elements:

> Element 3.3.1: Sustainable practices are embedded in service operations.
> (ACECQA 2011 revised 2013: 101)

> Element 3.3.2: Children are supported to become environmentally responsible and show respect for the environment.
> (ACECQA 2011 revised 2013: 102)

Context of the project

The Rainforest Project involved 22 children (aged three and a half to four and a half years) in learning experiences and action-taking around environmental and sustainability issues at their bayside kindergarten located in the outskirts of Brisbane, Australia. The project was an action research case study undertaken by the chapter co-author, Stuhmcke, as part of her doctoral studies.

The kindergarten teacher had a long-held personal interest in environmental issues, and had become interested in more recent times in ways to encourage and support young children's thinking about and acting for the environment. The kindergarten, for example, already had a strong environmental focus partly due to its location adjacent to an Environmental Reserve. The kindergarten's existing environmental practices (prior to the study taking place) are listed below:

- environmental policy
- large, natural playground
- eco-friendly cleaning practices
- sensor water taps and a water tank
- composting bins
- planting policy in line with the nature reserve
- litter-less lunch policy

Phase 1: getting the project started

The teacher employed her usual way of starting a project by discussing with the children their topics of interest. An outcome of this discussion was that one child constructed a collage communicating her understandings about the rainforest, camping, bush safety, rubbish and its impact on rainforest animals (Figure 10.7). This rainforest collage created a ripple effect of interest for the teacher and children, and hence, became the starting point for the whole group's Rainforest Project. Other children then began sharing their own experiences of the natural environment through camping trips and bushwalking.

I did 2 frogs, they're bouncing. The leaves are falling. The butterflies are flying. There are 3 stars falling from the sky. The vines are swinging. We should camp in a tent in the rainforest. You have to be careful of snakes. Look out for spiders. No rubbish – Don't put rubbish in the rainforest because all the animals will die. (Trina, 16 August 2010)

Figure 10.7 Child's collage about the rainforest

In Week 2 of the introductory phase of the children's Rainforest Project, the children and teacher built on the initial rainforest interest by collaboratively compiling an extended list of topics. Such negotiation is customary during this introductory phase according to Harris Helm and Katz (2011). The following list was suggested by the children: jungles, forests, waterfalls, rainforests, dinosaurs, water, dinghies (small boats) and beaches (Class discussion, 23/8/10). Together, each option for further exploration was discussed with the children, who ultimately suggested the construction of a large three-dimensional model as a way of representing their learning interest 'cos then we can see what a waterfall and a rainforest is like … because we don't have any at kindy' (Class discussion, 23/8/10). Following this collaborative discussion, the children began constructing their rainforest environment model.

During the initial phase of the Rainforest Project, the teacher also planned group times that included sharing picture books with environmental themes, for example, renowned Australian author Jeannie Baker's publications, *Where the Forest Meets the Sea* (1988a) and *Window* (1988b). The teacher shared these books, being mindful not to overtly point out their 'subtle' environmental messages. However, the children demonstrated that they well-understood both the overt and subtle environmental messages contained in the picture storybooks. For example, they noted instances where the book characters did not interfere with the various natural elements that they saw on the pages, 'you can't take creatures away from where they live 'cos they will die … you can only look, you don't pick things … you can only pick them up if they have already fallen off' (Teacher notes, 18/8/10). This was also evidenced by the following comments made by children: 'it's mean to the animals to cut down their trees' (Elise, 24/8/10) and 'animal homes and people homes should be together' (Mark, 24/8/10).

Children's understandings about, and interest in, their local environment continued to be evident as illustrated by their participation in a nature hunt in the kindergarten's playground. For example, when given further opportunities to explore the flora and fauna, many chose to use magnifying glasses to observe closely, rather than pick leaves or collect insects.

Phase 2: project in progress

The synthesizing phase of the Rainforest Project saw the children's interest in ways to care for the environment, develop even further. In particular, the children became interested in recycling and conservation. In this phase, the children devised their own 'rules' and practices around recycling and conservation within the kindergarten with many practices being additional to the centre-wide practices already in place, such as the use of sensor taps and a rainwater tank to reduce town water consumption. Many of these practices were also later introduced into the children's homes.

The children also expressed concern about polluted water and the impacts this could have on native animals and were observed enacting their ideas about how this problem could be solved. For example, when playing in the sandpit, they devised various ways to clean sand out of the water pipes. They made the comparison with pipes that showed pollution draining into a frog pond in the picture story book *Lester and Clyde* (Reece 1995) that the teacher had read to the children. Luke commented: 'we can see the baby animals ... we have to clean the water ... if there's rubbish in the water the baby animals will die' (Luke, 30/8/10). Then through their play, the children role-played pro-active environmental behaviours by pretending to clean the waterways. They showed their abilities to discriminate between what was natural to a waterway and what did not belong, and their dialogue further demonstrated that they understood the consequences of polluted water for native animals. Such role plays, focused on the theme of cleaning water, were repeated frequently over a number of weeks after the first occasion.

Similarly, the children continued to encourage each other to adhere to their new recycling 'rules' that they had developed then introduced into their daily practices until the end of 2010, long past the time that the Rainforest Project had concluded. To illustrate their interest in practical recycling strategies within the kindergarten, the teacher's aide shared the following observation:

> The children are very aware about their wrapping (glad-wrap) and the tops of their yoghurt containers, they tell one another 'quick, quick ... get it before an animal picks it up'. They (the children) seem to be transferring their learning into their practices without any intervention by us.
>
> (Conversation with teaching assistant, 6/9/10)

In response to the children's continuing environmental interest, the teacher also organized an incursion, a rainforest-themed puppet show (Stewart 1990), to visit the kindergarten. The puppet show actors identified features of the rainforest environment including the unique flora and fauna, discussed human impacts on rainforest habitats, and presented ways that the children could act to preserve and protect rainforests. After the puppet show, the children incorporated many new ideas into their play. For example, one child designed and constructed a 'rubbish crane' (see Figure 10.8) to 'scoop' pollution from the trees and the air, indicating her understanding that pollution cannot always be 'seen'. This child continued to use her rubbish crane in subsequent play in and around the rainforest environment model. Children also frequently made references to specific animals from the puppet show, these animals' survival needs, and the potential threats posed by humans. Harris *et al.* (2011) report that young children often process and extend their initial learning instigated in a project through play, and this was certainly the case here.

As indicated, these children continued to engage with the rainforest environment model during this phase of the Rainforest Project. They were observed incorporating new environment-related ideas into their play in and around the model. Harris *et al.*(2011) describe young children as being involved in increasingly advanced play throughout the course of a project, and that children often become protective of living things when involved in projects about nature. While

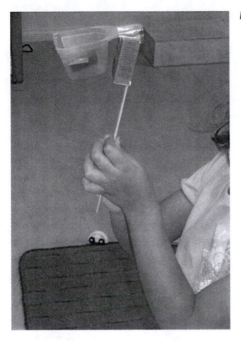

Figure 10.8 Child's construction – rubbish crane

immediately after the puppet show the children's play revolved around the animals they had learnt about, their later play broadened to include animals not featured in the show, such as uniquely Australian wombats and echidnas, thus indicating that the children were transferring their learning from the puppet show to broader content and contexts. For example, their play included creating and camouflaging animals' homes to protect the animals from predators.

As noted earlier, the project reported here was part of this co-author's doctoral studies. Hence, during the project, the teacher-researcher kept a reflective diary that included notes about her thoughts and interpretations of the children's learning as the project unfolded. An excerpt from this diary illustrates the depth and breadth of new learning that unfolded as a result of the Rainforest Project:

> My observations identified that the children had developed many under-standings about environmental issues and topics including:
>
> - human impacts on flora and fauna;
> - pollution (seen and unseen);
> - food chains and ecological systems;
> - appropriate practices for dealing with rubbish;
> - that native wildlife should not be caged;
> - that domestic animals need to be restrained, and;
> - pollution and polluted environments are harmful to wildlife and humans.
>
> (Reflective Diary, 15/9/2010)

Analysis of these reflections indicated that the children were able to make decisions about how to conserve and protect the natural environment and could act positively for the environment within local contexts such as their kindergarten and home.

Phase 3: concluding the project

Typically, the concluding phase of a project is characterized by communicating what has been discovered during its course (Chard 2011). This project culminated in two tangible products. The first was a collaboratively-constructed poster that documented the story of the children's participation in the project. The second was a class book created by the children to educate others about what they had learnt through the Rainforest Project. The poster was displayed in the kindergarten, and the class book was copied (on recycled paper) for distribution to families. While the poster told the 'story' of the children's environment project, the class book was aimed at teaching about what they had learnt 'so we can teach other people' (Class discussion, 5/10/10). The teacher adopted the role of scribe and editor bringing the children's ideas together, but the content and messages to parents was clearly the work of the children. One page of the class book is reproduced in Figure 10.9.

In summary, this project was different from previous projects that had used the Project Approach in the kindergarten because, not only were the children active

Figure 10.9 A page from the children's book *Ways to Act for the Environment*

co-constructors of their learning, they became active participants in creating change within their kindergarten and home contexts. The full extent of the environmentally-sustainable practices within the kindergarten that were a direct result of the project is listed in Table 10.1.

Table 10.1 Existing sustainability practices at the kindergarten and additional practices introduced during the Rainforest Project

Existing sustainability practices (prior to the Rainforest Project)	Additional sustainability practices resulting from the Rainforest Project
• kindergarten's environmental policy • kindergarten's large, natural playground • established eco-friendly cleaning practices • sensor taps/water tank to conserve water • established composting • planting policy in line with the nature reserve • kindergarten's litter-less lunch policy	• rainforest environment model • possum box installed in playground • further recycling measures introduced • further water conservation measures introduced • class book created to educate others about 'ways to act for the environment' • recycling posters created and distributed to local shops

Conclusions

Early childhood education has a clear role in promoting sustainability and can be shown to be effective. When children are involved in educational approaches and pedagogies that centre them in learning and action-taking and enable them to participate and contribute to their own futures, they become motivated and engaged. The first five years of a child's life are a natural starting point for education for sustainability (UNESCO 2008) and are recognized as a vital period on which future learning is built (DEEWR 2009). Beginning education for sustainability in this early period may potentially equip future generations to grow up with pre-established patterns of sustainable living and action-taking for the Earth.

In conclusion, we suggest that a meaningful way to implement an ecological ethic, as suggested by Bookchin (1990), is to involve young children in projects that deal with their own local environmental and sustainability issues. The Musim Stream Project in Korea and the Rainforest Project in Australia focused on familiar, local contexts, and both resulted in extensive new learning and action-taking within these contexts led by the children.

During the Musim Stream Project, children came to learn a great deal about the biological characteristics of otters out of concern for the decreasing otter population. They then made efforts to protect the otters in conjunction with local residents. These efforts helped instil pride in the children through being recognized as knowledgeable and caring members of their community. Hopefully, as anticipated by Carson (1956), the children who participated in the Musim Stream

Project will remember the pleasure of their engagement and learning in nature, and that such ecological sensibility will be the basis of a life-long, eco-friendly attitudes towards the natural world. The children also took their first steps in learning to be active citizens, learning ways to interact with their community and civic authorities on an issue that was meaningful to them. In the Rainforest Project, the children also had activist roles that demonstrated intergenerational impacts, particularly in relation to their own families. These children appeared empowered when they took on leadership and cast themselves as educators through the production of their class book.

The two case studies presented in this chapter challenge traditional views of children as 'becoming' adults. Instead, they support recent notions of children as competent, capable individuals, able to enact change within their communities and environments. Both studies provide examples of children caring about sustainability issues and enacting changes. Davis (2011) describes child participation and agency as central to early childhood education for sustainability and, as Robinson and Vaealiki (2010) state, 'Early childhood education for sustainability promotes the view that children have a voice that provides them with opportunities to influence their world' (p.162).

The Project Approach in early childhood education for sustainability

The Project Approach has recently been implemented as an effective strategy for early childhood education for sustainability in several countries. We believe that early childhood education for sustainability should not be based on a model of learning where knowledge and skills are conveyed to children; rather, it should be framed as a transformative approach which emphasizes meaning-making by learners, enhances their conceptual understandings and intellectual abilities (Jenkins 2009), and encourages action-taking to create change. Therefore, teachers should aim to scaffold children's construction of values and understandings about sustainability issues within their local communities, and support and motivate them to take relevant, meaningful and authentic actions. Both projects discussed in this chapter illustrate the potential of the Project Approach in early childhood education for sustainability. As chapter co-authors we value the contributions that the Project Approach can make toward children's co-construction of knowledge as well recognizing the power of strategies that encourage action-taking and creating change.

Co-author Sharon Stuhmcke illustrates the ways that co-constructivism and a transformative approach can be brought together. There now follows her model of the Transformative Project Approach (Stuhmcke 2012) (Figure 10.10) developed in the course of her doctoral studies. This model combines co-constructivist learning and teaching (drawn from the Project Approach in early childhood education) with transformative learning and teaching (drawn from education for sustainability). When employed together, a transformative Project Approach results, where children co-construct knowledge, direct their own learning around environmental and

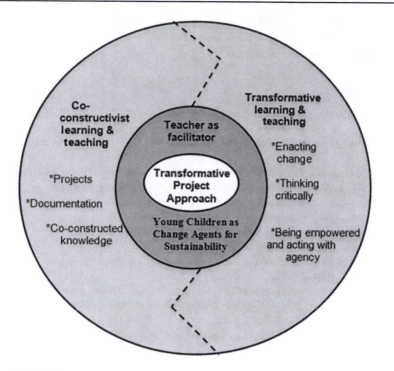

Figure 10.10 The transformative project approach
Source: Stuhmcke 2012

sustainability issues, and are empowered to take action based on their co-constructed understandings.

We believe we have demonstrated here that young children can be supported to co-construct knowledge about sustainability, and can act on this knowledge, and that changes can be achieved through utilizing a transformative project approach. It is through the opportunities where children are empowered to take action and to create change that transformative education for sustainability occurs.

Further, we conclude this chapter by posing a challenge to early childhood practitioners and researchers. To practitioners, we ask that you consider ways to strengthen your practices using transformative educational approaches and to design ways to support children to be active citizens. We also encourage practitioners to think about how to work authentically with their wider communities on sustainability-related topics and projects. To researchers, we ask that you turn your gaze to the research work that is beginning to occur around early childhood education for sustainability, and work to extend its conceptualization and reach. Through exposing current theory and practice to challenge and critique, this newly emerging field has the potential to make a significant contribution to reshaping early childhood education, more broadly, in dealing with twenty-first-century opportunities and challenges.

References

Australian Children's Education and Care Quality Authority (ACECQA) (2013) *Guide to the National Quality Standard*. Online. Available: http://files.acecqa.gov.au/files/National-Quality-Framework-Resources-Kit/NQF03-Guide-to-NQS-130902.pdf (accessed 10 March 2014).

Australian Government, Department of Education, Employment and Workplace Relations (DEEWR) (2009) *Belong Being Becoming: The Early Years Learning Framework for Australia*, Online. Available: www.deewr.gov.au/EarlyChildhood/Policy_Agenda/Quality/Pages/EarlyYearsLearningFramework.aspx (accessed 25 February 2010).

Baker, J. (1988a) *Where the Forest Meets the Sea*, London: Walker Books.

Baker, J. (1988b) *Window*, London: Walker Books.

Bookchin, M. (1990) *The Philosophy of Social Ecology: Essays on Dialectical Naturalism*, Montreal: Black Rose Books.

Carson, R. L. (1956) *The Sense of Wonder*, New York: Harper Collins Publishers.

Chard, S. (2011) *The Project Approach*. Online. Available: www.project-approach.com/definition.html (accessed 25 April 2012).

Cheongju City (2008) *Musim Stream Ecological Map*. Cheongju: Cheongju City Hall.

Davis, J. (2010) What is Early Childhood Education for Sustainability?, in J. M. Davis (ed.), *Young Children and the Environment*. Melbourne: Cambridge University Press, pp. 21–42.

Davis, J. (2011) 'Early Childhood Education', in J. Newman (ed.), *Green Education*. Los Angeles, CA: Sage Publications, pp. 115–17.

Davis, J. and Elliott, S. (2003) *Early Childhood Environmental Education Making It Mainstream*, Watson, ACT: Early Childhood Australia Inc.

Dewey, J. (1944) *Democracy and Education. An Introduction to the Philosophy of Education*. New York: The Free Press.

Education Research Institute of Village Community (2006) *Otters in Musim Stream*. Cheongju: Jikji.

Elkind, D. (1993) *Images of the Young Child*. Washington, DC: NAEYC.

Harris Helm, J. and Katz, L. (2011) *Young Investigators. The Project Approach in the Early Years*, New York: NAEYC and Teachers College Press.

Jenkins, K. (2009) 'Linking Theory to Practice: Education for Sustainability and Learning and Teaching', in *Australian Government Education for Sustainability in the Primary Curriculum*. South Yarra: Palgrave Macmillan, pp. 29–38.

Jensen, B. (2002) 'Knowledge, Action and Pro-environmental Behaviour', *Environmental Education Research*, 8(3): 325–34.

Ji, O. (2011) 'The Analysis of Young Children's Community Participation Contents in the "Musim Stream Project" As a Case for ECEfS', *The Journal of Korea Open Association for Early Childhood Education*, 16(6): 363–82.

Ji, O., Lee, H., Jang, J. and Oh, C. (2012) *The Program for Application of GGE for 3–5 Years Old Connecting Nuri Curriculum*. Seoul: Ministry of Education of Korea.

Katz, L. G. and Chard, S. C. (2000) *Engaging Children's Minds: The Project Approach*, 2nd edn. Stamford, CT: Ablex.

Kilpatrick, W. H. (1919) *The Project Method*. New York: Teacher's College, Columbia University.

Korean Education Ministry (2007) *The Revised 2007 Kindergarten Curriculum.* Seoul: The Korean Education Ministry.

Korean Education Ministry (2011) *The Teacher Guide Book for Application of Nuri Curriculum-10. Environment and Life.* Seoul: The Korean Education Ministry.

Presidential Committee on Green Growth of Korea (2009) *The Five Year Plan for Green Growth (2009–2013).* Online. Available: http://green.kosca.or.kr/down (accessed 10 November 2010).

Reece, J. H. (2005) *Lester and Clyde. Running Scared.* Sydney: Scholastic.

Robinson, L. and Vaealiki, S. (2010) 'Ethics and Pedagogy at the Heart of Early Childhood Education for Sustainability', in J. M. Davis (ed.), *Young Children and the Environment* (pp.154–181). Melbourne: Cambridge University Press.

Siraj-Blatchford, J., Smith, K. C. and Samuelsson, I. P. (2010) *Education for Sustainable Development in the Early Years.* Online. Available: www.ecesustainability.org (accessed 25 November 2010).

Short, V. M. (1991) 'Childhood education in a changing world', *Childhood Education,* 68(1): 10–13.

Stewart, J. (1990) *The Rainforest Experience (Puppet Show).* Online. Available: www.evergreenchildrenstheatre.com.au/ (accessed 10 October 2012).

Stuhmcke, S. M. (2012) *Children as Change Agents for Sustainability: An Action Research Case Study in a Kindergarten.* Unpublished thesis, Queensland University of Technology: Brisbane.

Taylor, N., Littledyke, M. and Eames, C. (2009) 'Why do we need to teach Education for Sustainability at the primary level?' in M. Littledyke, N. Taylor and C. Eames (eds), *Education for Sustainability in the Primary Curriculum.* South Yarra: Palgrave Macmillan, pp. 1–7.

UNESCO (2005) *Four Dimensions of Sustainable Development.* Online. Available: www.unesco.org/education/tlsf/mods/theme_a/popups/mod04t01s03.html (accessed 25 April 2012).

UNESCO (2008) *The Contribution of Early Childhood Education to a Sustainable Society.* Paris: UNESCO.

Vygotsky, L. S. (1978) 'Interaction between learning and development', in V. Steiner (ed.), *Mind in Society.* Cambridge, MA: Harvard University Press, pp. 79–91.

Chapter 11

Valuing agency in young children

Teachers rising to the challenge of sustainability in the Aotearoa New Zealand early childhood context

Glynne Mackey

Abstract

As teachers expand their understandings of how the early childhood curriculum for infants, toddlers and young children is able to confront issues of sustainability, they are also searching for ways to create a culture that embraces meaningful and transformative experiences that may empower children to become agents of change now and in the future. This chapter brings together the voices of kindergarten children, their teachers, and education services manager. The research data from teacher interviews explores the challenges, and successes involved in establishing sustainability programs in early childhood settings. Through a range of researcher recorded observations and experiences within the everyday kindergarten program, the children demonstrated their competence in understanding some of the issues, and their role as active participants capable of making valued contributions. The conversations and reflections of the teachers revealed how they valued young children's agency, and how this contributed to creating cultures of sustainability within these New Zealand early childhood settings.

Introduction

This chapter describes a participatory case study that was carried out in a New Zealand kindergarten where the curriculum focused on education for sustainability. The intent of the curriculum was to have children and teachers learning and working together to care for self, for each other, and for the environment. The study involved three teachers working with 35 children aged three to five years, and one education services manager from the kindergarten's umbrella organization whose role was to visit regularly, and to advise and support the teaching team. In the first section of this chapter, the research context, theoretical frame and methodology are briefly outlined. The second section describes the challenges faced and successes achieved by the teachers and manager in establishing their environmental program. Analysis of their conversations and reflections demonstrated how they perceived that the children, their families and broader communities responded to their vision for sustainability. The final chapter section focuses on the children's learning, and comments on selected experiences and observations in relation to principles and strands embedded in the bicultural New Zealand Early Childhood Curriculum, *Te Whāriki* (New Zealand Ministry of Education 1996: 9), as highlighted in the following:

> In early childhood education settings, all children should be given the opportunity to develop knowledge and an understanding of the cultural heritages of both partners to Te Tiriti o Waitangi. The curriculum reflects this partnership in text and structure.[1]

The research context

Recent research undertaken in early childhood settings has demonstrated how the role of the teacher, when working collaboratively with children, family and communities, has been instrumental in creating cultures of sustainability in which young children have agency, and are supported to actively bring about change (Davis 2005, Pratt 2010, Vaealiki and Mackey 2008). The New Zealand early childhood context, guided by *The New Zealand Early Childhood Curriculum, Te Whāriki* (New Zealand Ministry of Education 1996), takes the ecological theoretical position of Urie Bronfenbrenner (Lee *et al.* 2013) where the child is at the centre of several systems that impact either directly or indirectly on the child and, also, recognizes that the child impacts on the systems. The position taken in this chapter is to focus on the way in which education for sustainability aligns with the four principles of *Te Whāriki*: empowerment, holistic development, family and community, and relationships. These principles reflect a sociocultural approach to learning and development (Lee, *et al.* 2013) that recognizes children's agency and the importance of building responsive and reciprocal relationships within early childhood learning communities. This research allowed for the voices and experiences of children, teachers and parents to be recognized and respected so that teachers could potentially better understand the importance of valuing each child's agency when situated centrally in Bronfenbrenner's *Ecological Model of Child Development* (Bronfenbrenner 2005).

The study context

A local urban kindergarten, in the South Island city of Christchurch, for children aged three to five years agreed to participate in the case study as they were already part of a nation-wide EnviroSchools program (www.enviroschools.org.nz/about-enviroschools). Enviroschools was established in New Zealand schools, independent of the Ministry of Education, in the late 1990s and, wisely – as most other similar international programs do not – the EnviroSchools Foundation invited kindergartens to become involved. The program provided a sustainability focus for teachers within a framework of guiding principles aimed at empowering children and young people to explore relevant issues within their communities.

The teachers in this case study kindergarten received support from the local EnviroSchools coordinator, as well as the education services manager from the kindergarten's umbrella organization, to create a program focused on education for sustainability.

Theoretical frame

In a community where there is active participation in local cultural activities, individuals make a dynamic contribution to the learning community according to Rogoff (2003); this was the case here. The existing kindergarten program often invited members of the local community into the setting and encouraged wide participation and consultation with community and families. As sociocultural theory underpinned the kindergarten program and informed the pedagogies; the voices and perspectives of children, teachers and the community needed to inform and be reflected in the research (Mackey and Vaealiki 2011). The study intent was to uphold the rights of the children, their families and their teachers, therefore the researchers chose a participatory approach within a sociocultural frame. As the research project was planned and implemented, the synergy between using a participatory approach and the key tenets of early childhood education for sustainability (ECEfS) became apparent: the child as a rights holder; meaningful dialogue and engagement with children; respecting and appreciating diverse contributions; and embedding democratic values and principles of participation (Pramling Samuelsson and Kaga 2008).

Methodology

To help us appreciate how ECEfS was understood and practised, 35 children, three teachers, one education services manager, and three parents, were invited to work with us to understand how children participated and contributed in working towards sustainability. Ethical approval from the researchers' College of Education was granted, information about the research was communicated, and consent forms were signed by the adult participants. Respectful communication was central in consulting with the children about the research. Researchers engaged in conversations with children about what constitutes research, with information being shared at kindergarten group time, as well as via a letter read with their parents at home. Steps were taken to minimize the impact of researchers being in children's place of play and learning. For example, we attended sessions two weeks before data was recorded in order to build familiarity, communicated regularly with staff and children throughout the data-gathering phase, and respected the everyday experiences as they unfolded, even if this meant that we were unable to keep to our planned data-gathering schedule. In summary, the research was seen as a partnership with the participants, where there were shared understandings about the intent of the study and the importance of their contributions.

After talking with the teachers in a focus group and interviewing the kindergarten's education services manager, their data was placed alongside that gathered from the children to offer a more complete picture about how children's agency was valued at the research site. Children's data was obtained through observations, learning stories, drawings, constructions, photos and digital voice recordings over a four-week-period. This range of methods was important as it honoured the child's right to expression and to make a contribution to the research in an individually relevant manner.

Creating a culture of sustainability

Through a sociocultural lens, a culture for sustainability was created through the involvement of the early childhood professional community along with kindergarten families and the local community, each contributing with their strengths, knowledge and skills.

The education services manager

The education services manager initiated professional development and goal setting for the kindergarten staff, and met regularly with staff to discuss issues about setting up sustainability-focused projects, accessing suitable resources, and identifying community members with similar sustainability interests. Her perspectives as an early childhood professional outside the teaching team were of particular interest to us as researchers, as she was able to be objective, probe, and reflect with teachers on their progress towards creating a culture of sustainability in the kindergarten. She saw her role as a 'provocateur, an encourager, and a facilitator walking alongside' the staff as they embarked on their sustainability journey.

Early in her interview, the manager described the challenges of working to build a whole centre approach while the kindergarten community was in a state of flux – teachers, children and families were coming and leaving the service. In the early stages, as momentum was gathering, frequent personnel changes within the kindergarten presented a challenge in terms of working with/maintaining the sustainability vision of the original staff team. As the one constant individual, this manager endeavoured to keep the vision alive through regular discussion with staff about the meanings and practices of sustainability. Having to continually return to these matters seemed, at times, to be at odds with sustainability as a concept where ideas should be deepening, rather than continually being re-explored in shallow ways. However, as the kindergarten community stabilized over a longer period, the manager identified a tipping point where interest and momentum for sustainability increased through the implementation of two new projects within the kindergarten. She stated:

> Really, it's when people have a passion that the scales tip … through getting community on board and through the teachers having a passion for biculturalism and also environmental issues, people in the community come

forth. The teachers themselves – one in particular – would say that she was not born with a passion for this, but what she is doing is tapping into people who do, growing that community of learners that permeates other areas of their work.

(Manager June 2006)

The longevity of the ECEfS program at this kindergarten was finally secured when its community was invited to contribute, and when all members of the kindergarten community could connect with passion and commitment to the projects, despite the dynamics of changing families, children and staff.

The community

Within the wider community there were some members who had little or no direct link to the kindergarten, but who valued and supported the contributions of young children as citizens. The centre manager observed that, being a small community within the greater Christchurch urban area, there were already strong links with a range of community groups, local primary schools and other early childhood settings that made it possible for this kindergarten to link into local sustainability initiatives.

In her interview, one of the kindergarten teachers gave an example of such local community participation. She had invited the local Year 1 primary school teacher to attend various kindergarten events which not only encouraged a supportive relationship with the children before their transition to school, but demonstrated the kindergarten children's capacities as change agents for ECEfS. At the time of interview, the school had not engaged with environmental or sustainability issues. The kindergarten teacher was aware that 'her' children would ask questions of the school teachers such as 'Where do we put our recycling? Do we have a worm farm for our food scraps?' Thus, as a result of their interactions with the school, the kindergarten children influenced the school's decision to embrace the sustainability principles and actions of the EnviroSchools program. This is an example of how the influence of an early childhood setting, and particularly of the young children in the setting, can ripple out into the wider community (Vaealiki and Mackey 2008). As one of the kindergarten teacher commented in her interview:

It's got far-reaching benefits. At the [EnviroSchools] awards ceremony where people are coming together to talk about environmental education – we were there with primary and secondary [teachers] – people were saying 'Oh, so it starts in early childhood!' Our teachers were able to stand up and talk about children's participation and community involvement, that they inspired other people.

(Teacher June 2006)

The teachers

Through an ongoing focus on reflections and discussions about ECEfS, the kindergarten teachers determined that involving children in collaboration and listening to their ideas and perspectives not only impacted on the children and the local environment, but resulted in significant shifts in the teachers' curriculum and pedagogical practices. The following points, extracted from the teacher interviews, highlight key shifts in the teachers' practices as a result of their focus on ECEfS:

- Teachers now involve children in creating the vision through planning, mapping and altering the physical environment.
- Teachers now seek children's ideas and ask questions such as 'What's your favourite space? Where do you like to play? What parts don't you like? Why don't you like them? What can we do to fix it?' Children's inputs are designed to guide changes within the kindergarten setting and to acknowledge the children as active participants in creating these changes.
- Teachers now appear undeterred by past barriers. For example, they are more prepared to challenge the risk and safety policies of their management organization and the government regulations that the teachers have identified as impacting negatively on their community. To illustrate, children are now included in some of the 'family work' within the setting such as spreading bark soft-fall and gardening, and are involved in other playground working groups. Teachers stated that they have confidence in their revised risk management plan to ensure everyone's safety, rather than banning all children's participation in these family and community activities.

Living the culture of sustainability

The adults' engagement with creating a culture of sustainability in the kindergarten provided a firm basis for the ongoing journey of this kindergarten community and continues to offer challenges and insights for others wanting to create their own sustainability journeys. In the journey ahead, the culture of sustainability needs to weave through the philosophies, policies and practices that encourage young children's agency. The following section shares data showing some of the children's learning experiences within the kindergarten setting where the policies and practices were underpinned by the emerging ethos of sustainability. We advised the children that, as researchers, we were interested in their ideas about how to look after the environment. We recorded our conversations with the children, read about the children's learning that was documented regularly by the teachers as part of usual practice in the kindergarten, observed children taking the initiative and offering their ideas to teachers and peers, and listened as children explained to us their good ideas and helpful actions for the environment.

The kindergarten children are the focus of this section. The research data as mentioned above gave valuable insights into how the children in the kindergarten demonstrated their agency through playing, living and learning within a culture of sustainability. A selection of children's experiences and examples of agency from the children's documentation are linked here to each of the five strands of *Te Whāriki* (New Zealand Ministry of Education 1996) that weave through the four principles of early childhood curriculum. These strands are: *mana whenua* – belonging; *mana atua* – wellbeing; *mana aotūroa* – exploration; *ana reo* – communication; and *mana tangata* – contribution.

Belonging – *mana whenua*

Example 1

During a festival in the local community that identified Māori culture and historic settlement, the children became interested in the place where they lived and belonged. This included the rich local history where Māori had settled and where, many years later, in the 1840s the first British settlers arrived in sailing ships. A walk in the surrounding hills was organized to include parents and community members so that the children could get a perspective of how their place looked from an elevated position and to consider how early settlement might have occurred. The education services manager commented:

> They experience and appreciate the local history of the local community. They utilize the natural environment, and study the natural environment like the hills. They've been up in the Gondola to look at it from a different angle and they've involved the community in that. They've thought about the explorers and pioneers that were there before them ... education in the environment; education about the environment; education for the environment. These three things are now present, whereas in the past it might have been just education in the environment.
>
> (Manager June 2006)

Example 2

On another occasion, local contractors who were working next to the kindergarten gathered up a pile of volcanic rocks. The teacher asked that these be put by the gate so that the children could load them onto their carts to bring back to the kindergarten playground. The children often talked with teachers about the local landscape and past historical events. One child assembled the rocks to create a 'dinosaur playground' (see Figure 11.1) that he possibly imagined was part of the pre-history around the local harbour. The geography of the local landscape was clearly reflected in this outdoor play.

Example 3

In another example, part of the kindergarten's outdoor playground with a sloped, wooded area that the children referred to as 'the high hills', represented the terrain

Figure 11.1 The dinosaur playground

of the many hills and valleys in the local landscape (see Figure 11.2). Children in the study appeared to have a sense of belonging related to where they lived and played, with views of the harbour and related harbour activity – ships coming into port; trains and trucks delivering goods for shipping; and, the steep hills surrounding the harbour area once formed by a volcano.

Since the devastating effects of the earthquakes in 2010 and 2011 in the Christchurch region of the South Island, community vitality is returning to the city and to this kindergarten community, bringing with it, restrengthening a sense of

Figure 11.2 Exploring the 'high hills'

belonging and identity. Belonging and learning about interconnectedness with the surrounding environment links closely with wellbeing (Elliott 2010). Children who develop strong community links through understanding the history, culture, landscape and social issues of their local area, are likely to also appreciate and care for the natural world, and to be active citizens with a desire to participate (Sobel 2005).

Wellbeing – *mana atua*

Central to a child's sense of wellbeing is how others respond to and respect her/him. The following story from the research data gives hope that trust and acceptance – in this case generated through children's responses to a butterfly – can contribute to children's emotional wellbeing. A teacher described during her interview how a four-year-old boy had recently started at the kindergarten and that his ways of relating to others was posing a challenge for both teachers and children. However, the teachers were respectful and understanding of the disruption caused by his transition, so encouraged the children with comments such as 'He's still learning how we do things here.' On one occasion, she described that the child was clearly upset after an incident with another child, so entered the outdoor area with an angry expression as he navigated his way through the groups of engaged children, looking to join in, but finding that these children seemed to be avoiding him. The teacher observed how he then found a butterfly on the ground, barely alive. Carefully cradling the butterfly in his hands, he moved towards some children who noticed his empathy and expressions of tenderness. This display of empathy was interpreted by the teacher as a beacon to his peers who then moved around him in a caring and supportive circle.

On reflection, Noddings (2003) discusses the meaning of 'natural caring', an unconscious obligation to care that became the way this child responded immediately to a creature in need of help. As we learn to care and show empathy to improve the life of others, it is hoped that the skills learnt will be transferable between the human and the non-human world. As sensory and relational beings, children interact with the natural world and, as a consequence, better understand how to be caring and be appreciative of others in their lives (Ritchie *et al.* 2011). The data here reaffirms that it is through such opportunities to express themselves that children continually reshape their sense of identity, their relationships with others, as well as what it feels like to be trusted and respected.

Exploration – *mana aotūroa*

Our observations in this kindergarten, and our discussions with the teachers, provided many opportunities to view children as 'problem solvers and solution seekers' (Davis 2010: 32). Children were active participants in exploring relationships, ideas and materials in collaboration with others as they sought ways to improve the kindergarten's sustainability practices. The teacher described how group discussions canvassed a range of sustainability issues and led to problem-solving, and how democratic principles were applied as the children offered suggestions, participated in voting, and reached consensus.

The following observation was made while we were present at a group morning session in the kindergarten and demonstrates how a child's creativity engendered a sense of agency through problem-solving and seeking solutions.

A small group of children were helping a teacher cut up an old calendar of photographs of Antarctica. One child in the group, listening to a discussion between the teacher and another child about a movie depicting penguins dying in Antarctica, sat thoughtfully with a construction set and then created a penguin-saving device. His explanations to us about how the machine worked were complex, and his understandings of the conditions in the icy continent seemed well-informed. The child was encouraged further in his exploration of ideas when the teachers conveyed strong interest in his invention by taking photographs, displaying his ideas, and providing further materials and resources. What this observation suggests is that the child was attempting to deal with an environmental and moral dilemma and that he sees himself as having agency in making a difference for the penguins.

Johansson (2009) identified in her research how young children are competent in recognizing and responding to moral and ethical problems, which further supports the notion of competent children. Children are capable of taking action to care for environments around them and, through participation in experiences where their interests, ideas and concerns are explored; they are likely to display action competence (Jensen and Schnack 1997). Action competent children have knowledge of possible actions, believe in their own influence, and feel confident in taking action, either individually or as part of a group.

Communication – mana reo

The United Nations Convention on the Rights of the Child states that children have the right to express their ideas and opinions on matters that affect them (Article 12, UNESCO 1989). Children in the kindergarten that was the focus of this research were active within everyday democratic processes where they were consulted on possibilities for environmental action and were encouraged by teachers to communicate these through a variety of avenues such as offering suggestions to wash used containers; explaining recycling processes to new children; making labels for containers for food scraps; making constructions to save the penguins; and children taking responsibility for planning a concert for parents and community. We also observed an example of democracy in action where children were given an opportunity to vote. At the kindergarten entrance, the teacher had placed a poster illustrating different playground swing designs that were being considered for the playground. Under each picture she created a space for each child to make a pen mark to indicate the style of swing they preferred (see Figure 11.3). The teacher described how this allowed the children to see democracy in action and furthered their understandings that the decision of the individual is not always the final decision.

Figure 11.3 Voting for the best swing

The act of listening and consultation was only part of the process – teachers were aware that this must not be treated as a token gesture of consultation with no follow through. Kinney (2005) challenges educators to think about *how* they are listening and if they have heard the important messages. She asks, 'How well are we hearing, seeing and feeling children's voices?' (p.121). The opportunity for children to take the lead in voting for the best swings gave voice and decision-making power to the children, rebalancing the often inequitable adult/child power relationship. Practice in communication and participation in the swing voting supported the children's understandings of citizenship and democratic processes where consensus was integral to democratic decision-making. Hearing, seeing and feeling children's voices in the research present a constant challenge for researchers as we try to better understand and value children's agency.

Contribution – *mana tangata*

In *Te Whāriki*, contribution is viewed as equitable opportunities, learning alongside and with others, where children are affirmed as individuals (New Zealand Ministry of Education 1996). During the study, we observed how the children in the kindergarten contributed to several collaborative projects in the most individually meaningful and relevant ways that they could. The project list included:

- Making decisions about plants, weeding and putting up garden signs.
- Sorting the recycling and reusing materials and taking the bins to the kerbside on collection day.
- Sorting food scraps at the lunch table and helping younger children to understanding what to place in the bowl for the worms and what to place in the compost (see Figure 11.4).

Figure 11.4 Sorting food scraps at the lunch table

- Bringing items from home such as fresh, free range eggs so that the children could then add parsley from the garden to make egg sandwiches for everyone to share.
- Writing to the art supply company expressing concern at the amount of plastic wrap that was used to secure bundles of paper or paints.

These observations reinforced the notion that, as competent citizens, children have the right to make meaningful contributions to caring for the Earth in a way that is appropriate for their culture, place of play and learning, and to the best of their abilities. Recent research affirms children are capable of being agents of change (Elliott and Davis 2009, Johansson 2009, Mackey 2012, Vaealiki and Mackey 2008) who can make meaningful contributions through their daily play experiences, and through working alongside and sharing with adults in authentic real life experiences.

Final thoughts

It is important to acknowledge that this was a case study approach to research, involving one kindergarten in a specific early childhood context in New Zealand. Although this means that there are limitations to the way the data can be related to other contexts, it is intended that early childhood educators who are committed to promoting the empowerment of children will find that the research presented here will give strength to their practice. Teachers will continue to be challenged to develop programs that reflect the issues of the day such as children taking action for a more sustainable world. Practices such as those described here in one kindergarten in New Zealand need to become part of the wider research literature in both early childhood education and education for sustainability that demonstrates the competence and agency of the youngest citizens. Young children can and already do make a difference and have influence on others and the broader human and ecological systems they inhabit.

Conclusion

Valuing young children's agency for sustainability requires teams of committed teachers who can readily collaborate with community and families and children to identify local issues and who wish to see in children an excitement and love for life.

The teachers and education services manager in the kindergarten where we researched had a vision for an early childhood program where young children had a voice, a sense of belonging, and could make both valuable and readily visible contributions. The kindergarten community in this study was successful in creating and maintaining the sustainability focus because there was a service manager with a vision for sustainability, while the teachers were open to new ideas and showed courage to step into the unknown. Furthermore, they were able to work creatively with *Te Whāriki* (New Zealand Ministry of Education 1996), which embraces notions of belonging, wellbeing, exploration, communication and contribution, a complement to the transformative frame of ECEfS. As a researcher, my eyes and mind have been opened, inspired by the children and their teachers. Thus, I see more clearly children as experts in their own lives, with wishes, and hopes in a world full of possibilities. This research has demonstrated that when we, as adults, respect the child as an expert in their lives, we open a pathway for young children to have a voice and influence adult decisions and actions – it is not only the systems within the kindergarten, the family and the community that impact on the child but this research helps to show how the children in this study were able to impact on these systems. With a more open mind, I now reflect often on what, as teachers and researchers, we can achieve with children, their families and communities, when we seek to uncover what is possible for children, the planet and the future.

Note

1   The Treaty of Waitangi (Te Tiriti o Waitangi) is New Zealand's founding document signed in 1840 by representatives from Māori tribes and representatives from the British Crown. The Treaty is an exchange of promises between Māori and Pakeha (non-Māori), hence, the importance of a bicultural approach to policies and practices in education. For further information www.treatyofwaitangi.govt.nz.

References

Bronfenbrenner, U. (2005) *Making Human Beings Human: Bioecological Perspectives on Human Development*. Thousand Oaks, CA: Sage.

Davis, J. (2005) 'Educating for sustainability in the early years: Creating cultural change in an early childhood centre', *Australian Journal of Environmental Education*, 21: 47–55.

Davis, J. (ed.) (2010) *Young Children and the Environment: Early Education for Sustainability*, Melbourne: Cambridge University Press.

Elliott, S. (2010) 'Children in the natural world', in J. Davis (ed.), *Young Children and the Environment: Early Education for Sustainability*, Melbourne: Cambridge University Press, pp. 43–75.

Elliott, S. and Davis, J. (2009) 'Exploring the resistance: An Australian perspective on educating for sustainability in early childhood,' *International Journal of Early Childhood*, 41(2): 65–77.

Jensen, B. and Schnack, K. (1997) 'The action competence approach in environmental education', *Environmental Education Research*, 3(2): 163–78.

Johansson, E (2009) 'The preschool child of today – the world citizen of tomorrow?' *International Journal of Early Childhood*, 41(2): 79–95.

Kinney, L. (2005) 'Small voices – powerful messages', in A. Clark, A. Kjørholt and P. Moss (eds). *Beyond Listening: Children's Perspectives on Early Childhood Services*, Bristol: The Policy Press.

Lee, W., Carr, M., Soutar, B. and Mitchell, L. (2013) *Understanding the Te Whāriki Approach: Early Years Education in Practice*, London: Routledge.

Mackey, G. (2012) 'To know, to decide, to act: The young child's right to participate in action for the environment', *Environmental Education Research*, 18(4): 473–84.

Mackey, G and Vaealiki, S. (2011) 'Thinking of children: Democratic approaches with children in participatory research', *Australasian Journal of Early Childhood*, 36(2): 82–6.

New Zealand Ministry of Education (1996) *Te Whāriki: Early Childhood Curriculum*, Wellington: Learning Media.

Noddings, N. (2003) *Caring: A Feminine Approach to Ethics and Moral Education*. Los Angeles, CA: University of California Press.

Pramling Samuelsson, I. and Kaga, Y. (2008) *The Contribution of Early Childhood Education to a Sustainable Society*, Paris: UNESCO.

Pratt, R. (2010) 'Practical possibilities and pedagogical approaches for early childhood education for sustainability', in J. Davis (ed.), *Young Children and the Environment: Early Education for Sustainability*, Melbourne: Cambridge University Press, pp. 104–53.

Ritchie, J., Lockie, C. and Rau, C. (2011) 'He tatau pounamu. Considerations for an early childhood peace curriculum focusing on criticality, indigeneity, and an ethic of care, in Aotearoa New Zealand'. *Journal of Peace Education*, 8: 333–52.

Rogoff, B. (2003) *The Cultural Nature of Human Development*, New York: Oxford University Press.

Sobel, D. (2005) *Place-based Education. Connecting Classrooms and Communities*, Great Barrington, MA: The Orion Society.

UNESCO (1989) *Convention on the Rights of the Child*. Online. Available: www.unicef.org/crc (accessed 4 April 2013).

Vaealiki, S and Mackey, G (2008) 'Ripples of action: Strengthening environmental competency in an early childhood centre', *Early Childhood Folio*, 12: 7–11.

Chapter 12

I want to do real things

Explorations of children's active community participation

Louise Gwenneth Phillips

Abstract

Framed within communitarianism, this chapter explores possibilities for young children's active participation in the sustainability of Earth and its inhabitants, via attention to the interdependence of natural, social, economic and political systems. How embedded social and political structures limit and control the scope of children's participation is brought to the fore, with insights from two studies offering possibilities for adult practices to work with children to circumnavigate barriers to children's participation. In particular, possibilities for innovations in pedagogy in early childhood education for sustainability are discussed. One study explored a living theory of storytelling pedagogy, whilst another study investigated the scope of public pedagogy to cultivate shifts in social perceptions of children and citizenship. Data from both studies demonstrate that children want to be active citizens. They want to do 'real things', which challenges the metanarrative of young children existing in worlds of play, domesticity, and school. The ideas discussed alert educators, policy makers and community workers to the complexities that surround notions of young children's active citizenship and provide guidelines for practice to open doors to the breadth of possibilities for young children's inclusion in civic participation for sustainability.

Introduction

Stephen Sterling states that 'education for sustainability relates to just about everything' (2012) to which I fully agree. The UNESCO (2010) definition of the four interdependent pillars of sustainability provides a useful frame of the interdependent systems that humans exist within: natural/biophysical, economic; social and cultural; and political. We live on planet Earth, which is a complex ecosystem that supports life. To manage co-existence, humans have constructed social and cultural systems. Humans have also constructed economic systems, with the advancement of division of labour, ownership and trading. Political systems are enacted to make policies and decisions about the way social and economic systems use resources in the natural environment. We are all embedded in these interdependent systems. To consolidate recognition that sustainability relates to everything, consider an issue and assess how it fits into these interdependent systems. For example, reduced government funding for public transport services, are evidence of a political system restricting an economic system, the impact of which would see people increasing motor vehicle usage placing greater strains on road infrastructure, and increasing use of natural resources (e.g. petroleum, copper, rubber, iron ore) thereby placing further stress on Earth's biophysical systems.

Sustainability is a problematic term due to its ambiguous nature thus producing somewhat diverse interpretations (Garrard 2007). Interpretations that have most conflict with the call for urgent action to sustain the planet are those that take a 'business as usual' view generally acknowledged as embedded in an individualist view of sustaining personal life styles (Mayall 2000). The reality is that Earth cannot sustain exponential use of resources (made alarmingly visible through ecological footprint calculators),[1] what John De Graaf et al. (2005) refers to as 'affluenza', the Global North's epidemic of overconsumption. Rather than sustaining current practices, we should be reducing consumption and the environmental impacts of everyday decisions. A radical shift from attitudes of complacency, comfort and egocentricism is vital. Humans must take action with consideration for others by questioning how our actions impact other people, animals, living things, ecosystems and future generations.

Children's participation in sustainability

Such a transformational shift can be cultivated through a communitarian approach to citizenship, which views citizenship participation as purposeful group action to create a cohesive, just society and a strong sense of community responsibility (Delanty 2002, Etzioni 1993, Janoski 1998). The human population of Earth currently exceeds 7 billion, yet Earth can only sustain 2 billion people, at an equivalent consumption rate to the average European (World Population Balance 2013). Given such alarming statistics, I see environmental, social, political and economic responsibility as necessitated shared responsibility for all inhabitants of Earth. Communitarian citizenship as shared responsibility provides an approach that can be possible for, and inclusive of, children. Recent theorizing of children's citizenship builds on communitarian understandings of citizenship, making a case for children's agency in the wider community (e.g. Kulynych 2001, Lister 2007, 2008, Phillips 2010a, 2011). This is not to say that communitarian citizenship is an easy fit for children's citizenship. Millei and Imre (2009) argued that the idea of children acting as citizens based on a communitarian version of citizenship is problematic due to their limited access to civic institutions and full participation in political life.

Though the social demarcation between adulthood and childhood is clearly delineated through legislation, regulations, social infrastructures and metanarratives of children as developing, innocent, and protected, there is a growing body of evidence that demonstrates children's desires to be active contributors in society (e.g. Hayward 2012, Holden 2006, Nichols 2007, Phillips 2010a, 2011). Hence, the title for this chapter 'I want to do real things': words spoken by six year old

Denmark (a self-selected pseudonym) during a study (see Phillips 2010b) that investigated how social justice stories might provoke young children's active citizenship. Denmark voiced this rebuke when I (as researcher) had been listening to Denmark and a group of his peers' responses to hearing stories of children's experiences of working in carpet factories in Pakistan, which included suggestions from the children to address child exploitation, such as gathering supplies to build schools. I suggested we could build a model of a school to which Denmark replied, 'I want to do real things' (Week 8 workshop 10/09/2008). This assertion of a genuine desire to engage as a citizen in the wider community alerted me to how young children today are typically ascribed pretend or play situations rather than participation in real life, an observation noted generally by sociologists (e.g. Roche, 1999) and educators (e.g. Nimmo 2008).

Denmark's comment signalled how patronizing my suggestion to build a model school had been for him. Though my suggestion was in alignment with the typical practices of an early years setting, Denmark had the confidence to assert motivation for real action with real impact. The romance of play as advocated by Froebel (1887) and Rousseau (Rousseau 1762/2007) continues to be a core principle of early childhood pedagogy, that shelters children from the 'corrupting influence' of society. An assertion for 'real things' challenges the metanarrative of young children existing in worlds of play, domesticity, and school (Roche 1999). It also emphasizes the limitations young children can experience when opportunities for meaning-making are consistently restricted to the world of play.

Denmark's comment signalled the marginalization that children often experience in regard to their active community participation. Such a marginalized and deficit experience of citizenship is acknowledged by Arvanitakis (2008) in his typology of four citizenship spaces. In the marginalized and deficit experience category, citizens feel they are not listened to or represented by civic institutions; they consider participation pointless because they claim their opinions will not be heard. The other spaces Arvanitakis refers to are: privatization and citizenship deficit (citizens look to the private sector for action as they feel civic institutions do not meet their needs); citizenship surplus – empowered not engaged; and insurgent citizenship – empowered and engaged. Citizenship in this typology is understood as fluid and diversified lived experiences. Denmark's declaration of wishing to perform actions in the real world, demonstrates that he was empowered and engaged (insurgent citizenship) in that moment. He was not satisfied with the conventional experiences offered to children aged five to six years where real world contexts may be played with, drawn, built, talked about, but rarely engaged with directly through participation as communitarian citizens. These six words spoken by Denmark make visible how children's experiences of citizenship (environmental, social, political and economic responsibility) may have moments of ignition for action (insurgence) that then collide with deficit spaces due to social, political, and civic demarcations that restrict children's access to participation and action.

Early childhood education for sustainability can provide children with the opportunity to be active communitarian citizens, and build their capacities to negotiate access to the public sphere (e.g. civic institutions, public spaces, media), especially if early childhood education for sustainability is understood as 'the enactment of transformative, empowering and participative education around sustainability issues, topics and experiences within early education contexts' (Davis 2010: 28). Such an approach to early childhood education enables participation in 'real action' with 'real things', equipping children with capacities, knowledge, skills and dispositions to be active local and global community contributors. This is not about burdening children with the world's problems, but rather cultivating care, empathy, and questioning minds, and empowering children with knowledge and possibilities for action. If children are sheltered from sustainability issues and from active citizenship participation in addressing such issues, children remain in a marginalized and deficit space. In short, young children *are* aware and concerned about many issues pertaining to sustainability, and have the capability to understand the complexities, problem-solve and act for the environment.

Based on the provocations and principles pertaining to children's active participation in sustainability discussed above, the following section discusses pedagogical possibilities for early childhood education for sustainability drawn from two empirical studies. Though the studies involved young primary-school-aged children, the core ideas of the pedagogies discussed have applicability across all sectors of education.

Pedagogical foundations

Attention to discussion of pedagogy, as the art (Eisner 1979) and science of teaching (Simon 1981) and learning, has been a largely neglected component of education discourse in the English-speaking west, as attention to curriculum and assessment dominate (Alexander 2004). An emphasis on pedagogy in education for sustainability has been advocated for and prioritized by key education for sustainability authors (e.g. Grunewald 2003, Sterling 1996, Tilbury 1995). Pedagogy is signalled in Davis' (2010) definition of early childhood education for sustainability through her use of words such as 'transformative', 'empowering' and 'participative education'. These are critical pedagogy elements that support and cultivate communitarian citizenship participation. Critical pedagogues, such as Freire (1974), and Greene (1995), support communitarian citizenship through education for social change by cultivating critical awareness of unjust practices and taking action to address these. For Freire (1974), the awakening of critical awareness, or what he called *conscientização*, was necessary for education to provoke social change. He explained that critical awareness could only occur in 'active dialogical educational programs concerned with social and political responsibility and [that are] prepared to avoid the danger of massification' (p. 19). The concept of massification defines the process in which people remain susceptible to the magical, mythical, illogical, and irrational practices of power by blindly following such practices. To reduce overuse of natural resources, Shove (2003) argues that we need to question and reassess our 'illogical' practices for example taking a shower every day when we know that water is a precious and limited resource. Critical awareness is, thus, necessary for education for sustainability to engage children in critical dialogue that questions blind practices and enables social action to change these practices.

Maxine Greene (1995) also advocated for critical awareness by asking us to treat the world as more than simply 'there', by stirring 'wide-awakeness that leads to imaginative action, and to renewed consciousness of possibility' (p. 43). The sustainability agenda calls for a similar response to the Earth. For Greene, the experience of *wide-awakeness* can occur when teachers teach to arouse vivid, reflective experiential responses by releasing imagination through the arts. She suggests that the motivation to act for social change can, in part, be created by stories. By stories Greene meant the voice of personal perspectives as well as listening to the stories of others in the spaces of dialogue. Greene saw that people could come together through spoken words and action to create something in common. From this understanding, Greene envisioned classrooms that valued multiple perspectives, democratic pluralism, life narratives and ongoing social change. Engagement in education for social change can relate and bind people together in the same way that communitarianism aims to create a cohesive and just society. The theoretical frames of critical pedagogy (or education for social change) provided by Freire and Greene therefore, offer a foundation for pedagogical possibilities for early childhood education for sustainability.

Storytelling pedagogy for sustainability

In 2007, I drew on the above theoretical foundations to inform a social justice storytelling program with a class of children aged five to six years, to explore possibilities for young children's active citizenship. The study was inspired by previous encounters as a storytelling teacher of sharing stories of injustices, with young children who readily expressed concern about the injustices and were motivated to take action. I have come to appreciate storytelling as an aesthetic encounter that can provoke social change as advocated by contemporary thinkers such as Maxine Greene (1995) and Martha Nussbaum (1997), as they both recognize the capacity of story to captivate people to see and feel the perspective of others, which motivates changes in relations, possibilities and actions. A greater fullness of understanding can be achieved through story rather than through information-giving, because it is up to the listener to interpret the content of the story in the way she/he understands it (Benjamin 1955/1999).

The investigated program involved weekly visits to a prep[2] class (for 13 weeks) with whom I led a 90-minute storytelling-based session. I began each session by telling a story, in the tradition of oral storytelling, that is, being performative and interactive. Each story was purposefully crafted to provoke critique of social justice issues and to build knowledge about issues with current relevance for the children (e.g. an endangered local bird, sharing of resources). After the storytelling, the teacher and I co-facilitated a critical discussion of the story, based on a community of inquiry approach (Lipman 1988) in which children and adults dialogue to search out the problematic borders of pertinent issues. Further exploration of the story occurred in small group activities where the children employed modes such as drawing, sculpting/building and dancing. They also developed social actions to redress the injustices highlighted by the stories. These small group activities provided space for aesthetic engagement to help process affective responses (Greene 1995) to the stories, along with opportunities for the children to work on self-selected social actions to redress injustices. Two to three days after each story-telling workshop, I visited the class to gain feedback about that week's storytelling session through separate follow-up conversations with the teacher and a group of five to six self-nominated children. My practice was investigated through a living theory approach to practitioner research (Whitehead and McNiff 2006), by questioning, reflecting and amending practice to form explanations of influence in practice, 'in the learning of others, and in the learning of social formations' (p. 68). In the context of this study, the practice of inquiry was my practice of social justice storytelling with a prep class. The 'learning of others' was the participation of young children as active citizens and the 'learning of social formations' was the exploration of possibilities for young children's active citizenship.

By questioning, reflecting and amending my practice I came to form a 'living theory of social justice storytelling as pedagogy' by identifying key elements of my practice, which, I believe, offer pedagogical possibilities for early childhood education for sustainability. I refer to these elements as motifs, which are understood in storytelling as recurring themes with underlying meanings (MacDonald 1982), such as the wolf motif being equated with danger and destruction. The four motifs that explain social justice storytelling as pedagogy are: story-tailoring, 'walk in the shoes of another', spinning and weaving, and freedom of expression. These motifs are metaphors for how I crafted the stories, and facilitated the workshops as endeavours to provoke and promote young children's active citizenship (see Phillips 2010b). A motif of story-tailoring highlights a need for responsiveness to build community and meaning with listeners, by tailoring subsequent stories based on children's responses to preceding stories; the key issues that the children discussed were further explored in the subsequent story offering a different angle or counter perspective. A motif of 'walk in the shoes of another' encapsulates storytelling qualities that cultivate the lived experience and empathy for another, such as biographic material of tragedy, aesthetic qualities (e.g. eloquent, descriptive language), active participation of children in the story, and opportunities for the children to express opinions and feelings about the stories. A motif of spinning and weaving acknowledges attention to the interconnectivity between stories, issues (environmental, social and cultural, political, economic) and social actions set in motion for children's meaning-making. A motif of freedom of expression emphasizes the requirement for ongoing critical reflection of endeavours to support agency and multiplicity in young children's free expression of contributions, opinions, choices, and decisions. Collectively, these four motifs form a living theory of social justice storytelling as pedagogy that provokes and promotes young children's active citizenship. It is important to note, however, that this living theory was formed through my reflection of practice in a particular time period; it is not fixed, nor replicable; rather it is alive and open to ongoing intersections and experiences with others.

To provide insight to the workings of social justice storytelling as pedagogy, the following is a brief synopsis of the first three storytelling sessions in the study. The first story I told was a metaphoric Thai folktale *The Freedom Bird* (see Livo 1988), selected from my existing repertoire for its humorous yet provocative nature to incite deep thinking about freedom, tolerance, and survival. In this story, the song of the freedom bird annoys a hunter who employs numerous methods such as bagging, chopping, burying and drowning to stop the song, yet the bird continues to sing. Young audiences are readily engaged as they laugh and participate in the 'na-na-nana-na' and raspberry blowing.[3] I read the significance of this story as the injustice of being silenced and the enduring pursuit of freedom, and as such bears relevance to the social and political systems in which the concept of sustainability is embedded. The children's responses mostly focused on the harming of the bird, as exemplified in the following comment from Max.

> Max: Because if we have no animals it will be s-o-o quiet. A little bit Noise
>   … If people kill them and tie them down and so we have to help to
>   save the animals.
>
> (Week 1 workshop 16/07/2007)

Later, Max asked, 'Who protects the animals from the hunters?' (Week 1 conversation 18/07/2007). I explained about recovery programs for endangered animals, and Denmark suggested a plan for creating an enclosure for the birds to protect them, with no gate so the hunters could not get in. The children's attention was on stopping the practice of hunting. They were expressing care and concern for others and motivation to take action to stop the harmful practices of hunters. The children's disapproval of cruel hunting was what I heard as a teacher and storyteller and provided the inspiration for the next story.

To craft the second story, I looked at what aspects of the story were not worn out, that is, they still had presence for the children, to shape another story (motif: story-tailoring). I chose to present an alternative view to hunting, guided by the concept of counter narratives (Lankshear and Peters 1996) and counter stories (Solarzano and Yosso 2001, 2002). It was a worldview in which humans do not aim to dominate nature, but rather are embedded with nature. Keeping balance and harmony with nature (Raley 1998) was fostered through selection of the Cherokee story *Awi Usdi* (see Caduto and Bruchac 1997), in which hunters sought guidance and forgiveness from the spirits of animals.

The children's energy and interest in stopping the hunters continued into this second story, to which I listened and responded, and considered Hart's plea (1997) for adults to support children's participation in matters that interest them within their local environments. According to Hart (1997), a local focus enables children to be involved directly, and in turn deepens their understandings and connections with the issue. This informed my decision to source a story that could motivate citizenship participation in the children's local environment. I realized that if I wanted to present storytelling that provoked meaningful local social action, a story based on an animal that needed support in our local environment was required (motif: spinning and weaving). This was a conscious decision to build real world connections; these needed to be orchestrated because I was not the children's usual class teacher with the breadth of insight and knowledge of the children's social and environmental awareness and interests, or the school and community's sustainability issues.

I sourced information on a critically endangered bird in South-East Queensland, the Coxen's fig-parrot to craft the next story. A bird was chosen, as opposed to any other animal, to follow the children's attention to the vulnerability of a bird first aroused in *The Freedom Bird* story (motif: spinning and weaving). I wrote the story, *The Lonely Coxen's Fig-parrot,* as if colonization and urban development had occurred across the lifetime of just one parrot, so that the children could come to understand the environmental and social changes that have caused drastic reduction in the parrot population, whilst also enabling them to empathize with a central character (motif: walk in the shoes of another). The children did connect and empathize with the fig-parrot, as evidenced by their self-initiated petition to seek greater support for the recovery of the Coxen's fig-parrot population, and the nurturing of fig tree seedlings for reforestation of a local habitat area (see Figure 12.1).

Figure 12.1 Class display of signs children made to plead for support for the recovery of the Coxens' fig-parrot population

Although the children readily became engaged and empowered to take action (insurgent citizenship), enacting their social action initiatives were fraught with barriers. For example, the prep class wanted to walk around the school to collect signatures from students and teachers of other grades; however, the school principal did not support this initiative. When the teacher informed the class, the children decided to collect signatures from their other available networks – their parents and visiting teachers (motif: freedom of expression). (For further discussion of enablers and constrainers of young children's active citizenship from this study see Phillips 2010a.) This is the challenging, yet perhaps the most important work of early childhood education for sustainability: negotiating barriers to children's social, political and civic access. Deficit views of children and social, political, and civic restrictions for children invariably present barriers to enabling child-initiated social actions. To support children's engagement, educators and other supportive adults need to work with children to navigate circumventing these barriers. If we do not, we are at risk of sending messages to children that their ideas and actions do not matter. Once this message is entrenched, it can be difficult to reignite motivation to action into the future.

Such barriers to children's participation have been constructed with a view of children as welfare dependents – incompetent, vulnerable, needing protection and their childhoods primarily determined by adults (Neale 2002). Further, Neale (2004) argues that a view of children as citizens, given their dependence on adults, fits with a definition of citizenship as an entitlement of recognition, respect and participation. Adult insistences on child restrictions to social, political and civic access (or neglect to navigate these restrictions) do not honour children's entitlement to recognition, respect and participation. Neale (2004: 9) warns that

> without due recognition and respect, participation may become an empty exercise, at best a token gesture or, at worst, a manipulative or exploitative exercise. "Real" citizenship, then, involves a search for ways to alter the culture of adult practices and attitudes in order to include children in meaningful ways and to listen and respond to them effectively.

In recent decades, fortunately, early childhood education has shifted from a central view of children as developing, to children as competent and capable social actors. This shift has largely been cultivated by international interest in the teaching and learning practices applied in the schools of Reggio Emilia, Italy (e.g. Cadwell and Rinaldi 2003, Edwards *et al.* 1993, 1998) that are based on a view of children as competent and having rights forged by the work of sociology of childhood (e.g. see Corsaro 2005, James *et al.* 1998). Early childhood educators thus hold a pivotal role in furthering views of children as competent and capable social actors across society through education for sustainability.

Public pedagogy for sustainability

Challenging the constructions of children as vulnerable and incompetent that are embedded in legislation, social infrastructure and civic institutions is a necessary requirement to opening up more avenues for young children's active participation in 'real things' in early childhood education for sustainability. In response to this dilemma, a community cultural development project, 'Walking Neighbourhood' emerged in collaboration with Contact Inc., community cultural development artists. The project was hosted by children who curated and led walks of the local neighbourhoods to provoke shifts in perceptions of children's place in the public sphere. The aim of the project was to counter the metanarrative of children as vulnerable and incompetent, and to cultivate civic learning and changes in roles and perceptions for both children and adults through co-negotiation of public spaces. To date this project has taken place in the Brisbane neighbourhood of Fortitude Valley,[4] Queensland, Australia, the old city region of Chiang Mai, Thailand (as part of revitalization and sustainability initiatives for this region), and the Indigenous community of Bagot as part of the Darwin Festival. There are plans for further Australian and international communities currently being confirmed.

The Fortitude Valley venture of 'Walking Neighbourhood' involved a series of eight workshops with 12 children aged 8–12 years to develop the child-curated walks for a public event of walks across two sessions each on a Saturday and Sunday. Over 330 audience members attended the event including professionals working in community development, urban planning, arts and education sectors. Critical ethnographic analysis of pre and post interviews and workshop recordings identified multiple accounts of civic learning for both the child hosts and adult audience members. The child hosts and their parents commonly spoke of gains in confidence in negotiating public spaces (e.g. sibling participants now independently walk home from school and shop at local shops). For adult audience members, a key theme was how the experience provoked them to engage differently with children, letting go of their adult caregiver behaviours (e.g. managing conversation), seeing the urban space through the eyes of a child, and sharing concepts as equals.

Though this project was not located in a formally recognized early childhood educational setting, there is growing recognition and interest in learning and teaching that takes places outside formal educational settings, often referred to as public pedagogy (Sandlin et al. 2011). Recognition of the learning that takes place in the public sphere investigates the development of identities and social formations in the public sphere, and the relationships that play out between pedagogy, democracy and social action (Sandlin et al. 2010). Public spaces, as informal sites, can cultivate a more subtle, embodied mode of learning that moves 'towards notions of affect, aesthetics and presence' (Sandlin et al. 2011). Walking the streets of Fortitude Valley provided the opportunity to partake in embodied learning, connecting with the real world, which in this case included local businesses, road crossing, pedestrians, street art, street signage and unknown adult audience members. There are multiple stories to tell of the children's experiences in this project, however, the most pertinent point to this chapter is the kind of learning noted by the adult audience members. This was best exemplified by Brian's comment:

> I had a preconception that we'd talk about childish things, whereas actually we talked about shared concepts.

In summary, the experiences challenged adult perceptions of children. Adult audience members explicitly noted how the experience of child-curated walks altered their perceptions of children, hence widening the possibilities for children's future participation and contributions to the public sphere. For example, urban planners realized how consultation with children has been typically neglected in their field and proposed to proactively consult children in future planning decision-making. Further, the project has growing recognition of its potential to make valuable contributions to each of the areas of community development, urban planning, arts and education sectors by opening possibilities for children's active participation, agency, decision-making and voice on what matters to them in their local communities.

What can you do with what remains?

A range of rationales for early childhood education for sustainability resounds throughout this book, but the core lies in acknowledging and exemplifying children as agents of change for sustainability. Children are interested in the world in which they live and want to take part in decision-making and actions that affect them and other inhabitants of Earth. To achieve this requires engagement with the real world. The lesson for early childhood teachers is, first, to critically examine the everyday practices of the early learning setting, for example, use of water, energy, distribution, access and manufacturing factors of the resources used. Important, too, is to actively listen and genuinely respond to children's concerns, ideas and choices and to welcome collective decision-making and action-taking for the sustainability of Earth and its inhabitants.

As this chapter demonstrates, one way to open dialogue about sustainability issues is through story. Teachers can share stories of lived experiences from the perspective of animals, people, plants, water, or planet Earth as a whole. They can take the listener for a walk in the shoes of another, as if the story is happening to them. From such lived experience, empathy sprouts along with unsettledness that only action can appease. Early childhood teachers can work with children on their ideas for taking action. In our practices with children, it is imperative that we honour children's entitlement to recognition, respect and participation and, also, to continually question whether children's opinions, choices and participation are supported and responsively interconnected with those of others. We can cultivate meaning-making like an artisan spinning and weaving stories, ideas, thoughts, questions and actions. We can tailor content/issues to fit the children, their cultures, their communities, their socio-political contexts with attention to recycling content, just like the tailor in the folktale *The Tailor* (see Schimmel, 2002). The tailor wore garments until they were all worn out and then, from close examination of the tattered garment, assessed what was salvageable and crafted a new garment. We need, though, to take care to closely listen and notice what resonates with the children (the remnants) to shape and craft the next story so that a part of the previous story remains. Such remnants sustain continuity of meanings. The real skill in this recycling practice of story-tailoring is calculating which parts to cut off and which to retain. Such practice of recycled tailoring offers a pertinent message for education for sustainability: to look to the resources that are salvageable and craft anew for current and future needs.

As discussed, children have reduced access to social structures (Kulynych 2001), are economically dependent (Lister 2007), and endure a strong emphasis on care and protection in policy and practices (James *et al.* 2008). Thus adults – in whatever their role, be it educator, community worker, parent, politician, artist, policy maker, councillor or ... – should use their greater access to resources to bring young children's initiatives on sustainability issues into the public sphere. We have the capacity to open doors to the breadth of possibilities for young children's inclusion in civic participation for sustainability; to enable children's participation in 'doing real things'.

Notes

1 Ecological footprint calculators measure human consumption of Earth's ecosystems, based on individual everyday living practices.
2 Prep is the first year of schooling in Queensland, Australia.
3 Raspberry blowing is a noise of feigned or real derision made by placing tongue between lips and blowing.
4 An adult entertainment district, commonly perceived as child-unfriendly.

References

Alexander, R. (2004) 'Still no pedagogy? Principle, pragmatism and compliance in primary education'. *Cambridge Journal of Education,* 34: 7–33.
Arvanitakis, J. (2008) 'The heterogeneous citizen: How many of us care about Don Bradman's average?' *MC Journal*, 11. Online. Available: http://journal.media-culture.org.au/index.php/mcjournal/article/viewArticle/27 (accessed 15 March 2009).
Benjamin, W. (1955/1999) *Illuminations.* London: Pimlico.
Caduto, M. J. and Bruchac, J. (1997) *Keepers of the Earth: Native American Stories and Environmental Activities for Children.* Colorado: Fulcrum Publishing.
Cadwell, L. and Rinaldi, C. (2003) *Bringing Learning to Life.* New York: Teachers College Press.
Corsaro, W. (2005) *The Sociology of Childhood.* Thousand Oaks, CA: Pine Forge Press.
Davis, J. M. (2010) 'What is early childhood education for sustainability?' in J. M. Davis (ed.) *Young Children and the Environment: Early Education for Sustainability.* Cambridge: Cambridge University Press, pp. 21–42.
De Graaf, J., Wann, T. and Naylor, T. (2005) *Affluenza: The All Consuming Epidemic.* San Francisco, CA: Berrett-Koehler.

Delanty, G. (2002) 'Communitarianism and citizenship', in E. F. Isin and B. Turner (eds) *Handbook of Citizenship Studies*. London: Sage, pp. 159–74.

Edwards, C., Gandini, L. and Forman, G. (1993) *The Hundred Languages of Children: The Reggio Emilia Approach to Early Childhood Education*. Norwood, NJ: Ablex.

Edwards, C., Gandini, L. and Forman, G. (1998) *The Hundred Languages of Children: The Reggio Emilia Approach – Advanced Reflections*. Greenwich, CT: Ablex.

Eisner, E. W. (1979) *The Educational Imagination*. London: Macmillan.

Etzioni, A. (1993) *The Spirit of Community: Rights, Responsibilities, and the Communitarian Agenda*. New York: Crown.

Freire, P. (1974) *Education for Critical Consciousness*. London: Sheed and Ward.

Froebel, F. (1887) *The Education of Man*. New York: D. Appleton Company.

Garrard, G. (2007) 'Ecocriticism and education for sustainability'. *Pedagogy*, 7: 359–83.

Greene, M. (1995) *Releasing the Imagination: Essays on Education, the Arts, and Social Change*. San Francisco, CA: Jossey-Bass.

Grunewald, D. A. (2003) 'The best of both worlds: A critical pedagogy of place'. *Educational Researcher*, 32: 3–12.

Hart, R. (1997) *Children's Participation: The Theory and Practice of Involving Young Citizens in Community Development and Environmental Care*. London: Earthscan Publications.

Hayward, B. (2012) *Children, Citizenship and Environment*. Abingdon: Routledge.

Holden, C. (2006) 'Concerned citizens: Children and the future'. *Education, Citizenship and Social Justice*, 1, 231–47.

James, A., Curtis, P. and Birch, J. (2008) 'Care and control in the construction of children's citizenship', in A. Invernizzi and J. Williams (eds) *Children and Citizenship*. London: Sage, pp 85–96.

James, A., Jencks, C. and Prout, A. (1998) *Theorizing Childhood*. Oxford: Polity Press.

Janoski, T. (1998) *Citizenship and Civil Society: A Framework of Rights and Obligations in Liberal, Traditional and Social Democratic Regimes*. Cambridge: Cambridge University Press.

Kulynych, J. (2001) 'No playing the public sphere: Democratic theory and the exclusion of children'. *Social Theory and Practice*, 27: 231–65.

Lankshear, C. and Peters, M. (1996) 'Postmodern counternarratives', in H. Giroux, C. Lankshear, P. Mclaren and M. Peters (eds) *Counternarratives: Cultural Studies and Critical Pedagogies in Postmodern Spaces*. New York: Routledge.

Lipman, M. (1988) *Philosophy Goes to School*, Philadelphia: Temple University Press.

Lister, R. (2007) 'Why citizenship: Where, when and how children?' *Theoretical Inquiries in Law*, 8: 693–718.

Lister, R. (2008) 'Unpacking children's citizenship', in A. Invernizzi and J. Williams (eds) *Children and Citizenship*. London: Sage, pp. 9–19.

Livo, N. (ed.) (1988) *Joining In: An Anthology of Audience Participation Stories and How to Tell Them*. Cambridge, MA: Yellow Moon Press.

Macdonald, M. R. (1982) *The Storyteller's Sourcebook: A Subject, Title, and Motif Index to Children's Folklore Collections*. Detroit, MI: Neal-Schuman Publishers in Association with Gale.

Mayall, B. (2000) 'The sociology of childhood in relation to children's rights'. *The International Journal of Children's Rights*, 8: 243–59.

Millei, Z. and Imre, R. (2009) 'The problems with using the concept "citizenship" in early years policy'. *Contemporary Issues in Early Childhood*, 10: 280–90.

Neale, B. (2002) 'Dialogues with children: Children, divorce and citizenship'. *Childhood*, 9, 455–75.

Neale, B. (2004) 'Introduction: Young children's citizenship', in B. Neale (ed.) *Young*

Children's Citizenship: Ideas into Practice. York: Joseph Rowntree Foundation, pp. 6–18.

Nichols, S. (2007) 'Children as citizens: Literacies for social participation'. *Early Years: An International Research Journal,* 27: 119–30.

Nimmo, J. (2008) 'Young children's access to real life: An examination of the growing boundaries between children in child care and adults in the community', *Contemporary Issues in Early Childhood,* 9: 3–13.

Nussbaum, M. (1997) *Cultivating Humanity: A Classical Defense of Reform in Liberal Education,* Cambridge, MA: Harvard University Press.

Phillips, L. (2010a) 'Social justice storytelling and young children's active citizenship'. *Discourse: Studies in the Cultural Politics of Education,* 31: 363–76.

Phillips, L. (2010b) *Young Children's Active Citizenship: Storytelling, Stories and Social Actions.* Doctor of Philosophy monograph, Queensland University of Technology.

Phillips, L. (2011) 'Possibilities and quandaries for young children's active citizenship'. *Early Education and Development,* 22: 778–94.

Raley, K. (1998) 'Maintaining balance: The religious world of the Cherokees'. *Tar Heel Junior Historian,* 37: 2–5.

Roche, J. (1999) 'Children: Rights, participation and citizenship'. *Childhood,* 6: 475–93.

Rousseau, J. (1762/2007) *Emile: Or, on Education.* Sioux Falls, SD: Nu Vision Publications.

Sandlin, J. A., O'Malley, M. P. and Burdick, J. (2011) 'Mapping the complexity of public pedagogy scholarship: 1894–2010'. *Review of Educational Research,* 81: 338–75.

Sandlin, J. A., Schultz, B. D. and Burdick, J. (2010) 'Understanding, mapping, and exploring the terrain of public pedagogy', in J. A. Sandlin, B. D. Schultz and J. Burdick (eds) *Handbook of Public Pedagogy: Education and Learning Beyond Schooling.* New York: Routledge.

Schimmel, N. (2002) 'The tailor', in E. Brody, J. Goldspinner, K. Green, R. Leventhal and J. Porcino (eds) *Spinning Tales, Weaving Hope: Stories, Storytelling and Activities for Peace, Justice and Environment,* 2nd edn. Gabriola Island, Canada: New Society Publishers.

Shove, E. (2003) *Comfort, Cleanliness and Convenience: The Social Organization of Normality (New Technologies/New Cultures).* Oxford: Berg.

Simon, B. (1981) 'Why no pedagogy in England?' in B. Simon and W. Taylor (eds) *Education in the Eighties: The Central Issues.* London: Batsford.

Solarzano, D. G. and Yosso, T. J. (2001) 'Critical race and LatCrit theory and method: Counter storytelling'. *Qualitative Studies in Education,* 14: 471–95.

Solarzano, D. G. and Yosso, T. J. (2002) Critical race methodology: Counter storytelling as an analytical framework for educational research. *Qualitative Inquiry,* 8: 23–44.

Sterling, S. (1996) 'Education in change', in J. Huckle and S. Sterling (eds) *Education for Sustainability.* London: Earthscan.

Sterling, S. (2012) *The Future Fit Framework: An Introductory Guide to Teaching and Learning for Sustainability in HE.* York: The Higher Education Academy.

Tilbury, D. (1995) 'Environmental education for sustainability: Defining the new focus of environmental education in the 1990s'. *Environmental Education Research,* 1: 195–212.

UNESCO (2010) *Teaching and Learning for a Sustainable Future: A multimedia teacher education program.* Online. Available: www.unesco.org/education/tlsf/mods/theme_a/mod04.html?panel=1#top (accessed 28 January 2014).

Whitehead, J. and Mcniff, J. (2006) *Action Research: A Living Theory.* London: Sage.

World Population Balance (2013) *Frequently Asked Questions.* Online. Available: www.worldpopulationbalance.org/faq (accessed 29 January 2013).

Chapter 13

Education for sustainability in Swedish preschools

Stepping forward or out-of-step?

Ingrid Engdahl and Eva Ärlemalm-Hagsér

Abstract

This chapter brings the reader to Sweden where the two authors, both former preschool teachers, now holding doctorates and lecturing and researching at universities, share their understandings of education for sustainability in Swedish preschools. This chapter begins with a review of Swedish research in this emerging field, then offers a discussion about education for sustainability projects in Swedish preschools. To conclude, we present our understandings of high quality education for sustainability (EfS) pedagogy, along with provocations for the field to stimulate deeper thinking about education for sustainability (EfS) in early childhood education (ECE) in Sweden.

Introduction

Throughout the 150 year history of Swedish preschools, a recurrent purpose has been making a contribution towards a better world. One focus has been to improve children's health and well-being, especially through interactions with nature and the outdoors; another has been aimed at addressing broad social issues such as alleviating poverty or dealing with alcohol and drug addictions. More recently, this tradition of seeking to address social issues has included environmental education while, now, questions linked to sustainability are on the national agenda. As Dahlbeck and Tallberg Broman (2011: 202-3, 211) comment, striving to make the world a better place has informed Swedish early childhood education from the outset.

In Sweden, there are some common characteristics between education for sustainability and early childhood education – using children's everyday lives, integrated curriculum approaches, thematic orientated teaching, authentic topics to guide children's learning, and relational and contextualized learning (Arnér 2009, Engdahl and Ärlemalm-Hagsér 2008, Hägglund and Pramling Samuelsson 2009, Pramling Samuelsson and Asplund-Carlsson 2008). There are also some overarching pedagogies that can be used to describe both education for sustainability and early childhood education and care: a holistic approach, experiential learning; values clarification; creative thinking; problem-solving; storytelling; and, inquiry learning (Pramling Samuelsson 2011, UNESCO 2005).

With the above descriptions as starting points, we refer to the research utilized in this chapter as a bricolage, where, as researchers, we have consciously strived for creative use of different theoretical and methodological approaches to understanding early childhood education for sustainability (ECEfS) (Denzin and Lincoln 2005: 4–6), with a result that could be understood as a Nordic 'quilt'. Our purpose is to highlight knowledges from different sources and in various environments, but all related to education for sustainability.

Before beginning our discussion about sustainability and research into this newly emerging field in the Swedish preschools, however, we introduce some background to the Swedish preschool.

All children from the age of one are offered preschool education in Sweden. In 2011, the attendance level for children in preschool was 47 per cent of one year olds, 87 per cent of two year olds, 92 per cent of three year olds, and 94 per cent of four and five year olds (National Agency for Education 2011: 9). In other words, there is a high uptake of preschool education in Sweden. There are three categories of staff in Swedish preschools: 54 per cent are preschool teachers with a 3.5-year Bachelor's degree, 41 per cent are preschool attendants with a vocational qualification, mainly a 3-year Diploma, while 5 per cent of employees have no professional training for working with young children (National Agency for Education 2011: 10). Preschools in Sweden are managed and staffed by their owners, of which around 80 per cent are owned by local municipalities while the rest are run by independent owners, such as private enterprises and parent and/or teacher cooperatives (National Agency for Education 2011). Overall, the field, as in many other countries, presents great diversity that offers considerable challenges in understanding the 'state of play' of a relatively new field such as education for sustainability.

The following questions provide provocations for both early childhood teachers and researchers in relation to education for sustainability in Swedish preschools. They also offer a framework for consideration of current early childhood sustainability research in Sweden.

Q1 How do Swedish preschools address sustainability?
Q2 How does the preschool curriculum support education for sustainability?
Q3 How do Swedish preschool teachers respond to the children's rights agenda on participation in everyday early childhood education practices?
Q4 Are preschool teachers in Sweden stepping forward or are they out-of-step in terms of education for sustainability?

Q1 How do Swedish preschools address sustainability? A review of research

This section begins with an overview of recent discussions and theorizing about education for sustainability in Swedish preschools to highlight contemporary thinking about early childhood education for sustainability.

In Sweden, the present National Curriculum for the Swedish Preschool (National Agency for Education 2011: 3, 7–8) does not explicitly use the concepts education for sustainability or sustainable development (Ärlemalm-Hagsér and Davis forthcoming). While there has been a call by sections of the early childhood education community for this to be strengthened, Dahlbeck and Tallberg Broman (2011: 206–8) and Dahlbeck (2012: 28–39) problematize these calls for education for sustainability and for the child as an actor for creating change. They state, as mentioned earlier, that these ideas are not new, originally emanating from the early preschools where the aim was for children to bring home new knowledge and ideas to families to improve their quality of life and, ultimately, to lead to an improved society.

Further discussion highlights the fact that activities in and about the natural environment involving, for example, outdoor play, gardening and natural science practices, are profoundly rooted in ECE traditions in Sweden (Ärlemalm-Hagsér 2013a: 121–2), beginning with the importation of ideas about the role of nature and the upbringing of children for good citizenship emerging from the enlightenment era. The continuing focus on nature and environment in the current national curriculum (National Agency for Education 2011) is expressed as: 'environmental and nature conservation issues and an ecological approach' (p. 7); and 'a positive belief in the future and acquiring a caring attitude towards nature and the environment' (p. 11). Swedish preschools are also expected to work with democratic values as a foundation for learning and social interactions. Children are described in the curriculum as individuals with competencies – active human beings with experiences, interests, knowledge, skills and understandings that should be the starting-point for everyday activities in early childhood settings. The stated purpose of this orientation is 'to give children opportunities to understand how democracy works, to take part in democratic decision-making and to take responsibility for their actions in the preschool and for the environment, both indoors, outdoors and in the nature' (National Agency for Education 2011: 12).

It has also been noted recently that broad interest in sustainability is evident from the growing number of Swedish preschools currently working with sustainability issues (Ärlemalm-Hagsér and Pramling Samuelsson 2013: 146–7; Sandberg and Ärlemalm-Hagsér 2011: 48). Although Sweden is often seen as a pioneer country working towards sustainable development, however, the number of empirical studies within this field in Swedish early childhood education research has only recently begun to grow (Ärlemalm-Hagsér and Pramling Samuelsson 2013: 148–9, Ärlemalm-Hagsér 2012a: 1–2, 2012b: 1, 2013a: 41–3). Nevertheless, some vibrant discussion within Swedish early childhood educational research is emerging, focusing on how sustainability is relevant content for preschool-aged children. Examples of this discussion are highlighted below.

Hägglund and Pramling Samuelsson (2009: 50–2) argue that children have competencies and skills as well as rights to participate in working for a sustainable world. Sustainability is generally recognized as having three dimensions – social, economic and ecological sustainability – that are closely related to other fields of research, such as peace education, ethics, citizenship and education for democracy. As Hägglund (2011: 252) suggests, ethical perspectives of justice and equality could be used as tools to understand preschool practice and the various intersections could be analysed. For example: *What is inequality or inequity in preschool? How are justice and equality connected to gender, age or ethnicity?* Hägglund (2011: 253–4) argues that such an analysis could create opportunities for challenging taken-for-granted-assumptions in preschool practice and in the longer term contribute to a sustainable future.

Johansson (2009: 90-91) identifies another perspective, discussing the relationship between education for sustainable development and the child as a world citizen. She states that the idea of children as global citizens involves both individualism and solidarity, where caring for oneself, others and the world are fundamental concepts. According to Johansson, ethical and moral values, for example rights, justice and concern for others' well-being, can be negotiated and developed through preschool children's experiences and play. These values are crucial and related to how children perceive themselves and others, as well as being linked to global sustainable development and democracy.

Dahlbeck (2012) also focuses on children's moral development. He argues that there are hidden ethical values about individuality, attitudes and behaviour embedded in some forms of education for sustainability 'according to a fixed scale of "right" and "wrong"/"good" and "evil" in a universal sense' (p. 37). These values, he states, are seldom problematized or challenged in the preschool setting. Dahlbeck (2012: 106–12) advocates for a philosophical approach to education for sustainability where fundamental values and perspectives are critically analysed and related to a specific preschool context in order to develop opportunities for new understandings.

To summarize, in this section we have put forward some recent examples of the kinds of discussions that are beginning to occur around early childhood education for sustainability in Sweden, illustrating growing interest amongst researchers and theorists in discussing, critiquing and problematizing education for sustainability. Of particular note is interest in sustainability as an issue linked to values, ethics, and democracy. These discussions also emphasize that preschool education can address sustainability as part of ongoing Swedish traditions of concern for nature and the environment, drives to improve society and a commitment to building democracy.

Q2 How does the preschool curriculum support education for sustainability?

In this section, we discuss how the Swedish preschool curriculum is understood and supported in Swedish preschools and link this to the implementation of education for sustainability.

An overview of the preschool sector suggests that around 20 per cent of Swedish preschools are involved in education for sustainability through participating in certificated programs such as Green Flag, the Schools for Sustainable Development program (a Swedish government sponsored program), and through association with the 'In Rain and Shine' forest schools (Breiting and Wickenberg 2010: 14-15). These programs have their origins in the 1980s, and are recognized as stressing the importance of environmental education and education for sustainability. A recent study of 30 preschools in five Swedish municipalities revealed that many more preschools beyond these specific programs are engaged in activities connected to environment and sustainability. This indicates considerable interest in sustainability and education for sustainability, but how sustainability is understood and implemented is as yet under-researched.

In one of the few studies that has sought to address these topics, 32 practising preschool attendants who had participated in an in-service education course about sustainability and young children were asked, as part of their assessment, to describe and document their understandings of the concept 'sustainable development' and pedagogical practices linked to sustainable development (Ärlemalm-Hagsér and Sandberg 2011). The findings, using qualitative content analysis, revealed several key themes in these preschool attendants' understandings, notably that sustainable development is about: *fundamental democratic values* (such as respecting children's views, supporting positive social relations, gender equality, and cultural diversity); *nature* (such as outdoor play, natural cycles, seasonal changes, animals and plants, cultivation and gardening); *learning* (such as developmental pedagogies, pedagogical documentation, play, children as co-researchers); and, children's *physical needs* (such as physical play, health promotion, nutrition and food). Taking the analysis further, the researchers identified three ways that further explained these childcare workers understandings of sustainable development: (1) as a holistic concept underpinning all education; (2) primarily as an environmental concern; and (3) as a democratic concern. These different ways of approaching the concept were reflected in different day-to-day practices in the educational programs of the preschools in which these carers worked. Additionally, the data revealed that almost all participants indicated that preschools only minimally addressed questions related to education for sustainability. On a positive note, however, they also indicated that they were working on improving education for sustainability within their settings.

In another study, 18 applications to the Swedish National Agency for Education from preschools seeking a 'Diploma of Excellence in sustainable development' were analysed (Ärlemalm-Hagsér 2012a: 8, 11). The aim was to scrutinize how these applications framed the *content knowledge* about sustainability and whether and how young children were described as being able to actively participate in daily decisions about program activities and if they were looked upon as active participants in change. Content knowledge here refers to different objectives that were highlighted as part of education for sustainability.

Table 13.1 illustrates how the applications for the Diploma of Excellence framed the content knowledge of sustainability. There were two main categories: (1) sustainability as being about preschoolers' sense of self and other people within which there were five sub-categories; and (2) sustainability as being about preschoolers' relationships with place, technologies and materials, with four sub-categories.

Table 13.1 Knowledge content areas that describe sustainability

Preschoolers' sense of self and other people

Sustainability knowledge content areas	Children having influence	Health and wellbeing	Cultural diversity	Gender equality	Social skills
	e.g. everyone should have their say and have influence	e.g. to take care of their health and wellbeing	e.g. expand and enhance understandings among children of other cultures and approaches	e.g. reinforcing children's possibilities of expanding their gender roles	e.g. to be kind to each other

Preschoolers' relationships with place, technologies and materials

Sustainability knowledge content areas	Importance of a physical and close relationship with nature	Knowledge of and respect for nature	Knowledge of garbage management and taking responsibility for their environment	Reuse and be gentle with materials
		e.g. becoming aware of how it all fits together		e.g. how to be careful with materials

Source: Ärlemalm-Hagsér 2012: 8, 11

In the second part of the analysis about children's participation and agency, these concepts were mostly described as 'listening' and 'taking part in', even when the overall rhetoric in the documents indicated that teachers were taking a child rights' perspective to their sustainability work with children. In other words, children were not readily recognized as participants or as agents of change within the preschool programs described in the applications being interrogated.

Nevertheless, these studies demonstrate that working with sustainability issues *is* becoming an important task in the Swedish preschool and, furthermore, that preschools are working with a broad range of sustainability issues across social, economic and environmental dimensions. However, there are few signs of critical thinking about sustainability or challenging taken-for-granted assumptions within preschool practice in relation to children's active participation and agency (Ärlemalm-Hagsér 2013a: 121–2, 2013b: 38–40). Drawing on this groundwork, in the next section we consider the issues of empowerment and citizenship in preschool programs.

Q3 How do Swedish preschool teachers respond to the children's rights agenda on participation in everyday early childhood education practices?

In response to the above question we highlight and discuss some examples of child-orientated approaches as a way of facilitating empowerment and citizenship. As previously mentioned, child participation is a pillar in the Swedish national curriculum (National Agency for Education 2011: 11) and is also an essential aspect of early childhood education for sustainability.

Striving for a child-orientated approach in an early childhood setting means implementing daily pedagogical practice that aligns with children's ways of thinking and communicating (Johansson and Pramling Samuelsson 2003: 4). By attending to children's own ways of expressing their meanings and ideas, early childhood teachers may further develop their understandings of children's perspectives (Arnér 2009: 90, OMEP Sweden 2010: 7–8, Qvarsell 2011: 72–3). However, several Swedish studies show that children's possibilities for influencing the preschool's everyday practice are quite limited (Ärlemalm-Hagsér 2012a: 13–14, Pramling Samuelsson and Sheridan 2003: 80). Here, though, we outline sustainability projects and investigations aimed at addressing this.

Use of documentation to seek and acknowledge children's ideas about sustainability

One strategy utilized to both explore and change this situation was an action research project conducted in 2009 in 10 Swedish early childhood settings where the purpose was to promote children's participation and to identify suitable methods aimed at extending children's participation in the preschool (Engdahl and Ärlemalm-Hagsér 2010: 17). At the start of this study, preschool staff developed their skills and understandings through joint lectures, seminars held between different preschools to share and critique their practices, focus group discussions and tutorials. All together, these activities contributed to transformative changes in the educators, for instance in their views about children and of child participation. For example, it was reported that the preschool teachers and preschool attendants in the study developed their skills in seeing children as capable individuals with competencies to participate in decision-making and able to make their own choices in play and other activities (Engdahl and Ärlemalm-Hagsér 2010: 18). Learning to listen to children's voices, and learning to respect their ideas, thoughts and interests, can facilitate interactions and communications for high quality early childhood education (Pramling Samuelsson and Asplund-Carlsson 2008: 633).

The Swedish national preschool curriculum (National Agency for Education 2011: 15) states the importance of pedagogical documentation as a means for making children's learning processes visible. Pedagogical documentation has been shown to promote teachers' critical thinking, enhance teachers' and preschool attendants' professional awareness and their abilities to create new teaching practices. The case studies presented below – all part of this larger project – include pedagogical documentation drawn from interviews, walk-and-talk approaches, observations, tape recordings and photographs taken in the preschool settings.

In 2009, the Swedish national committee of OMEP[1] (Organisation Mondiale pour l'Éducation Préscolaire) initiated a world project on education for sustainable development. The overall aims of the project were to collect information about young children's thoughts, comments and understandings of education for sustainability (Engdahl and Rabušicová 2010: 3), and to encourage local preschool initiatives.

Here, we discuss the first part of this international project. In 2009–2010, teachers were asked to conduct informal interviews with children employing a drawing of children cleaning the Earth as a stimulus (see Figure 13.1). OMEP members (mainly early childhood teachers) in 28 countries from all regions of the world interviewed 9,142 children aged between two and eight years. The participating countries from Europe in particular were Bulgaria, the Czech Republic, Denmark, Finland, Greece, France, Ireland, Norway, Poland, Russia, Slovakia, Sweden, Turkey and the United Kingdom (Engdahl and Rabušicová 2011: 163). Interview and analysis guides were sent out to all the participants.

Specifically in the Swedish part of this case study, the children interviewed interpreted the drawing in a variety of ways. Most commonly, in answer to the question 'What are the children doing?' children identified that the children in the picture

Figure 13.1 Child interviews were conducted employing this drawing by Anna-Karin Engström as a stimulus for conversations

were cleaning the Earth because it was dirty, though some children thought that the children were painting the Earth. The reasons cited to explain why the children were cleaning or painting were mainly aesthetic or about feelings: 'to make the Earth beautiful and shining' for better health; 'the children want everybody to be healthy and everybody has happy life'; or to address a problem with garbage or pollution, namely 'the rubbish made me feel sad, I didn't want it to be there' (Engdahl and Rabušicová 2011: 167–70).

As expected, the term, 'sustainable development' is not a concept that young Swedish children have necessarily heard before. One eight year old, however, did show that she was aware of the term and had an understanding of its meaning: 'The Earth shall last longer, if the sun becomes too strong, it will be too hot for the people on Earth' (Ärlemalm-Hagsér 2010: 5). Overall, for Sweden, the results showed that just a few of the children who were interviewed were able to express a sense of environmental awareness with only one child mentioning that his father had spoken about environmental issues.

The responses of the Swedish children were similar to those of children in other countries and, as expected, most reports from around the world identified that the children did not recognize the concept of sustainable development. In some countries, the term does not even exist with no direct translation into the local language. However, many interviewers were surprised by the depth of knowledge the children demonstrated about the state of the Earth. The children had ideas about environmental issues and human responsibilities for the Earth, and ideas about actions to address unsustainable practices: 'We should clean the earth, because on the earth live the animals, there are the plants and we live there' (Engdahl and Rabušicová 2011: 169). It was noted by those participating in the project that the technique of interviewing children by using a drawing in conjunction with open-ended questions was a research method well received by both children and teachers (pp. 171–5) and we believe it offers a useful tool for further investigations of education for sustainability within early childhood education.

Respecting children's rights to be involved

A second part of the OMEP project – ESD[2] in practice – involved 413 preschools across the world. Participants in this project were asked to work with children around seven concepts linked to education for sustainability – Respect, Reflect and Rethink (related to socio-cultural dimensions of sustainability), Reuse and Reduce (highlighting environmental aspects), and Recycle and Redistribute (drawing on economic perspectives).

One of the Swedish case studies was implemented in 2011 in a Green Flag preschool in the centre of Stockholm (Engdahl et al. 2012: 12–15). The teacher was asked to document the pedagogical processes utilized in the case that ran over a number of weeks. This documentation included a teacher's reflective diary, records of children's conversations, photographs and interviews with professional waste collectors and gardeners. Researchers then analysed the data to discover how the teacher interpreted education for sustainability and implemented it in practice. Below is a segment of the teacher's data with the researchers' analytical comments.

The teacher's story

The preschool's general theme for the semester was sorting garbage as proposed by the Green Flag Program. To commence, the teachers and children, aged 2–4 years, brainstormed what they already knew about the topic, then they identified a range of activities to support learning. As an ongoing activity, the children regularly visited a local recycling station, as illustrated in Figure 13.2 below.

Following is an edited account of the Using Again project that arose from the sorting garbage theme as told by Camilla the preschool teacher:

> One day on the way to the station, the children started to play with the empty milk cartons assembled in the preschool kitchen, although the walk originally was planned to recycle the cartons. What resulted was that these were carried back to the preschool for creative play, thus reused. This initiated a focus for the class project which the children named 'Using Again'. As the project proceeded, children's questions arose, for example: *How can we reuse our garbage? How can we cooperate with our neighbours to have them recycle garbage rather than throwing it in the streets?* This was a project driven by the children, their questions, and their investigations.
>
> Using garbage to create something new was exciting and the children worked many hours to create new things with different types of garbage. One

Figure 13.2 Children visiting a local station for recycling paper, glass, plastic, etc.

day, the children asked about what happened to the garbage: *Where does it go?* and *How can we find out what happens to the waste?* After discussion, we decided to talk to someone who could give us some answers – the man who collects our preschool's garbage, who the children called 'the waste collector'. We decided to approach one of the waste collectors when he collected the garbage in the local preschool area.

Following is the transcript of the teacher's and children's conversation about rubbish with the waste collector:

Camilla (preschool teacher):	Hi! Can we ask you a few questions?
Waste collector:	Yes, just ask me.
Loraine:	Is it heavy with the cart?
Waste collector:	Yes, a little, but I'm strong, yes.
Thomas:	What do you do with the trash?
Waste collector:	We load the trash in the truck, and then we go off to the dump.
Thomas:	What happens to the garbage then? At my country house, we burn leaves …
Waste collector:	You know a lot about it, but I load more than leaves. We bring plastic, food waste, metal and tons of other garbage …
Nanny:	What happens then? Do you save them?
Waste collector:	No, we sort them. Some things go to become other things … and some we take to another place.
Vanne:	How?
Waste collector:	You make bottles, cartons, aluminium, and lots of new things … The children turned quiet.
Waste collector:	You know, have you seen commercials for returning bottles and cans, 'Panta mera' (Cash in more)?
Vanne:	Yes. I have seen 'Panta mera'.
Waste collector:	Exactly, so you use the bottles again, but you have to sort, clean and prepare them carefully.
Lorraine:	Yeah, but how do you do that?
Waste collector:	I collect the garbage and others do the sorting and send it on to the other places for preparation. We kind of use the material again for new things that we then can use again. The children looked questioning …
Thomas:	Like we do here when we build new toys out of the trash.
Waste collector:	Maybe, but now I have to go.

After this interview, the children discussed the content and reflected further. They were very excited about what happened to the garbage after the garbage truck left the waste disposal site. They wanted to know what the waste collector meant by 'they make new things out of the garbage'. *What kind of things? How?* The children concentrated on the idea of following the garbage truck, to see what happened to the garbage.

Nanny: We can stay outside the preschool and follow the garbage truck.
Martin: It can drive really fast. Should we run or?
Thomas: We can take bikes ... Yes, that should work ...

The children were confident that we could follow the garbage truck to the waste disposal site. We tried it out the next Thursday, when the garbage truck came. We waited and we followed on our bicycles. We did so for a full hour, but then the garbage truck drove away and we could not keep up. Tired, we returned to the preschool. We needed a new plan!

As the children's interest grew, they came up with many more questions such as how paper and cartons are recycled into new things. These topics, too, were explored. So, while the initial goal for the learning was about seeking answers to the children's questions about sorting garbage, quite soon the children also wanted to play with the materials to construct and create new items. The creative construction and play became a source of inspiration for children, teachers and parents. Deeper understandings of the recycling process and respect for the complex process began to grow. Shared thinking about this sustainability issue became evident (Ärlemalm-Hagsér and Pramling Samuelsson 2013: 157–9, Engdahl and Ärlemalm-Hagsér 2008: 118–20).

Parents also informed the teacher that the children's learning was being transferred beyond the preschool – they were sorting garbage at home. The children also kept reminding and encouraging the adults to produce less garbage, reuse and recycle, and to take care of the environment and the neighbourhood. The adults had to rethink their practices in order to meet the challenges put to them by the children. The adults became responsive to the children's observations and suggestions, and the children continued to develop many new thoughts about the environment. The adults also learnt that young children's learning and actions can make a difference.

Conclusion

In this chapter, we began with three questions or provocations about early childhood education and education for sustainability. In responding to Question 1, we provided a review of some of the current thinking about early childhood education for sustainability in Sweden which suggested that education for sustainability is not so much a new trend, but an extension of earlier environmental and social traditions aimed at improving Swedish citizens' quality of life. We also raised the connection between education for sustainability and children as global citizens, and other moral issues related to democracy. These discussions illustrate the beginnings of robust discussion and critique about the place and purpose of early childhood education for sustainability in Sweden.

Regarding Question 2, we discussed recent research that illustrated how preschool teachers are engaging with education for sustainability, but which illustrates that there are significant gaps in their understandings of key concepts. This has implications for how education for sustainability is enacted, often with a lack of child-orientated perspectives and few examples of child-led actions of change.

With respect to Question 3, we outlined two OMEP research projects related to early childhood education for sustainability. The first of these showed that young children can demonstrate sophisticated ideas about sustainability matters. If adults make an effort to ask and use suitable techniques, for example non-verbal prompts such as drawings, then children's ideas can be brought to light. In the second project, we provided an account of how preschoolers, aged 2–4 years, and their teacher explored recycling. This account revealed the extensive learning that the children were involved in, and how this also impacted on the thinking and practices of their parents. Together, these two projects illustrate that quality practice and interesting research in early childhood education for sustainability is beginning to occur in Sweden. Overall, we have reported on a number of projects and case studies that cover a broad spectrum of theoretical and methodological approaches – a bricolage. This now takes us to our final, synthesizing question.

Q4 Are preschool teachers in Sweden stepping forward or are they out-of-step in terms of education for sustainability?

Here, we link our previous discussions to the rhetoric common in Swedish society that implies that Sweden is a model state in sustainability practice. As previously indicated, many preschools in Sweden have signed up to programs linked to sustainability and environmental education (Ärlemalm-Hagsér 2013a: 38–40). However, it seems that teachers still do not fully acknowledge and act upon a view of children as active citizens, capable of being collaboratively involved in the common task of reorientating society towards a sustainable future.

So, are Swedish preschool teachers stepping forward for education for sustainability or are they out-of-step? Perhaps it is both. On the one hand, Swedish teachers firmly identify with a connectedness to nature and a respect for the social and economic priorities in a welfare state; on the other, there seems to be a lack of critical political awareness amongst many teachers today. The principles of equity and democracy as fundamental values, as well as necessary for forming a society based on active citizenship, seem to be taken for granted.

Our subsequent questions are:

- Why don't more, or all, early childhood educators and researchers address these principles?
- How is it that researchers still underestimate children's agency when designing their studies?
- Why don't educators regularly use children's questions and curiosities as legitimate starting points for their teaching, for preschool projects?

As has been discussed, early education traditions in Sweden promote improved living conditions for children and the society at large. Perhaps if curriculum developers, teacher educators and preschool teachers begin to see early childhood education for sustainability as a continuation of this tradition, they will be more inclined to engage. Instead of seeing it as something new, education for sustainability simply becomes part of the ongoing societal project of contemporary early childhood education. The same argument can be used in support of nature education, resource conservation, and child participation/democracy. These are aspects of Swedish preschool culture; giving them increased emphasis, within a sustainability framework, is not such a significant conceptual and/or pedagogical leap. Teachers could serve as the bridge between children and learning for sustainability. The research projects described here – where children's ideas and understandings were listened to and children were encouraged to 'make a difference' – highlight how teachers in early childhood settings can begin to engage effectively with education for sustainability.

As previously stated, children have a right to participate in the decision-making in their daily lives. It is now time to recognize that children should be given priority in decision-making and creativity; they are the inhabitants of the twenty-first century, after all. From where are new ideas, solutions and discoveries to come? From the generation who is responsible for the crisis situation currently on Earth, or, from children and young people? In conclusion, we are certain that how sustainability is currently addressed within early childhood pedagogical practice needs to be challenged and questioned in order to promote transformative change in this era of uncertainty and instability. One clear option is to acknowledge children's thoughts, ideas and initiatives and to create opportunities for shared critical thinking (Ärlemalm-Hagsér 2013: 122). It is time for adults to favour the capabilities of children. This is especially so within early childhood education where there are real and exciting opportunities for children to learn to make a difference to both current and future sustainability options.

Notes

1   OMEP, World Organization for Early Childhood Education, is an international, non-governmental and non-profit organization concerned with early childhood education and care (ECEC) for children from birth to eight years. OMEP is established in over 73 countries and is represented at meetings of UNESCO, UNICEF, and other international organizations.

2   In Sweden, the term 'Education for Sustainable Development' (ESD) is widely used in policy and politics, and also in research (Bretings and Wickenberg, 2011, Öhman, 2011). The OMEP project was started in 2009, and also uses ESD. In this chapter, we use the term 'Education for Sustainability' (EfS) and Early Childhood Education for Sustainability (ECEfS), in line with the critique of equating development with economic growth (Knutsson 2011).

References

Ärlemalm-Hagsér, E. (2010) *National Report ESD Project Sweden.* Stockholm: OMEP Sweden.

Ärlemalm-Hagsér, E. (2012a) 'Lärande för hållbar utveckling i förskolan – Kunskapsinnehåll, delaktighet och aktörskap kommunicerat i text (Education for sustainable development: Knowledge content, participation and agency)'. *Nordisk barnehageforskning,* 5(2): 1–21.

Ärlemalm-Hagsér, E. (2012b) 'Minds on Earth hour – a theme for sustainability in Swedish Early Childhood Education'. *Early Child Development and Care,* 1–14, iFirst Article.

Ärlemalm-Hagsér, E. (2013a) *'An Interest in the Best for the World'? Education for Sustainability in the Swedish Preschool* (doctoral thesis, Gothenburg Studies in Educational Sciences 335). Gothenburg: Acta Universitatis Gothoburgensis.

Ärlemalm-Hagsér, E. (2013b) 'Respect for nature: A prescription for developing environmental awareness in preschool'. *Center for Educational Policy Studies Journal,* 3(1): 25–44.

Ärlemalm-Hagsér, E. and Sandberg, A. (2011) 'Sustainable development in early childhood education: In-service students' comprehension of SD'. *Environmental Education Research Journal,* 17(2), 187–200.

Ärlemalm-Hagsér, E. and Pramling Samuelsson, I. (2013) 'Kulturer av hållbarhet – förskolebarns aktörskap och meningsskapande (Cultures for sustainability: preschool children's agency and meaning-making)'', in I. Tallberg Broman and I. Pramling Samuelsson (eds), *Barndom, Lärande och Ämnesdidaktik.* Lund: Studentlitteratur, pp. 157–9.

Ärlemalm-Hagsér, E. and Davis, J. (forthcoming) 'Examining the rhetoric: A comparison of how sustainability and young children's participation and agency are framed in Australian and Swedish early childhood education curricula'. *Contemporary Issues in Early Childhood.*

Arnér, E. (2009) *Barns inflytande i förskolan: En fråga om demokrati* (Children's participation in preschool: A question about democracy). Lund: Studentlitteratur.

Breiting, S. and Wickenberg, P. (2010) 'The progressive development of environmental education in Sweden and Denmark'. *Environmental Education Research,* 16(1): 9–37.

Dahlbeck, J. (2012) *On Childhood and the Good Will. Thoughts on Ethics and Early Childhood Education* (doctoral Thesis, Malmö Studies in Educational Sciences 65). Lund: Lund University.

Dahlbeck, J. and Tallberg Broman, I. (2011) 'Ett bättre samhälle genom pedagogik: högre värden och barnet som budbärare (A better society through education: values and the child as a messenger)', in P. Williams and S. Sheridan (eds), *Barns lärande i ett livslångt perspektiv.* Stockholm: Liber, pp. 202–14.

Denzin, N.K. and Lincoln, Y.S. (2005) *The Sage Handbook of Qualitative Research.* London: Sage.

Engdahl, I. and Ärlemalm-Hagsér, E. (2008) 'Swedish preschool children show interest and are involved in the future of the world', in I. Pramling Samuelsson and Y. Kaga (eds) *The Contribution of Early Childhood Education to a Sustainable Society.* Paris, UNESCO, pp. 116–21.

Engdahl, I. and Ärlemalm-Hagsér, E. (2010) *Barns delaktighet i det fysiska rummet: Svenska OMEP:s utvecklingsprojekt med stöd av Allmänna arvsfonden 2007–2010* (Child participation outdoors in the Swedish preschool: A development project from OMEP Sweden supported by the Swedish Inheritage Fund 2007–2009). Stockholm: OMEP. Online. Available: www.omep.org.se (accessed 31 January 2013).

Engdahl, I. and Rabušicová, M. (2010) *Children's voices about the state of the Earth and sustainable development* (A report for the OMEP World Assembly and World Congress on the OMEP World Project on Education for Sustainable Development 2009–2010). Stockholm: OMEP. Online. Available: www.omep.org.gu.se (accessed 31 January 2013).

Engdahl, I. and Rabušicová, M. (2011) 'Children's voices about the state of the Earth'. *International Journal of Early Childhood*, 43(2): 153–76.

Engdahl, I., Karlsson, B., Hellman, A. and Ärlemalm-Hagsér, E. (2012) *Lärande för hållbar utveckling – är det någonting för förskolan eller?* (Education for sustainable development: Something for the preschool, or not?) Online. Available: www.omep.org.se (accessed 31 January 2013).

Hägglund, S. (2011) *Förskolebarnet och rätten till lärande för hållbar utveckling: Några tankar om förutsättningar, möjligheter och utmaningar* (Preschool children and the right to education for sustainable development. Some thoughts about conditions, possibilities and challenges). In P. Williams and S. Sheridan, (eds), *Barns lärande i ett livslångt perspektiv*. Stockholm: Liber, pp. 245–57.

Hägglund, S. and Pramling Samuelsson, I. (2009) 'Early childhood education and learning for sustainable development and citizenship'. *International Journal of Early Childhood*, 41(2): 49–63.

Johansson, E. (2009) 'The preschool child of today – the world citizen tomorrow?' *International Journal of Early Childhood*, 41(2): 79–95.

Johansson, E. and Pramling Samuelsson, I. (2003) 'Barns perspektiv och barnperspektiv i pedagogisk forskning och praxis [Children's perspectives and child perspective; in Swedish]', in E. Johansson and I. Pramling Samuelsson (eds), Barns perspektiv och barnperspektiv. Temanummer av *Pedagogisk Forskning i Sverige* 1–2: 1–5.

National Agency for Education (2011a) *Curriculum for the Preschool, Lpfö 98*. Stockholm. Sweden: The Swedish National Agency for Education. Online. Available: www.skolverket.se/publikationer?id=2704 (accessed 31 January 2013).

National Agency for Education (2011b) *Facts and Figures 2011 Preschool Activities, School-age Childcare, Schools and Adult Education in Sweden* (Summary of Report 363). Stockholm. Sweden: The Swedish National Agency for Education. Online. Available: www.skolverket.se/publikationer?id=2768 (accessed 31 January 2013).

OMEP Sweden (2010) *Child Participation Outdoors in the Swedish Preschool. A Development Project from OMEP Sweden supported by the Swedish Inheritage Fund 2007–2009*. Stockholm: OMEP. Online. Available: www.omep.org.se (accessed 31 January 2013).

Pramling Samuelsson, I. (2011) 'Why we should begin early with ESD: The role of Early Childhood Education'. *International Journal of Early Childhood*, 43(2): 103–18.

Pramling Samuelsson, I. and Sheridan, S. (2003) 'Delaktighet som värdering och pedagogik (Participation as value and pedagogy)'. *Pedagogisk Forskning i Sverige*, 8(1–2): 74–88.

Pramling Samuelsson, I. and Asplund-Carlsson, M. (2008) 'The playing learning child: towards a pedagogy of early childhood'. *Scandinavian Journal of Educational Research*, 52(6): 623–41.

Qvarsell, B. (2011) 'Demokrati som möjlighet i små barns liv och verksamhet (Democracy as a possibility in young children's life and activities)'. *Nordisk barnehageforskning*, 4(2): 65–74.

Sandberg, A. and Ärlemalm-Hagsér, E. (2011) 'The Swedish National Curriculum – lay and learning with the fundamental values in focus'. *Australasian Journal of Early Childhood*, 36(1): 44–50.

UNESCO (2005) *United Nation's Decade of Education for Sustainable Development*. Online. Available: http://portal.unesco.org/education (accessed 31 January 2013).

Chapter 14

Innovative approaches to early childhood education for sustainability in England

Case studies from the field

Robert Barratt, Elisabeth Barratt-Hacking, and Pat Black

Abstract

Although there are innovative local examples of projects and programmes associated with ECEfS in England there has been no sustained policy commitment to this important aspect of young children's educational experience. The authors argue that natural play, that is, free play in natural environments, provides the foundations for ECEfS using the metaphor, nature as teacher. Despite England's rich heritage of providing outdoor nature experience for young children, current early years policy negates opportunities to develop natural play and children's engagement with nature. This combined with reduced experience of the natural world denies children essential developmental experiences and the underpinnings of EfS.

Four case studies of early years settings are used to illustrate ECEfS approaches in England. An analysis of documentation and external inspection reports from the settings found four distinctive approaches to EfS including: (1) sustained authentic outdoor play; (2) place-based learning; (3) free play and risk-taking in the outdoors; and (4) participation in developing a sustainable school curriculum. It is suggested that staff interest and enthusiasm, children's needs, the local context and external agencies influence the approach to ECEfS adopted by some settings. For each case study there is evidence of positive impact of EfS on children's learning. The authors propose that future ECEfS learning opportunities should incorporate natural play, familiar and unfamiliar environments, participation and models of sustainable living.

Introduction

This chapter sets out to critique the extent to which the education policy context in England for the Early Years Foundation Stage (birth–5 years) and the National Curriculum for Key Stage 1 (5–7 year olds) (Box 14.1) is able to support opportunities for early childhood education for sustainability (ECEfS). It is argued that in recent years there has been a growing international focus on the importance of ECEfS and 'the value of starting early with Education for Sustainability ... even if the practice and research is yet to fully emerge' (Davis 2009: 228). In England, this trend has led to locally inspired ECEfS projects, but there has not been a sustained

Box 14.1 A summary of early years provision in England

Early years education up to the age of four years takes place in a range of different types of pre-school provision including playgroups, local authority and private nurseries, nursery classes in schools, workplace nurseries, child and family centres run by social work departments and community childcare centres. This varies by region 'reflecting Local Authority funding and geographical conditions (i.e. urban/rural and local access to centres)' (Sylva *et al.* 2004: 2). Schools (maintained and independent) provide the remainder of early years education ('reception classes' – four to five year olds) and Key Stage 1 education (five to seven year olds).

national policy commitment to this essential phase and dimension of education. On the contrary, it is argued here that the current standards-driven agenda and the framing of the natural world by a readiness for school agenda is undervaluing the importance of children's access to the natural world and their opportunities to learn and develop relationships (early values) with their environments through natural play. We define natural play as free play experience in the natural environment where the environment stimulates the child to think and behave, as opposed to structured play where adults direct the activity. We consider natural play as the essential foundation for education for sustainability (EfS) in the early years. From this standpoint, we argue that the standards and readiness agendas leave little room for considering, with children themselves, how to sustain an environment.

The chapter begins by providing a brief overview of the origins of early years education in England and the opportunities this affords for natural play and education for sustainability. Four case study settings are presented which illustrate the development of distinctive, innovative and effective ECEfS curricula that provide children with access and opportunity to engage in, and learn through, natural world experiences. The chapter concludes by proposing ways in which the early years curriculum in England could be enhanced to secure the essential educational experiences needed to support children's natural engagement with matters to do with environmental sustainability. We use the term natural engagement to illustrate the opportunities afforded to children to access and engage with the natural environment, for example, wild places, urban green spaces or gardens.

Early years education: the foundations for Education for Sustainability (EfS)

Outdoor play

The pioneers of early years education in England recognized the importance of outdoor play, in the fresh air, for promoting good health and development; this linked with the open air nurseries and schools movement which started in the early 1900s and continued to the middle of the century (Cruikshank 1977). The open air schools movement was a public health response to urbanization, industrialization and health issues. At this time the urban poor were living in slum conditions and also suffering from air pollution with consequent effects on children's health in cities. This and other concerns about children's health, such as malnutrition, asthma and eczema led to the adoption of the open air approach, originating in Germany, which combined educational architecture to maximize fresh air alongside the provision of health education through modelling the importance of healthy lives (Hille 2011). Buildings and classrooms were designed to have direct access to outdoor areas with open sides throughout the year. Children played and learned outside and even slept outside during rest times. One of the early open air schools was established in Peckham in 1914 by the sisters and educationalists, Margaret and Rachel McMillan. These educationalists were 'strong advocates of fresh air and play in the outdoor environment' (Santer *et al.* 2007: 8). In 1928, educationalist Susan Isaacs supported the establishment of the Chelsea Open Air Nursery school, which still functions today and is a case study in this chapter.

The emphasis on the outdoors in early years education continued with the forest schools movement that had developed in Sweden and Denmark. This rich legacy of open air education in England together with our 'outstanding diversity of wooded habitats' (Plantlife 2011: 5) which are a 'familiar part of the landscape' (p. 6) may have influenced our interest in the forest school concept. Forest schools began to emerge in the mid-1990s supported by the UK Forestry Commission; by 2006 there were 100 in England (O'Brien and Murray 2006). The achievement of this initiative in England and the United Kingdom more widely has been significant in encouraging other countries to implement forest schools. The research associated with forest schools has demonstrated the benefits of outdoor learning (O'Brien and Murray 2006) and the forest school philosophy is having a widespread impact on early years philosophy and provision in England (Knight 2009; Maynard 2007).

Today, almost all early years settings provide outdoor spaces for activity and learning. Further, there is a policy requirement for all nurseries to provide an outdoor experience every day, weather permitting; however, the policy emphasis appears to focus more on physical activity than engagement with the natural environment (DfE 2012) (Box 14.1). Play is recognized as so important to a child's well-being and development that the right to play is made explicit in the United Nations Convention on the Rights of the Child (UNICEF 1989). The centrality of both indoor and outdoor play in early years learning and development is 'among one of the fundamental continuities in early years ... Play is an almost hallowed concept for teachers of young children' (British Educational Research Association Early Years Special Interest Group (BERA) 2003: 13).

The concept of play in England tends to be associated with child–centred learning and hands-on experience (Kwon 2002). Recently, however, play has become a contested concept, both in definition and value; for example, whether to employ child- or teacher-initiated play (free play or structured play) and how play can address educational objectives and outcomes. As such, there is no agreed 'pedagogy of play' and 'play in practice is deeply problematic' (BERA Early Years Special Interest Group 2003: 14). This may reflect, first, the variation in professional development opportunities and qualifications held by early years professionals (Siraj-Blatchford *et al.* 2002) and second, the differing curriculum requirements within the early years age range.

> 'During the Foundation Stage (3–5 year olds), they have many opportunities to learn outside through play … At age 5 or 6, their educational experience becomes guided by the National Curriculum. Opportunities to learn experientially outside become restricted as increasingly teacher-directed lessons focus on prescribed learning outcomes'.
>
> (Waite *et al.* 2011: 2)

Experience of the natural world

The value of free outdoor play for child development and learning is widely accepted, not least because 'the outdoor environment provides unique opportunities for children to relive their experiences through movement, and learn about the natural world' (Santer *et al.* 2007: 41; see also Barratt-Hacking *et al.* 2007). Natural play, free choice activity, and other experiences in the natural environment such as growing plants, making dens, and dam building on streams provide opportunities for children to act independently in the environment, modify it and develop understandings, skills and values. Barratt *et al.* (2011) discuss their research into the impact of sustained experience of growing food in schools; they found it promoted 'a pro-sustainability disposition: an ethos of care towards the Earth and its peoples' (p. 36). In one example in an infant school, a parent helper recalls the impact on the children of a broad bean crop being unexpectedly destroyed by caterpillars. At first the children are upset, but then they become fascinated, 'my five year old … he'd be telling you all about that caterpillar … It was huge and … obviously caterpillars are green, the same colour of the leaf … (so) you can't see them!' (Parent interview, ibid.: 32). This illustrates how, through sustained nature-based experiences, children can get to know and develop a relationship with the natural world, thus providing foundational experiences for EfS.

Yet there is evidence that children's experience of the natural environment is reducing in terms of time spent outdoors and the quality of children's experience. We have reported previously on this trend (Barratt-Hacking *et al.* 2007) including reasons – such as parental anxiety, increased traffic, children's growing engagement with virtual worlds and the commodification of childhood and play – as adversely affecting children's experiences of the outdoor environment. Underlying this trend is the destruction or modification of urban and other habitats, for example, through renovation, infill or new developments, so reducing natural diversity. England's flowering plants, for example, are reported to be decreasing by 60 per cent per year (RSPB 2013). On the local scale, Pyle (2010) suggests this results in the 'extinction of experience' (p. 157) with reduced opportunities for children to experience wildlife and specific species in their locality. Further, a recent study in England drawing on 43,000 interviews with families, including those with young children, has identified different behaviours by social groups in respect of the natural environment (Burt, Hunt, Rickinson, Andrews and Stewart, in press reporting on MENE project data).[1] Data analysis revealed that, amongst people with children in their household, ethnicity and socio-economic group were the demographic variables that had most influence on visit frequency; with members of the Black, Asian and minority ethnic population and people in the lowest socio-economic groups being the least likely to make frequent visits, compared to the rest of the population. A small qualitative investigation to explore these quantitative findings observed that aspirations for visits to the natural environment may be different between adults and children. Many parents seek leisure experiences which provide a product that has been 'commoditized' and which will keep children occupied. This contrasted with the views of some of the children interviewed who perceived a visit to the outdoors as an opportunity for an unstructured experience to 'explore a less familiar environment, such as the beach, farmland or woodland, without necessarily knowing what might lie in store'. These findings suggest that young children may prefer unstructured, natural play, although this may not be available to them. Concerns about the loss of children's independent outdoor experience are shared by a range of researchers, practitioners and policymakers in England, 'children today have fewer opportunities for outdoor play than their predecessors. … In play children seek out risks … Adult caution and fear reduce children's opportunities to set themselves challenges and take risks' (Santer et al. 2007: xiii).

Early years' policy: opportunities for natural play and engagement

Given these trends, it is clear that early years education in England has an important responsibility to ensure all children, no matter what their background, have regular opportunities for natural play. The evidence suggests that children living and attending educational provision in areas of the greatest social and urban deprivation have the most to gain from natural play opportunities. This is not only because of the dearth of local natural habitats, but also because these are the groups that are least likely to have opportunities for regular natural play. There seems, however, to be some misalignment of policies with respect to these opportunities. On the one hand, the Natural Environment White Paper (2011) promotes outdoor experience: 'as well as having important health benefits, access to the natural environment can also improve children's learning. We want to see every child in England given the chance to experience and learn about the natural environment' (Department for Environment, Food and Rural Affairs 2011: 47). One of the four key reforms set out in the White Paper for reconnecting people and nature is 'action to get more children learning outdoors, removing barriers and increasing schools' abilities to teach outdoors' (ibid.: 45). On the other hand, successive education policies have challenged opportunities for free play in the early years and added pedagogical, curricular and assessment requirements; increasingly these policies permit limited time for play.

In recent years, government intervention in early years education has increased significantly in order to raise standards and improve readiness for school. Readiness for school is, however, a contested concept. The traditional view of this concept is about developing social and communication skills that will help a child to learn (Whitebread and Bingham 2011). The government's current view seems to relate readiness for learning to literacy and numeracy skills;

> This leads to a situation where children's basic emotional and cognitive needs for autonomy, competence and relatedness, and the opportunity to develop their metacognitive and self-regulation skills, are not being met. The problem is not that children are not ready for school, but that our schools are not ready for children.
>
> (Whitebread and Bingham 2011: 4)

The greater emphasis on school readiness is reflected strongly in the England Early Years Foundation Stage statutory framework (DfE 2012) which sets the standards for all English early years settings. The framework focuses on learning, child development, and health and safety. Importantly, it highlights that settings must promote a model of teaching and learning that 'ensures children are ready for school,' and further, enables children to 'learn the skills … and provide the right foundation for good future progress through *school* and life' (DfE website).[2]

It is argued that this, overtly school-framed agenda for the early years, narrows the curriculum on offer and limits the development of meaningful outdoor and natural play curricular experiences for children which are based upon reliable United Kingdom and international research (see, for example, Palaiologou 2009). What appears to be undervalued are the notions that (1) best practice in early years foundation stage learning is premised upon the capacity of the curriculum to be predicated on children's play (Garrick *et al.* 2010); and (2) outdoor play is a fundamental dimension of a child's life experience as proven by England's long tradition of pioneering and researching its impact. To reduce the opportunity for outdoor play seems to be inconsistent with an international agreement (UNICEF 1989) and offers a limited educational experience. Opportunities for ECEfS are not specified in the statutory framework (DfE 2012), nevertheless settings could, and some still do, provide outdoor natural play curricula that focus on children's interests in sustainability.

Opportunities for ECEfS

We argue that natural play and other experiences in the natural environment provide foundational experience for ECEfS; if a young child becomes familiar with a natural environment, observing changes over time, they can begin to understand the rhythm and cycle of life; in this way, nature becomes a teacher. The metaphor, 'nature as teacher', is offered by Webster and Johnson (2008) as a way forward for

EfS. They explain this as 'In nature, "waste=food". Natural systems are self-sustaining and abundant. ... Everything connects and is closed loop, circular feedback mechanisms help to ensure a dynamic balance and continuity in the system' (p. 15).

Therefore, if young children can understand the idea of life cycles and that in nature waste is recycled, this may also help them to understand recycling in the nursery setting, and thus the idea of living more sustainably. Further, facilitating other experiences in nature such as making secret dens, building shelters and overnight camping extends this by developing skills for sustainability and providing a glimpse of what it means to live sustainably, to depend on what is around you in the environment whilst sustaining it for the future. This suggests a plan for early progression in EfS; first, getting to know, understand and connect with natural environments in the locality (and elsewhere) and second, beginning to think about how to protect and sustain such environments. Simply, spending sustained periods of time outdoors, engaged in the challenge of interacting with the real-world would lead to an authentic curriculum experience. There is much to learn here from the place-based education movement (Barratt 2011; Gruenewald and Smith 2007; Sobel 2004) premised upon the interactions of people with their locale. This would include the interest in indigenous knowledges in contexts such as Canada, Alaska, Australia and African countries (see also, Bates *et al.* 2009; and Nakashima *et al.* 2000).

Opportunities for ECEfS: the policy context

The curricular frameworks for this age range provide some limited opportunities for EfS. The early years framework for birth to five years of age requires schools and early childhood settings to provide activities and experiences for children relating to a number of areas, including 'understanding the world' (DfE 2012). 'This involves guiding children to make sense of their physical world and their community' (ibid.: 5) 'and talk about changes' (ibid.: 9). For 5–7 year olds the demise of the former government's sustainable schools framework (Box 14.2) in 2010 led to a reduction in emphasis on EfS in schools, resulting in 'increased uncertainties amongst educational institutions and practitioners about how much emphasis to place on sustainability within teaching and learning' (UK National Commission for UNESCO 2013: 17). The remaining EfS requirements for 5–7 year olds are the National Curriculum references to 'environmental change and sustainable development in the local area' (geography), 'living things in the local environment' (science) and 'care for the local environment' (science).

The development of EfS is now, therefore, largely a matter for individual settings to decide upon thus depending on staff commitment to EfS and the contribution of EfS champions.[3] The champion can be from the staff, children, parents or other community members. There are examples of good practice across early years settings in the form of small-scale projects or programmes and regional initiatives. The impact of the former sustainable schools framework, together with the work of

---

Box 14.2 The sustainable schools framework in England (2006–2010)

The sustainable schools framework introduced in 2006 comprised three interlocking parts: a commitment to care; an integrated approach (developing EfS through the curriculum, campus and community); and eight doorways or entry points developing sustainability practices. The eight doorways were food and drink; energy and water; travel and traffic; purchasing and waste; buildings and grounds; inclusion and participation; local well-being; global dimension. This initiative was seen to bring educational benefits to schools and children where the framework was well-developed (Barratt *et al.* 2010).

---

environmental organizations, has been significant in stimulating this work, for example, Ecoschools claims considerable reach into English schools (Ecoschools website). The inconsistency of EfS in early years settings and schools in general, however, has been evidenced in a meta-analysis of research which 'suggests that there is a big difference in practice between those schools identified as actively engaged with sustainability and the majority of schools for whom it is not a high priority' (SEEd 2008). UK UNESCO believes that the widespread adoption of EfS requires 'an overall strategic framework which puts it firmly at the core of the education policy agenda' in order to provide 'coherence, direction and impetus to existing initiatives and ... build on existing good practice' (2013: 4; see also the SEEd website).

Case studies

Approach to the case studies

The following case studies illustrate how different early years settings have successfully provisioned for outdoor play, including meeting a sustainability agenda within the current statutory framework. All four settings are graded as 'outstanding' the highest grade awarded by England's independent auditor of educational standards, the Office for Standards in Education, Children's Services and Skills[4] (Ofsted, see the Ofsted website). These settings have been selected for analysis due to their educational interest in the natural environment and/or EfS.

An analysis of Ofsted inspection reports forms the basis of these cases together with evidence from the setting and its EfS project documentation and websites. The subjective nature of inspection suggests the possibility of bias in this evidence. Nevertheless, Ofsted claim independence and rigour in moderating all inspection assessments before confirming their reports. A four-year research study has shown recently that: 'the inspection system appears to be effective ... inspectors produce ratings which are valid and ... they are able to identify poorly performing schools' (Hussain 2012). Given that Ofsted inspection reports are online and freely available to the public the consequent scrutiny of inspectors' grades and evidence may increase their validity. Hence, the analysis of Ofsted reports in the case studies attempted to (1) verify the evidence obtained through setting documentation and (2) identify the impact of EfS in the setting.

Each case study includes an introduction to the setting and its local context, how EfS originated in the setting, how EfS is developed including its underpinning rationale, the approach to EfS with children and evidence of the impact of the approach on the setting and on children's learning and development. The findings of the analysis have been summarized in a statement that describes the distinctive approach to EfS adopted by each of the settings as follows:

- sustained authentic outdoor play leading to sustainable learning
- using place-based learning to support education for sustainability
- valuing the outdoors, fresh air, free play and risk-taking as a foundation for sustainability
- advancing a participatory-framed sustainable school curriculum.

These statements appear at the start of each case study along with the URL for the setting website.

Case study 1: Redcliffe Children's Centre and Maintained Nursery School

www.redcliffechildrenscentre.ik.org/p_Home.ikml

DISTINCTIVE APPROACH TO EDUCATION FOR SUSTAINABILITY

Sustained authentic outdoor play leading to sustainable learning.

INTRODUCTION

Redcliffe Children's Centre is a National Teaching school[5] with 86 full-time equivalent places for children from birth to four years of age. It holds the highest grade 'outstanding' awarded by Ofsted (2011a); this judgement included evidence of the success of the forest-based curriculum.

CONTEXT

This local authority children's centre is located in the south-west of England in an inner city area of Bristol. 'The nursery building is set amidst a group of high-rise flats close to the city centre … The Centre is in the 30% band of the most deprived areas in England' (Redcliffe Children's Centre website).

> Nearly two-thirds of the children are of ethnic minority backgrounds; this is well above the average for England. The largest ethnic group is Black

Somalian. Twelve different languages are spoken at the centre and nearly all of the children are at the early stages of learning to speak English. Just over a tenth of children in the centre have special educational needs and/or disabilities. Their needs include autism, speech and language disorders, complex emotional needs and physical difficulties. A quarter of the youngest children have special educational needs and/or disabilities; this is above average. The range and nature of their needs includes Down's syndrome, cerebral palsy and autism.

(Ofsted 2011a: 3)

HOW EDUCATION FOR SUSTAINABILITY STARTED

The forest experience was established in 2006 due to the commitment of the head teacher who believed in introducing children to the natural world because they lived in a built environment. The head teacher and staff recognized that 'children living in the high-rise flats had low levels of physical development as they did not have access to the outdoors' (Ofsted 2011a: 7). In 2011, a minibus was purchased to facilitate ease of travel to the forest; three locations situated a few miles from the centre are used.

HOW EARLY CHILDHOOD EDUCATION FOR SUSTAINABILITY IS DEVELOPED

The centre focuses on outdoor play and 'wild experience' (setting website) as an opportunity to develop EfS; its statement of beliefs includes, 'outdoor experiences are as important as indoor experiences. We need to look after the earth to survive' (setting website). The setting's principles are illustrated through weekly forest experiences for every child, which provides 'awe inspiring matter, challenge, adventure, and ecology' (setting website). The forest is also brought into the classroom; logs and leaves can be seen inside. The setting views the forest experience as beneficial to children as well as their families and parents/carers who are invited to join the forest experience at any time. This reflects the centre's commitment and contribution to education within the wider community. These aims and commitment to outdoor experiences move well beyond the curricular expectations of the national Early Years' Foundation Stage. This setting also sets out to promote children's physical development and risk-taking through forest experiences, thus supporting the children's confidence in, and enjoyment of, natural environments. This is seen to be especially important by the staff because, as mentioned earlier, many of the children live in high-rise flats and/or have little opportunity for adventurous play in natural environments.

APPROACH TO EDUCATION FOR SUSTAINABILITY

All children spend one day a week at one of three forest sites 'finding freedom and adventure' (setting website) and using their senses to get to know the forest in different seasons and weather conditions. A child-initiated and 'hands-on', experiential learning approach is adopted with an emphasis on 'exploration, experimentation, observation, problem-solving, prediction, critical thinking, decision-making and discussion' (setting website). The approach could be described as providing authentic learning experiences (Rule 2006) in which learning occurs through collaborative real-world experiences involving children and adults.

EVIDENCE OF IMPACT

The centre staff report that children benefit from regular experiences in the forest in that they become familiar with it and observe change over time. They identify how children begin to appreciate the changes in the natural state of the environment throughout the year and as the seasons change in relation to colour, smell, sound and touch. The staff also identify that, through regular experience and opportunities to explore freely, the children become familiar and develop a personal relationship with the forest. Ofsted describe the forest as: 'an excellent outdoor classroom where children develop their love of nature and sense of responsibility for the environment. This makes a very positive contribution to their spiritual, moral, social and cultural development' (Ofsted 2011a: 6).

Further, Ofsted report that the outdoor experience contributes to children's physical development and resilience where:

> children demonstrate a very keen sense of adventure, tempered by a sensible approach to risk-taking. This enables them to understand the concept of safety and to develop highly complex problem-solving skills. For example, wanting to climb a tree, two boys figured out that by leaning sturdy branches onto the trunk they could climb up into the tree and be 'owls.'
>
> (Ofsted 2011a: 5)

Case study 2: Bishop Sutton Primary School

www.bishopsutton.bathnes.sch.uk/

DISTINCTIVE APPROACH TO EDUCATION FOR SUSTAINABILITY

Using place-based learning to support education for sustainability.

INTRODUCTION

This is an Ofsted-graded (2012) 'outstanding' primary school with children aged 4–11 years. The Ofsted report contains evidence of the place-based learning project referred to in this case study. The school 'has been at the heart of village life since it was built in 1842' (school website). It now consists of Victorian buildings, newer extensions and outdoor spaces including a field in which the school has developed 'a conservation area with a pond, and a variety of trees, shrubs and plants' (school website). The school is located in an area of outstanding natural beauty including a lake that serves as a reservoir for neighbouring villages.

CONTEXT

The school is situated in the south-west of England in the village of Bishop Sutton with approximately 1,200 people. There is less social and economic deprivation than average for schools in England. Almost all of the pupils are White British with the proportion of disabled pupils and those who have special educational needs well below average for England. There are four mixed-age classes in Key Stages 1 and 2 and a Reception class.

HOW EDUCATION FOR SUSTAINABILITY STARTED

A significant focus on EfS was inspired by the school's involvement in a place-based learning project with Bath Spa University designed to integrate place-based learning into the curriculum. The school was interested in developing EfS in the context of the local environment and its rich ecological and historical heritage. Prior to the place-based project, the school had not focused, in any depth, on EfS. However, with the support of the head teacher, an enthusiastic early career teacher became involved in the project supported by a university teacher educator.

HOW EARLY CHILDHOOD EDUCATION FOR SUSTAINABILITY IS DEVELOPED

The school motto is 'learning together for tomorrow'. One of the school's aims is to develop a positive self-image in children – respecting themselves, others and the environment and 'a sense of awe and wonder in the world' (school aims for the early years, school website). The development of EfS in the school has largely been as a result of a place-based learning project. The school has therefore developed EfS through the local place and by using an integrated approach to learning across subjects in the curriculum.

The school's involvement in a project to develop a community place-based curriculum through science, technology, sustainability and the environment (Bath Spa University, funded by the Astra Zeneca Science Teaching Trust, 2010–2012) has made a key contribution to its EfS work. The purpose of this project was to research the benefits and impact of place-based learning (PBL) on children's education.

APPROACH TO EDUCATION FOR SUSTAINABILITY

Children's interests provided the stimulus and ongoing direction for the place-based learning project; the project focused on the 'life of the lake', through a local reservoir, the Chew Valley Lake. The project also involved an investigation of environmental changes in the local area and their impacts (including before and after the building of the reservoir) and to identify the distinguishing characteristics of the locality/village identity by asking questions such as, 'What does it mean to be a Bishop Suttoner?' The project approach was place-based, that is, designed to develop learning with the community that is grounded in the locale. Local community partners included historians, villagers and older people, parents/carers, farmers, a community farm and Avon Valley Wildlife trust. Activities with villagers included planning and hosting a community tea party to gather local perceptions and experiences of the village and lake. Activities with the wildlife trust included 'a day of environmental studies where the children used their science skills to carry out ... surveys and pond dipping activities in both the lake and our school pond' (project teacher) (Children Environment Research Centre Bath Spa University, Children Environment Research Centre 2013: 10).

Although the emphasis of the project was to develop EfS through science, environment, and technology this has been a genuinely integrated cross-curricular approach with EfS being supported through mathematics, English, music, art and history.

EVIDENCE OF IMPACT

The Ofsted school report included reference to the place-based project in its report:

> the exceptionally well planned creative curriculum inspires learning, motivates pupils and staff and makes a very strong contribution to pupils' outstanding spiritual, moral, social and cultural development. This can be seen in the exceptionally high quality work arising from the Lakes project. This project exemplifies the school's use of links with other organizations to extend opportunities for learning as it was carried out in partnership with other schools and Bath Spa University. It also enabled pupils to work alongside experts such as artists and scientists from the community.
>
> (Ofsted 2012a: 8)

As a result of the project, the school has established new relationships within the community and with other organizations and has further recognized the opportunities and value of intergenerational learning. In the 'end of project' interviews the project teacher reported that 'children are 'impassioned' about the location and lifestyle ... there was a sense of excitement' (Bath Spa University 2013: 11). Through this project, the school considered the relationship between the school curriculum (National Curriculum subjects and dimensions) including science and technology, and the local environment/community. The school believes that student progress and achievement in numeracy, literacy and science was enhanced by their involvement in this project. The project teacher cited the motivation of the children involved and how their standards improved. Interestingly, the teacher (who was not from the local area) also developed sophisticated understanding and respect for the value of the local environment as a learning resource. Place-based learning is now being embedded across the school curriculum

> The project has raised the profile and significance of local studies and curriculum topics within our school. It has proven that learning about your local area need not be dry or un-ambitious and that children really do have a genuine fascination and interest in learning about their local environment.
> (End of project teacher interview, Bath Spa University 2013: 16)

The evaluation of the project by the Bath Spa University researchers (ibid. 2013) found evidence that the children in the project developed:

- deep learning
- new enquiry skills as active researchers (e.g. using data loggers, science software, developing a digital archive and questionnaires and online surveys)
- personal engagement with the local environment and community
- personal aspirations for their local environment and community.

Case study 3: Chelsea Open Air Nursery and Children's Centre

www.chelseaopenairnursery.co.uk/

DISTINCTIVE APPROACH TO EDUCATION FOR SUSTAINABILITY

Valuing the outdoors, fresh air, free play and risk-taking as a foundation for sustainability.

INTRODUCTION

The Chelsea Open Air Nursery is internationally recognized for its ethos and focus on indoor and outdoor learning. This is a community nursery with 59 children and has an extensive outdoor space (gardens). It has been graded 'outstanding' by Ofsted (2012b). This nursery has a rich heritage having been established in 1928 by an American, Natalie Davies, with the involvement of the educationalist Susan Isaacs. The early principles of the nursery were to 'combine a healthy and invigorating lifestyle with the most recent discoveries in child development' (Chelsea Open Air Nursery and Children's Centre, School website). Susan Isaacs inspired the nursery with her child-centred approach to education and belief in the importance of fresh air for young children.

CONTEXT

This nursery is situated in inner London in the affluent area of Kensington and Chelsea. There is a diverse range of children with 'one-third of children ... of

White British heritage and the remainder come from a range of minority ethnic backgrounds' (Ofsted 2012b: 3). Evidence of social and economic deprivation is lower than average for England. At the time of inspection there were three children with special educational needs (SEN), these 'Children enter the nursery with levels of skills, knowledge and understanding that are below those typical for their age' (Ofsted 2012b: 4).

HOW EDUCATION FOR SUSTAINABILITY STARTED

The nursery has a history of outdoor play and learning beginning with the contribution of educationalist, Susan Isaacs and the open air philosophy.

Susan Isaacs believed that the 'outdoors was as valuable a learning environment as indoors. The open air philosophy, also, recognized that many city children did not have enough access to fresh air, sunlight and exercise for healthy development (Chelsea Open Air Nursery and Children's Centre Prospectus, no date). The head teacher has a special interest in outdoor learning and has had several articles on outdoor play published (see, for example, Solly 2007) and is completing her first book about adventure, risk and challenge in the early years.

HOW EARLY CHILDHOOD EDUCATION FOR SUSTAINABILITY IS DEVELOPED

The 'open air philosophy' combined with indoor activity provides 'a complete and balanced learning environment' (school website) with a combination of free play and structured activities. Risk and challenge is seen to be 'a strong ethic for children's learning and play, and this is reflected in how the provision is run' (Play England website, case study).

Amongst the aims of the nursery are for children to:

- have free access to outdoors
- play in an environment which stimulates the imagination and allows reasonable risk-taking
- explore, discover, experiment and plan to be independent, creative and inventive learners
- make their own choices and decisions
- experience privacy and seclusion, joy and celebration
- develop an appreciation of beauty as perceived through all the senses
- develop a love and understanding of nature, the local community and the world further afield.

APPROACH TO EDUCATION FOR SUSTAINABILITY

The nursery adopts a play-based approach to learning with a balance of free play and structured activity. 'A child's play is work. Young children learn through play by active investigation and exploration' (school website). There is a great deal of choice and space for children to play, both indoors and outdoors; 'children are encouraged to play outside and make the most of the outdoor space, which contains various play structures, flowerbeds, trees, a hut and a sand-filled pirate ship' (Play England website). Children are also involved in gardening and growing food that they then have the opportunity to cook and try, for example, 'using the juicer, growing beans, making soup' (school website).

Both inside and outside areas of the nursery are seen as learning spaces, or 'workshop areas', 'the outdoor area is ... carefully planned to offer children ... a variety of learning opportunities appropriate to the weather.' As well as outdoor activity in the school grounds the nursery provides 'expeditions' into the local environment, for example, 'going on an expedition to Holland Park Ecology Centre, Natural History Museum and Albert Bridge' (school website).

EVIDENCE OF IMPACT

'The strong focus on outdoor learning all year round and the "expeditions" to places beyond the school are very special and very effective features of provision' (Ofsted 2009: 4). Children are encouraged to explore, investigate, experiment and above all question (Ofsted 2012b: 4). Children feel very safe in the nursery, 'they are confident to take risks in the outdoor area, but listen carefully and respond to adults when they feel children are entering an activity that is potentially dangerous' (Ofsted 2012b: 5).

Case study 4: Emscote Infants School

www.emscoteinfants.co.uk

DISTINCTIVE APPROACH TO EDUCATION FOR SUSTAINABILITY

Advancing a participatory-framed sustainable school curriculum.

INTRODUCTION

Emscote Infants School is a smaller than average infant school in England with 157 children aged 4–7 years. It has continued to improve, moving from Ofsted 'good' to 'outstanding' between 2009 and 2013. The school has been awarded the Ecoschools green flag.

CONTEXT

A large majority of children are of White British heritage. The school is situated in Warwickshire in an urban area. It has average numbers for England of (1) children with special educational needs (SEN) and (2) children from backgrounds with social and economic deprivation.

HOW EDUCATION FOR SUSTAINABILITY STARTED

The focus on EfS arose from the work of a champion (a committed teacher) and their involvement in the Ecoschools initiative; the international award program for developing sustainability in schools. 'One teacher's passion got us started and the Green Flag Award in 2004 was both a measure of our early success and a stimulus to do more' (Ofsted 2011b).

HOW EARLY CHILDHOOD EDUCATION FOR SUSTAINABILITY IS DEVELOPED

The school believes that 'sustainable development runs through everything we do' (Ofsted 2011b: 1). This school adopted the previous government's sustainable schools strategy (Department for Children Schools and Families (DCSF), 2008; Box 14.2), using the 'eight doorways' as a structure to build and evaluate the curriculum and as a way of embedding sustainable development in its work. The doorways are fundamental to the way England's previous sustainable schools strategy was to be implemented in schools (DCSF 2008). This school has focused on embedding sustainability in the curriculum, developing a sustainable campus and working with the local community.

APPROACH TO EDUCATION FOR SUSTAINABILITY

The school makes good use of the outdoor environment to provide learning opportunities for children through, for example, gardening, exploring, and play. A participatory approach to EfS is adopted ensuring that all stakeholders are involved (leaders, teachers, children, governors, administrative and other staff, parents/carers, and community members). The school claims that sustainability is now 'completely embedded throughout the school' (Ofsted 2011b: 2).

Children take a lead in decision-making and action through the eco team; the caretaker helps to save energy and administrative staff lead the reduction of paper use and other resources. Children's ideas are acted upon where possible, for example,

> the pupils have introduced a water saving scheme for rainwater which is used for the flower pots and beds. Outdoor play equipment and the gardening club were also their suggestions. Children monitor electricity use and lead initiatives to save electricity.
>
> (Ofsted 2011b: 2)

EVIDENCE OF IMPACT

The grounds have been developed to include woodlands, raised garden beds, bird boxes, bike parks and play areas. Classes are named after tree species and there are attractive wall displays throughout the school. 'The hugely attractive outdoor area with its screening, natural shelters, composting and recently planted fruit trees reflects the level of care taken in all aspects of the school's work' (Ofsted 2013: 7). Effective use is also made of the outdoor spaces to promote children's social and physical development.

The school was selected by Ofsted as an example of good practice in respect of education for sustainable development. It was commended for its focus on outdoor learning for the youngest children (4–5 year olds) for whom 'a wide range of opportunities help children to learn very quickly through play and investigation, both inside and outside the classroom' (Ofsted 2013: 5). Ofsted also noted its links with organizations in Finland, France, Bo in Sierra Leone and Italy including involvement in a Comenius[6] funded project about sharing best practice in water conservation with partners in Finland, France and Italy (ibid. 2013).

Summary

The case studies illustrate that effective ECEfS can be approached in distinctive ways according to the philosophy, interests and expertise of staff and others in the setting community as well as the influence of outside agencies and local characteristics. An ECEfS curriculum that considers the needs of the child and the local context can provide significant opportunities for natural play, nature as teacher and meaningful learning. We have argued that learning in natural environments can lead to sustained knowledge creation, action taking and value building. Chawla's (2007) 'significant life experience' research argues convincingly that positive nature experiences in childhood contribute to a lifelong interest in sustaining and caring for the environment. The case studies also demonstrate the passion and commitment of individuals and/or external agencies to ensure that children have experience of the natural world. Together, an appropriate curriculum and professional commitment to EfS, can lead to the development of concepts, skills and behaviours for sustainable living.

Independent reviews of the curriculum in England for the Early Years Foundation Stage (birth to 5 years) (Early Childhood Action 2012) and for primary children (5–11 years) (Hofkins and Northen 2009; Rose 2009) espoused an entitlement to EfS for young children. Yet this chapter has shown that a commitment to EfS is not evident in the educational policy context or curriculum for birth to years in England today. The 'schoolification' (Early Childhood Action 2012) and standards-driven approach to the early years curriculum in England is a conceptually narrow response to raising educational standards in the primary years. This approach undervalues the importance of play that practitioners and researchers in the field acknowledge should be central to any early years curriculum. Further, the reduced opportunity for outdoor play in England due to the concerns and perspectives of many contemporary parents together with reduced access to natural spaces, is affecting children's life and educational experiences.

Any future ECEfS curriculum should consider the relationship of the child to the natural environment (local–global), the child's engagement with nature and the importance of play. In particular, future curricula should consider a range of EfS learning and development opportunities that incorporate natural play, familiar and unfamiliar places and environments, participation and sustainable living (Box 14.3).

Box 14.3 EfS Learning experiences for the early years

In the early years children should have the opportunity to experience:

- free play, natural play and outdoor structured 'activity' (e.g. growing, physical activity)
- natural play as an essential dimension of children's development
- caring for the environment, for example, gardening, tree planting, improving a small-scale environment
- natural play with other children from other places
- learning *about* and *through* the environment
- regular and return visits to a natural place
- sustained periods of time in the natural environment, for example a camp in which children, teachers, families and community members live in a natural space and are challenged to think and act responsibly in relation to food, water and shelter
- visits to different environments and places including coastlines, mountains, forests, farmland and built environments
- a night-time expedition to a natural environment
- learning which is focused on global perspectives
- a (national) curriculum that reflects a global environmental agenda taking account of how people live and interact with the planet
- intergenerational learning to share knowledge across the generations and provide role-models
- planned progression in learning about the environment and sustainability
- recognition as global, national and local citizens
- being listened to about their perspectives on the (local) environment
- planned learning about how to live more sustainably in their local environment (skills, knowledge, understanding and values)
- participation in developing and using sustainable practices in the setting that replicate nature's cycles and systems (for example, reusing waste, walking to school, collecting and using water …)
- roles as sustainability leaders, champions and ambassadors in their setting or local community (helping or persuading others to live more sustainably)
- a dialogue with adults about the nature of their educational experiences including what they see as meaningful learning
- researching their own environment (e.g. species counts, bird watching, how environments have changed …)
- what local and distant habitats, places and environments are like at different times (day and night) and seasons using digital technology (e.g. webcam in a nest or burrow, webcam in a city centre).

Notes

1   The Monitor of Engagement with the Natural Environment (MENE) project aims to provide baseline and trend data on how people (including children) use the natural environment in England. For the purposes of this project the natural environment is defined as the green open spaces in and around towns and cities, as well as the wider countryside and coastline (Burt *et al.* in press) www.naturalengland.org.uk/ourwork/research/mene.aspx.

2   All settings are subjected to inspection by the independent regulatory body, Office for Standards in Education, (Ofsted) who through their inspection framework, 2012, are required to grade each setting in respect of the Early Years Foundation Stage statutory framework.

3   Champion is used here in the sense of championing a cause. The term is used in corporate sustainability literature on the role of individuals as environmental or social champions (or change agents) for corporate sustainability (Visser and Crane 2010). In corporate sustainability champions can be sustainability managers or any other individuals working in an organization with a commitment to sustainability.

4   Of inspections in 2011–2012, 12 per cent of early years registered provision was outstanding, 62 per cent good, 23 per cent satisfactory and 3 per cent inadequate (Ofsted website). Ofsted is an independent organization which reports to Parliament. Ofsted inspects and regulate all services that care for children and young people as well as educational and skills providers for learners of all ages. All inspection reports are made public.

5   'Teaching schools are outstanding schools with a strong track record of supporting other schools' (National College website). Any phase or type of school in England, including nurseries, can apply for this national initiative. However, there are stringent criteria and schools must demonstrate successful experience in providing support to other schools. Teaching schools provide school-to-school support for school improvement. At the time of writing, there are more than 360 teaching schools designated in England.

6   'The Comenius Programme is named after Jan Amos Comenius (1592–1670), often considered the father of modern education. Comenius is aimed at schools, colleges and local authorities across Europe and has two main objectives:
    (1) to develop knowledge and understanding among young people and education staff of the diversity of European cultures and languages, and the value of this diversity;
    (2) to help young people to acquire basic life skills and competences for their personal development, for future employment and for active European citizenship' (British Council website).

References

Barratt, R. (2011) *Developing a Community Place-based Curriculum through Science, Technology, Sustainability and the Environment: Interim report for Astra Zeneca Science Teaching Trust*. Bath: Bath Spa University.

Barratt-Hacking, E., Barratt, R. and Scott, W. (2007) 'Engaging children: Research issues around participation and environmental learning'. *Environmental Education Research*, 13(4): 529–44.

Barratt-Hacking, E., Scott, W. and Lee, E. (2010) *Evidence of Impact of Sustainable Schools*. London: Department for Children, Schools and Families (DCSF).

Bates, P., Chiba, M., Kube, S. and Nakashima, D. (2009) *Learning and Knowing in Indigenous Societies Today*. Paris: UNESCO.

Bath Spa University (2013) 'Advancing a Place Based Learning (PBL) Science Curriculum

Through a Community of Practice, Final Report, January 2013'. Children Environment Research Centre, Bath Spa University.

British Educational Research Association (BERA) Early Years Special Interest Group (2003) *Early Years Research: Pedagogy, Curriculum and Adult Roles, Training and Professionalism*. BERA. Online. Available at: www.bera.ac.uk/system/files/beraearlyyearsreview 31may03.pdf (accessed 28 January 2014).

Burt, J., Hunt, A., Rickinson, M., Andrews, R. and Stewart, D. (in press) *Visits to the Natural Environment by Households with Children: Analysis of MENE data 2009–2012 and Supplementary Qualitative Research*. Natural England Data Report.

Chawla, L. (2007) 'Childhood experiences associated with care for the natural world: a theoretical framework for empirical results'. *Children Youth and Environments*, 17(4): 144–70.

Chelsea Open Air Nursery School and Children's Centre (no date) *Prospectus*. Online. Available: www.chelseaopenairnursery.co.uk/ckfinder/userfiles/files/COA_prospectus_ web.pdf (accessed 28 January 2014).

Children Environment Research Centre (CERC) (2013) *Advancing a Place-based Learning (PBL) Science Curriculum through a Community of Practice. Final report for Astra Zeneca Science Teaching Trust*. Bath: Bath Spa University.

Cruikshank, M. (1977) 'The open air school movement in English education'. *Paedagogica Historica. International Journal of the History of Education*, 17(1): 62–74.

Davis, J. M. (2009) 'Revealing the research 'hole' of early childhood Education for Sustainability: A preliminary survey of the literature'. *Environmental Education Research*, 15(2): 227–41.

Department for Children, Schools and Families (DCSF) (England) (2008) *Sustainable Schools – A Brief Introduction*. London: DCSF.

Department for Education (DfE) (2012) *Statutory Framework for the Early Years Foundation Stage*. London: DfE. Online. Avaliable www.education.gov.uk/publications/standard/ AllPublications/Page1/ (accessed 28 January 2014).

Department for Environment, Food and Rural Affairs (Defra) (2011) *The Natural Choice: Securing the Value of Nature*. London: Defra. Online. Available: www.official-documents.gov.uk/document/cm80/8082/8082.pdf (accessed 28 January 2014).

Early Childhood Action (2012) *Unhurried Pathways: A New Framework for Early Childhood*. Winchester: Early Childhood Action.

Garrick, R., Bath, C., Dunn, K., Maconochie, H., Willis, B. and Wolstenholme, C. (2010) *Children's Experiences of the Early Years Foundation Stage*. London: Department for Education. Online. Available: www.gov.uk/government/uploads/system/uploads/ attachment_data/file/182163/DFE-RR071.pdf (accessed 28 January 2014).

Gruenewald, D.A. and Smith, G.A. (2007) *Place-based Education In the Global Age*. New York: Lawrence Erlbaum Associates.

Hille, T. (2011) *Modern Schools: A Century of Design for Education*. Holboken, NJ: John Wiley and Sons, Inc.

Hofkins, D. and Northen, S. (2009) *Introducing the Cambridge Primary Review*. Cambridge: University of Cambridge. Online. Available: www.primaryreview.org.uk/publications/ introductory_booklet.php (accessed 28 January 2014).

Hussain, I. (2012) *Subjective Performance Evaluation in the Public Sector: Evidence from School Inspections. Centre for the Economics of Education Discussion Paper No. 135*. London: Centre for the Economics of Education, London School of Economics.

Knight, S. (2009) *Forest Schools and Outdoor Learning in the Early Years*. London: Sage.

Kwon, Y. I. (2002) 'Changing curriculum in early childhood education in England'. *Early Childhood Research and Practice*, 4(2): n2.

Maynard, T. (2007) 'Forest schools in Great Britain: an initial exploration'. *Contemporary Issues in Early Childhood*, 8(4): 320–31.

Nakashima, D., Prott, L. and Bridgewater, P. (2000) 'Tapping into the world's wisdom'. *UNESCO Sources*, 125, July–August, 12.

O'Brien, L. and Murray, R. (2006) *A Marvellous Opportunity for Children to Learn. A Participatory Evaluation of Forest School in England and Wales*. Farnham, Surrey: Forest Research. Online. Available: www.forestry.gov.uk/pdf/fr0112forestschoolsreport.pdf/ $FILE/fr0112forestschoolsreport.pdf (accessed 28 January 2014).

Ofsted (2009) 'OFSTED School Report: Chelsea Open Air Nursery School and Children's Centre'. Online. Available: www.ofsted.gov.uk/inspection-reports/find-inspection-report/provider/ELS/100474 (accessed 28 January 2014).

Ofsted (2011a) *Redcliffe Children's Centre and Maintained Nursery School Inspection Report*. Online. Available: www.ofsted.gov.uk/inspection-reports/find-inspection-report/provider/ELS/108904 (accessed 28 January 2014).

Ofsted (2011b) *Sustainable Development at the Heart of a School: Emscote Infants School*. Online only. Available www.ofsted.gov.uk/resources/good-practice-resource-sustainable-development-heart-of-school-emscote-infants-school (accessed 28 January 2014).

Ofsted (2012a) *Bishop Sutton Primary School Inspection Report*. Online. Available: www.ofsted.gov.uk/inspection-reports/find-inspection-report/provider/ELS/109061 (accessed 28 January 2014).

Ofsted (2012b) *OFSTED School Report: Chelsea Open Air Nursery School and Children's Centre*. Available at: www.ofsted.gov.uk/inspection-reports/find-inspection-report/provider/ELS/100474 (accessed 28 Janaury 2014).

Ofsted (2013) *OFSTED School Report: Emscote Infant School*. Available at: www.ofsted.gov.uk/inspection-reports/find-inspection-report/provider/ELS/125566 (accessed 28 January 2014).

Palaiologou, I. (2009) *The Early Years Foundation Stage – Theory and Practice*. London: Sage.

Plantlife (2011) *Forestry Recommissioned: Bringing England's Woodlands Back to Life*. Salisbury: Plantlife.

Pyle, R. M. (2010) 'No child left inside: Nature study as a radical act', in D. A. Gruenewald and G. Smith (eds) *Place-Based Education in the Global Age: Local Diversity*. New York: Routledge, 155–72.

Rose, J. (2009) *Independent Review of the Primary Curriculum: Final Report*. Nottingham: Department for Children, Schools and Families.

Royal Society for the Protection of Birds (RSPB) (2013) *England: The State of Nature*. Online only. Available www.rspb.org.uk/stateofnature (accessed 28 January 2014).

Rule, A. C. (2006) 'The components of authentic learning'. *Journal of Authentic Learning*, 3(1): 1–10.

Santer, J. and Griffiths, C. with Goodall, D. (2007) *Free Play in Early Childhood. A Literature Review*. London: National Children's Bureau.

Siraj-Blatchford, I., Sylva, K., Muttock, S., Gilden, R. and Bell, D. (2002) *Researching Effective Pedagogy in the Early Years. DfES Research Report RR356*. Norwich: HMSO.

Sobel, D. (2004) *Place-Based Education, Connecting Classrooms and Communities*. Great Barrington, MA: The Orion Society.

Solly, K. (2007) 'Once upon a time – a story of early years outdoor learning in Central London'. *Horizons*, 38(summer): 25–29. Online. Available: www.outdoor-learning.org/Portals/0/IOL%20Documents/Horizons%20Documents/Horizons%20pdf%20archive/h38_c_chelsea_open_air.pdf (accessed 28 January 2014).

Sustainability and Environmental Education (SEEd) (2008) *Practice, Barriers and Enablers in Education for Susutainable Development and Environmental Education: A Review of the Research.* Shrewsbury: SEEd. Online. Available: http://se-ed.co.uk/edu/ (accessed 28 January 2014).

UK National Commission for UNESCO (2013) *Education for Sustainable Development (ESD) in the UK – Current Status, Best Practice and Opportunities for the Future.* Policy brief 9. London: UK National Commission for UNESCO.

United Nations (1989) *Convention on the Rights of the Child.* New York: United Nations.

UNICEF (1989) *United Nations Convention on the Rights of the Child.* Online. Available: www.unicef.org/crc/ (accessed 14 February 2014).

Waite, S. J., Rogers, S. and Evans, J. (2011) *Opportunities Afforded by the Outdoors for Alternative Pedagogies as Children Move from Foundation Stage to Year 1. ESRC End of Award Report, RES-000-22-3065.* Swindon: ESRC.

Whitebread, D. and Bingham, S. (2011) *School Readiness; A Critical Review of Perspectives and Evidence.* Occasional Paper number 2, TACTYC (Association for the Professional Development of Early Years Educators). Online. Available: www.tactyc.org.uk/occasional-papers.asp (accessed 28 January 2014).

Websites

Bishop Sutton Primary School: www.bishopsutton.bathnes.sch.uk/

British Council Website (Comenius Project): www.britishcouncil.org/comenius.htm

Chelsea Open Air Nursery and Children's Centre: www.chelseaopenairnursery.co.uk/

Department for Education (DfE): www.education.gov.uk

Emscote Infant School: www.emscoteinfants.co.uk

EcoSchools England: www.keepbritaintidy.org/ecoschools/

National College website – Teaching Schools: www.education.gov.uk/nationalcollege/teachingschools

Natural England: www.naturalengland.org.uk/ourwork/research/mene.aspx

Ofsted: www.ofsted.gov.uk/

Play England: www.playengland.org.uk/resources/chelsea-open-air-nursery-school-and-children's-centre.aspx

Redcliffe Children's Centre and Maintained Nursery School: www.redcliffechildrenscentre.ik.org/p_Home.ikml

Sustainability and Environmental Education (SEEd): http://se-ed.co.uk/edu/

Chapter 15

Early childhood education for sustainability in the United States of America

Louise Chawla and Mary Rivkin

Abstract

Research on significant life experiences in the development of active care for the environment indicates the importance of extended free play in nature in early childhood, and adults who encourage appreciation for the natural world. Ecological psychology provides a framework for understanding these research outcomes, and highlights the importance of children having opportunities to assume responsible roles in their communities, including collective environmental action. After reviewing the literature, this chapter identifies initiatives in the United States which illustrate these components of education for sustainability, including nature-based preschools, forest kindergartens, nature-based play at childcare centers, and Green Schools. The chapter closes with two examples from a community-wide partnership to integrate children into actions for sustainability – one involving preschoolers in urban planning and design, and the second involving elementary school children in park management.

Sustainability and the sense of wonder

If early childhood educators were to pick a patron spirit for early education for sustainability, it would likely be Rachel Carson. When people gather to discuss the development of appreciation and care for the natural world in early childhood, they frequently quote *The Sense of Wonder*, Carson's essay on introducing young children to nature that originally appeared in the magazine *Women's Home Companion* in 1956. She intended to expand it into a longer book, but her death from cancer in 1964 stopped her plans. Instead, the essay was issued as a book posthumously in 1965. Carson urged parents and other special adults in children's lives to share adventures in nature, beginning in infancy. This sharing, she recommended, 'includes nature in storm as well as calm, by night as well as day, and is based on having fun together rather than on teaching' (Carson 1956: 10). Her examples included taking time with a child to watch the full moon ride the sky, listening to the wind, feeling rainfall, following birds' migrations, hunting the source of cricket songs, and pondering the sprouting of a seed. She reassured parents who might feel poorly equipped for this role because they were not naturalists:

It is not half so important to *know* as to *feel*. If facts are the seeds that later produce knowledge and wisdom, then the emotions and the impressions of the senses are the fertile soil in which the seeds must grow. The years of early childhood are the time to prepare the soil.

(p. 45)

The Sense of Wonder is remarkable for at least three reasons. One is its lasting resonance. The text has gone through numerous reprintings and a new edition, and remains widely cited whenever people write about children and nature. As Sideris (2008) observes, Carson expressed principles of the nature study movement that began in the late nineteenth century and deeply penetrated American thinking. The movement arose out of concern for children in a rapidly urbanizing and industrializing nation, increasingly removed from nature and agrarian rhythms. It sought to awaken reverence for life, a sense of life's mystery, and sympathy for all living things by encouraging children's curiosity and connection with the natural world. Similar concerns and ideas echo in the contemporary movement, 'Leave No Child Inside,' that was sparked by the bestselling book *Last Child in the Woods* by journalist Richard Louv (2008).

Second, it is remarkable that, as Carson neared death, the topic that occupied her mind was the cultivation of love and care for the natural world in early childhood. She was a painstaking scientist whose investigations into the effects of toxic chemicals on human health and ecosystems launched a new wave of the environmental movement when she published *Silent Spring* in 1962. If Carson can be called the patron spirit of early childhood education for sustainability, she is also considered, by many, the guiding spirit of contemporary environmentalism. Her message is that humanity must cease its destruction of the biosphere, and for our own wellbeing as well as the survival of other species, align human activities in harmony with nature. Despite the seriousness of her message and the immense scale of the challenge, Carson did not consider the experiences of young children insignificant, but intrinsic to her message.

A third reason why *The Sense of Wonder* is remarkable is that Carson wrote it from her personal experience, without the benefit of formalized research on the impacts of early childhood ventures into nature for later life. From her relationship with her nephew, whom she introduced to the coastal woods and shores of Maine from the time he was a baby, and perhaps with the memories of her own immersion in the woods and fields of Pennsylvania when she was a girl, she generalized the principle that children require opportunities to explore nature with 'the companionship of at least one adult who can share it, rediscovering with him the joy, excitement and mystery of the world we live in' (p. 45). Her conclusion was prescient, for looking backwards now from the vantage point of more than 30 years of research that has sought to understand the 'significant life experiences' that form lasting habits of awareness and care for nature, this body of research can be summarized as 'proving Rachel Carson right.' When current researchers have investigated factors that predict whether people will take action to protect the environment, or develop a keen interest in natural history, or simply seek out natural areas for recreation, they repeatedly find that those who protect the environment as adults or visit forests and natural parks for recreation enjoyed free play and discovery in nature in childhood (Asah et al. (2012) 2011, Chawla and Derr 2012, Ward-Thompson et al. 2008). This finding holds in different cultures and contexts across the world and with diverse samples – from activists who have dedicated their lives to environmental causes to ordinary people who take the trouble to recycle or install solar panels on their roofs. The frequency of this finding dwarfs references to formal education as a catalyst for responsible care and activism for the environment (Chawla and Derr 2012).

Another frequent research finding is the importance of role models who communicate their own enjoyment and appreciation of nature to the child: the 'companion in wonder' identified by Carson (Dunlap and Kellert 2012). Most often, this person is a family member, often a parent; however, an inspiring teacher can play this role. What unfolds, according to James et al. (2010, see also Chawla 1999), is a process of 'environmental socialization' in which early childhood play and discovery in nature is fostered by adults around the child. If formal education or out-of-school programs also encouraged connections to the natural world, young people might integrate being a naturalist or environmentalist into their emerging identities.

Using the theoretical lens of ecological psychology, the following section looks closely at what happens when young children play and explore in natural areas in collaboration with adults who encourage their appreciation for what they find and do. While these processes of shared discovery constitute education *in* and *about* the environment, as Davis (2010) argues, education for sustainability also requires education *for* the environment, as children learn how to take informed action to create conditions of respect and harmony between humans and the natural world. Therefore, this section notes key processes of this kind as well. Concluding sections examine initiatives that are underway in the United States to provide young children with a holistic education *in*, *about* and *for* the environment. It is noted that education for sustainability is still largely missing from discussions of best practices in early childhood education in this country, but nevertheless, key elements are now beginning to emerge.

Significant processes in developing care for the environment in early childhood

It is generally accepted that young children take cues about how to respond to the world from people around them who are important to them. Therefore, it is not surprising that when researchers explore factors associated with the development of caring actions for the environment in childhood, they frequently find that parents and other family members exemplify this form of care (Chawla and Derr 2012). Less evident is why free play in nature emerges as an equally, if not more, important reason. This section reviews theories in psychology that account for these results.

When Davis (2010) writes about education *in* the environment, she refers to standard interpretations of this phrase in the field of environmental education – the deliberate use of the natural environment as a medium for outdoor nature study, gardening, play with natural materials, and other experiential activities. What emerges from research on significant life experiences, however, is the importance of children's informal play in their yards and neighborhoods and on family vacations, where there are no adults in the background watching for 'teachable moments' to offer lessons about the environment. What, then, is profoundly formative about free play in nature, in and of itself?

The branch of psychology that is best equipped to answer this question is the ecological psychology of James Gibson (1979), Eleanor Gibson and Anne Pick (2000) and Edward Reed (1996a, 1996b). Unlike most branches of psychology, ecological psychology is grounded in the evolutionary theory of Darwin and the radical empiricism of William James (1912). These share the belief that organisms – including human beings – have direct sensory experiences of the physical world and, in the process, learn what the environment affords them, in terms of potentials for action relative to the organism's intentions and capabilities (Heft 2001). Given this principle that people act in a world of real possibilities and limits, one irreplaceable value of nature play is that children become familiar with the elements of the Earth on which human survival depends – as much today as when our species first evolved. Although books and digital screens may represent the natural world with detailed fidelity – and although there is much that children can learn from these resources – these mediated experiences do not grow food, purify water, encompass creatures in life-giving air, or generate biodiversity (Monke 2005). Therefore, Reed (1996a) argued for the 'necessity of experience' in the form of full-bodied encounters with the world that enable people to make discoveries for themselves in fields of information that are, for all purposes, infinite in their detail and depth. Books, digital screens and other people's stories can direct children's attention to important features of this world, but they remain second-hand representations.

Ethnographic studies of children's play in naturalized schoolyards and natural areas in neighborhoods show their absorption in creative activities and discovery (Blizard and Schuster 2004, Hart 1979, Moore 1986, Moore and Wong 1997, Sobel 2002, Stanley 2011). They observe small animals such as birds and salamanders, build forts, dam streams, trade found objects, give names to special rocks or trees and wonder about the hidden lives of insect galls and turtle shells. As Chawla (2007) has noted, the natural world offers recurring patterns and cycles at the same time as it never does anything exactly the same way twice, so that every time children return to a natural play area they find a place that is both reassuringly familiar and intriguingly new.

James Gibson (1979) observed that as people learn about the affordances and qualities of the natural world, they simultaneously learn about their own capacities for perception and action. One reason why nature play attracts and holds children's attention – and one likely reason why people often recall it as a formative experience – is that it is a fertile ground for the development of competence (Chawla

2007). It is filled with graduated challenges that enable children to reach beyond past accomplishments to the next level of possibility – a higher tree branch that they could not grasp before but find accessible today, a heavier stone to lift, a larger log to roll, a more distant path to navigate. As White (1959) observed, the development of competence is intrinsically motivating, giving people a sense of agency that they can have an impact on the world, as well as a sense of efficacy that they can achieve goals that they set for themselves. Education for sustainability requires both knowledge about nature and a sense of competence to influence the environment; free play in nature provides abundant opportunities for both forms of learning.

Although children need no formal instruction to engage with nature in this way, adults do play a pivotal role. From infancy, children learn how to respond to the world through processes of joint attention and social referencing (E. Gibson and Pick 2000, Reed 1996b), looking where others look and, in the process learning what others consider worthy of attention and engagement. Babies quickly learn to direct the attention of others; if they are fortunate, they live among people who willingly share their interests (Crain 2003). Is the pigeon that captivates a toddler in a park, for example, a fascinating animal worth close observation and discussion about its iridescent feathers and its nimble mating dance, or is it a 'dirty bird' to be avoided and disregarded?

When people identify role models of care for the natural world in childhood, they rarely recall explicit exhortations that the natural world needs their protection. What they describe is a 'contagious attitude of attention' through which others communicate elements of nature that have value (Chawla 2007, Matthews 1992). These memories confirm Rachel Carson's (1956) advice to parents in *The Sense of Wonder* that it is not so important to know the names of all the birds, insects, rocks and stars that they see with their child as it is to share emotions such as 'a sense of the beautiful, the excitement of the new and unknown, a feeling of sympathy, pity, admiration or love' (p. 45). This type of close attention to another creature's way of being cultivates the perspective-taking that is critical for the development of sympathy for other living things (Chawla 2009). In addition, adults show children how to express care through actions such as filling a bird feeder or planting and tending a tree.

Additionally, adults play a vital role by creating opportunities for children to encounter nature. As Reed (1996b) notes, children grow up in fields of 'free action,' 'promoted action' and 'constrained action.' Even when children engage in free action as they explore and play in natural areas, adults have usually promoted this possibility in some way, such as by choosing to live near a park or natural area and allowing their child free-ranging play in these places, letting a corner of their yard grow wild, volunteering to help plant a natural habitat at their child's preschool, choosing vacations on the beach or in the countryside, tolerating dirty clothes, or trusting their child to manage increasing levels of risk. At the same time, adults inevitably establish fields of constrained action as they seek to protect children from risks that they consider unmanageable.

The dependence of fields of free action on ample fields of promoted action and limited fields of constrained action applies to early childhood education as much as to parenting. For example, Malone and Tranter (2003) discovered in their comparison of five Australian primary schools that although three of the schools had natural areas in their grounds, children engaged in creative play in nature at only one school. This was at a Steiner school, the only setting where the teaching philosophy overtly encouraged children's connection with nature.

In his book *Last Child in the Woods*, Louv (2008) sounded the alarm that spontaneous play in nature has been largely lost within just one or two generations in high income nations like the United States, as children have become increasingly constrained indoors, and outdoor spaces have become increasingly urbanized, built over, trafficked, fenced and feared. Responding to these conditions, there are initiatives in the United States aimed at recreating conditions for children's free play and discovery in nature. The next section provides examples of childcare centers, nature centers and elementary schools which respect children's agency and seek to foster their sense of wonder.

Although these initiatives may be identified as efforts to restore 'lost worlds' of access to nature, they also present new possibilities for education for sustainability. Because they involve deliberate collective action by parents and teachers on behalf of children and nature, they have the potential to create spaces where children, too, can learn skills of collective organizing for environmental goals. Ecological psychologist Roger Barker (1968) argued that children require not only opportunities for autonomous exploration of their world, but also many 'behavior settings' where they can try out different roles and learn social as well as physical skills. These include opportunities to help decide courses of action and to execute decisions in a group (Heft and Chawla 2006). Just as wooded areas provide immediate feedback when children seek to dam a stream or climb to the top of a tree, children begin to learn what works and does not work in social and political spheres when they join with peers and adult partners to improve a school yard or restore a city park. The following sections highlight initiatives that exemplify education *for* as well as *in* and *about* the environment, enabling young children to work cooperatively toward sustainability at the same time as they learn in and about nature through play and exploration.

Three aspects of the United States context

The United States has long been ambivalent towards the urgency of sustainability efforts. The United States Congress famously declined to ratify the Kyoto Protocol to reduce greenhouse gas emissions, for example. Coal and oil production have historically been significant parts of the national economy, and these industries fiercely defend their interests. A current national controversy about importing unrefined oil from Canada in a pipeline through the United States – the Keystone XL Pipeline – pits jobs against sustainability, a contentious argument in an economy struggling to rise from a deep recession.

A second aspect of the United States context is the limited role of the federal government in education. Education is not specifically enumerated in the Constitution of the United States as a federal responsibility, thus, it is a state responsibility. Ever since the United States Department of Education was established in 1979, some conservative politicians have sought to abolish it on grounds that it takes power away from the states. The third aspect of the national context relates to this federal-state divide, but also to the culturally-enshrined practice of leaving the care and education of young children to their families. The United States, in contrast to Nordic countries for example, simply does not provide much support for its youngest citizens (Economist Intelligence Unit 2012). In 2008, local, state and federal governments spent about half as much per capita on children aged birth–5 years as on children aged 6–11 years (Edelstein *et al.* 2012: 9). Nonetheless, there are currently several federal initiatives aimed at promoting environmental education, including for young children.

These initiatives include those of the Environmental Protection Agency (EPA), established in 1970 as part of the national reaction to *Silent Spring*. Additionally, the National Education and Environment Fund (NEEF) was chartered by Congress in 1990 to support education and training activities, including the development of environmental education guidelines, training, and publications by the North American Association for Environmental Education (NAAEE). In 2012, the EPA, Department of Education, and Department of the Interior reconvened the 1990 Federal Interagency Task Force on Environmental Education, which works across all educational levels. A bill entitled 'Leave No Child Inside,' aimed at providing outdoor and environmental education in P-12 public schools has had two favorable hearings in the House of Representatives. This bill is widely supported; the Coalition for No Child Left Inside has more than 2,000 member organizations across 30 states. It is likely that this bill will be incorporated into a comprehensive education bill for all of the United States.

Another recent federal initiative focuses on Green Schools. The Green School movement began in various places, partly with home schooling parents, partly in states like Maryland which has a vigorous environmental education tradition. The movement received a boost when the federal government created a Green Ribbon Schools program in 2012 (US Department of Education 2012). To receive a prestigious Green Ribbon, a school must be nominated by its state Department of Education for showing excellence in:

- Reduced environmental impact and costs for its buildings, grounds and transportation
- Improved health and wellness for students, visitors and staff
- Effective environmental and sustainability education

The improved health and wellness criterion includes a 'quantity of quality outdoor time for both students and staff,' meaning that children must be outdoors some of the time. This time outdoors could include utilizing the environment for 'effective

Figure 15.1 The Lucy School in Middletown, Maryland, a Green Ribbon School, uses the surrounding farmland as an outdoor classroom and playground. The younger children enjoy much outdoor time. Photo by Lucy School

environmental and sustainability education.' Through these objectives, the outdoor environment is now being nationally recognized as an important dimension of education from pre-kindergarten through grade 12.

One of the first recipients of a Green Ribbon award, the Lucy School in Middletown, Maryland, began as a preschool for 3 and 4 year olds, situated in a renovated barn and surrounded by meadows, woods and a pond (see Figure 15.1). The curriculum emphasized nature and the arts. While maintaining the preschool, the Lucy School next built for the now primary-aged children a school that meets the highest environmental standards for construction and operation. The combination of the natural environment, its green technology building, and a curriculum that engaged children in the study of their buildings and grounds forms a powerful model for sustainability education. The Green Ribbon award signifies recognition of such education for young children.

Recently too, young children have become a focus of North American Association for Environmental Education (NAAEE) which has published *Guidelines for Excellence in Early Childhood Environmental Education* (2011), founded the *International Journal of Early Childhood Environmental Education* (2012) and launched an alliance for early childhood environmental education (2013). The *Guidelines* embody Carson's philosophy with their emphasis on play and rich experiences in nature. They come at an opportune time, as there is growing national concern at the lack of universal preschool education in the United States. Sustainability education must find its place in the overall education for young children as the nation responds to the reality that early years education is critical for optimal development, and eventually for a healthy citizenry now and into the future.

Nature-based preschools – models for sustainability education

One of the first nature-based preschools opened at the New Canaan Nature Center in Connecticut in the 1980s and others have since followed. Guided by the belief that they are raising the next generation of conservationists and nature center supporters, staff at such centers facilitate young children's access to the centers' generous acreages and diverse habitats on a daily or twice-weekly basis (see Figure 15.2). More than 20 preschool programs now exist in nature centers (Bailie 2012). The curriculum is usually based on the surrounding land and follows the seasons, and is augmented indoors with books, binoculars, toy animals, and other resources that reinforce the outdoor experiences. A recent study of these preschool programs found, not surprisingly, that the most successful centers had teachers with backgrounds in both environmental studies and early childhood (Bailie 2012).

Figure 15.2 Dodge Nature Center Preschool, St. Paul, Minnesota. Photo by Sheila Ridge Williams

In addition to preschool programs at nature centers, there are a handful of 'forest kindergartens' or 'forest schools' based on Northern European models. Although each program is different, basic practice immerses preschool children in rich outdoor environments in all weathers, with little or no indoor time. Models of this approach in the United States are: Forest Gnomes in Natick, Massachusetts; the Waldkindergarten of the Waldorf School in Saratoga Springs, New York; the Mother Earth School in Portland, Oregon; and the Cedarsong Forest Kindergarten on Vashon Island, Washington. Cedarsong in particular offers Forest School Teacher Certification in an effort to promote nature-immersion experiences for young children facilitated by knowledgeable and skilled teachers. These skills equip teachers to lead school-ground greening and nature study in preschools of all kinds (Rivkin 2013).

Nature-based preschools may be the forerunners of the next generation of preschools in the United States. They return early childhood education to its historical roots in gardening and nature play as promoted by Froebel, Montessori, Dewey and Steiner. For the last three decades, early childhood education has focused on literacy and social-emotional development, in line with school priorities. These priorities do not typically encompass outdoor learning. This limited understanding of the possibilities of outdoor learning is suggested in one of the key documents of early childhood education in the United States, *Developmentally Appropriate Practices* (Copple and Bredekamp 2009) that has shaped early childhood pedagogical practice since its first edition in 1987. Consistent with this neglect of outdoor learning, regulations governing childcare facilities now typically require minimal outdoor spaces. The state of Maryland, for example, requires only 75 square feet (6.97 square meters) of outdoor space per child. However, there is increasing national concern about growing rates of childhood obesity in the United States, and playing outdoors is associated with more vigorous as well as moderate activity (McCurdy *et al.* 2010). When Kimbro *et al.* (2011) reviewed data from more than 1,800 children in the United States Fragile Families and Child Wellbeing Study, they found a significant positive correlation between obesity and limited time spent in outdoor play, after controlling for potential confounding factors. Acting on data of this kind, the Natural Learning Initiative (NLI) in North Carolina initiated an extensive project for 'Preventing Obesity by Design' that develops nature-based play experiences outdoors for childcare centers throughout the state (http://naturalearning.org/pod-3). Partnering with the North Carolina State Department of Education, NLI has also participated in training for staff, families and communities about how to plan a high quality outdoor environment and to use it as an 'an extension of the indoor classroom and to model effective and meaningful teaching practices' (NLI 2010). This project sets a new standard for the early childhood field nationally.

Putting the elements of early childhood education for sustainability together

This chapter closes with two examples of early childhood programs that combine education *in, about* and *for* the environment in the context of a commitment to children's rights, and, specifically, the right to a voice in environmental decisions that affect their lives. Both programs are part of Growing Up Boulder, an initiative in the city of Boulder, Colorado, to include young people in participatory urban design and planning. Growing Up Boulder combines methods from the UNESCO Growing Up in Cities program (Chawla 2002, Driskell 2002) with principles of UNICEF's Child Friendly Cities Initiative (www.childfriendlycities.org) that guide municipal governments in aligning their laws and practices with the United Nations Convention on the Rights of the Child (UNICEF 1989). Although the United States is not a signatory to the Convention, city governments may independently choose to honor its principles.

The 'capabilities' approach to human development (Nussbaum 2011) bridges principles of human rights with psychological research that emphasizes the importance of human agency. This approach claims that it is not enough for governments to grant citizens legal rights; they also have an obligation to enable citizens to realize their rights. In the sphere of democratic participation, this implies that governments are obliged to provide opportunities for citizens to learn how to gather information about public issues and to express their views. Hayward (2012) reviewed research into children's ideas about citizenship, and found that many children feel either, socially isolated and excluded from citizenship, or believe that their possibilities for action are limited to individual behaviors such as turning out lights or reducing and recycling consumables. She argued that children need opportunities to learn that individual actions are good, but they can achieve more by working in partnership with others. This 'strong ecological citizenship,' as Hayward called it, goes beyond independent agency to valuing an interdependent sense of agency – interdependence amongst people and between people and the natural world.

The Growing Up Boulder program seeks to provide children and youth with experiences of this kind. Established in 2009, the program is an ongoing partnership between city government, the Boulder Valley School District, the Children, Youth and Environments Center for Community Engagement at the University of Colorado, and a number of other local non-government organizations that advocate for children's inclusion in civic processes and public spaces. The program reflects the city's commitment to honor children's civil rights to freedom of association and peaceful assembly, freedom of thought and expression, access to information, participation in the cultural life of their society, and expression of their views on matters that affect them. The Department of Community Planning and Sustainability and the Children, Youth and Environments Center fund part-time coordinators who have office space in the Center. They convene partners, oversee undergraduate interns and work with classes in Environmental Design to help implement program activities. Using a variety of methods such as walking tours, photography, digital stories, mapping, model making, letter writing, and public speaking (Driskell 2002), staff of partner organizations and undergraduate students engage children and youth in investigating issues in their community, developing ideas to improve city places and programs, and constructing enhancements such as public art. In effect, the program provides an organizational structure to create behavior settings where children can learn skills for active environmental citizenship. Although the city staff value this dimension of child and youth development, they have an immediate interest in understanding young people's perspectives so that they can create parks and public places that serve all ages well. The following examples represent two of many program initiatives, with a focus on young children.

Civic Area Redevelopment

In 2012, a major redevelopment of the Civic Area at the heart of the city commenced. The designated area included the main branch of the public library and its surrounding land, municipal offices, a tea house, art museum, farmers' market, and a central park that is the site of seasonal festivals. The Boulder Creek greenway, a linear park, runs through this area. To ensure that young people's ideas would be considered, the Growing Up Boulder team worked with different groups with an interest in the redevelopment. Project coordinators and undergraduate design interns, for example, engaged children who visited the area with their families in on-the-spot photovoice activities. Children took photos and wrote captions about features that they disliked, such as trash in the creek and parked cars, as well as those they liked, such as bike racks and lawns for running and playing. The coordinators also introduced more extended design and planning activities to school classes and the I Have a Dream after-school program for children from low-income families. A core partner in this work was the Boulder Journey School, which serves young children from six weeks to six years old.

A guiding principle of the Boulder Journey School is respect for children's rights. In the words of the school's director, Ellen Hall, this requires listening to young children and amplifying their voices (Hall and Rudkin 2011). 'Amplifying' does not necessarily mean making their voices louder, but translating what young children say in ways that enable adults to appreciate the value of their ideas. In order to include a class of four year olds in the redevelopment of the Civic Area, the school began by organizing a family picnic in the park beside the farmers market so that the children and their parents could familiarize themselves with the area destined for change. Back in the classroom, the children looked at pictures of the Civic Area and talked about their experiences (see Figure 15.3). Their teacher and the school's community specialist, who organizes events that connect the school and community, then held follow-up meetings with parents to explain the redevelopment process and how they, too, could participate through public meetings and online comments. The class divided into three groups of about six children each and, accompanied by parent volunteers, each group rode city buses on a field trip to explore the Civic Area more systematically. Once there, the groups played a game in which each child took turns leading the group to a place in the Civic Area that he or she wanted to explore. Everyone played at the chosen place for about 10 minutes, then it was the next child's turn. The teacher, community specialist and parents observed the children carefully, in the belief that children communicate through their actions as well as with words. After these visits, the teacher engaged the small groups in drawing and discussing their suggestions for Civic Area changes, and held conversations with the class as a whole about their ideas. From these activities and observations, the teacher, community specialist and a parent who was an environmental designer extracted five themes to share at a public forum and through the city's project website, using a collage and film composed from the children's pictures and words (www.growingupboulder.org/boulder-journey-school-research-process.html). The forum included the mayor, city council members, and urban planning and design staff. The children's contributions helped guide the selection of a final redevelopment plan to create a family friendly place that would appeal to all ages, including young children.

I would add a sandbox with lots of colors of sand. It can be in the sky so the birds can play there too.
—Lelah, age 4

I saw a butterfly. I want there to be lots of butterflies. We can just call them to come and then they will come. We can plant plants and they will like and they will come.
—Skyler, age 5

Figure 15.3 After four year olds at the Boulder Journey School visited the Civic Area and Boulder Creek greenway, many of their pictures and ideas recommended caring for the wildlife. Picture assembled by Ashley Bauer

Admiral Burke Park redevelopment

Another outcome of Growing Up Boulder was a partnership with the Department of Parks and Recreation to include children in the evaluation, design and restoration of city parklands. The city piloted its model with the Horizons School for kindergarten through eighth grade, a public school that borders Burke Park, a green space surrounded by a densely built neighborhood that includes a large retirement community (explorationsinburkepark.weebly.com). Growing Up Boulder coordinators and interns introduced the initiative in the school's 'Make a Difference' community service class. Children as young as eight began with a 'bioblitz' (an inventory of the park's plants and animals, including wetland species in and around a pond). They then photographed the site, identified their favorite places and potential areas for improvements, and built models of suggested changes. For the land adjacent to the school, they worked with the Department of Parks and Recreation to design a new nature-based playground. In public meetings, children presented their ideas to the Parks Department, school administrators, parents and local residents – including a contingent of elders. The children also interviewed older residents about their connections to the park and their goals for a park master plan. Although the youngest students in this initial phase of the project were eight year olds, the school has identified many ways to involve younger age groups in using the park as an outdoor classroom, and contributing to ongoing ecological restoration and park maintenance programs.

A significant aspect of these projects is that the line between school and community is becoming blurred. The city is viewed as a place that welcomes young children and youth into its parks and public spaces *and* respects their rights as active citizens now, not just in the future when they have become adults. To ensure that these projects are not one-time events, but steps toward having young people's participation a routine part of urban planning and park management, representatives of Growing Up Boulder's partner organizations meet every other month to review how projects are unfolding, share lessons learned, and generate ideas for future initiatives.

Concluding comments: building structures for strong ecological citizenship

Research on significant life experiences indicates that two primary sources of life-long care for the environment are free play and exploration in natural areas in childhood, with adults who encourage children's appreciation for the natural world. Acknowledging that fewer and fewer contemporary children have access to extended free play in nature around their homes, the initiatives described in this chapter represent efforts to bring nature to the preschools, childcare centers and primary schools where children now spend much of their time. When these places combine natural landscaping with philosophies that advocate for connecting children with nature, and when teachers are adequately educated to make the most of such sites, teachers can serve as 'companions in wonder' who encourage children's free play and discovery, share their interests in nature, and introduce supportive curricula that build on children's discoveries.

Essential as these steps are, however, the examples of children's participation in the Civic Area redevelopment and Burke Park master plan in Boulder suggest how education for sustainability can be taken beyond the buildings and grounds of schools and childcare centers. In both projects, schools served as springboards to children's involvement in planning how parks and open spaces in their city can be made as inviting as possible for young people. In both cases, children were asked to consider how public spaces serve multiple groups and think about how their interests could be integrated into intergenerational spaces. Spontaneously, the four year olds from the Journey School thought in terms of interspecies spaces. They found the wildlife in the Civic Area one of its most inviting features and they wanted to see habitats for wildlife enhanced. In the process, they introduced new ideas to the city's staff in urban planning and design. In Burke Park, children's engagement in ecological monitoring, restoration and management was part of the project's goals from the beginning, and Horizons School members enthusiastically embraced these activities. Children in these projects were not only engaged in education for sustainability in their schools, but also in improving opportunities for out-of-school encounters with nature for themselves and others.

While this chapter describes examples of good practice in early childhood education for sustainability, it also opens up questions about how to create community-wide structures to promote children's democratic participation as well as contact with the natural world. We see that these questions also offer potential for advancing research into what makes for successful early childhood education for sustainability partnerships. Schools and childcare centers are limited in what they can achieve by themselves. Everyone needs to think more boldly about the networks they belong to. To achieve this synergy, key questions include:

- *What types of partnerships can be forged to embed early childhood education for sustainability into the culture of collaborating institutions in the broadest possible way?* Partnerships work best when the interests of all partners are met. For example, the Natural Learning Initiative for childcare centers, 'Preventing Obesity by Design', was very much in the interest of the health care insurer, BlueCross/BlueShield, which provided major funding. Sometimes the specialized interests of a potential partner must be adopted but further developed as part of the project. The question for identifying partners is, 'Who is interested, and who else might be interested, if the goals were framed to meet their needs?'

- *What contributes to effective coordination when a variety of groups seek to work together for a common purpose?* In the example of Growing Up Boulder, a university center played a catalyzing and coordinating role to bring city agencies, the school district, and other local schools and organizations together to plan for children's inclusion in city planning and park management. How could staff in a city agency, a school administration, a local environmental group, or an organization for children be supported to assume this role?

- This coordinating role requires a secure source of funding for staff. *What different mechanisms can be found to fund staff who do the day-to-day work of identifying community partners, bringing them together, and ensuring the continuity that enables partners to become increasingly familiar with each other's capacities and resources and build on past collaborations?*

These are practical questions that early childhood programs and their communities can answer by sharing lessons learned through trial and error. Other important questions relate to challenges and benefits of these initiatives.

- *What tangible outcomes do these partnership experiences provide for young children, their teachers and/or childcare center staff?* Are there measurable impacts in terms of children's health, learning, sense of connection to nature, environmental behavior, and sense of agency in their schools and communities? What are impacts in terms of teacher and staff satisfaction, sense of wellbeing and retention?

An understanding that education extends beyond childcare centers and early childhood programs to the operation of program buildings, beyond buildings to their surrounding grounds, and beyond these grounds to the green spaces and civic areas of a town or city requires a shift in thinking in many quarters. Seeing children – including young children – as partners in building greener schools and communities requires a similar shift. In efforts to integrate sustainability into early childhood education, practice and research can be conceptualized as two feet moving forward in synchrony: one foot introduces and strengthens nature-based play and learning and supports children's agency in childcare centers, preschools, primary schools and cities; the other foot documents the outcomes of these efforts so that benefits can be widely communicated and programs can be continuously improved.

References

Asah, S.T., Bengston, D.N. and Westphal, L.M. (2012) 'The influence of childhood: Operational pathways to adulthood participation in nature-based activities', *Environment and Behavior*, 44(40): 545–69.

Bailie, P.E. (2012) 'Connecting children to nature: A multiple case study of nature center preschools', unpublished doctoral dissertation, University of Nebraska.

Barker, R. (1968) *Ecological Psychology*, Stanford, CA: Stanford University Press.

Blizard, C. and Schuster, J. (2004) '"They all cared about the forest": Elementary school children's experiences of the loss of a wooded play space at a private school in upstate New York', *Proceedings of the Northeastern Recreation Research Symposium*, GTR-NE-326: 57–63.

Carson, R. (1956) *The Sense of Wonder*, New York: Harper and Row.

Carson, R. (1962) *Silent Spring*, New York: Houghton-Mifflin.

Chawla, L. (1999) 'Life paths into effective environmental action', *Journal of Environmental Education*, 31(1): 15–26.

Chawla, L. (ed.) (2002) *Growing Up in an Urbanizing World*, London: Earthscan Publications.

Chawla, L. (2007) 'Childhood experiences associated with care for the natural world', *Children, Youth and Environments*, 17(4): 144–70.

Chawla, L. (2009) 'Growing up green', *Journal of Developmental Processes*, 4(1): 6–23.

Chawla, L. and Derr, V. (2012) 'The development of conservation behaviors in childhood and youth', in *The Oxford Handbook of Environmental and Conservation Psychology*, S. Clayton (ed.), New York: Oxford University Press, pp. 527–55.

Copple, C. and Bredekamp, S. (2009) *Developmentally Appropriate Practice in Early Childhood Programs*, Washington, DC: National Association for the Education of Young Children.

Crain, W. (2003) *Reclaiming Childhood*. New York: Henry Holt.

Davis, J.M. (2010) 'What is early childhood education for sustainability?' in *Young Children and the Environment: Early Education for Sustainability*, J.M. Davis (ed.), Melbourne: Cambridge University Press, pp. 21–42.

Driskell, D. (2002) *Creating Better Cities with Children and Youth*, London: Earthscan Publications.

Dunlap, J. and Kellert, S.R. (eds) (2012) *Companions in Wonder*, Cambridge, MA: MIT Press.

Economist Intelligence Unit. (2012) *Starting Well: Benchmarking Early Education Across the World*. Online. Available: www.lienfoundation.org/pdf/publications/sw_report.pdf (accessed 7 April 2013).

Edelstein, S., Isaacs, J., Hahn, H. and Toran, K. (2012) *How Do Public Investments in Children Vary with Age? A Kids' Share Analysis of Expenditures in 2008 and 2011 by Age Group.* Washington, DC: Urban Institute. Online. Available: www.urban.org/projects/kids_share.cfm (accessed 14 April 2013).

Gibson, E. and Pick, A. (2000) *An Ecological Approach to Perceptual Learning and Development,* Oxford: Oxford University Press.

Gibson, J.J. (1979) *The Ecological Approach to Visual Perception,* Boston, MA: Houghton-Mifflin.

Hall, E.L. and Rudkin, E. (2011) *Seen and Heard: Children's Rights in Early Childhood Education,* New York: Teachers College Press.

Hart, R. (1979) *Children's Experience of Place,* New York: Irvington.

Hayward, B. (2012) *Children, Citizenship and Environment,* London: Routledge.

Heft, H. (2001) *Ecological Psychology in Context,* Mahwah, NJ: Lawrence Erlbaum.

Heft, H. and Chawla, L. (2006) 'Children as agents in sustainable development', in *Children and Their Environments,* C. Spencer and M. Blades (eds), Cambridge: Cambridge University Press, pp. 199–216.

James, J.J., Bixler, R.D. and Vadala, C.E. (2010) 'From play in nature, to recreation then vocation,' *Children, Youth and Environments,* 20(1): 231–56.

James, W. (1912) *Essays in Radical Empiricism,* Cambridge, MA: Harvard University Press.

Kimbro, R., Brooks-Gunn, J. and McLanahan, S. (2011) 'Young children in urban areas: Links among neighborhood characteristics, weight status, outdoor play, and television-watching', *Social Science and Medicine,* 72(5): 668–76.

Louv, R. (2008) *Last Child in the Woods,* 2nd edn, Chapel Hill, NC: Algonquin Books.

Malone, K. and Tranter, P. (2003) 'Environmental learning and the use, design and management of school grounds', *Children, Youth and Environments,* 13(2). Online. Available: www.colorado.edu/journals/cye (accessed 25 January 2013).

McCurdy, L.E., Mehta, S.S., Winterbottom, K.E. and Roberts, J.E. (2010) 'Using nature and outdoor activity to improve children's health', *Current Problems in Pediatric and Adolescent Health Care,* 40(5): 102–17.

Matthews, J.R. (1992) 'Adult amateur experiences in entomology', in *Insect Potpourri: Adventures in Entomology,* J. Adams (ed.), Gainesville, FL: Sandhill Crane Press, pp. 321–8.

Monke, L. (2005) 'Charlotte's webpage' *Orion,* September/October, pp. 24–31.

Moore, R.C. (1986) *Childhood's Domain,* London: Croom Helm.

Moore, R.C. and Wong, H.H. (1997) *Natural Learning,* Berkeley, CA: MIG Communications.

Natural Learning Initiative (2010) 'North Carolina Department of Public Instruction (DPI) Outdoor Learning Environments Initiative'. Online. Available: www.naturalearning.org/content/north-carolina-department-public-instruction-dpi-outdoor-learning-environments-initiative (accessed 27 January 2013).

Nussbaum, M. (2011) *Creating Capabilities,* Cambridge, MA: Harvard University Press.

Reed, E.S. (1996a) *The Necessity of Experience,* New Haven, CT: Yale University Press.

Reed, E.S. (1996b) *Encountering the World,* New York: Oxford University Press.

Rivkin, M.S. (2013) *The Great Outdoors,* 2nd edn, Washington, DC: National Association for the Education of Young Children.

Sideris, L.H. (2008) 'The secular and religious sources of Rachel Carson's sense of wonder', in *Rachel Carson: Legacy and Challenge,* L.H. Sideris and K.D. Moore (eds), Albany: State University of New York Press, pp. 232–50.

Sobel, D. (2002) *Children's Special Places,* 2nd edn. Detroit: Wayne State University Press.

Stanley, E. (2011) 'The place of outdoor play in a school community', *Children, Youth and Environments*, 21(1): 185–211.

UNICEF (1989) *United Nations Convention on the Rights of the Child*. Online. Available: www.unicef.org/crc/ (accessed 14 February 2014).

United States Department of Education (2012) 'Green Ribbon Schools eligibility'. Online. Available: www2.ed.govprograms/green-ribbon-schools/eligibility.html (accessed 3 January 2013).

Ward-Thompson, C., Aspinall, P. and Montarzino, A. (2008) 'The childhood factor: Adult visits to green spaces and the significance of childhood experience', *Environment and Behavior*, 40: 111–43.

White, R. (1959) 'Motivation reconsidered: The concept of competence', *Psychological Review*, 66: 297–333.

Chapter 16

The Arts and education for sustainability

Shaping student teachers' identities towards sustainability

Lyndal O'Gorman

Abstract

The Arts are acknowledged for their potential in providing learners with multiple 'languages' with which they might make their learning visible across all levels of education. This chapter explores how the integration of the Arts and education for sustainability can provide expanded opportunities for seeing, understanding and responding to the sustainability imperative. Such approaches encourage broad engagement and expression of ideas about sustainability that extend beyond more common approaches that have mostly responded to sustainability through the languages of the Sciences and geography. Traditionally, the Arts have been valued highly by the early childhood education field and typically lie at the heart of early childhood programs. Increasing engagement with the sustainability agenda in early childhood contexts suggests that teachers might find ways to integrate early education for sustainability with the Arts in meaningful ways. This chapter explores how an integrated Arts and Humanities subject in an early childhood teacher education course in Queensland, Australia provides a context for the integration of sustainability as a cross-curricular thread in teacher education, reflecting recent national curriculum innovation in Australia.

Integrating the Arts and sustainability

The Arts are recognized as powerful ways of knowing, providing learners with multiple 'languages' with which they might make their learning visible. Put succinctly, 'the Arts offer universal languages that connect people with big ideas' (Everett *et al.*2009: 181). Throughout history, the Arts have served to confront, and to raise consciousness about controversial social issues (Leavy 2009). Increasingly, visual artists across the world are using the languages of painting, sculpture, photography, media and installation to advance the cause of sustainability (Curtis *et al.*2012; Steiner 2007; Young 2012). For centuries the Arts have provided humans with a vehicle for exploring their identities and developing the skills of creativity and flexibility that are required to address pressing and shifting local and global issues (Gibson and Ewing 2011; Robinson and Aronica 2009). A transformative view of sustainability, in which people are prompted to enact change at a personal and communal level, may be supported by engagement with the Arts; such engagement has the potential to change the ways in which people see their world.

In early childhood education contexts such as kindergartens and preschools, and in wider society, integrating the Arts and sustainability provides new opportunities of seeing, understanding and responding to the sustainability challenge that extends beyond more common approaches grounded in the fields of Science and Geography. A report of the International Alliance of Leading Education Institutes (IALEI) (Læssøe et al. 2009) provided an overview of ten nations' approaches to climate change and sustainable development and confirmed that, in a number of countries, education for sustainability sat firmly within school science curricula. Leavy (2009) proposes that the Arts and Sciences actually share common ground in their efforts to shed light on the human condition. The Arts, however, also have the capacity to communicate complex messages about sustainability by connecting with people emotionally and intellectually in ways that traditional approaches in the Sciences cannot (Curtis et al. 2012).

There could be many benefits from using approaches that enrich conversations about sustainability through integration with the Arts. According to Wright (2012) integrated approaches provide teachers and children with powerful opportunities for deep and enhanced learning across traditional subject boundaries. Ewing (2012) endorses this view, calling for broad and integrated approaches to knowledge and the development of learners' thinking skills and related attributes, rather than focusing on separate academic disciplines which risk the fragmentation of knowledge into 'meaningless chunks' (Gibson and Ewing 2011: xviii). Without integration, Ewing warns that new curriculum frameworks, such as those recently introduced in Australian early childhood services and in schools, risk disconnection with children. Also, the frameworks are in danger of becoming obsolete because of restricted possibilities for creativity and imagination. This is troublesome because creativity and imagination are key for learning in both the Arts and education for sustainability.

The Arts and sustainability in early childhood

The early childhood education field has a long history of interest in, and advocacy for, the Arts. With the Arts traditionally lying at the heart of early childhood programs, it is both possible and important to find ways of meaningfully integrating early education for sustainability with the Arts. The human capacity for art-making, for the flourishing of imagination, ingenuity, flexibility of thought and attraction to fiction, is at its peak in early childhood (Wright 2012). Across the spectrum of education contexts, if we expect anywhere to see children engaged in extended periods of high quality Arts education as active participants, it is within early childhood settings.

Children have a right to a rich, high quality Arts education (Gibson and Ewing 2011, MCEETYA 2007). However, current trends in Australia suggest that high quality Arts programs are at risk of being available only to the privileged few who might access extra-curricular Arts experiences (McArdle 2012). Likewise, children have a right to high quality education for sustainability. It is especially important that within education for sustainability, children be given opportunities to imagine and create their futures and to make their learning visible. The Arts make this possible (for example, Lewis *et al.* 2010). Further, Wright (2012) argues that the Arts provide young people with options to actively create their futures through critical thinking, problem-solving and openness to change. The transformative potential of the Arts (Ewing 2012; Gibson and Ewing 2011) can, in turn, enrich transformative approaches to education for sustainability. Ewing (2012) argues that the Arts can act as 'a catalyst for personal and social transformation' (p. 106). She argues that integration of the Arts facilitates transformation through students' active involvement in learning, by providing enhanced opportunities for collaboration, encouraging risk-taking, challenging stereotypical assumptions, and allowing students to see the world from different perspectives. Each of these benefits of Arts integration is potentially enhanced through integration with sustainability. The transformational potential of the Arts to alter habitual patterns of thought, sight and behaviour (Ewing 2012), and to envision different futures for ourselves and our planet (Everett *et al.* 2009), provides a powerful fit with transformational approaches to education for sustainability which seek to change the ways in which people see, know and act in the world.

Preparing teachers for Arts and sustainability curriculum integration

A critical factor in advancing education for sustainability is teacher education (UNESCO 2005). The research described in this chapter explored the ways in which an integrated Arts and Humanities subject in an Australian University early childhood teacher education course provided a powerful context for the integration of sustainability as a cross-curricular thread. Until recently, the Humanities, in Australian schools have been referred to as Studies of Society and Environment (SOSE) with sustainability embedded as a key concept into this key learning area. It remains to be seen how sustainability will be affected by the replacement of SOSE with separate History and Geography learning areas in the new Australian National Curriculum (Gibson and Ewing 2011), currently in the process of being implemented across the country.

Recent Australian national school curriculum documents – the first in Australia's history – name sustainability as a 'cross-curriculum priority' to be embedded in all learning areas (Australian Curriculum, Assessment and Reporting Authority 2011). This is similar to a Canadian approach (Læssøe *et al.* 2009), where education for sustainability in schools is also infused across the curriculum. However, such an approach has its critics. Doherty's (2012) critique of the new Australian Curriculum approach suggests that cross-curriculum priorities contribute to a 'complex web of cross-hatched perspectives that pull the citizen in different directions in their assemblage' (p. 2). The inclusion of sustainability as a cross-curriculum priority can also be seen to weaken its position, with advocacy groups such as the Australian Association for Environmental Education (AAEE) bemoaning the lack of real presence for cross-curriculum integration in the new Australian framework (Gough 2011), and in the overarching curriculum frameworks in nations such as the United Kingdom, United States, Canada and Korea (Læssøe et al. 2009). Such complexity is illustrated by Gough's (2011) exploration of a jigsaw metaphor to unpack the uncertain place of environmental education/education for sustainability in Australian education sectors, both prior to school and in school. In response to this complexity, robust examples of how integration of sustainability across the curriculum might work and what it might look like are timely.

Within the Australian early childhood field, the recent introduction of a national curriculum framework, *Belonging, Being and Becoming: The Early Years Learning Framework for Australia* (DEEWR 2009) for children in the birth to five age group, profiles early childhood education for sustainability by the inclusion of two learning outcomes – 'children are connected with and contribute to their world' and 'children become socially responsible and show respect for the environment' (DEEWR 2009: 29). Notably, Gough (2011) posits that linking the 'jigsaws' of early childhood and school curricula will add to the complexities of education for sustainability implementation in Australia especially if children move from one way of incorporating sustainability in the birth to five curriculum to a different way in the school curriculum. In addition, traditional views of childhood and children's relationships to nature may serve as stumbling blocks to critical approaches that value the ethics of care and children's active engagement in sustainability (Duhn 2012) at the early childhood level

Because of the recent curriculum changes, the Australian teacher education field is obliged to respond to the inclusion of sustainability more overtly than it has in the past, but within a potentially more complex curricular landscape. While many schools and early childhood services are demonstrating interest in sustainability, teacher education (including early childhood teacher education) has been slow to respond (O'Gorman and Davis 2012). That said, the introduction of these new Australian Curriculum frameworks in schools and early childhood settings has prompted renewed action towards the inclusion of sustainability content in teacher education.

The integrated Arts and Humanities subject

Authors such as Summers *et al.* (2003) highlight a number of complex issues surrounding teacher professional development in education for sustainability. These include varying emphasis on sustainability in different curriculum documents, dilemmas around learner engagement with local versus global topics (also mentioned by Duhn 2012), how to make a difference through action, and finding a balance between feelings of helplessness and empowerment. The integrated Arts and Humanities subject described in this chapter aimed to assist student teachers (the cohort was a mix of both in-service and pre-service teachers) to see the transformational possibilities of the Arts and education for sustainability while negotiating these complexities. The majority of students were enrolled in the subject as part of a one year Graduate Diploma in Education program specializing in the education of children from four to eight years of age. The program was offered in multiple delivery modes: internal, external, full-time or part-time. While the Arts and Humanities were initially placed together more for reasons of expediency within the course structure, the potential for deepening learning and engagement across both areas was ultimately enhanced through the inclusion of the cross-curricular concept of sustainability.

During their semester of study in this integrated subject, students engaged with content through a combination of online and face to face lectures and workshops, electronic discussion forums, links to video presentations, websites, virtual art galleries and a plethora of other online resources and learning activities. The following statement was included in the subject's rationale:

> The integration of the Arts and Humanities is at the core of this unit, defining ways of knowing and teaching that encourage and support young people to understand themselves and to be proactive in shaping peaceful, healthy, just and sustainable futures.
>
> (Unit Outline 2013: 1)

Typically, the student teachers engaged with new knowledge, reflected on their attitudes and values, and were challenged to adopt new practices – within both the Arts and Humanities. O'Gorman and Davis (2012) have already described in detail how these student teachers' engaged with an ecological footprint calculator tool as part of their learning, prompting powerful reactions and reflections on the causes of their large 'footprints'. These students identified their willingness to take individual actions such as reducing meat and electricity consumption, considered the early childhood teaching implications of large ecological footprints, made suggestions for social change, and indicated their strong support for the integration of sustainability with the Arts as a powerful curriculum approach.

The theoretical underpinnings of this subject were two-fold. Critical theory underpinned the education for sustainability component, and identity theory underlaid the Arts aspects as represented in a self-portrait or identity project that students undertook as a synthesizing task at the conclusion of the semester. Examples of the self-portrait are included in Figures 16.1 and 16.2, along with further details about the task. It has been suggested that Australian education for sustainability emerges out of critical theory (Davis and Elliott 2009) and aligns with Henderson and Tilbury's (2004) call for a model of education for sustainability that moves away from traditional approaches to environmental education such that 'it focuses sharply on more complex social issues such as the links between environmental quality, human equality, human rights and peace and their underpinning politics' (p. 8). Transformative education for sustainability also aligns closely with what Sauvé (2005) describes as 'social criticism' (p. 24), one of 15 'currents' that have shaped thinking about environmental education since the 1970s. According to Sauvé, a socially critical view of environmental education challenges individuals to confront their own beliefs, attitudes and actions and to challenge taken-for-granted social realities. In the subject described in this chapter, student teachers were engaged with how the Arts can speak to social issues, provide languages to express important thoughts about identities and beliefs, and encourage articulation of ideas that might challenge the status quo.

The second theoretical underpinning for this integrated Arts subject is identity theory. In their text on identity theory, Burke and Stets (2009: 3) state:

> Identity theory seeks to explain the specific meanings that individuals have for the multiple identities they claim; how these identities relate to one another for any one person; how their identities influence their behaviour, thoughts and feelings or emotions; and how their identities tie them in to society at large.

Throughout the semester, student teachers were challenged to consider how their attitudes towards social, environmental and political issues were shaped by and, in turn, acted to shape their sense of identity. Sustainability provided a context for enabling students to examine their behaviours, thoughts, feelings and emotions, and to reconsider their place in the local and global society, as Burke and Stets (2009) outline.

The subject was designed to profile the ways in which the Arts provides languages for artists to explore issues of identity, belonging, social justice, solidarity, environment, indigenous perspectives and sustainability. The work of these student teacher artists typically prompted discussions about what are appropriate visual images for sharing with young children. For example, Chris Jordan's photographs of dead albatross chicks – that were starved because their parents had fed them plastic marine debris – prompted questions such as *'Yes, but these wouldn't be appropriate to show to young children, would they?'* This example illustrates the potential disruptive power of visual imagery, both as a vehicle for confronting student teachers with global sustainability concerns, but also as a challenge to dominant views of childhood as a 'sheltered enclave dominated by romantic notions of childhood and nature' (Duhn 2012: 27). Indeed, the Arts have a role in mitigating feelings of helplessness and apathy that can put optimistic approaches to education for sustainability at risk (Summers *et al.* 2003, Taylor *et al.* 2009), by their capacity for confirming the positive processes of care and repair (Everett *et al.* 2009).

Overall, the integrated Arts and sustainability subject described in this chapter provided opportunities for these student teachers to encounter some powerful messages about sustainability delivered through the Arts. Such an approach gives these students alternative ways of viewing issues and, therefore, learning about sustainability while at the same time underscoring the power of the Arts as a language for communication. Thus, the subject provided student teachers with an example of how curriculum integration supports meaningful interactions between multiple learning areas, thus deepening, rather than diluting, the learning in seemingly disparate areas.

The culminating experience of the semester was an opportunity for these student teachers to use the language of the Arts to express their ideas about these issues through a self-portrait – their 'identity project' – which was shared with their tutor and peers by electronic uploading to an online gallery. Students were asked to create an artwork, using any medium that would express aspects of their identity. The self-portrait task provided students with a concrete example of an integrating device that brought together the Arts and Humanities. Several students chose to explore ideas about sustainability in their artwork. Two examples of these self-portraits and artist statements are provided here in Figures 16.1 and 16.2:

Online discussions of the Arts and sustainability

Another aspect promoting learning in the integrated Arts and Humanities subject was the online discussion forum. A large proportion of the student teachers who enrolled in the subject did so as external students who were encouraged to participate in a range of online engagement opportunities such as the discussion forum. At the end of Semester 2 (July–October 2010) I sought these student teachers'

In light of the integration of arts and SOSE, I felt compelled to explore the connection between self and the environment. 'Landscape' has a new relevance because of climate change. I am deeply passionate about environmental sustainability so to be able to communicate this through painting is strangely liberating and proactive.

Figure 16.1 Student self-portrait and artist's statement

My identity project explores the SOSE strand of place and space. I used oil pastels and paint as my medium for this piece. The tree is connected to my mouth, which signifies the relationship I have with nature. When I am outside and the natural environment surrounds me I feel at peace. I have always been in awe of the beauty that Mother Nature has provided us with.

Figure 16.2 Student self-portrait and artist's statement

consent to include their discussion forum conversations in a research project aimed at investigating their experiences of learning in this integrated Arts and Humanities subject. The study was conducted with ethical approval from the University's Human Research Ethics Committee, and 12 of the 18 students who had participated in the forum gave their consent. A three-step analysis process of their online discussions – as outlined by Creswell (2005) – was used. This involved *familiarization* with the data through multiple readings, followed by *thematic analysis* (cf. Denzin and Lincoln 2005). In the thematic analysis, students' responses were (1) compared with other responses in the forum; (2) compared with emergent categories or themes; and, (3) themes were compared with other themes (Creswell 2005). The third and final step, *synthesis*, required deeper investigation of the themes for further refinement and combination. For the purposes of this chapter, I refer to only one theme – the one that related to how this subject integrated the Arts and sustainability – and I only refer to a select number of entries from this theme. All five themes are detailed elsewhere (O'Gorman and Davis 2012).

A key idea emerging from the students' discussions about this subject was that the deep learning the students experienced involved high levels of discomfort, with one participating noting 'this unit is all about taking us out of our comfort zones, right?' The use of the Arts to connect people with big ideas (Everett *et al.* 2009) and to raise their consciousness about controversial social issues (Leavy 2009), is bound to cause discomfort from time to time; this subject provided fertile ground for such feelings, although it is important to note that those who taught the subject aimed to balance discomfort with suggestions for action-taking to mediate this discomfort.

As already discussed, the identity project that student teachers completed at the end of the semester supported the possibility of integration of Arts and SOSE concepts through the tangible creation of an artwork. The potential for the Arts to facilitate exploration and expression of identities (Gibson and Ewing 2011) was illustrated for these student teachers through their engagement with this task. The following forum participant illustrated the ways in which the subject contributed towards her growing awareness of personal and practical aspects of sustainability as she described her proposal for the artwork:

> As we have been talking so much about education for sustainability I wanted my work to really fit into the category where it won't need lighting or air-conditioning to be displayed. ... My passion for trees, leaves and native plants inspired me to make my face green.

The possibilities of integrating Arts and sustainability for the expression of 'big ideas' (Everett *et al.* 2009) and controversial issues (Leavy 2009) such as human rights is further illustrated by this student teacher's use of metaphor in her project as she planned to integrate the Arts and social justice themes:

> I seem to be in the endless loop as to the aspects of my identity I want to represent (or feel comfortable about representing). One aspect I keep returning to is my interest in social justice and the barriers that are faced by children, women and families in accessing basic human rights (education for example!). I have thought about using familiar images, such as the scales of justice for example, but they feel clichéd.

The following quote further illustrates how the opportunity to share identity projects helped these student teachers to consider the power of the Arts to express thoughts and emotions that lie deeply centred within the human experience. This forum participant was providing feedback on another student's proposal for the identity project:

> I love your idea for your portrait – showing both sides. When I think of your plan to use broken pieces of mirror it makes me think that even in the midst of such turbulence, your positive and resilient nature is depicted because it is you who is reflected back when you look at the pieces.

As mentioned previously, student teachers enrolled in this subject were presented with carefully-selected online resources to support their learning in the Arts and sustainability. One such resource was Ken Robinson's provocative lecture *How schools kill creativity* (Robinson 2006). Having viewed the video clip, one student teacher discussed her reaction:

> I recently viewed the video clip on the Blackboard site, by Sir Ken Robinson 'Do schools kill creativity?' and I must say it is fascinating viewing. There were a number of important points that I took from his talk including:

- we must educate for 'unpredictability' – no one knows what the future will be like
- we are currently educating children *out* of their creativity
- intelligence is three things: diverse, dynamic and distinct.

This subject opened up possibilities for students to consider how thoughts about identity might be challenged and enhanced by consideration of sustainability issues and topics. Student teachers were encouraged to think about how attitudes towards social, economic and environmental issues are linked to how we see ourselves and our place in the world. The identity project provided a context for some students to explore and express the links between identity and sustainability, and how this might be expressed using the Arts as a medium. It was encouraging to see how some students, like the artists to whom they were introduced over the semester, used the Arts to explore their thoughts about sustainability. This student, for example, used the online forum to share some preliminary ideas about his identity project with other students:

> For me it [the identity project] will have to be something to do with environmental issues of which I have much interest in and passion for. I have been involved in a few environmental campaigns over the years (and the occasional protest) thus it has been a big part of my life. My two kids are a big part of my life too so [I] was wanting to portray both them and environmental issues perhaps in the theme of sustainability (i.e. sustaining the world for their future!).

The above entry echoes sentiments explored by Howarth's (1992) notion of a 'chain of obligation' (p. 133) which describes the responsibilities of current generations to sustain the world for future generations.

As discussed, integrating the Arts and Humanities (especially with respect to sustainability) provides alternative ways of exploring identities, issues and responses to current challenges. The following entry illustrates how such integration provides new contexts and lenses for student teachers to explore and express fundamental aspects of who they are in an ever-changing world:

> Both the Arts and humanities make up such a vital part of who we are as people and the way that we differ from other animals on this planet. Children are able to look at problems in 'new ways' from adults and are able to simplify the problems much better than we can.

While this student teacher suggested that children are well-placed to examine and respond to the problems facing the world, another student expressed an alternative view about adults' expectations of children's responses to environmental issues such as global warming. In the following entry, she pointed to the value of dance and music as alternative languages for children to express their knowledge of such issues. Interestingly, this student teacher constructed an insightful argument about adults leaving too much responsibility in the hands of children and future generations without taking action themselves in the present:

> It's so great to see kids getting into saving the planet and the awareness they have. However, I wonder if the people (the governments) who have the power to change things are listening to the children. It makes me sad that we educate the children about global warming etc. and yet the people who have the power to change it, just smile, clap and say 'good on you' to the kids, but are the adults really listening? Or are they merely passing on important information to children and hoping for … what? I'm not sure. Children unfortunately have to depend on the adults to change things. As a teacher, I plan to lead by example.

A final example is from a student teacher who used the forum to reflect on her learning across the semester, and how the Arts and sustainability integration helped to build her understandings of the connections between humans and nature:

> This subject certainly seems to have moved us all! I have learned the importance of nurturing a strong sense of connection between ourselves and other life forms/nature. I think we often see ourselves as 'above' or 'apart from' mother nature, but if we can change our perceptions, really accept that humans are in fact just one more link in the chain, perhaps we will take caring for that chain more seriously! I think the Arts is one way to help us build this understanding.

The reference to 'changing perceptions' in the above quote is noteworthy. This chapter has presented an argument for Arts-based approaches as potentially useful strategies for reshaping the ways in which people interpret, express and act upon complex issues such as sustainability. To respond to the (un)sustainability problem, a good starting point might be for teachers to address their own perceptions about their place in the world, their relationships with nature, and their responsibilities for caring for the planet, before – or at least along with – the children they teach. The Arts have significant potential to contribute to our understandings of these issues.

Conclusion

This chapter provides a snapshot of what is possible in teacher education when the Arts and sustainability are integrated and has presented the Arts as offering opportunities for seeing, understanding, and expressing, through multiple 'languages', ideas and concepts relating to sustainability. The discussion and data presented here suggest that the integration of the Arts and education for sustainability provides opportunities for student teachers to be unsettled, challenged and inspired to respond to sustainability issues. However, I also acknowledge the limitations of the study from which the data were drawn. Although consent was sought at the conclusion of the semester, the participants were, in a sense, a captive group and the number of participants was small. Twelve students of an enrolment of 120 consented, so it is not possible to claim that the data are representative of the total cohort. Nevertheless, the ideas presented here provide a useful starting point for discussing the possibilities of integrating the Arts and education for sustainability in early childhood teacher education contexts, and indeed, in education contexts more broadly.

The Arts provide an alternative lens to learning that enables deeper engagement with sustainability ideas in ways that move beyond conventional modes of communication and learning based in the traditional science and social science fields. Education for sustainability must not be limited to these fields of knowledge. To do so would require considerable lowering of ambitions of what is achievable (Læssøe *et al.* 2009). The Arts have a recognized capacity for touching emotions and for portraying ideas that cannot be encapsulated in words. As the education for sustainability field continues to evolve and as the sustainability imperative becomes more urgent, it is important that we find innovative and creative ways to communicate ideas about sustainability to broader audiences. These audiences include academics in teacher education, pre-service and in-service teachers and ultimately the children and families that student teachers encounter in early childhood education contexts. With a recognized tradition of interest in and advocacy for the Arts and a growing commitment to early childhood education for sustainability, early childhood teachers are well-placed to respond to the challenges of sustainability with creativity, energy and insight, in part through meaningful integration with the Arts. Effective teacher education, in which the Arts are considered as a lens and a language for exploring and expressing sustainability ideas is key, both for illustrating the value of well-considered curriculum integration in early childhood settings and for shaping early childhood teacher views about sustainability.

References

Australian Curriculum, Assessment and Reporting Authority (ACARA) (2011) *Cross-Curriculum Priorities*. Online. Available: www.acara.edu.au/curriculum/cross_curriculum_priorities.html (accessed 23 April 2013).

Burke, P. and Stets, J. (2009) *Identity Theory*, Oxford: Oxford University Press.

Commonwealth of Australia Department of Education, Employment and Workplace Relations (DEEWR) (2009) *Belonging, Being and Becoming: The Early Years Learning Framework for Australia*, Canberra: Department of Education, Employment and Workplace Relations.

Creswell, J. (2005) *Educational Research: Planning, Conducting, and Evaluating Quantitative and Qualitative Research*, Upper Saddle River, NJ: Pearson.

Curtis, D., Reid, N. and Ballard, G. (2012) 'Communicating ecology through art: What scientists think', *Ecology and Society*, 17(2): 3. Online. Available: http://dx.doi.org/10.5751/ES-04670-170203 (accessed 28 January 2013).

Davis, J. and Elliott, S. (2009) 'Exploring the resistance: An Australian perspective on educating for sustainability in early childhood', *International Journal of Early Childhood*, 41(2): 65–77.

Denzin, N. and Lincoln, Y. (eds) (2005) *Handbook of Qualitative Research*, 3rd edn, Thousand Oaks, CA: Sage.

Doherty, C. (2012) 'Forging the heteroglossic citizen: Articulating local, national, regional and global horizons in the Australian Curriculum', *Discourse: Studies in the Cultural Politics of Education,* DOI:10.1080/01596306.2012.745729.

Duhn, I. (2012) 'Making 'place' for ecological sustainability in early childhood education', *Environmental Education Research*, 18(1): 19–29.

Everett, L., Noone, G., Brooks, M. and Littledyke, R. (2009) 'Education for sustainability in primary creative arts education', in M. Littledyke, N. Taylor and C. Eames (eds), *Education for Sustainability in the Primary Curriculum*. South Yarra, VIC: Palgrave Macmillan.

Ewing, R. (2012) 'Competing issues in Australian primary curriculum: Learning from international experiences', *Education 3–13: International Journal of Primary, Elementary and Early Years Education*, 40(1): 97–111.

Gibson, R. and Ewing, R. (2011) *Transforming the Curriculum Through the Arts*, South Yarra, VIC: Palgrave Macmillan.

Gough, A. (2011) 'The Australianness of curriculum jigsaws: Where does Environmental Education fit?' *Australian Journal of Environmental Education*, 27(1), 9–23, DOI:10.1017/S0814062600000045.

Henderson, K. and Tilbury, D. (2004) *Whole-school Approaches to Sustainability: An International Review of Sustainable School Programs*. Report prepared by the Australian Research Institute in Education for Sustainability (ARIES) for the Department of the Environment and Heritage, Australian Government.

Howarth, R. (1992) 'Intergenerational justice and the chain of obligation', *Environmental Values,* 1(2): 133–40.

Læssøe, J. Schnack, K. Breiting, S. and Rolls, S. (2009) *Climate Change and Sustainable Development: The Response from Education* (A cross-national report from the International Alliance of Leading Education Institutes). Aarhus: Aarhus University.

Leavy, P. (2009) *Method Meets Art: Arts-Based Research Practice,* New York: The Guilford Press.

Lewis, E., Mansfield, C. and Baudains, C. (2010) 'Going on a turtle egg hunt and other adventures: Education for sustainability in early childhood', *Australasian Journal of Early Childhood,* 35(4): 95–100.

McArdle, F. (2012) 'The visual arts: Ways of seeing', in S. Wright (ed.), *Children, Meaning Making and the Arts*, 2nd edn, French's Forest, NSW: Pearson.

MCEETYA (2007) National education and the arts statement. Ministerial Council on Education, Employment, Training and Youth Affairs, Cultural Minister's Council. Online. Available: www.curriculum.edu.au/verve/_resources/National_Education_Arts_Statement.pdf (accessed 23 April 2013).

O'Gorman, L. and Davis, J. (2012) 'Ecological footprinting: Its potential as a tool for change in pre-service teacher education', *Environmental Education Research,* DOI:10.1080/13504622.2012.749979.

Robinson, K. (2006) *How Schools Kill Creativity* (video file). Online. Available: www.ted.com/talks/ken_robinson_says_schools_kill_creativity.html (accessed 28 January 2014).

Robinson, K. and Aronica, L. (2009) *The Element: How Finding your Passion Changes Everything*, Camberwell, VIC: Penguin.

Sauvé, L. (2005) 'Currents in environmental education: Mapping a complex and evolving pedagogical field', *Canadian Journal of Environmental Education,* 10(1): 11–37.

Steiner, A. (2007) *Art in Action: Nature, Creativity and our Collective Future*, San Rafael, CA: Natural World Museum, Earth Aware Editions.

Summers, M., Corney G. and Childs, A. (2003) 'Teaching sustainable development in primary schools: An empirical study of issues for teachers', *Environmental Education Research*, 9(3): 327–46.

Taylor, N., Littledyke, R. and Eames, C. (2009) 'Why do we need to teach Education for Sustainability at the primary level?' in M. Littledyke, N. Taylor and C. Eames (eds), *Education for Sustainability in the Primary Curriculum*, South Yarra, VIC: Palgrave Macmillan.

UNESCO (2005) *Guidelines and Recommendations for Reorienting Teacher Education to Address Sustainability*, Paris: UNESCO.

Wright, S. (2012) 'Ways of knowing in the arts', in S. Wright (ed.) *Children, Meaning Making and the Arts*, 2nd edn, French's Forest, NSW: Pearson.

Young Imm Kang Song (2012) 'Crossroads of public art, nature and environmental education', *Environmental Education Research*, DOI:10.1080/13504622.2012.670208

Chapter 17

Science in preschool – a foundation for education for sustainability?

A view from Swedish preschool teacher education

Bodil Sundberg and Christina Ottander

Abstract

In this chapter we elaborate on how science encounters can be used within education for sustainability (EfS) in preschool practice as a means of empowering children to engage with sustainability. We acknowledge recent research arguing for a rethink of what science teaching in preschool can be. Such rethinking involves a shift from viewing science in preschool as mainly nature experiences, towards introducing young children to science inquiry. By doing so, the interplay between knowledge, values and the ways in which humans build and make use of new knowledge can become visible, thus laying a foundation for EfS. Implementation of science inquiry processes in preschools would, however, necessitate changes in preschool teachers' personal and professional views of science, nature and pedagogy. In our research we have explored how competence in inquiry-based teaching may, or may not, develop during pre-service preschool teacher education. We have also observed how competence can develop, but still not be realized in practice due to culturally and historically grounded attitudes and notions about science and about teaching. Drawing on these findings, we initiate discussion about how pre-service and in-service teacher education can support a broader view of teaching and science to fit the 'community of practice' of preschools and hence, make a contribution to EfS. Our suggestions highlight the need for pre-service and in-service education to explore the historical/cultural contexts of preschool practices and teachers' roles in raising children's awareness of their own scientific observations and science learning processes. We also stress the need for stronger co-operation between teacher educators and teachers in practicum (teaching practice) settings to ensure that pre-service students experience preschool environments where they have opportunities to challenge norms and practise inquiry teaching skills that are foundational for EfS.

Introduction

In this chapter we elaborate if and how science in preschool can lay foundations for EfS. As a starting point, we elaborate how EfS and science are represented in the Swedish curriculum for the preschool, *Läroplan för förskolan (Lpfö) 1998 revised*

2010, (National Agency for Education 2011) compared with the United Nation's definition of education for sustainability (UNESCO 2005, 2009). We then discuss these topics in relation to results from a longitudinal study of preschool teacher students' development of attitudes towards, and competence in, science teaching. We also elaborate on how a change in science encounters can be used to strengthen EfS in preschool practice in Sweden.

Education for sustainability and science in the preschool curriculum

The overall goal of the United Nations Decade of Education for Sustainable Development (UN DESD) is to integrate the principles, values and practices of sustainable development into all aspects of education and learning (UNESCO 2005, 2009). The key educational principles for the UN DESD are identified as: interdisciplinarity, holism, critical thinking, problem-solving, multi-method approaches, participation, decision-making, applicability and local relevance. The overall goal of the UN DESD is relevant to preschool curricula; however, we question if this goal is being achieved in Swedish preschool practice.

EfS in Sweden, and in Scandinavia generally, has its roots in environmental education (Sandell *et al.* 2005) and, in schools, this has traditionally been dealt with during science sessions. As such, content has been concerned with understandings of biological, chemical and physical processes, mostly in relation to the environmental disturbances caused by humans (Ashley 2000, Öhman 2006). The shift from environmental education to education for sustainability according to Sandell *et al.* (2005) has been informed by three different traditions: fact-based (learning about nature in nature), normative (learning pro-environmental behaviours), and pluralistic (emphasizing different opinions and critical thinking in sustainable education).

Sustainability has a place in the new Swedish national preschool curriculum (National Agency for Education 2011) even though the actual terms ESD or EfS are never mentioned. Fundamental values and tasks to optimize children's potentials are included in the curriculum, for example, that the preschool should support children to create a positive image of themselves as learners and creative individuals. The curriculum describes supporting children to become confident in their abilities to think for themselves – to act, to move and to learn – that is, to fully develop in a broad range of ways. Moreover, the curriculum states that the preschool should emphasize issues concerning the environment and nature conservation. For example, an ecological approach and a positive belief in the future should typify the preschool's activities and the preschool program should stimulate caring attitudes towards nature and the environment. The preschool should also help children understand that daily living and work can be organized in such a way in order to contribute to a better environment, now and in the future (National Agency for Education 2011).

The science goals described in the curriculum state that the preschool should strive to ensure each child develops their:

- interest and understanding of the different cycles in nature, and how people, nature and society influence each other;
- understanding of science and relationships in nature, as well as knowledge of plants, animals, and simple chemical processes and physical phenomena; and
- ability to distinguish, explore, document, ask questions about and talk about science.

(National Agency for Education 2011)

The first two goals in the science curriculum have much in common with the knowledge-based traditions mentioned above. This is the way environmental teaching in Swedish preschools has been traditionally implemented; predominantly, it has been concerned with recycling, compost management and nature experiences. In particular, children's encounters with nature, their development of knowledge about nature, and the fostering of respect and care for each other and nature, have been central (Ärlemalm-Hagsér 2013). Within this discursive consensus, there is also a strong belief in nature experiences as fundamental to a lifelong commitment to the environment (Ärlemalm-Hagsér 2013, Bergnér 2009). This accords with Davis (2009) who reports that most research studies in early childhood EfS focus on education *in* and *about* the environment, namely about children's relationship with nature and children's understanding of the phenomena in nature, rather than reporting on education *for* the environment where children are actors. In this type of knowledge-based teaching *in* and *about* nature, science becomes reduced to a set of facts. The third goal of the curriculum however, opens up the potential for scientific processes to be explored and thereby an opportunity for children's participation, agency and critical thinking.

There is still a lack of studies showing how preschools actually interpret the goals of the Swedish curriculum. One exception is a recent study by Ärlemalm-Hagsér (2013) where she investigated how EfS was interpreted and implemented in Swedish preschools. In this study, EfS was seen as an important task and preschool children were participating in various sustainability-related activities. The study, however, also described EfS as affirming mainstream practices where underlying structures of knowledge, content or ways of working were not challenged or transformed. Ärlemalm-Hagsér also pointed out that in preschool practice as well as in the preschool curriculum, there was no discussion of the preschool child as a political, critical thinker and active subject. Her conclusion was that 'one way to move further is to acknowledge children's thoughts, ideas and initiatives and to create opportunities for shared critical thinking' (p. 122). In our opinion, this is the area where a broader view of science activities in preschools could be productive.

We argue that the implementation of EfS would benefit from this broader view of science. Rather than viewing science as a set of facts, we promote science as a process that uses specific methods to explore, investigate and practise critical thinking. By taking this stance, we acknowledge recent research arguing for a rethink about what preschool science teaching can be. Experiencing science as a critical knowledge-producing process introduces children to the interplay of knowledges and values, and the ways in which humans build and make use of new knowledge (Colucci-Gray *et al.* 2012). If science is introduced in such a way, science experiences have the potential to become a means of empowering children (Andersson and Gullberg 2012). The concept 'emergent science' (Johnston 2008, Siraj-Blatchford 2001) emphasizes such a shift, from mere concept learning and a means to reach pre-determined answers, to scientific questioning, and promoting children's scientific skills, attitudes, understandings and language through their shared investigations as a process (Larsson 2013).

Implementation of such an approach requires changes in preschool teacher's personal and professional views of science as well as their science teaching competence. In our research, we have explored how such competence may or may not be promoted in preschools. Drawing on these findings, we discuss how pre-service and in-service training can support teachers to widen their ideas about science learning, so that it supports EfS. We discuss our experiences based on a longitudinal study with student teachers who undertook practicum during their pre-service education, as well as drawing on observations of science activities conducted in Swedish preschools, interviews with preschool teachers, and a nationally distributed questionnaire to Swedish preschool teachers.

Preschool teacher students' competence and confidence in EfS and science teaching

Between 2008 and 2012, we followed 65 student teachers enrolled on a Swedish university preschool teacher education program in a longitudinal study (Sundberg and Ottander 2013). The aim was to explore how students described and developed competence in, and attitudes towards, science, science teaching and the teachers' role. The rationale for following these students was that they were enrolled in a teacher education innovation, and we wanted to explore how the new program impacted on students learning. The new program contained a full year of combined subjects in Science and Creative Arts, which offered more Science content than is usually offered in Swedish preschool teacher education programs. The students in this study, theoretically, would have greater possibilities to gain competence and confidence in implementing science activities with children because of their additional exposure to science knowledge and science education pedagogies through the science and arts combined-course focus.

Earlier reports have indicated that science teaching in preschool is often poorly developed or not evident at all. Preschool teachers seem to lack understandings of what science might look like in an everyday preschool context, which means they may miss science 'teachable moments' (Tu 2006). Reasons often cited for poor science teaching in preschools are preschool teachers' negative attitudes towards science, in combination with lack of competence and confidence in teaching the subject with young children (e.g. Appleton 2008, Garbett 2003, Harlen and Holroyd 1997, Spector-Levy *et al.* 2011). Suggestions have therefore been made, for more science in preschool teacher education in order to overcome negative attitudes and to enhance teaching competence and confidence. Preschool teachers' epistemological beliefs have also been put forward as an obstacle to high quality science education in preschools. For example, the argument that minimal input from teachers is the best learning environment for children has been reported (Fleer 2009, Thulin 2011), and that children are best left to 'discover' science knowledge and skills in the learning environment. Hence, we were interested in following these pre-service student teachers' development of competence and confidence to implement preschool science activities.

The combined Science-Creative Arts year was designed to provide both content knowledge and competencies appropriate to responding to young children's questions and experiences of nature and natural phenomena. Also, the students were introduced to the basics of scientific inquiry and the pedagogical aspects of these activities with children. Scientific themes were covered in various ways – lectures, excursions, group discussions, and individual and group assignments. Within all science themes, creative activities were integrated and a wide range of art techniques were taught. For example, when exploring a science theme about 'Space', students made models of planets in papier mâché and performed space dramas with shadow play, and a 'creepy crawly' theme involved making spider models from recycled materials. The purpose of integrating the Arts with Science was to give the students additional tools for developing skills such as questioning, observation and communication, all relevant for scientific inquiry and play-based preschool pedagogy.

The developing attitudes of the students were sampled using five different questionnaires distributed to all students at intervals during their program. The first questionnaire was handed out two weeks into semester one. The second, third and fourth questionnaires were distributed at the beginning, middle and end of the Science and Art year respectively. The final questionnaire was sent one month after the students had fully completed their studies.

Closed questions were constructed as Likert items with statements to disagree (1) or agree (5) to. The 1–5 scale probed the extent of student agreement with statements such as *The most important aspect of outdoor activities is that children have an opportunity to practise motor skills, Children need to learn inquiry skills early,* and *I will often arrange pedagogical activities with scientific content.* Open-ended questions related to the students' perceptions of science teaching and their role when teaching science. Typical questions were: *Describe the type of activities with scientific content you want to arrange? What is the purpose of this activity? How do you picture your role in the activity?* and *How do you think teachers can help children develop scientific process skills?* Later, based on student descriptions of their role and from their reports in the assignment that was set for the first practicum period, nine students were invited to participate in individual semi-structured interviews, and all agreed. The interviews focused on attitudes towards science activities in the preschool and, more specifically, how these students felt about the scientific activity they were expected to plan and implement as part of their assessment.

The results from this study, described in more detail below, led us to initiate an additional, and still ongoing, research project to explore how (or whether) current preschool practices meet science learning goals. This is an interpretative study underpinned by activity theory (Engeström 1987) and theories of cultural reproduction and communities of practice (Lave and Wenger 1991), thus focusing on how beliefs about preschool, the preschool teacher's role and the goals of science influence preschool pedagogy. Qualitative data has been collected from interviews with preschool teachers and principals, observations of staff meetings and science activities and video-recalled group interviews based on recorded preschool practices. To obtain a more comprehensive picture, questionnaires with, in part, similar questions to those of the longitudinal study described above, were also sent to 1,700 preschool teachers nationally. At the time of writing, we have preliminary results from 400 preschool teachers.

Results

As described above, reluctance to teach science in preschool has been connected to poor content knowledge and negative teacher attitudes towards science. Our results indicate that this issue is far more complex and involves attitudes towards 'teaching' in preschool generally, and towards teaching science, nature and environmental care in preschool, specifically. For clarity, we have divided our results into two themes: *nature experiences as science and environmental teaching* and *teaching without teaching*.

Nature experiences as science and environmental teaching

This first theme illustrates a complexity of views concerning *science and environmental teaching* in Swedish preschool practice. First, an implicit connection seems to be made between children *experiencing nature*, *science learning* and the development of *human-nature connectedness*. When starting the one-year Science/Creative Arts course, a majority (89 per cent) of students claimed that they were looking forward to arranging pedagogical activities with scientific content and many (75 per cent) believed they would often engage in such activities. However, when students were asked to describe the types of activities they would plan for in the future, we could not find any descriptions of purposefully-designed activities that focused on learning about nature or that were aimed at developing scientific skills. Rather, the vast majority of students described a range of nature experiences that lacked any evidence of planned educational interventions, for example, going to the forest for a picnic or having free play in nature. A typical student response was: *Excursions to the forest, playground etc.,* or *a lot of outdoor activities.* In a few cases, learning about or exploring nature was briefly described, simply as *exploring nature* with no further details provided.

In the same questionnaire, we also asked the students to freely associate the two words 'nature' and 'science'. Comparing these answers with other answers in the questionnaire revealed a picture where science was given quite different meanings by the students, depending on the contexts. Science, in a broad sense, was associated with rote learning of facts and concepts, school memories of experiments, and in a few cases, with negative feelings. In other words, science was associated with traditional school-based views. In a preschool context however, science was interpreted as nature experiences, often without any teacher/adult guidance. This view was in line with their free associations where nature was linked with forests, living organisms, physical activities outdoors, and having positive feelings. The same kind of reasoning was also common amongst the experienced preschool teachers in the later follow-up project. For example, when we approached preschool teachers to ask if we could visit during science activities, we were most often invited to take part in nature (forest) excursions. Results from the questionnaires sent to 1,700 experienced preschool teachers also revealed that almost all respondents saw general outdoor activities as providing most of the science teaching and learning.

In addition to science learning, nature experiences were also seen as a fundamental means for learning about human–nature connectedness. Often science and nature experiences were considered as two sides of the same coin. A typical response from an experienced preschool teacher was: *Nature provides good context for how everything is connected* (Preschool teacher, 197). This view is typified also by this student's view:

> To be in nature ... If you do that you will get more experiences of nature and will probably take care of it. Nature has much to be discovered. But to understand there is often also a need for scientific explanations. Nature is a very good environment for children to gain knowledge and come up with questions they then can find answers to. Nature also practises the kids' motor skills.
>
> (Student 22, questionnaire 4)

To sum up, we believe a more encompassing view of science in the preschool can be a tool for developing practice where children learn shared critical thinking through inquiry skills. However, our examples above illustrate that attitudes and beliefs related to preschool practice and science may cause challenges for the implementation of such activities. This, in turn, is tightly connected to the complex issue of *teaching* in preschool, the next theme we explore here.

Teaching without teaching

As a result of the intensive Science/Creative Arts year, the vast majority of the students expressed growing competence about science and science teaching as well as increasing appreciation of the competencies of young children. This is exemplified by the following student comment recorded at an end of year interview:

> At first I was a bit sceptical [towards science], because I haven't studied science ... or I'm not an outdoor person ... The children have so many ideas and thoughts, actually about things we have learned in this [science] course ... it

feels quite good. Sometimes, I have the answer when they ask a question. That means you can discuss it with the child directly, when they still remember it.

(Student 1)

Our results somewhat unexpectedly showed that, in spite of their growing science competence and confidence, many students still found implementing science activities to be awkward in the preschool, as they tried to protect children from early introduction of a school culture where rote learning of science prevails. A view of a rigid elementary school culture lay at the heart of the matter. Such an image simply did not align with the students' strong views of preschool as being very different from school. In the interviews, one of the students shared their point of view as follows:

I don't want to be a teacher ... that person who stands in front and gives information ... I want to be a support to inspire, so that they can do themselves. They [the children] learn by being interested. If it is something fun ... Like, you can play, and then you see, what sticks, sticks. You can't force anything onto them ... And there I see a big difference, how it changes when you enter the school world. That's what I want to protect the children from.

(Student 14)

In response to this school-based image of science learning and teaching, the idea of teaching science inquiry skills becomes problematic. Even though we could see a shift in attitudes towards greater appreciation of a preschool teacher who actually plans and leads science inquiry activities, the key characteristics of a science activity described by the students remained as something that was mainly fun, and evolved with as little interference by the teacher as possible. A typical response was: *I would choose something that interests the children. Something that is not too difficult. Talk about it, ask what they can see and feel etc.* (Student 55, questionnaire 4).

Only in a few student interviews was the actual purpose of engaging in the inquiry process clearly expressed:

I would take them out in nature and then listen to their questions. Drawing from that I would bring materials so that they could figure the answers out themselves. I would make them become familiar with the material and inquiry methods.

(Student 21, questionnaire 4)

Thus, in contrast to previous findings demonstrating that preschool teachers lack science knowledge and confidence (e.g. Harlen and Holroyd 1997, Saçkes *et al.* 2011), our results indicate that the clash of different learning cultures might be the major obstacle for purposefully-framed education focused on science inquiry skills.

During recent decades, different theories and paradigms have informed preschool practice (Woodhead 2006). In Sweden, these appear to have had little effect on preschool practice, as traditional values and approaches such as combining nurturing, caring and education have mostly remained in place within preschool culture (Tellgren 2008). These values include ideas about the teacher as the guide who follows children and their interests, rather than vice versa. When combined with a strong belief that preschool learning is very different from school learning, these values seem to have as much, or perhaps even greater, impact on the types of activities implemented in preschools, despite what might occur in pre-service teacher education courses.

According to our data, student teachers are already well acquainted with the preschool 'community of practice' (Lave and Wenger 1991) that effectively marginalizes science when beginning their studies, and their practicum periods do little to support changes towards using science inquiry. Not one of our interviewed students referred to preschool supervisors who guided them in planning and implementing science inquiry activities during practicum. Also, our observations of experienced preschool teachers' strategies to stimulate inquiry indicated that social learning, such as taking turns and listening to each other, rather than science content and skills, were the main learning foci (Sundberg et al. 2013). This is somewhat alarming as a number of studies indicate that adult guidance is a cornerstone in children's science inquiry learning experiences (Inan et al. 2010, Nayfeld et al. 2011, Peterson and French 2008).

The possibility of adding science inquiry as a means for promoting EfS in preschool practice might thus be problematic depending of traditional beliefs of what fits, and does not fit, into preschool practice. Adding to this complex situation in Sweden is the very special place nature has in Swedish preschools. Most preschool children experience free play outdoors at least for a couple of hours every day and many preschools have a weekly whole day outing. A key feature of these outdoor activities is that they are valued as a special zone for children's free play guaranteed not to be like school (Halldén 2009). In the context of EfS, the question arises: *If a cornerstone of children's learning is adult guidance (teaching), how is science and environmental learning to come about if it is supposed to happen automatically in a teaching free zone?* By posing this question we do not mean to devalue positive outcomes of free play in nature, but we do want to highlight the complexity of a situation where nature is meant to serve as both a teaching free zone *and* the place where learning of science, inquiry skills and environmental care is to take place.

Implications for early childhood teacher education

In summary, we have identified some epistemological beliefs within preschool practice that affect what types of science activities are considered appropriate in preschools. We have also identified a complicated set of views about nature, nature experiences, the development of environmental care, and teaching that directly impact the potential for implementing EfS. Here we discuss how pre-service and in-service teacher education can support future and current preschool teachers to broaden science learning to include inquiry skills so that it can become a foundation for EfS. We focus on discussing how a broader view of science might better fit into the community of preschool practice, and the science Pedagogical Content Knowledge (PCK) that preschool teachers require in order to realize purposeful emergent science education in preschools.

Broadening the perspective of teaching and science in preschool

The ability and competence to teach specific content is not only a matter of specific PCK. Attitudes towards science content knowledge also play an important role, as well as teachers' philosophical understandings about learning and the teachers' pedagogical role. As we have identified from our longitudinal study, pressure to take a more active role in 'instructing' young children can result in stressful situations in a community of practice that traditionally ranks 'adult instruction' as least important for enhancing children's learning (Broström *et al.* 2012, Lobman and Ryan 2007). This suggests that teacher educators may need to innovatively rethink *their* practices in order to meet the challenges that arise from new curricula that have more fully elaborated learning objectives. We believe the challenge here is to broaden both the view of teaching and the view of science.

First, the notion of dividing play and learning into separate entities needs to be problematized (Pramling Samuelsson and Johansson 2006). The *Belonging Being Becoming: Early Years Learning Framework for Australia* (DEEWR 2009), for example, has adopted 'intentional teaching' as a pedagogical practice, which involves educators being deliberate, purposeful and thoughtful in their teaching decisions and actions. This offers an intermediate alternative to teaching by rote learning or continuing almost exclusively with free play traditions, simply because things have 'always been done that way'.

Second, the concept of emergent science may fit more effectively into the preschool community than the tradition of school-based rote learning. Emergent science emphasizes the inquiry skills that we believe are an important ingredient for shared critical thinking between teachers and learners. Of course, for a preschool teacher to arrange purposeful, educational, emergent science activities, general science literacy competence is more than helpful. Teacher educators can be guided, for example, by the *Principles and Big Ideas of Science* (Harlen 2010). These principles describe the aim of developing and sustaining learners' curiosity about the world, enjoyment of scientific activity and understanding of how natural phenomena can be explained. The set of 'big ideas' in science includes ideas *of* science (e.g. that all material in the Universe is made of very small particles) and ideas *about* science and its role in society (e.g. that science assumes that for every effect there is one or more causes).

Further, in the paper by Andersson and Gullberg (2012), four specific skills to promote preschool children's inquiry skills are described: paying attention to and using children's previous experiences; capturing unexpected things that happen at the moment they occur; asking questions that challenge children and stimulate further investigation; and, creating a situated presence thus 'remaining' in the situation and listening to the children and their explanations. Similarly, Louca *et al.* (2013) have identified the necessity to develop teaching responsiveness to children's science inquiry. Teaching responsiveness includes (1) knowledge of various forms of in-class scientific inquiry; (2) abilities to evaluate elements of children's inquiry; and, (3) a repertoire of instructional strategies, from which to choose in order to respond to children's in-class inquiry.

Third, we believe that there is a requirement to highlight the complex situation where nature is meant to serve as both a teaching free zone *and* the place where learning of science, inquiry skills and environmental care take place. The uncritical view of nature as always inherently good, that children innately belong in nature, and a place where science and environmental learning comes about automatically needs to be opened up for discussion (Halldén 2009, Sandell and Öhman 2010).

Collaboration and critical discussion

In Kind's (2009) review of research concerning science Pedagogical Content Knowledge (PCK), she stressed that the practicum is the most important influential component involved in PCK development for student teachers. Significant changes take place in the early months and years of working as a preschool teacher; this is when turning subject competence into true PCK occurs (Lederman *et al.* 1994, Simmons *et al.* 1999). According to our data, the interviewed student teachers had gained effective and useful science knowledge during their Science/Creative Arts year. However, during the practicum experience, the preschool environment was rarely supportive of science education and inquiry processes. Thus, one could argue that the conditions in our study for fully developing science PCK during teacher education were not adequate. Especially worrying is that in the final questionnaire distributed after graduation, the majority of new teachers reported that they did not implement any science activities at all, similar to their experiences when they were student teachers undertaking practicum. If this is the common case, and we believe it is, then future student teachers will continue to experience no, or at best poor, science education in practicum, thus continuing to replicate the difficulties of developing PCK for teaching science and sustainability. Our suggestion is that pre-service and in-service education must collaborate in a critical discussion about views of science, nature and teaching within the preschool community (cf. Davis, 2009). Even though this research was conducted in Sweden, international research supports similar patterns of the tensions between different pedagogical frameworks for supporting play and learning in science, in other western countries (Fleer 2011).

Conclusion

Key educational principles for EfS have been identified by the United Nations as interdisciplinarity, holism, critical thinking, problem-solving, multi-method approaches, participation, decision-making, applicability and local relevance. In this chapter, we have elaborated how emergent science can be used to engage practically with these principles in the preschool setting. We have also identified two aspects that require consideration prior to employing science teaching as a means for implementing EfS in Swedish preschools. First, early childhood teacher educators should be given opportunities to investigate and discuss the learning cultures of preschools in relation to nature, science and environmental care. One way to approach this is to offer exemplars to pre-service students of inquiry-based pedagogical practice rather than models of traditional, transmissive approaches to science. Second, stronger co-operation between teacher educators and teachers in practicum settings is required. Teacher educators should aim for student practicum experiences in preschool environments where they have opportunities to challenge norms and practise inquiry teaching skills, thus laying a foundation for EfS. Of course, we recognize that such settings are in short supply – but we believe it is still possible to aim for such experiences. Development of teaching materials such as videos of exemplary practice is a way forward. We intend to seek permission to use videos illustrating such exemplary inquiry practice taken during our research project in order to produce teaching materials for our preschool teacher education program. Furthermore, student tasks to specifically implement science activities in practicum with follow-up group work where students conduct peer analysis and review to improve their inquiry practice would be professionally constructive. If such steps are taken, we believe we can change the direction for science in preschools so that it supports preschool children's critical thinking and empowerment. Science can thereby be used in preschool to support key educational principles of the UN DESD.

References

Andersson, K. and Gullberg, A. (2012) 'What is science in preschool and what do teachers have to know to empower the children?' *Cultural Studies of Science Education*. Online. doi10.1007/s11422-012-9439-6.

Appleton, K. (2008) 'Developing science pedagogical content knowledge through mentoring elementary teachers', *Journal of Science Teacher Education,* 19(6): 523–45.

Ärlemalm-Hagsér, E. (2013) '"An interest in the best for the world"? Education for sustainability in the Swedish preschool'. Doctoral thesis. Acta Universitatis Gothoburgensis Göteborg, Sweden.

Ashley, M. (2000) 'Science: An unreliable friend to environmental education?' *Environmental Education Research* 6(3): 269–80.

Bergnér, D. (2009) 'Nature, outdoor setting and the good childhood in the newspaper 'The preschool (in Swedish)', in G. Halldén (ed.) *Nature as a Symbol of the Good Childhood.* Stockholm: Carlsson bokförlag, pp. 59–77.

Broström, S., Johansson, I., Sandberg, A. and Frøkjær, T. (2012) 'Preschool teacher's view on learning in preschool in Sweden and Denmark', *European Early Childhood Education Research Journal,* iFirst Article, 1–14.

Colucci-Gray, L., Perazzone, A., Dodman, M. and Camino E. (2012) 'Science education for sustainability, epistemological reflections and educational practices: From natural science to trans-disciplinarity', *Cultural Studies of Science Education*, Online. doi:10.1007/s11422-012-9405-3.

Davis, J. M. (2009) 'Revealing the research "hole" of early childhood education for sustainability: A preliminary survey of the literature', *Environmental Education Research*, 15(2): 227–41.

DEEWR (2009) 'Belonging being becoming: The Early Years Learning Framework for Australia', Online. Available: http://deewr.gov.au/early-years-learning-framework (accessed 22 April 2013).

Engeström, Y. (1987) *Learning by Expanding. An Activity-theoretical Approach to Developmental Research*, Helsinfors: Orienta-Koskit Oy.

Fleer, M. (2009) 'Supporting scientific conceptual consciousness or learning in "a roundabout way", in play-based contexts', *International Journal of Science Education* 31(8): 1069–89.

Fleer, M. (2011) 'Kindergartens in cognitive times: Imagination as a dialectical relation between play and learning', *International Journal of Early Childhood*, 43: 245–59.

Garbett, D. (2003) 'Science education in early childhood teacher education: Putting forward a case to enhance student teachers' confidence and competence', *Research in Science Education*, 33(4): 467–81.

Halldén, G. (ed.) (2009) *Nature as Symbol for a Good Childhood*, Stockholm: Carlsson bokförlag.

Harlen, W. (ed.) (2010) *Principles and Big Ideas of Science Education*, Gosport: Ashford Colour Press Ltd.

Harlen, W. and Holroyd, C. (1997) 'Primary teachers' understanding of concepts of science: Impact on confidence and teaching', *International Journal of Science Education*, 19(1): 93–105.

Inan, H. Z., Trundle, K. C. and Kantor, R. (2010) 'Understanding natural sciences education in a Reggio Emilia-inspired preschool in America', *Journal of Research in Science Teaching*, 47(10): 1186–208.

Johnston, J. (2008) 'Emergent science'. *Education in Science*, 227: 26–8.

Kind, V. (2009) 'Pedagogical content knowledge in science education: potential and perspectives for progress', *Studies in Science Education*, 45(2): 169–204. Online. Available: www.ase.org.uk/ journals/education-in-science/2008/04/227/ (accessed 22 April 2013).

Larsson, J. (2013) 'Children's encounters with friction. Friction understood as a phenomenon of emerging science and as "opportunities for learning"', *Journal of Research in Childhood Education*, 27(3): 377–92.

Lave, J. and Wenger, E. (1991) *Situated Learning: Legitimate Peripheral Participation*. Cambridge: Cambridge University Press.

Lederman, N. G., Gess-Newsome, J. and Latz, M. S. (1994) 'The nature and development of pre-service science teachers' conceptions of subject matter and pedagogy', *Journal of Research in Science Teaching*, 31(2): 129–46.

Lobman, C. and Ryan, S. (2007) 'Differing discourses on early childhood teacher development', *Journal of Early Childhood Teacher Education*, 28(4): 367–80.

Louca, L. T., Tzialli, D., Skoulia, T. and Constantinou, C. P. (2013) 'Developing teaching responsiveness to children's inquiry in science: A case study of professional development for preschool teachers', *Nordic Studies in Science Education*, 9(1): 66–81.

National Agency for Education (2011) 'Curriculum for the preschool Lpfö 98', revised 2010. Stockholm: Fritzes. Online. Available: www.skolverket.se/publikationer?id=2704 (accessed 29 January 2014).

Nayfeld, I., Brennerman, K. and Gelman, R. (2011) 'Science in the classroom: Finding a balance between autonomous exploration and teacher-led instruction in preschool settings', *Early Education and Development*, 22(6), 970–88.

Öhman, J. (2006) 'Pluralism and criticism in environmental and sustainable education', *Environmental Education Research*, 12(2): 149–63.

Peterson, S. M. and French, L. (2008) 'Supporting young children's explanations through inquiry science in preschool', *Early Childhood Research Quarterly*, 23: 395–408.

Pramling Samuelsson, I. and Johansson, E. (2006) 'Play and learning – inseparable dimensions in preschool practice', *Early Child Development and Care*, 176(1): 47–65.

Saçkes, M., Cabe Trundle, K., Bell, R. L. and O'Connell, A. A. (2011) 'The influence of early science experience in kindergarten on children's immediate and later science achievement: Evidence from the early childhood longitudinal study', *Journal of Research in Science*, 48: 217–35.

Sandell, K. and Öhman, J. (2010) 'Educational reflections from a Swedish outdoor perspective'. *Environmental Education Research*, 16(1): 95–114.

Sandell, K., Öhman, J. and Östman, L. (2005) *Education for Sustainable Development: Nature, School and Democracy*. Lund: Studentlitteratur.

Simmons, P. E., Emory, A., Carter, T., Coker, T., Finnegan, B. and Crockett, D. (1999) 'Beginning teachers: Beliefs and classroom actions', *Journal of Research in Science Teaching*, 36(8): 930–45.

Siraj-Blatchford, J. (2001) 'Emergent science and technology in the early years, paper presented at the twenty-third World Congress of OMEP, Santiago, Chile, 31 July–4 August 2001', Online. Available: www.327matters.org/Docs/omepabs.pdf (accessed 22 April 2013).

Spector-Levy, O., Kesner Baruch, Y. and Mevarech, Z. (2011) 'Science and scientific curiosity in pre-school – The teacher's point of view', *International Journal of Science Education*, iFirst Article, 1–28.

Sundberg, B. and Ottander, C. (2013) 'The conflict within the role: A longitudinal study of preschool student teachers' developing competence in and attitudes towards science teaching in relation to developing a professional role', *Journal of Early Childhood Teacher Education*, 34(1): 80–94.

Sundberg, B., Areljung, S., Due, K., Ekström, K., Ottander, C., and Tellgren, B. (2013) 'Emergent science in preschool'. Conference proposal at the tenth Conference of the European Science Education Research Association (ESERA) Nicosia, Cyprus 2–7 September 2013.

Tellgren, B. (2008) 'From mother of society to a teacher qualified for post-graduate studies – continuity and change in a local preschool education' (doctoral thesis in Swedish). *Örebro Studies in Education*, 24.

Thulin, S. (2011) 'Teacher talk and children's queries: Communication about natural science in early childhood education' (doctoral thesis in Swedish). University of Gothenburg, Faculty of Education, Gothenburg, Sweden.

Tu, T. (2006) 'Preschool science environment: What is available in a preschool classroom?' *Early Childhood Education Journal*, 33(4), 245–51.

Woodhead, M. (2006) 'Changing perspectives on early childhood: Theory, research and policy'. Paper commissioned for the Education for All Global Monitoring Report 2007, Strong foundations: Early childhood care and education. Online. Available: http://unesdoc.unesco.org/images/0014/001474/147499e.pdf (accessed 22 April 2013).

UNESCO (2005) *UN Decade of Education for Sustainable Development*, Paris: UNESCO.

UNESCO (2009) *Review of Contexts and Structures for Education for Sustainable Development 2009*. Paris: UNESCO.

Chapter 18

Early childhood education for sustainability in the United Kingdom

Generating professional capital

Louise Gilbert, Mary Fuller, Sally Palmer, and Janet Rose

Abstract

A growing body of literature highlights the important role that early childhood education (ECE)[1], and therefore early years practitioners, can and should play in education for sustainability (Britto, Yoshikawa and Boller 2011; Elliott and Davis 2009). This chapter reviews the ways in which higher education can engender professional capital to facilitate and normalize a 'culture of sustainability' (Davis 2005) in the early years. Two recent studies conducted by the authors demonstrate the transformative effect that active engagement in a variety of sustainability issues can have on the development of practitioners' professional capital, and how this can be translated into the promotion and implementation of early childhood education for sustainability (ECEfS). In seeking to promote transformative mind-sets, opportunities were created for practitioners to become agents of change (Gilbert *et al.* 2013; Rose *et al.* 2011) and, as influential role-models, to empower children to contribute actively to the creation of sustainable futures.

The UK context

Education is fundamental to the promotion, development and maintenance of sustainable human, social and environmental capital (Elliott and Davis 2009), and is recognized as promoting personal and national economic benefits (Fien *et al.* 2009). Education can also be viewed as a source of community strength, providing focused opportunities for co-operation, partnership, synergy and symbiosis: all conducive to the promotion of transformational learning about sustainability (Lange 2012).

Nutbrown and Clough (2009) advocate that inclusion, citizenship and belonging should underpin ECE policy. The Early Years Foundation Stage (EYFS) (Department for Education 2012a) provides statutory guidance on educational practice for children from birth to five years old, and has recently been revised to strengthen the above elements. Although no reference is made to the term 'sustainability', the promotion of supportive relationships, nurturing experiences, and enabling environments to ignite 'children's curiosity and enthusiasm for learning,

[and] build their capacity to learn, form relationships and thrive' (DfE 2012a: 4) supports a connection with ECEfS.

However, ECE as a newly recognized specialism, is vulnerable to the vagaries of the traditional long-established education system, which is heavily influenced by both national and international political and economic forces, both in the United Kingdom and elsewhere (Hagglund and Pramling Samuelsson 2009). Although the UK government rhetoric advocates health promotion and early intervention for greater well-being (Allen 2011), economic forces are leading to sweeping cuts in social and welfare services. The reform of education funding models, and planned structural and professional reorganization have led to some key advocates, who were integral to government educational policy, now challenging current ECE proposals. Nutbrown (2013:10) warns that such proposals 'will shake the foundations of quality provision for young children ... [who] must not bear the costs of the government getting this wrong'. As 'values, attitudes, skills and behaviours acquired in this period may have a long-lasting impact in later life' (Pramling Samuelsson and Kaga 2008: 9), ECE is responsible for laying foundations for personal development and life-long learning. The EYFS (DfE 2012a), therefore, must act as a vehicle to promote active engagement in learning.

The value of active engagement

Promoting physically active engagement in learning can facilitate higher conceptual understandings (Pundak *et al.* 2009), greater retention of information (Smith and Cardaciotto 2011) and increased creativity (Gino *et al.* 2010). In Hong Kong, Chan *et al.* (2009) identified that young children were willing *and* able to engage harmoniously in practices that promoted sustainable, ecological and social well-being, and Johansson (2009) demonstrated how young Swedish children were capable of developing foundational notions of global citizenship and social justice. Vaealiki and Mackey (2008) recognized that children of three and four years old were not only able to actively engage in a recycling project in their centre, but also influence environmental practices within their family homes and wider communities.

However, Mumford (2006: 69) cautions that learners can become 'prisoners of their own often limited experiences or the victims of experiences of others' if those who design learning environments underestimate the contribution of practical engagement in learning. For true learning, there must be opportunities to challenge and reflect on tangible personal experiences; easily accessible knowledge sourced from 'others' should not be considered a substitute for real life experience (Billet 2009; Hope 2009). Respectful communication, trusting relationships and democratic participation are essential to 'empower young children to strengthen their role as citizens in their communities, today and for tomorrow' (Mackey and Vaealiki 2011: 85).

Therefore adaptations to existing early years curricula necessitate both a greater focus on developing shared understandings of the symbiotic relationships between economic, environmental and social worlds (Fien *et al.* 2009) and ensuring children are recognized and promoted as active participants. But, how might practitioners do this? With no consensus on what constitutes excellence, providers of early childhood services and early childhood practitioners can feel confused and isolated about how to take the practice agenda forward (Nolan *et al.* 2005). In this chapter, we offer a way forward for higher education institutions to assist prospective early years practitioners to support and develop practices that reflect and utilize the recursive and symbiotic relationships found within a child's lived experience.

Generating professional capital for sustainability

Historically, limited regulations have existed in England to guide ECE provision where, until fairly recently, few or no professional qualifications were required. Radical alterations to the structure and delivery of ECE included the creation of a specialist, graduate-led early childhood education workforce and the establishment of the Early Years Professional Status (EYPS), which was accredited through a set of professional standards accessed via higher education institutions. In 2013, the EYPS practitioner was replaced with the term 'Early Years Teacher' and a revised set of professional standards. The aim of these policy changes is to raise professional status and further integrate ECE into the educational experience. Like the EYFS (DfE 2012a), the professional standards for graduate early years practitioners, contain no reference to sustainability issues.

To provide early childhood practitioners with ECEfS skills and knowledge, and to create inter-generational understandings of sustainable practices, requires a more 'holistic view of life-long learning that encompasses the full life cycle' (European Panel on Sustainable Development 2010: 11). ECE has to provide formal and informal stimulating, reflective, active learning opportunities that invite children 'to be, to do, to learn and live together' (Hughes 2009: 140). These are 'not techniques but rather attitudes of the spirit' (Ettling 2012: 545) that are fundamental to the construction of a person's identity. It is through inclusion and engagement that interpersonal and intercultural social and civic competencies are shaped.

Roberts and Roberts have highlighted that sustainability is concerned with the maintenance and enhancement of 'five types of capital, namely: natural, human, social, manufactured and financial' (2007: 4). The notion of professional capital has roots in both human and social capital since it is concerned with the building of individuals to meet the needs of society in professional contexts. The intention is to improve provision and contribute to communities of practice, professional capital is both productive *and* purposive (Brodie 2003). We propose that by developing early years professional capital, through improving practitioner education, children's potential to make meaningful contributions to a sustainable society can be better facilitated. Therefore, early childhood practitioners must be given opportunities in their training to explore what ECEfS means and how this informs the way they understand and engage in their personal and professional settings. Through active engagement they will discover and experience sustainability and identify how this then relates and informs their practice with children, families and colleagues. The next part of this chapter reports on two studies that focus on the generation of professional capital in promoting and implementing ECEfS.

The research context

The two studies were informed by transformative learning theory (Mezirow 1991), which identifies adult learning as an ongoing process that allows an individual to adapt their knowledge-base to better understand the world in which they live. It rests upon the notion that 'we interpret our experiences in our own way, and that how we see the world is a result of our perceptions and our experiences' (Cranton and Taylor 2012: 5). New information and experiences can reveal and/or challenge assumptions and value systems, which are often tacit. Engagement with and reflection on new information also promotes metacognition and the resulting knowledge reflects better understandings. This then informs subsequent personal and professional practice. Our research sought to explore ways in which understandings of sustainability and sustainable futures could be developed amongst final year early childhood education degree students. As the degree programme involved students simultaneously working in early childhood settings and on-campus study, these diverse personal experiences became the students' 'living textbook' (Lindeman 2011: 9), providing opportunities for embodied learning that emanates from living with and through experience.

We explored how these tertiary students' understandings of sustainability issues were manifested in the real world of practice and how, when confronted with alternative perspectives, they adopted and/or adapted their beliefs. The methodology for both studies was interpretive, employing both deductive and inductive approaches to analysing qualitative, narrative data derived from focus group discussions, semi-structured questionnaires, interviews and written essays. The findings identified the role of tertiary students in adopting, adapting and disseminating environmental and pedagogical practice, and how transformative learning played a key role in the development of their understandings about sustainability.

Study 1: early childhood practitioners as agents of change for sustainability

A key goal for any early years practitioner is to operate as a change agent facilitating the development of people and organization (Hadfield et al. 2012; Rose and Rogers 2012a). In operationalizing a transformational leadership approach, early years practitioners need to be able to articulate an educational vision that examines and re-examines policies, procedures and relationships within settings to achieve genuine and lasting change (Elias et al. 2006). Jucker (2004) argues for such practitioners to embody principles of 'ecojustice' into their practice that engenders shared ownership and is both integral to service functioning and lies at the heart of policies, procedures and practices. The process of permeating early childhood higher degree programmes with sustainability perspectives includes acknowledging and then raising awareness of sustainable futures, so that tertiary students can apply these perspectives to the early childhood education settings in which they work, or will work in the future.

With these ideas in mind, we explored various ways in which tertiary students could be supported to create visions, insights and understandings designed to bring about changes in their own thinking about sustainable futures, and to engage and empower young children as an integral part of this process. Initiatives were built around the seven Rs, – reduce, reuse, repair, recycle, respect, reflect and responsibility advocated by UNESCO (Pramling Samuelsson and Kaga 2008). The tertiary students liked this framework as it accommodated their differing initial knowledge-base, whilst also providing clear guidance from which progress could be monitored.

A total of 40 tertiary students participated in the study. They were either studying for the early childhood studies degree or undertaking the graduate EYPS training. Many were already practitioners in early years settings (studying part-time) or had been on work-based learning placements. They completed a questionnaire to ascertain their initial conceptual understandings about ECEfS. Many of the students' understandings centred on traditional environmental concepts of sustainability, that is, on activities that mainly focused upon *reduce, reuse, repair, and recycle* (Pramling Samuelsson and Kaga 2008). Yet employers are increasingly seeking employees who show an awareness of, and responsibility for, social sustainability as well as environmental concerns (Park *et al.* 2009). Therefore, broadening the students' perspectives beyond environmental issues, to include the wider sustainability agenda of *respect, reflect and responsibility,* became a clear task for us as early childhood teacher educators.

Questionnaire responses were used to inform the semi-structured focus group discussions (10 per group), in which the students explored questions such as *'What does sustainability mean to me?' 'What does sustainable practice entail?'* and *'What aspects of their early childhood setting's practice reflected sustainability endeavours?'* Focus group discussions also provided a forum for students to engage in peer-led, professionally reflective discourse (Mezirow 2000) providing 'opportunities to question and challenge taken-for-granted beliefs and practices' (Pramling Samuelsson and Kaga 2008: 13).

We identified the following themes within the focus group discussion data:

Theme 1: identification of sustainable practices

One participant described how their nursery that catered for 1–5 year olds, had branded itself as organic in order to advertise their commitment to promoting healthier lifestyles. She reported that the staff considered that their organic, nursery-grown vegetables and fruit not only enhanced healthy living, but provided a model for both children and families.

Another participant reported that their nursery had decided to return to the practice of milk delivery in glass bottles, to reduce plastic and cardboard waste, and to re-educate children about portion size. 'Pouring what you would like' instead of receiving a set amount of milk in a carton reduced milk wastage and raised child-ren's awareness and involvement in health promotion.

Yet another participant reported that her initiative to start using a locally-based supplier that sold environmentally-friendly products, led to the setting reviewing their entire product usage to ensure greater consistency in more sustainable prod-ucts. This 'ripple effect' (Vaealiki and Mackey 2008) for other aspects of practice is discussed further in Theme 2 below.

Theme 2: what helped students change to more sustainable practices in early childhood education services?

Participants identified that small monetary rewards helped services consider their sustainability practices. For example, one participant reported that the inducements given by commercial recycling companies for agreeing to be the collection site for recycled clothes and shoes, provided a mutually beneficial focus on sustainability for the wider community. Having a convenient place to recycle children's clothes and shoes provided opportunities to develop community cohesion, as well as raised awareness about recycling and reusing. Several settings saw themselves as 'voucher collection centres' capitalizing on the 'generosity' of large supermarket chains. Encouraging families and friends to donate their vouchers enabled the setting to trade in larger quantities of the vouchers for equipment to supplement the centre.

The need to enhance partnership with parents, a requirement of the EYFS (DfE 2012), was identified by one participant as the motivation to 'embrace the twenty-first century and the digital era', and her setting started to use emails and text messaging to disseminate the parent newsletters. She found a greater number and range of parents now read and responded to the newsletters, and savings were made on staff time, paper and printing costs.

Theme 3: children's engagement

Early years practitioners are educated to support and facilitate each individual child's development to reach their full potential – this is guided through observa-tion and research-based practice (DfE 2012b). Central to early childhood practice are beliefs that children can, and should, be active informed learners, capable of impacting positively on their own setting, family and local environment (Layard and Dunn 2009; Trevarthen 2011). Through peer discussion, participants designed provocations and carried out sustainability projects in their settings that encouraged children's greater awareness and actions.

One participant, following the children's interest in the effects of cold weather on their nursery garden, used a story-book to sustain engagement and further curiosity in climate as well as extend understandings about the impact of climate change on animals. 'You must turn off the power switch to save the polar bears' was heard from a four year-old after the reading of *The Polar Bears' Home: A Story about Global Warming* (Bergen and Nguyen 2008).

In another example, a participant reported on a four-year-old child, who, after sharing the story-book *The Treasure of Trash: A Recycling Story* (Mandel 1994), had later returned to tell her that now 'We [her family] take all our bottles to the bank; they make new bottles you know'. She felt that this was evidence of the child's thinking and demonstrated an ability to transfer personal knowledge into community practice.

Theme 4: sustainability and the wider community

Focus group participants identified parent and staff education as central to promoting understandings of the life-long impacts of early education for children, and its potential contribution to sustainable living. To ensure ECEfS was a shared commitment between early years settings and the home, the fostering of positive partnerships with parents was identified as critical. Although it is known that informal education opportunities, promoted through social interactions and links between families and friends, can generate valuable social and human capital, it is often overlooked and its potential not harnessed (Newton 2006).

Therefore, to become confident and competent leaders for sustainable practices participants identified a need for greater personal and shared community commitment. Acknowledging this, they were also aware that a workplace action plan for sustainability should be visible to all, clearly situated and linked to the setting's current self-evaluation tools. Since none of the participants' early childhood settings had sustainability policies, they agreed that this was a starting point for action. They proposed that if the staff, children, parents and families worked together to create such a policy, the consequences of shared responsibility and ownership could generate both personal and community empowerment.

Theme 5: professional development

Another clear priority that participants identified was the value of peer-shared professional development, which had broadened their understandings of sustainability and, specifically, about three of their commonly-discussed dimensions: human, social and environmental. They considered that this enhanced knowledge-base supported their abilities to reflect upon, audit and plan for purposeful and lasting change through their work. However, there was little discussion on the economic dimensions of sustainability and the reasons for this were not explored since discussion was student-led.

As a result of the focus group discussions more than half the participants now believed that, to successfully engage children in sustainability projects, the setting needed effective, secure relationships between staff, children, parents and the wider community. These relationships should recognize and value both individual and collective contributions.

A knowledge-based society must be value-centred, with a foundational focus on respecting life and human dignity. The participants, in recognizing that they were 'as much fellow travellers as guides' (Taylor and Elias 2012: 160), developed an understanding of the ongoing critical role of education and experience in promoting human capacity for life-long learning and ECEfS. This small-scale study is now being extended through integration of focus group discussions on sustainability to all in the degree programme. We are continuing to explore tertiary students' perceptions of their role in contributing to sustainable futures, and the particular place that early years education has within such a vision. Some of the participants are now working as university associate researchers and are involved in developing a series of practice-informed principles to improve knowledge, understanding and application of ECEfS.

Study 2: early years student-practitioners² generating human and professional capital for a sustainable society

The second study focused on promoting human capital and practice change through the active engagement of early years student-practitioners on an international visit to Sweden. One aim of the visit was to reveal and challenge student-practitioners' tacit belief systems. Experiencing alternative learning environments increased their awareness of the effects of cultural attitudes on learning opportunities and refocused attention on the 'processes of learning through intent participation' (Rogoff et al. 2003: 197).

Sweden is considered to provide models of exemplary practice in early childhood education and care (Pugh 2009), and offers an alternative perspective to challenge and develop existing knowledge and understanding of pedagogy and practice. Swedish culture traditionally reflects an expectation of inclusivity: 'allemansratten', for example, is the Swedish framework that recognizes the 'universal right to move in and enjoy nature' (Asano 2011: 25). It also has well-established universal access to early years provision and globally is in the top three countries for child well-being (Hertzman et al. 2010).

This study investigated the experiential learning of 50, tertiary student-practitioners with an age range of 20 to 40 years, who visited early year settings in Sweden. The impact of the Swedish visit on their practice, once they had left university, was also investigated (Rose et al. 2011).

Analysis of qualitative, narrative data derived from semi-structured questionnaires, interviews and written essays revealed that the student-practitioners afforded a catalytic value to the physical, emotional and cognitive aspects of their active learning experiences. The combined stimulations generated a more coherent, meaningful and relevant learning to support their professional development (Gilbert et al. 2013). A key finding was that these student-practitioners recognized their capacity to implement improvements and become 'agents of change' (Fullan 1993). This 'transformative mindset' (Rose et al. 2011: 56) also gave rise to an increased awareness of, and reflection on, what they considered constrained their abilities to adapt practices.

As a result of engaging in the visits to Swedish preschools, over 90 per cent identified a new sense of empowerment that could transcend their current work-place situation. At the core of their learning was a re-evaluation of the traditional pedagogic role and the way they, as adults, related to children. They considered how their experiences led them to re-conceive their practice as more child-centred in terms of addressing the needs and rights of the children. By raising awareness and being able to challenge often tacit restrictive and prescriptive expectations in relation to child competence and rights, their practice became more reflective of the vision of children and children's rights as portrayed in the United Nations Convention on the Rights of the Child (UNICEF 1989). This is a central tenet of the Swedish education system and, arguably, ECEfS.

A common theme emerging from the research was the change in student-prac-titioners' perceptions about children's capabilities. For example: 'I was impressed by the fact the children as young as two were so independent … [which] in turn made me think what I could do in my setting to improve the children's independence.' This respect for children's individual potential led the student-practitioners to promote children's freedom to be active decision-makers, and agents in directing their own learning agendas. This was one of the most consistent themes in the study. Another student-practitioner claimed that the visit had raised her expecta-tions of children, resulting in provision that was more self-directing and enabling:

> Now I have an ethos that the children will find out more by themselves. I now think we just need to stand back and let them lead and explore and do their own things and only when they come to you; then we get involved.

Increased confidence to invite children to take more responsibility and to be more independent, was key to her revised expectations. An older student-practitioner, who owned and managed a private day-care nursery, testified to changes in her practices resulting from the transformational visit to Sweden. She believed that the trip had 'enabled me to think outside the box' and had given her the confidence to support her staff, through role-modelling and training, to adopt an alternative view of children. She considered that before the trip she had a 'narrow, blinkered view of what children should and shouldn't do'. Since visiting different settings and witnessing the ways in which Swedish preschool teachers created co-learning envi-ronments for children, she re-evaluated her role from that of a 'policeman' to a 'facilitator'. As she put it: 'I am now more aware of joining the children and play-ing with them rather than just "watching" them'.

Another student-practitioner's willingness to accept the status quo of educa-tional provision in the United Kingdom was challenged. She declared the visit 'has let me see a different way to educate children'. In particular, she had noticed 'the trust between the children and the practitioners about safety and freedom'. She said that her observations of Swedish children 'made me realise that children like to choose' so that now 'I try to bring a new approach or attitude to the way children learn. I let children have more choice when I teach. I really believe in this approach and that it works. I have seen it work'. This is a significant issue in the light of current practice in early years classrooms in UK schools, where adult-directed and formalized forms of learning predominate with an emphasis on literacy and mathematics (Rose and Rogers 2012b).

Through actively engaging in intercultural experiences, student-practitioners had the opportunity to reflect upon the complex, interconnected and interactional relationships between child, practitioner, learning context and society; the student-practitioners were in effect 'living to learn and learning to live' (Gilbert *et al.* 2013: 12). Our research demonstrated how they came to re-evaluate their role and the way they related to children; how they came to re-conceive their practice to become more child-centred in addressing the needs of children; and how they now recognized their capacity to implement improvements and become 'agents of change' (Fullan 1993) for promoting children's rights. This process was summarized by a student-practitioner:

> My visit to Sweden had a profound effect on my views on early years education as a whole and what can be done to improve provision in my country. I feel that the visit offered the opportunity to critically analyse teaching experience and curriculum philosophy which I can now relate to my own practice and make important changes.

The study revealed the power of personal engagement and intercultural learning in transforming student-practitioners' values in terms of roles, rights and responsibilities. Further research is needed to augment these findings, which were based on a specific location and a small group of tertiary early childhood students, spanning a diversity of age, practice experience and workplace settings. Future studies could investigate the learning experiences of a more homogeneous student grouping and include a wider variety of locations and settings to consider the cultural transferability and contextual specificity of the findings. However, as a result of such active learning, these student-practitioners evidenced transformations in their personal and professional capacities to view children as capable and competent, and to see their own role as facilitators of learning.

Concluding comments

ECE has much to offer as a vehicle for advancing sustainability, and can make a vital contribution to the interdependent pillars of social development, economic development and environmental protection (UN World Summit Outcome 2005). At both individual and professional levels, our research 'celebrates small victories, as well as personal learning, thereby [continually] building momentum for innovation toward a preferred future' (Bradbury 2007: 292). It promotes an evolutionary rather than a revolutionary approach to ECEfS (Davis 2009), and recognizes that 'in the work of sustainable development ... all change must be implemented by *people*' (Bradbury 2007: 279, original emphasis). Our research concurs with the claim that systemic change in education must include human change, developed through the processes of personal transformation and experimentation, in order to 'eventually evolve the system as a whole' (ibid.). We claim that these tertiary students have started on both personal and shared journeys to better understand and facilitate ECEfS. They report that their engagement in these projects has resulted in feeling more empowered and increased awareness of their roles and responsibilities as role-models and facilitators of change.

Early years practitioners are required to sensitively translate the concept of sustainability into relevant, everyday practice. As Engdahl and Rabusicova suggest 'a way to integrate sustainability into the agenda for pedagogical activities is to handle it as a vision or a perspective rather than [focus on] specific content' (2010: 7). Thus, ECEfS can be viewed as 'a way of being *and* as a way of becoming' (Gilbert *et al.* 2013: 12), promoting a sense of shared commitment and responsibility to ensure learning addresses the interests and abilities of all.

Higher education programmes that provide space and opportunities for tertiary students to actively participate in, and reflect on their engagement and contributions to ECEfS, have the potential to generate transformative and professional capital. Therefore, early childhood higher education courses must reflect and promote the pedagogical principles of critical and creative thinking, participation and participatory learning, system and futures thinking and community partnerships (University of Gloucestershire 2011). They need to be seen to address the content of children's learning as well as acknowledge and incorporate child and family voices (Heikka and Waniganayake 2011). To lay the foundations for sustainable human and social capital, early years practitioners not only require sound knowledge of child development, curriculum, early learning and pedagogy, but also the skills, knowledge and values to nurture empowerment, resilience, and a willingness to create change. Such principles will provide opportunities for early years practitioners to develop professional capital that helps them to acknowledge and understand the sustainability agenda as a philosophical approach to ECE, and as a practice to inform learning experiences and projects.

Elliott (2012) recognizes the complexity of promoting and integrating ECEfS into early years practice and further research is needed to substantiate the findings of our studies. Evidence-based models of early years curricular and tertiary programmes of study that reflect a holistic, integrative approach to ECEfS, will help to clarify the most effective ways of generating professional capital. A shared understanding of ECEfS will endorse and reinforce the rights of children to be recognized as competent and integral members of the community, now and into the future.

Notes

1   It should be noted that although similar developments are taking place in the rest of the United Kingdom, this chapter focuses attention on developments in the early years workforce in England. The term early childhood education (ECE) is used in this chapter, but an educare framework is assumed.

2   The term 'student-practitioner' was used to signify simultaneous status as final year early childhood degree students and practitioners, novice and seasoned, currently working in early years settings whilst engaged in degree study.

References

Allen, G. (2011) *Early Intervention: The Next Steps; An Independent Report to Her Majesty's Government*, London: The Cabinet Office. Online. Available: www.dwp.gov.uk/docs/early-intervention-next-steps.pdf (accessed 10 January 2012).

Asano, Y. (2011) 'The comparative study of education for sustainable development in early childhood in Sweden and Japan: Through the environmental epistemological model of 5 aspects', *Problems of Education in the 21st Century*, 32: 23–32.

Bergen, L. and Nguyen, V. (2008) *The Polar Bears' Home: A Story about Global Warming.* London: Little Simon.

Billet, S. (2009) 'Conceptualizing learning experiences: Contributions and mediations of the social, personal and brute', *Mind, Culture and Activity*, 16(1): 32–47.

Bradbury, H. (2007) 'Social learning for sustainable development: Embracing technical and cultural change as originally inspired by The Natural Step', in A.E.J. Wals (ed.), *Social Learning Towards a Sustainable World*, Wageningen: Wageningen Academic Publishers.

Britto, P., Yoshikawa, H. and Boller, K. (2011) 'Quality of early childhood development programs in global contexts, rationale for investment, conceptual framework and implications for equity', *Social Policy Report*, 25(2): 1–23.

Brodie, P. (2003) '*The Invisibility of Midwifery: Will Developing Professional Capital Make a difference*', PhD thesis, University of Technology Sydney. Online. Available: http://utsescholarship.lib.uts.edu.au/dspace/handle/2100/339?show=full > (accessed 2 April 2010).

Chan, B., Choy, G. and Lee, A. (2009) 'Harmony as a basis for education for sustainable development: A case example of Yew Chung International Schools', *International Journal of Early Childhood*, 41(2): 35–48.

Cranton, P. and Taylor, E. (2012) 'Transformative learning theory: Seeking a more unified theory', in E. Taylor and P. Cranton (eds), *The Handbook of Transformative Learning, Theory, Research and Practice*, San Francisco, CA: Jossey Bass.

Davis, J. (2005) 'Educating for sustainability in the early years: Creating cultural change in a child care setting', *Australian Journal of Environmental Education*, 21: 47–55.

Davis, J. (2009) 'Revealing the research "hole" of early childhood education for sustainability: A preliminary survey of the literature', *Environmental Education Research*, 15(2): 227–41.

Department for Education (DfE) (2012a) *Statutory Framework for the Early Years Foundation Stage*, Nottingham: DCSF Publications.

Department for Education (DfE) (2012b) *Longitudinal Study of Early Years Professional Status: An Exploration of Progress, Leadership and Impact – Final Report*, London: Department for Education. Online. Available: https://www.gov.uk/government/uploads/system/uploads/attachment_data/file/183418/DfE-RR239c_report.pdf (accessed 12 June 2013).

Elias, M. J., O'Brien, M. U. and Weissberg, R. P. (2006) 'Transformative leadership for social-emotional learning', *Principal Leadership*, 7(4): 10–13.

Engdahl, I. and Rabusicova, M. (2010) *Children's Voices about the State of the Earth and Sustainable Development*, Sweden: World Organization for Early Childhood Education.

Elliott, S. (2012) 'Sustainable outdoor playspaces in early childhood centres: Investigating perceptions, facilitating change and generating theory', PhD thesis. Online. Available: https://e-publications.une.edu.au/vital/access/manager/Repository/une:11715 (accessed 26 April 2013).

Elliott, S. and Davis, J. (2009)' Exploring the resistance: An Australian perspective on educating for sustainability in early childhood', *International Journal of Early Childhood*, 41(2):
65–77.

Ettling, D. (2012) 'Educators as change agents', in E. Taylor and P. Cranton (eds), *The
Handbook of Transformative Learning: Theory, Research and Practice*, San Francisco, CA: Jossey
Bass.

European Panel on Sustainable Development (2010) *Taking Children Seriously: How the EU
can Invest in Early Childhood Education for a Sustainable Future, Report 4*, Sweden: Centre
for Environment and Sustainability.

Fien, J., Maclean, R. and Park, M. G. (eds) (2009) *Work, Learning and Sustainable Development,
Opportunities and Challenges*, Dordrecht: Springer.

Fullan, M. (1993) 'Why teachers must become change agents', *Educational Leadership*, 50(6):
12–17.

Gilbert, L., Rose, J., Palmer, S. and Fuller, M. (2013) 'Active engagement, emotional impact
and changes in practice arising from a residential field trip', *International Journal of Early
Years Education Years Education*. Online. Available: http://dx.doi.org/10.1080/
09669760.2013.771320 (accessed 4 March 2013).

Gino, F., Argote, L., Miron-Spektor, E. and Todorova, G. (2010) 'First, get your feet wet: The
effect of learning from direct and indirect experience on team creativity', *Organizational
Behaviour and Human Decision Processes*, 111(2): 102–15.

Hadfield, M., Jopling, M., Needham, M., Waller, T. and Coleshaw, L. (2012) *Longitudinal Study
of Early Years Professional Status: An Exploration of Progress: Leadership and Impact – Final
Report, Research Report DFE-RR-239cDFE*. London: Department for education. Online.
Available: www.education.gov.uk/publications/eOrderingDownload/DfE-RR239c%20
report.pdf (accessed 13 January 2013).

Hagglund, S. and Pramling Samuelsson, I. (2009) 'Early childhood education and learning
for sustainable development and citizenship', *International Journal of Early Childhood*, 41(2):
49–63.

Heikka, J. and Waniganayake, M. (2011) 'Pedagogical leadership from a distributed perspective within the context of early childhood education', *International Journal of Leadership in
Education: Theory and Practice*, 14(4): 499–512. Online. Available: http://dx.doi.org/
10.1080/13603124.2011.577909 (accessed 10 October 2012).

Hertzman, C., Siddiqi, A., Hertzman, E., Irwin, L. G., Vaghri, Z., Houweling, T. A., Bell, R.,
Tinajero, A. and Marmot, M. (2010) 'Bucking the inequality gradient through early child
development', *British Medical Journal (Overseas and Retired Doctors Edition)*, (340): 346–8.

Hope, M. (2009) 'The importance of direct experience: A philosophical defence of fieldwork
in human geography', *Journal of Geography in Higher Education*, 33(2): 169–82.

Hughes, P. (2009) 'Education for all and TVET: The creative synergy', in J. Fien, R. Maclean
and M. Park (eds), *Work, Learning and Sustainable Development: Opportunities and
Challenges*, Berlin: Springer.

Johansson, E. (2009) 'The preschool child of today–The world citizen of tomorrow',
International Journal of Early Childhood, 41(2): 79–95.

Jucker, R. (2004) 'Have the cake and eat it: Ecojustice versus development? Is it possible to
reconcile social and economic equity, ecological sustainability, and human development?
Some implications for ecojustice education', *Educational Studies*, 36(1): 10–26.

Lange, E. (2012) 'Transforming transformative learning through sustainability and new
science', in E. Taylor and P. Cranton (eds), *The Handbook of Transformative Learning, Theory,
Research and Practice*, San Francisco, CA: Jossey Bass.

Layard, R. and Dunn, J. (2009) *A Good childhood – Searching for Values in a Competitive Age*, London: Penguin.

Lindeman, E. (2011) 'For those who need to be learners', in S. Merriam and A. Grace(eds), *Contemporary Issues in Adult Education*, San Francisco, CA: Jossey Bass.

Mackey, G. and Vaealiki, S. (2011) Thinking of children: Demographic approaches with young children in research, *Australasian Journal of Early Childhood*, 36(2): 82–86.

Mandel, L. (1994) *The Treasure of Trash: A Recycling Story*, London: Avery Publishing Group.

Mezirow, J. (1991) *Transformative Dimensions of Adult Learning*. San Francisco, CA: Jossey Bass.

Mezirow, J. (2000) 'Learning to think like an adult: Core concepts in transformation theory', in J. Mezirow and Associates (eds), *Learning as Transformation: Critical Perspectives On a Theory in Progress*. San Francisco, CA: Jossey Bass.

Mumford, A. (2006) 'Action learning: Nothing so practical as a good theory', *Action Learning: Research and Practice*, 3: 69–75.

Newton, K. (2006) 'Political support: Social capital, civil society and political and economic performance', *Political Studies*, 54(4): 846–64.

Nolan, A., Raban, B. and Waniganayake, M. (2005) 'Evaluating a strategic approach to professional development through guided reflection', *Reflective Practice*, 6(2): 221–9.

Nutbrown, C. (2013) 'Shaking the foundations of quality. Why childcare policy must not lead to poor-quality early years education and care', Sheffield: University of Sheffield. Online. Available: www.shef.ac.uk/polopoly_fs/1.263201!/file/Shakingthefoundations ofquality.pdf (accessed 2 April 2013).

Nutbrown, C. and Clough, P. (2009) 'Citizenship and inclusion in the early years: Understanding and responding to children's perspectives on belonging', *International Journal of Early Years Education*, 17(3): 191–206.

Park, M., Majumdar, S. and Dhameja, S. (2009) 'Sustainable development through a skilled, knowledge-based workforce', in J. Fien, R. Maclean and M. Park (eds), *Work, Learning and Sustainable Development: Opportunities and Challenges*, Berlin: Springer.

Pramling Samuelsson, I. and Kaga, Y. (eds) (2008) *The Contribution of Early Childhood Education to a Sustainable Society*, Paris: UNESCO.

Pundak, D., Herscovitz, O., Shacham, M. and Wiser-Briton, R. (2009) 'Instructors' attitudes toward active learning', *Interdisciplinary Journal of E-learning and Learning Objects*, 5: 215–32.

Pugh, G. (2009) *Contemporary Issues in the Early Years*, London: Paul Chapman.

Roberts, C. and Roberts, J. (2007) 'Greener by degrees' in C. Roberts and J. Roberts (eds), *Greener by Degrees: Exploring Sustainability through Higher Education Curricula*, Cheltenham: Centre for Active Learning, University of Gloucestershire.

Rogoff, B., Paradise, R., Mejía Arauz, R., Correa-Chávez, M. and Angelillo, C. (2003) 'First hand learning through intent participation', *Annual Review of Psychology*, 54(1): 175–203.

Rose, J. and Rogers, S. (2012a) *The Role of the Adult in Early Years Settings*, Maidenhead: Open University Press.

Rose, J. and Rogers, S. (2012b) 'Principles under pressure: Student teachers' perspectives on final teaching practice in early childhood classrooms', *International Journal of Early Years Education*, 20(1): 43–58.

Rose, J., Fuller, M., Gilbert, L. and Palmer, S. (2011) 'Transformative empowerment: Stimulating transformations in early years practice', *Learning and Teaching in Higher Education*, 5: 56–72.

Smith, C. and Cardaciotto, L. (2011) 'Is active learning like broccoli? Student perceptions of active learning in large classes', *Journal of the Scholarship of Teaching and Learning* 11: 53–61.

Taylor, K. and Elias, D. (2012) 'Transformative learning, a developmental perspective' in E. Taylor and P. Cranton (eds), *The Handbook of Transformative Learning, Theory, Research and Practice,* San Francisco, CA: Jossey Bass.

Trevarthen, C. (2011) 'What young children give to their learning, making education work to sustain a community and its culture', *European Early Childhood Education Research Journal,* 19(2): 173–93.

United Nations (1989) *United Nations Convention on the Rights of the Child (UNCRC),* Geneva: United Nations.

United Nations (2005) *World Summit Outcome.* Online. Available: www.un.org/womenwatch/ods/A-RES-60-1-E.pdf (accessed 14 February 2014).

UNICEF (1989) *United Nations Convention on the Rights of the Child.* Online. Available: www.unicef.org/crc/ (accessed 14 February 2014).

University of Gloucestershire (2011) '*Education for Sustainability: A Guide for Educators on Teaching and Learning Approaches*', Cheltenham: University of Gloucestershire.

Vaealiki, S. and Mackey, G. (2008) 'Ripples of action: Strengthening environmental competency in an early childhood centre', *Early Childhood Folio,* 12: 7–11.

Chapter 19

Expanding worlds of early childhood education for sustainability

Looking back, looking forward

Ann Farrell and Susan Danby

Transnational dialogues in early childhood education for sustainability represent a confluence of two globally significant fields of research and practice: early childhood education and education for sustainability. The dialogues discussed in this book are emblematic of the new hybridized field of early childhood education for sustainability. At international, national and local levels, although not evident universally, we are witnessing a sharpened focus on the early years and the ways in which young children, and their families and communities, (may) live and learn in sustainable ways. For those working within an early childhood education for sustainability agenda, there is increasing awareness of the everyday lives of young children and those around them, with a sharpened focus on what happens *in situ*, that is, in everyday lives and in everyday contexts in education and care settings, in family contexts and in communities.

While the fields of early childhood education and education for sustainability have been afforded international prominence for more than a decade, the confluence of the two is relatively recent. The transnational dialogues captured in this book exemplify such a confluence, and at a critical time for young children and their worlds. While in its infancy, the hybrid field is calling for new priorities in research and practice to ensure that young children, both now and in the future, are participatory, ethical and sustainable.

The transnational dialogues presented in this book typify a global movement of awareness and advocacy for young children and their worlds. While there is a legitimate focus on the present and the future, it is also timely to consider the past; not least of all, to consider the histories and epistemologies of the disciplines that gave rise to the dialogues in the first instance, and to consider the importance of education as a prime vehicle for transformational change, for individuals and their societies. The reader of this book is invited to consider the three-fold focus: core values and ethics; historical, cultural and political contexts; and, curriculum and pedagogy.

We draw on the conceptual thread that weaves works from the past, to the present and into the future, seen in the work of John Dewey (1938). His call for education, in its broadest sense, is education:

as a continuous process of reconstructing experience. This occurs only when the educator can look to the future with the perspective of viewing each present experience as a moving force that influences future experiences. The challenges for the educator are in the formation of ideas, putting those ideas into action, observing the conditions that result, and in organizing facts and ideas for future use.

(Dewey 1938: 87–8)

Dewey's emphasis on the educator's challenges is no less important today than when he first wrote about education in 1938. The challenge of putting 'ideas into action' is a central agenda for educators and researchers working within the field of early childhood education for sustainability today. The chapters within this book reflect that international agenda and the momentum over the previous decade. The formation and transformation to which Dewey alludes is a catalyst for participatory dialogue around educational research in early childhood education for sustainability, and consideration of its approaches, methodologies, results and impacts. Against these, we can draw on Dewey's conceptual framing of children and childhood as being as relevant today as when he first wrote about children and pedagogy over a century ago.

The social construction of children as agents in enacting and promoting sustainable practices is evident through the contributions in this book. In the introductory chapter, Julie Davis and Sue Elliott introduce the concept of children as social agents of change; not children as saviours of a world ruined by adults, nor as those perpetuating its ruin. A key focus, then, is how children and young people work collaboratively with adults, including parents, teachers and members of the community.

An underlying and fundamental principle is the view of children, as competent and capable agents, can bring about momentum in terms of social change through putting 'ideas into action'. This idea of children and their power to effect social change is not new. In Dewey's own words, in his pedagogic creed published over a century ago in 1897, he proposes that children are active agents in their own social interactions and in promoting agendas for the good of the community:

I believe that the only true education comes through the stimulation of the child's powers by the demands of the social situations in which he finds himself. Through these demands he is stimulated to act as a member of a unity, to emerge from his original narrowness of action and feeling and to conceive of himself from the standpoint of the welfare of the group to which he [sic] belongs. Through the responses which others make to his own activities he comes to know what these mean in social terms.

(n.p.)

More recently, within the past few decades, the view of children as agents has risen again to prominence. For example, Hutchby and Moran-Ellis (1998) point out that the construction of the child can only be a local and particular description based on the situatedness of the activity: competence has 'to do with the children's ability to manage their social surroundings, to engage in meaningful social interaction within given interactional contexts' (p. 16). Understanding the work of children themselves to organize and maintain their social worlds, and concurrently participate in adults' social worlds, offers conceptual ways forward to consider how children and young people participate as active agents of change.

Looking back

It is no coincidence that the editors of this book, Julie Davis and Sue Elliott, in their introductory chapter, quote famous anthropologist of the early twentieth century, Margaret Mead, and her view that 'a small group of thoughtful people could change the world.' While Mead was not referring specifically to education for sustainability, her perspective still holds true today, and the chapters in this book are testament of that standpoint.

The fields of early childhood education and of education for sustainability have their own histories of empirical research, practice and advocacy. So too, they have their own futures. Historically, each has been identified internationally as a priority area. Early childhood, for example, has been championed by the Organization for Education Cooperation and Development (OECD) (2001, 2006, 2012) and the United Nations Children's Education Fund (UNICEF) (2008) as a priority for investment of human, social and economic capital. In turn, education for sustainability has been championed by the United Nations Millennium Development Goals (2000), the United Nations Educational, Scientific and Cultural Organization (UNESCO 2005; UNESCO UNEP 1975), and the United Nations Environment Program (UNEP) (2012).

The two fields go hand-in-hand. Early childhood, as an international policy phenomenon, focuses on children's optimal life chances and outcomes, operationalized through the agenda of starting strong and its policy corollary, of investing in the early years. The OECD has promoted the starting strong/investing early agenda through a series of international comparative reports on early childhood education and care (ECEC) (OECD 2001, 2006, 2012). Other premier bodies such as UNICEF (2008) have given further impetus to the agenda, by contributing international benchmarks for ECEC. The agenda is underpinned by a substantial body of developmental and neuroscientific research and cost-benefit analysis research (cf. Cunha *et al.*, 2006); and substantiated by a meta-analysis of 120 research studies conducted by Camilli and colleagues (2010) in support of the move to invest in ECEC for short- and long-term outcomes and life trajectories for children and for society.

Despite this weight of evidence, the early childhood/starting strong/investing early agenda is challenged by major geo-political shifts evidenced by rapid urbanization (UNHCR, 2012), child poverty, HIV/AIDS and family dislocation (UNDESA 2011; UNICEF 2012). UNICEF's report *Children in an Urban World*

(2012) demonstrated, for instance, that almost half of the world's children live in urban areas, urban populations are growing fastest in Africa and Asia, educational attainment is the most unequal in high density urban areas, and children of the urban poor are more likely than others to be undernourished. We see, therefore, the co-existence of both agendas, that is, the starting strong/investing early agenda and the global sustainability agenda.

Looking forward

The work begun by the transnational dialogues has a history and a trajectory into the future. The dialogues presented in this book have exemplified the capacity and commitment of researchers to draw upon and contribute to early childhood for sustainability in ways that are global, ethical and, hopefully, sustainable.

The dialogues provide a platform for significant conceptual, methodological and analytic work in research with and about young children and their worlds. The process of engaging in dialogue and of sharing research is, in turn, generating new dialogues and research ideas, such that a new research 'movement' may begin to emerge. Propelled by further conceptual and empirical work, the group, platform and/or movement is well poised to take a leading role in advocacy for practice and policy, such that children and those around them are afforded authentic opportunities to learn and grow.

Transnational dialogues have the capacity to further strengthen the substantive fields of early childhood and education for sustainability in ways unforeseen to each field and to engender genuine dialogue between these and other substantive fields such as geo-politics, economics, architecture, health, happiness and wellbeing.

Conclusion

By focusing on children, in the context of their everyday lives, including their lives within families and communities, transnational dialogues have the capacity to address human rights and/or breaches of human rights for children, families and communities. While advocating transformational change, the dialogues give permission to those engaged in research, practice and policy to 'learn to live in the middle of things, in the tensions of conflict, confusion and possibility; and we must become adept at making do with the messiness of that condition' (Merriam 2002, p. 401). Transnational dialogues are calls for actioning change, with children and young people in local, national and international arenas of action.

References

Camilli, G., Vargas, S., Ryan, S. and Barnett, S. W. (2010) 'Meta-analysis of the effects of early education interventions on cognitive and social development'. *Teachers College Record*, 112(3), 579–620.

Cunha, F., Heckman, J. J., Lochner, L. J. and Masterov, D. V. (2006) 'Interpreting the evidence on life cycle skill formation', in E. Hanushek and F. Welch (eds). *Handbook of the Economics of Education.* Amsterdam: Elsevier, pp. 697–812.

Dewey, J. (1938) *Experience and Education.* Toronto: Collier-Macmillan.

Hutchby, I., and Moran-Ellis, J. (1998) 'Situating children's social competence', in I. Hutchby and J. Moran-Ellis (eds), *Children and Social Competence: Arenas of Action.* London: Falmer Press.

Merriam, S. B. (2002) *Qualitative Research in Practice.* San Francisco, CA: Jossey-Bass.

Organization for Economic Cooperation and Development (OECD) (2001) *Starting Strong.* Paris: OECD.

Organization for Economic Cooperation and Development (OECD) (2006) *Starting Strong II.* Paris: OECD.

Organization for Economic Cooperation and Development (OECD) (2012) *Starting Strong III. A Quality Toolbox for ECEC.* Paris: OECD.

United Nations Children's Fund (UNICEF) (2008) *Innocenti Report Card. The Child Care Transition. A League Table of Early Childhood Education and Care in Economically Advanced Countries.* Florence: UNICEF Innocenti Research Centre.

United Nations Children's Fund (UNICEF) (2012) *Children in an Urban World. State of the World's Children.* Geneva: UNICEF.

United Nations High Commission for Refugees (UNHCR) (2012) *Global Trends. Global Displacement. The New 21st Century.* Statistical Yearbook. Geneva: UNHCR.

United Nations Department of Economic and Social Affairs (UNDESA) (2011) *Estimates of Urban Population.* Geneva: UNDESA.

United Nations Educational, Scientific and Cultural Organization (UNESCO) (2005) *Decade of Education for Sustainable Development 2005–2014: Draft International Implementation Scheme.* Paris: UNESCO.

United Nations Educational, Scientific and Cultural Organization, United Nations Environment Program (UNESCO UNEP) (1975) *The Belgrade Charter: A framework for environmental education.* Online. Available: http://unesdoc.unesco.org/images/0001/000177/017772eb.pdf (accessed 20 December 2010).

United Nations Environment Program (UNEP) (2012) *The Emissions Gap Report.* Nairobi: UNEP.

Transnational dialogues participants

Transnational Dialogues in Research in Early Childhood Education for Sustainability I

Stavanger University, Stavanger, Norway
16–18 August 2010

Dr Eva Ärlemalm-Hagsér, Sweden
Associate Professor Julie Davis, Australia
Dr Sue Elliott, Australia
Professor Susan Danby, Australia
Dr Ingrid Engdahl, Sweden
Professor Ann Farrell, Australia
Professor Solveig Hägglund, Sweden
Professor Eva Johansson, Norway
Glynne Mackey, New Zealand
Elizabeth Morkeseth, Norway
Monica Rothle, Norway
Dr Barbara Sageidet, Norway

Transnational Dialogues in Research in Early Childhood Education for Sustainability 2

Queensland University of Technology, Brisbane, Australia
13–15 July 2011

Dr Jo Ailwood, Australia
Dr Eva Ärlemalm-Hagsér, Sweden
Hui-Ling Chua, Singapore
Associate Professor Julie Davis, Australia
Professor Susan Danby, Australia
Dr Sue Elliott, Australia
Dr Ingrid Engdahl, Sweden

Dr Karin Engdahl, Sweden
Professor Ann Farrell, Australia
Professor Solveig Hägglund, Sweden
Estelle Harris, Australia
Glynne Mackey, New Zealand
Professor Michiko Inoue, Japan
Dr Melinda Miller, Australia (unable to attend)
Professor Okjong Ji, Korea
Dr Lyndal O'Gorman, Australia
Dr Louise Phillips, Australia
Dr Jenny Ritchie, New Zealand
Dr Barbara Sageidet, Norway
Dr Sharon Stuchmke, Australia
Dr Bodil Sundberg, Sweden
Sue Vaealiki, New Zealand (unable to attend)
Tracy Young, Australia

Appendix 2

Our chronology of selected key events, research and publications that chart the development of ECEfS

Year	Event or publication	Origin
1782–1852	Froebel cited the term 'kindergarten' and envisioned children as playing and developing in nature.	Germany
1950s	Scandinavian forest preschools movement emerged.	Scandinavia
1956	Carson, R. (1956 republished 1998) *The Sense of Wonder*, New York: Harper and Row.	USA
1962	Carson, R. (1962) *Silent Spring*, New York: Houghton Mifflin Company.	USA
1977	First intergovernmental conference on Environmental Education held in Tiblisi, USSR.	International
1987	World Commission on Environment and Development (WCED) (1987) *Brundtland Report: Our Common Future,* Oxford: Oxford University Press.	International
1991	Elliott, S. and Emmett, S. (1991) *Snails Live in Houses Too, Environmental Education for the Early Years*, Sydney: Martin Educational (second edition 1997).	Australia
1992	Earth Summit, Rio de Janeiro, Agenda 21 supported education initiatives in some countries such a Scandinavia.	International
1992	Environmental Education in Early Childhood Victoria. (EEEC Vic Inc.) established and ongoing, www.eeec.com.au.	Australia
1993	Wilson, R. (1993) *Fostering a Sense of Wonder During the Early Childhood Years*, Columbus, Ohio: Greyden Press.	USA
1994	Wilson, R. (ed.) (1994) *Environmental Education at the Early Childhood Level,* Troy, Ohio: NAAEE.	USA

Year	Event or publication	Origin
1995	Queensland Early Childhood Environmental Education Network established, now ongoing as Queensland Early Childhood Sustainability Network (QECSN) www.qecsn.org.au	Australia
1996	New Zealand Ministry of Education (1996) *Te Whāriki: Early Childhood Curriculum.* Wellington: Learning Media.	New Zealand
1998	Davis, J. (1998) 'Young Children, Environmental Education and the Future', *Early Childhood Education Journal*, 26 (2), 117–23.	USA/ Australia
1998	National Agency for Education (1998) *Curriculum for the Preschool Lpfö 98*, Stockholm: Fritzes (later revised 2010).	Sweden
1999	New Zealand Government Environmental Guidelines promoted education for sustainability and linked to later Enviro schools program.	New Zealand
1999	First symposium in an environmental education conference, Australian Association for Environmental Education (AAEE).	Australia
1999	Davis, J. (1999) 'Early Childhood Environmental Education – Mainstream not Marginal', *OzEEnews*, 76: 2.	Australia
2002	Rio Plus 10 UNESCO meeting in Johannesburg and Japan proposed the United Nations Decade of Education for Sustainable Development (UNDESD).	International
2003	New South Wales Environment Protection Authority (NSW EPA) (2003) *Patches of Green: A Review of Early Childhood Environmental Education*, Sydney: NSW EPA.	Australia
2003	Australian Association for Environmental Education Early Childhood Special Interest Group established and ongoing, www.aaee.org.au.	Australia
2003	Davis, J. and Elliott, S. (2003) *Early Childhood Environmental Education: Making it Mainstream*, Canberra: Early Childhood Australia.	Australia
2003	New South Wales Early Childhood Environmental Education Network (NSW ECEEN) established and ongoing, www.eceen.org.au.	Australia

Year	Event or publication	Origin
2004	Enviro Kindergartens Pilot Program based on National Enviro schools Program commenced supported by local and national government and universities.	New Zealand
2005	Louv, R. (2005) *The Last Child in the Woods: Saving our Children from Nature Deficit Disorder,* Chapel Hill, NC: Algonquin Books.	USA
2005	Davis, J. (2005) 'Education for Sustainability in the Early Years: Creating Culture Change in a Childcare Setting', *Australian Journal of Environmental Education,* 21, 47–55.	Australia
2005	Davis, J., Gibson, M., Pratt, R., Eglington, A. and Rowntree, N. (2005) 'Creating a Culture of Sustainability: From Project to Integrated Education for Sustainability at Campus Kindergarten' in Filho, W.L. (ed.) *The International Handbook of Sustainability Research,* Paris: UNESCO, pp. 563–94.	International
2005	UNESCO (2005) Decade of education for sustainable development 2005–2014 Draft International Implementation Scheme, Paris: UNESCO.	International
2005	Tilbury, D., Coleman, V. and Garlick, D. (2005) *A National Review of Environmental Education and its Contribution to Sustainability in Australia: School Education,* Canberra: Australian Government Department of the Environment and Heritage and Australian Research Institute in Education for Sustainability. Section on ECEfS by Davis and Elliott.	Australia
2005	UNESCO Chair for Early Childhood Education and Sustainable Development appointed, Ingrid Pramling Samuelsson.	International
2006	Inaugural Australasian Early Childhood Education for Sustainability Conference, Christchurch, NZ.	New Zealand/ Australia
2007	Second Australasian Early Childhood Education for Sustainability Conference, Sydney Australia	Australia/ New Zealand
2007	Kinsella, R. (2007) *Greening Services Practical Sustainability,* Canberra, ACT: ECA.	Australia

Year	Event or publication	Origin
2007	*Little Green Steps* program developed by local government, Gosford and Wyong Councils www.livingthing.net.au/rc/PP/ClimbLittleGreenSteps.pdf	Australia
2007	Safe and Sustainable Indoor Cleaning (SASI) Project, Victorian State Government funded research project in four early childhood centres re cleaning practices undertaken by Bridget Gardner, Fresh Green Clean www.sasiclean.com.au/	Australia
2007	Early Childhood Australia, Victorian Sustainability Special Interest Group established, www.ecavic.org.au	Australia
2007	Davis, J. (2007) 'Climate Change and its Impact on Young Children', Early Childhood Australia, www.eca.org.au.	Australia
2007	Young, T. (2007) 'Why do young children need to know about climate change?' Early Childhood Australia, www.eca.org.au.	Australia
2008	Vaealiki, S. and Mackey, G. (2008) 'Ripples of Action: Strengthening Environmental Competency in an Early Childhood Centre', *NZCER Early Childhood Folio* 12, 7–11.	New Zealand
2008	Kinsella, R. (2008) *Everyday Learning About Being Green*, ECA, Canberra, ACT.	Australia
2008	UNESCO (2008) The Gothenburg Recommendations on Education for Sustainable Development omep.vrserver2.cl/cgi-bin/procesa.pl?plantilla=/archivo.html&bri=omep&tab=art_6&campo=c_file&id=270.	International
2008	UNESCO (2008) *Early Childhood and its Contribution to a Sustainable Society*, Paris: UNESCO.	International
2008	Davis, J., Miller, M., Boyd, W. and Gibson, M. (2008) *The Impact and Potential of Water Education in Early Childhood Care and Education Settings,* Brisbane, Queensland: Rous Water Board, Queensland University of Technology and Institute of Sustainable Resources.	Australia
2009	Davis, J. (2009) 'Revealing the Research "Hole" of Early Childhood Education for Sustainability: A Preliminary Survey of the Literature', *Environmental Education Research*, 15 (2), 227–41.	Australia

Year	Event or publication	Origin
2009	Elliott, S. and Davis, J. (2009) 'Exploring the Resistance: An Australian Perspective on Educating for Sustainability in Early childhood', *International Journal of Early Childhood*, 41(2), 65–77.	Australia
2009	*Green Kinders Toolkit* launched by Hobson's Bay Council Australia, based on research with two early childhood centres www.hobsons.vic.gov.au/files/GreenKinderBro_Final2.pdf.	Australia
2009	Department of Education and Early Childhood Development (DEECD) (2009) *Looking Ahead Report*, inclusive of ECEfS initiatives www.eduweb.vic.gov.au/edulibrary/public/schadmin/environment/lookahead.pdf.	Australia
2009	Third Australasian Early Childhood Education for Sustainability Conference, Melbourne Australia.	Australia/New Zealand
2009	Young, T. (2009) "The Crack Where the Light Gets In": An Examination of Sustainable Education in Early Childhood Education. Master of Education Thesis. Monash University, Melbourne.	Australia
2009	OMEP Asia Pacific Conference, Singapore, Sustainability Strand	Asia Pacific
2009	*International Journal of Early Childhood*, 41(2) Special themed edition on sustainability.	International
2009	Siraj-Blatchford, J. and Pramling Samuelsson, I. (2009) 'The Sustainable Development Case', in I. Siraj-Blatchford and M. Woodhead, (eds) *Early Childhood in Focus 4: Effective Early Childhood Programmes*. Milton Keynes: The Open University, pp. 10–11.	UK/Sweden
2009	UNESCO DESD mid-term review includes an ECEfS case study. UNESCO (2009) *Review of Contexts and Structures for Sustainable Development 2009*, Paris: UNESCO.	International
2010	Davis, J. (ed.) (2010) *Young Children and the Environment: Early Education for Sustainability*. Melbourne: Cambridge University Press. In 2014 republished in Korean and in 2015 second edition to be available.	Australia

Year	Event or publication	Origin
2010	Siraj-Blatchford, J., Smith, K. C. and Pramling Samuelsson, I. (2010) *Education for Sustainable Development in the Early Years*, Gothenburg, Sweden: OMEP.	UK/Sweden
2010	Duhn, I. with Bachmann, M. and Harris, K. (2010) 'Becoming Ecologically Sustainable in Early Childhood Education', *NZCER, Early Childhood Folio*, 14(1), 2–6.	New Zealand
2010	Ellwood, A. (2010) 'Caring for Papatūānuku: Yesterday, Today and Tomorrow', *Early Education*, 47 Autumn/Winter, 15–18.	New Zealand
2010	Ritchie, J. (2010) 'Fostering Communities: Ecological Sustainability within Early Childhood Education', *Early Education*, 47, Autumn/Winter, 10–14.	New Zealand
2010	Elliott, S. (2010) 'Essential not Optional: Education for Sustainability in Early Childhood Centres', *Childcare Information Exchange*, March/April, 34–37.	Australia/ USA
2010	First Transnational Dialogues on Research in ECEfS, Stavanger, August 16–18.	Australasia/ Scandinavia
2010	North American Association for Environmental Education (2010). *Early Childhood Environmental Education Programs: Guidelines for Excellence*, www.naaee.org/programs-and-initiatives/guidelines-for-excellence/early-childhood.	USA
2010	United Kingdom Preschool Alliance (2010) *My Favourite Colour is Green*, London: United Kingdom Preschool Alliance.	UK
2010	First Japanese Ecosystem Conservation Society Study Tour to Australia for ECEfS.	Australia/ Japan
2010	UNESCO DESD International Symposium on Reorientating Teacher Education in Paris May 19–21, inclusive of early childhood education.	International
2010	First accredited AuSSI Early Childhood Centre in Australia, St Kilda and Balaclava Kindergarten.	Australia
2010	OMEP World Conference, Gothenberg, Sweden, Sustainability strand.	International

Year	Event or publication	Origin
2010	Siraj-Blatchford, J., Smith, K. C. and Pramling Samuelsson, I. (2010) *Education for Sustainable Development in the Early Years,* Gothenburg, Sweden: OMEP.	Sweden
2011	Second Japanese Ecosystem Conservation Society Study Tour to Australia for ECEfS.	Australia/ Japan
2011	World Environmental Education Congress Brisbane, Early Childhood Strand including Second Transnational Dialogues on Research in ECEfS, July 13–15.	International
2011	Mackey, G. and Vaealiki, S. (2011) 'Thinking of Children: Democratic Approaches with Young Children in Research', *Australasian Journal of Early Childhood,* 36(2), 82–6.	New Zealand
2011	Edwards, S. and Cutter-Mackenzie, A. (2011) 'Environmentalizing Early Childhood Education Curriculum through Pedagogies of Play', *Australasian Journal of Early Childhood [E],* 36(1), 51–59.	Australia
2011	Sandberg, A. and Ärlemalm-Hagsér, E (2011) 'Play and learning with fundamental values in focus', *Australasian Journal of Early Childhood,* 36(1), 44–50.	Sweden
2012	North American Association for Environmental Education (NAAEE), established *International Early Childhood Environmental Education Journal,* www.naaee.org.us.	USA/ International
2012	Smith, K., Wheeler, L. Guevara, J. R., Gough, A. and Fein, J. (2012) *Conversations on School-Community Learning Partnerships for Sustainability: A Guidebook,* Bundoora, Victoria: RMIT University (includes early childhood case study).	Australia
2012	Elliott, S. (2012) 'Sustainable Outdoor Playspaces in Early Childhood Centres: Investigating Perceptions, Facilitating Change and Generating Theory', Unpublished doctoral thesis, University of New England, Armidale, NSW.	Australia

Year	Event or publication	Origin
2012	Ärlemalm-Hagsér, E. (2013) 'An Interest in the Best for the World'? Education for Sustainability in the Swedish Preschool, Doctoral thesis. Acta Universitatis Gothoburgensis Göteborg, Sweden.	Sweden
2012	Stuhmcke, S. M. (2012) *Children as Change Agents for Sustainability: An Action Research Case Study in a Kindergarten.* Unpublished thesis, Queensland University of Technology: Brisbane	Australia
2012	Australian Children's Education and Care Quality Authority (ACECQA) (2011 revised 2013) *Guide to the National Standard.* Retrieved 10 March 2014 from: http://files.acecqa.gov.au/files/National-Quality-Framework-Resources-Kit/NQF03-Guide-to-NQS-130902.pdf. Inclusive of sustainability standard.	Australia
2013	Third Japanese Ecosystem Conservation Society Study Tour to Australia for ECEfS.	Australia
2013	Elliott, S., Edwards, S., Davis, J. and Cutter-Mackenzie, A. (2013) *ECA Best of Sustainability: Research, Theory and Practice,* Watson, ACT: Early Childhood Australia.	Australia/ New Zealand
2013	OMEP World Conference, Shanghai, China, Sustainability Strand.	International

Index

Aborigines: children learning the culture and history of 73; embedding Indigenous perspectives 67; First Peoples of Australian lands and territories 66, 70; NAIDOC (National Aborigines and Islanders Day Observance Committee) week 68; right for all children to engage with 64, 66; wisdom of 28

Admiral Burke Park redevelopment: bioblitz 260; children's presentation of their ideas 260–1; 'Make a Difference' community service class 260; children as active citizens 261

affluenza 195

agency 26, 34, 50, 132, 159, 176, 180–1, 183, 185–6, 189–92, 195, 199, 204, 213, 221, 252, 253, 258, 262–3, 282

Agenda 21 28, 89

agents of change 1–2, 33, 64, 152, 180, 191, 204, 213, 294, 297, 301, 303, 310–1

Allen, P. G. 53

Amazon rainforests 30

Ang, L. 104

Anthropocene: concept of 29–30

anthropocentricism: distortion of sensitivity to nature 50; interconnectedness with biocentric/ecocentric rights 30; meaning of 30

Ärlemalm-Hagsér, E. 282

Arts and Humanities: adopting new practices 270; critical theory 270, 270–1; discomfort of students 273; ecological footprint calculator tool 270; engagement with a variety of contents 270; expression of big ideas 273, 274; identity theory 270, 271, 274–5; integrated 269–71; online discussions of the Arts and sustainability 272–6; powerful messages of sustainability for students 271–2; self-portrait 270, 272; student teachers' sense of identity 271; synthesis 273

Arts: advantages over traditional approaches in the Sciences 267; Arts and Humanities integrated subject see Arts and Humanities; children's capacity for art-making 267; early childhood education and 267–8; integrated approaches 267; integration with sustainability 266–7; opportunities for children to create their futures 268; visual artists advancing the cause of sustainability 266

Arvanitakis, J. 196

Atua 55

AuSSI (Australian Sustainable Schools Initiative): community engagement 150–2; implementation at grassroots level 143; partnership statement 146; significance and effectiveness of 144; sustainable early childhood project see SECP; twelve-step action plan 145–6; 'whole-school' framework 145

Australia: background to ECEfS 169; Belonging, Being and Becoming: The Early Years Learning Framework for Australia (EYLF) 34, 66, 140, 143, 169, 269, 289; inclusion of environmental education into children's services 144; National Curriculum 268; National Quality Standards 169; pressure to integrate sustainability across all education sectors 143–4; reform agenda for early childhood profession 143; scholarly output on early childhood environmental education 79; Studies of Society and Environment (SOSE) 268;

see also Aborigines; Arts and Humanities; Arts; Torres Strait Islanders
Australian Association for Environmental Education (AAEE) 269
Australian Curriculum 66
Australian Research Institute for Education for Sustainability (ARIES) 7
Australian Sustainable Schools Initiative (AuSSI) *see* AuSSI
autonomy: self-determination theory 117
Avon Valley Wildlife Trust 237
Awi Usdi 200–1

Baker, J. 171
Banksia Childcare Centre: active participation by children 133; apparent lack of education for sustainability 129–30; fully nested systems 136, 139; outdoor playspaces 130; play opportunities offered by natural playspaces 137; positive images of children held by teachers and parents 133; teachers' adopting principles of education for sustainability 131–2, 138; worm farm 129
Barker, R. 253
Barrett, R. 228
Barrett-Douglas, R. 54
Barrett-Hacking, E. 225–47
Basic Act on Education 82
Bath Spa University 236
Beder, S. 29
The Belgrade Charter 8
belonging: children's sense of where they live and play 186–7; dimension of world citizenship 42; future others 42; 'the Other' 42; relationship between child and society 43; return of community vitality 187–8; right to be involved 42–3; world citizen 42
Belonging, Being and Becoming: The Early Years Learning Framework for Australia (EYLF) 34, 66, 140, 143, 169, 269, 289
Bingham, S. 230
biocentric/ecocentric rights: Anthropocene 29–30; anthropocentrism 30; assigns value to the Earth's non-living systems 30; Earth Charter 28, 32–3; ecocide 31; equal value of all living beings 30; Gaia Hypothesis 30; interconnectedness with anthropocentrism 30
Bishop Sutton Primary School: activities with villagers and wildlife trust 237;

background to 235–6; context 236; developing a positive self-image in children 236; impact of Chew Valley Lake project 237–8; inspiration for EfS 236; 'life of the lake' project 236–7; partnership with Bath Spa University 236; place-based learning 236, 237, 238
Bixler, R. D. 250
Black, P. 225–47
BlueCross/BlueShield 262
Bonnett, M. 13
Bookchin, M. 158, 175
Boulder Journey School 259
Boulder Valley School District 258
Brennhaugen, Gabriele 118
bricolage 209
Bronfenbrenner's Ecological System Theory 134
Bronfenbrenner, U. 134, 181
Brooks-Gunn, J. 257
Brundtland Report 9, 112–13
Burke, P. 271
Burnett, B. 65

Campbell, B. 56
Carson, Rachel 6, 248–9, 252
Cedarsong Forest Kindergarten 256
Centres for Early Childhood Education and Care 80
CERES (Centre for Education and Research into Environmental Strategies): lack of expertise in early childhood sector 145; lack of relevance to young children 145
Chai, M. 100
Chard, S. C. 159, 160, 161
Chawla, L. 242, 251
Chelsea Open Air Nursery and Children's Centre: background to 238; context 238–9; establishment of 227; impact of outdoor learning 240; inspiration for EfS 239; open air philosophy 239; play-based approach to learning 239–40
child exploitation 196
Child Friendly Cities Initiative 257
children: action competence 189; active in everyday democratic processes 189–90; active social agents 3; becoming part of the local community 45; benefits of positive interactions with natural world 100; centrality of 1; child exploitation 196; collectively-formed social knowledge 43; communitarian citizenship 195, 197; creation of shared

worlds and belongings 43, 45;
dimension of belonging 45; disengaged
from community life 152; distance from
natural, wild spaces 50; early childhood
education for sustainability for 196–7;
ecological citizenship 258; evidence of
desire to be active contributors in
society 195–6; experience of citizenship
196; fields of free action 252–3; global
citizens 211; learning about nature with
adults 252; learning experiences for the
early years 243; marginalization as active
participants 196; moral development
211; National Quality Framework
campaign 63–4; natural caring 188;
outdoor play *see* outdoor play;
participation in sustainability 195–7;
physical health benefits playing outdoors
100; reduced experience of natural
environment 228; responsibility for a
common world 45; responsive to moral
and ethical problems 189; rights and
respect for 46; romance of play 196;
sedentary lifestyle of Singaporean
children 101; value conflicts 45; working
authentically 1–2; *see also* rights of
children
Children and Nature Network 32
Children, Youth and Environment Center
for Community Engagement 258
Christchurch (kindergarten case study):
active participation of local community
182; children's learning experiences
185–6; community 184; creating a
culture of sustainability 183–5, 192;
dinosaur playground 186, 187;
earthquakes 187–8; ecological
theoretical position of Urie
Bronfenbrenner 181; links with other
groups 184; living the culture of
sustainability 185–6; *mana aotūroa*
188–9; *mana reo* 189–90; *mana tangata*
190–1; *mana whenua* 186–8; meanings
and practice of sustainability 183;
participatory approach 182; partnership
with participants 182; teachers' changing
practices 185; theoretical frame of case
study 182
Chua, H.-L. 91–111
citizenship: belonging dimension of world
citizenship 42; children's rights as active
citizens 261; communitarian 195, 197;
ecological 258; learning for

sustainability dimension of world
citizenship 42; typology of spaces 196
City Area redevelopment: amplifying
children's voices 259; Boulder Creek
259; Boulder Journey School 259;
children's contribution to final
redevelopment 259; children's
exploration of Civic Area 259;
combined different groups 259;
designated area 258–9; family picnic 259
climate change: crisis 49
Clough, P. 294
Cluster 1: core values and ethics 10
Cluster 2: contrast between different
countries 11; historical and sociocultural
contexts 10–11
Cluster 3: connections with nature 12;
curriculum and pedagogy 11–12;
transformative agenda 11–12
Coalition for No Child Left Inside 254
collective rights: error of pursuing
individual interests 27; global nature of
problems and solutions 27; inadequacy
of existing human rights treaties 26;
Indigenous peoples' rights 27–8; tragedy
of the commons 27
commons 27
communication: children active in
everyday democratic processes 189–90;
children voting for the best swings 190
communitarian citizenship 195, 197
competence: self-determination theory 117
Comstock, D.E. 129
conflicts: enable possibilities for change 44;
prerequisite for democracy 44
conscientização 197
contribution, of children to project 190–1
*The Contribution of Early Childhood
Education to a Sustainable Society* 4
Convention on Biological Diversity 28
Corney, G. 269
Course of Study for Kindergarten 80, 83
Coxen's fig-parrot 201–2
CPAR (Critical Participatory Action
Research): Acacia Kindergarten *see*
Acacia Kindergarten; Banksia Childcare
Centre *see* Banksia Childcare Centre;
methodology 128–9; nested systems
theory *see* nested systems theory;
participating case study centres 129;
systems theory *see* systems theory;
theoretical framework *see* theoretical
framework (CPAR)

Creswell, J. 273
critical awareness 197–8
Critical Participatory Action Research
    (CPAR) *see* CPAR
critical theory 270, 270–1
critical thinking 91
Crutzen, P. 30
cultural systems 194
Cutter-Mackenzie, A. 143–57

Dahlbeck, J. 208, 210, 211
Danby, S. 309–13
Davies, N. 238
Davis, J. M. 4, 197, 250, 251, 270, 282
Decade of Education for Sustainable
    Development 2005–2014 (DESD) 7, 9,
    82, 89, 281
Declaration on the Rights of Indigenous
    Peoples 27
deep ecology 115–16
De Graaf, J. 195
democracy: children active in 189–90;
    conflicts and political struggles 44
Denmark 215
Developmentally Appropriate Practices 257
Dewey, J. 91, 309–10
dialogical interpenetration 51
dinosaur playground 186, 187
distance moral 42
Dreise, M. 67
Durie, M. 52

early childhood education: achieving
    intercultural goals 66; combined with
    sustainability 257–61; concept of 8;
    contribution to sustainability 4; Earth
    Charter 28, 32–3; environmental
    education research 5; focus/refocus on
    rights and values 32; holistic standpoint
    33; in Japan *see* Japan; literature on 5;
    narrow conceptualization of rights 22;
    rethinking philosophies to connect with
    the natural world 32; rethinking the
    socio-constructivist frameworks 33;
    rights of children *see* rights of children
Early Childhood Education for
    Sustainability (ECEfS) *see* ECEfS
early childhood environmental education
    84–6, 87–92; *see also* Japan
early childhood pedagogy: romance of play
    196
Early Years Foundation Stage (EYFS) 225,
    242, 294, 295

Early Years Professional Status (EYPS) 296
Early Years Teacher 296
Earth: complex ecosystem 194; human
    population 195; shared environmental,
    social, political and economic
    responsibility 195
Earth Charter 28, 32–3
earthquakes (Christchurch) 187–8
Earth Summit 28
ECEfS (Early Childhood Education for
    Sustainability): conferences 1; in
    England *see* England; environmental
    socialization 250; foundations 3; gaps in
    research and how it is reported 74;
    intercultural dialogues *see* intercultural
    dialogues; National Quality Framework
    campaign 63–4; research in 10; role
    models for 250; transnational dialogues
    309; *see also* early childhood education;
    education for sustainable development;
    EfS; environmental education; Norway
Eco-Agents 118
ecocentrism: assigns value to the Earth's
    non-living systems 30
ecocide 30
ecojustice 297
ecological citizenship 258
Ecological Model of Child Development
    181
ecological psychology: behaviour settings
    for children 253; capabilities approach
    to human development 258;
    evolutionary theory of Darwin 251;
    'necessity of experience' 251; sensory
    experiences of the physical world 251
ecology, deep 115–16
economic systems 194
Ecoschools 232
Ecuadorian Constitution: buen vivir 30–1;
    Rights of Nature 30–1
Education for Sustainability (EfS) *see* EfS
education for sustainable development:
    concept of 9; interpretations of values in
    peer-cultures 39; knowledge learning
    and learning for sustainability 38–9;
    learning for sustainability 40–1; studies
    in Nordic countries 39; *see also*
    environmental education
educators *see* teachers
EfS (Education for Sustainability):
    characterized by a list of principles 9;
    concept of 9, 22; in England *see*
    England; ethical principles of early

childhood education for sustainability
159, 175; frame of mind 13;
interconnection of environment, society,
economics and politics 158–9; learning
experiences for the early years 243; in
Norway see Norway; programme for
creating change 33; supporting children
as agents of change 33–4; in Sweden see
Sweden; transformative education
approaches 33; see also education for
sustainable development; environmental
education
Elliott, S. 33, 34, 35, 47, 50, 59, 70, 76, 103,
108, 127, 128, 130, 132, 133–5, 139,
141, 143–4, 156, 159, 178, 188, 191,
193, 270, 277, 294, 304, 305, 310–11,
314, 316, 317, 320, 321
embedded processes: limitations on non-
Indigenous teachers' practices 71–3;
positioning Indigenous individuals on
the periphery 72; protocols 72–3
embedding processes: issues with fear 70–1;
misrepresentation of perspectives in
mainstream education 68; partnerships
between Indigenous and non-
Indigenous peoples 71; partnerships
with members of local Indigenous
communities 68; practices aligning with
intercultural education goals 67;
understanding whiteness in relation to
Indigenous peoples 69; Walking whole-
school approaches to 68
emergent science 283, 289
Emscote Infants School: background to
240; context 240; 'eight doorways'
structure 241; impact of using outdoor
grounds 241–2; inspiration for the EfS
241; participatory approach to include
stakeholders 241
endangered animals 200
endangered birds 201
Endahl, I. 208–24
England: Bishop Sutton Primary School
235–8; Chelsea Open Air Nursery
School and Children's Centre 227,
238–40; development of meaningful
outdoor natural play 230; Early Years
Foundation Stage 225; early years
framework 231; early years' policy
229–30; Ecoschools 232; Emscote Infants
School 240–2; England Early Years
Foundation Stage 230; forest schools
movement 227; government intervention

in early years education 230; National
Curriculum for Key Stage 225; Natural
Environment White Paper 229; natural
play 226; 'nature as teacher' 230–1;
opportunities for ECEfS 230–2; outdoor
play 226–8; Redcliffe Children's Centre
and Maintained Nursery School 233–5;
right to play 227–8; sustainable schools
framework 231–2; urban poor 227; see
also United Kingdom
England Early Years Foundation Stage 230
environment: children acting for 4–5; deep
ecology philosophy 115–16
environmental education: active child
participation 91; concept of 8–9; critical
thinking 91–2; cultural differences 92;
failure to build sustainable societies 89;
global recognition of 89; in Japan see
environmental education in Japan;
learning from diverse cultures 91–2;
promotion of sustainability 89; see also
education for sustainable development
environmental education in Japan: concepts
for rethinking existing early childhood
education for sustainability 89–90;
critical thinking 91–2; definition of
83–4; early childhood environmental
education 84–6, 87–92; history of 82;
Japanese Society of Environmental
Education 84; learning from diverse
cultures 91–2; meaning of education for
sustainability 87, 88; meaning of
environmental education 87, 88;
omission from early childhood
education 83; part of the nation's
environmental policies 82; researchers in
84, 86; teachers introducing an
ecological worldview 90
environmental socialization 250
Enviroschools: awards ceremony 184;
sustainability focus for teachers 181
EnviroSchools Foundation 181
ESD (Education for Sustainable
Development) 4, 7, 8, 9, 41–2, 82–3, 84,
87, 88–9, 91, 93, 113, 143, 211, 215,
216, 222, 281
ethnography 146–7
European Environment and Schools
Initiatives (ENSI) 145
Ewing, R. 267, 268
exploration: action competence 189;
children as problem solvers and solution
seekers 188–9

Farrell, A. 309–13
Flannery, T. 57
forest experiences 234
Forest Kindergarten 32
forest schools movement 227
Forest School Teacher Certification 256
Foundation for Environmental Education
    (FEE) 118, 145
Framework Plan for Preschool Teacher
    Education 114
France 215, 242
The Freedom Bird 200, 201
freedom of expression 199, 202
Freire, P. 197
Froebel, F. 32, 196, 257, 316
Fuller, M. 294–308

Gaia Hypothesis 30
Galbraith Kindergarten 55
Gibson, E. 251
Gibson, J. 251
Gilbert, L. 294–308
global financial crises: unsustainable
    economic systems 6
globalization: individualization and
    liberation of people 116
Global North 195
*Gothenburg Recommendations on Education for
    Sustainable Development* 4
Gough, A. 5, 269
Gould League 145
Greene, M. 197, 198
Green Flag (Sweden) 211
Green Growth Education 162
Green Ribbon Schools program 254, 255
Green School movement 254
Green Schools Award (Sweden) 145
Green Schools Program (China) 145
Growing Up Boulder program: Admiral
    Burke Park redevelopment 260–1; aim
    of 257; Civic Area redevelopment
    258–60
Growing up in Cities program 257
Gruenewald, David 51
*Guideline for Care and Education in Nursery
    Centres* 80
*Guidelines for Excellence in Early Childhood
    Environmental Education* 255
Guidelines on Intercultural Education 64, 65

Hägglund, S. 210, 211
Hall, Ellen 259
Hart, R. 200–1

Hawera Kindergarten 56
Hayward, B. 258
Henderson, K. 270–1
Higgins, P. 31
Holmes, H. 54
Horizons School 260
Howarth, R. 29, 275
How schools kill creativity 274–5
humanity: capabilities approach to human
    development 258; management of co-
    existence 194; population growth 195;
    shared environmental, social, political
    and economic responsibility 195

identity theory 270, 271
imagery, of children 25–6
Imre, R. 195
Indigenous and Tribal Populations
    Convention 27
Indigenous peoples: Australian 52–3;
    building relationships with and learning
    from 57; care of the country worldview
    53; connectedness to geographical area
    28; conventions 28; Declaration on the
    Rights of Indigenous Peoples 27; formal
    education systems 92; historical
    misrepresentations and assumptions
    about 67; learning connected with daily
    lives 92; misrepresentation of
    perspectives in mainstream education
    68; models for facing challenges of
    climate change 53; protocols 73;
    recognizing diversity within cultural
    groups 68; rights of 27–8; Rights of
    Nature 30–1; understanding
    particularities of place 51;
    understandings local ecologies 49;
    wisdoms 52–3; *see also* Aborigines;
    Māoris; Torres Strait Islanders
Inoue, M. 79–96
institutional racism 70
insurgent citizenship 196
intercultural dialogues: in an Australian
    context 66–7; call for 64; challenging
    stereotypes, racism and discrimination
    65; embedding Indigenous perspectives
    67–73; intercultural goals 66; non-
    Indigenous people require
    understanding of Indigenous peoples'
    history 67; self-awareness and
    understanding 65; shared characteristics
    of environmental education and
    multicultural education 65; shared

understandings between different groups 65–6
intergenerational rights 28–9, 29
International Alliance of Leading Education Institutes (IALEI) 267
International Criminal Court (ICC) 30
The International Handbook of Research on Environmental Education 5
The International Journal of Early Childhood Environmental Education 5, 255
International Labour Organization (ILO) 27
Isaacs, S. 227, 238, 239
iwi (tribes) 54, 55

James, J. J. 250
Japan: commendation by OECD 81; early childhood education in 80–2; environmental education in *see* environmental education in Japan; initiation of DESD 82–3; kindergartens 80, 81, 86–7; national standards for early childhood education 80; nature-based activities 90; nursery centres 80, 86–7; policies and curriculum guidelines for early childhood education 81; promotion of education for sustainable development (ESD) 82–3; qualifications required by teachers 80–1
Japan Council 83
Japanese Society of Environmental Education 84
Japan Society of Research on Early Childhood Care and Education 84
Jickling, B. 23
Ji, O. 163
Johansson, E. 189, 211
Jones, A. 73
Jordan, C. 271
Journal of Action Research Today in Early Childhood 5
Jucker, R. 297–8

kaitiakitanga 52
Katz, L. G. 159, 160, 161
kaupapa 55
Kemp, P. 42, 45
Kimbro, R. 257
Kindergarten Curriculum Guide (Singapore) 101
kindergartens: Acacia Kindergarten 129, 129–30, 132, 133, 136, 137–8, 138; Cedarsong Forest Kindergarten 256; *Forest Kindergarten* 32; Froebel's original

conception of 32, 196, 257, 316; Galbraith Kindergarten 55; Hawera Kindergarten 56; in Japan 80, 81, 86–7; Meadowbank Kindergarten 54–5; in New Zealand *see* Christchurch; in Norway 113, 114–15, 116, 118–21; Papamoa Kindergarten 55; Rainforest Project *see* Rainforest Project; Singapore 101; Waldkindergarten 256
Kinney, L. 190
Korea: background to ECEfS 162; government commitment to low-carbon, green growth strategy 162; Musim Stream Project *see* Musim Stream Project; 'Nuri' curriculum 162
Korzak, J. 46
Kyoto Protocol 253

Läroplan för förskolan (Lpfö) (Sweden) 1998 revised 2010 280–1
Last Child in the Woods 249, 253
Laszlo, E. 6
Law for Enhancing Motivation on Environmental Conservation and Promoting of Environmental Education (Japan) 82, 83
learning for sustainability: belonging 41–3; concept of sustainability 41; conflicts 44–5; dimension of time 42; dimension of world citizenship 42; inviting children to partnerships 41; relationship between child and society 43; resistance to children as holders of rights 40; rights and respect for children 46; rights of children 40–1; right to be involved 42–3; values and value conflicts 43–5
Leavy, P. 267
Lester and Clyde 172
The Lonely Coxen's Fig-parrot 201
Louv, R. 249, 253
Lovelock, J. 30
Lowan-Trudeau, G. 28
Lucy School (Middletown) 255

Mackey, G. 180–93
Malone, K. 253
manaakitanga 52
mana aotūroa: action competence 189; children as problem solvers and solution seekers 188–9
mana atua 188
mana reo: children active in everyday democratic processes 189–90; children

voting for the best swings 190
mana tangata, project contribution 190–1
mana whenua: children's sense of where
    they live and play 186–7; dinosaur
    playground 186, 187; high hills 186–7;
    local history tour 186; return of
    community vitality 187–8
Mang, P. 74
Māoris: close relationship with nature 52;
    honouring the specificities of different
    birds and trees 54; Indigenous wisdoms
    52; models of education 52; research
    projects 54–6; settlement in
    Christchurch 186
massification 197
McArdle, F. A. 65
McLanahan, S. 257
McMillan, M. 227
McMillan, R. 227
Mead, H. 55
Mead, M. 1, 311
Meadowbank Kindergarten 54–5
Millei, Z. 195
Miller, M. I. 63–9
Ministry of Education, Culture, Sports,
    Science and Technology (Japan) 80
Ministry of Health, Labour and Welfare
    (Japan) 80
Mipyung Childcare Centre 163
Monitor of Engagement with the Natural
    Environment (MENE) project (UK)
    243n1
more-than-human realm: meaning of term
    50; respect for 51
Moreton-Robinson, A. 69
Mother Earth School 256
motifs 199
Mouffe, C. 44
Mumford, A. 295
Mundine, K. 70–1
Murata, K. 92
Musim Stream Project: biotape map for
    young children 166–7; children learning
    to be active citizens 166; children's
    misunderstandings about the stream
    164; children's proposition to Cheongju
    City Hall 166; conclusion 168; context
    of project 162–3; culminating event in
    Sangdang Park 168; educational goals
    163; excursion 165; learning of children
    166; legacy/impact 168–9; preparation
    for 163; problem solving 164–5; Project
    Learning Community 163; the prompt

164; social and political dimensions of
    sustainability 161; starting the project
    163–4

Næss, A. 115–16
NAIDOC (National Aborigines and
    Islanders Day Observance Committee)
    week 68
Nakata, M. 68
National Agency for Education (Sweden)
    281–2
National Curriculum (Australia) 268
National Curriculum for Key Stage (UK)
    225
National Curriculum for the Swedish
    Preschool 34, 210
National Education and Environment
    Fund (NEEF) (USA) 254
*National Framework Plan for the Content and
    Tasks of Kindergartens* (Norway) 112, 113
National Green Plan (Singapore): activities
    of 97; greening plan 98; green network
    98; 'Singapore Clean and Green Schools
    Carnival' 99; study and preservation of
    tropical biodiversity 98; 'Thumbs up for
    Earth' program 99
National Quality Framework (Australia) 63
National Quality Standards (Australia) 143,
    169
National Teaching schools (UK) 233
Natural Environment White Paper (UK)
    229
Natural History Museum 240
Natural Learning Initiative (NLI) (USA)
    257, 262
nature: *Children and Nature Network* 32;
    collective rights 27; connections with
    12; deep ecology philosophy 115–16;
    embedded with 200; *Forest Kindergarten*
    32; free play 251; impact of urbanization
    on 99; Māoris' close relationship with
    52; outdoor play *see* outdoor play;
    principle of wholism 116; rethinking
    philosophies to connect with 32; Rights
    of Nature 30–1; and science *see* Science
    (Sweden)
Naylor, T. 195
Neale, B. 202
nested systems: description of 134;
    framework 134–5; outdoor playspace
    physical context 134–5, 137–8, 139
New Canaan Nature Center 255–6
Newman, B. 70, 73

New Zealand: early childhood curriculum *see Te Whāriki* kindergarten case study *see* Christchurch
New Zealand Teaching and Learning Research Initiative 54
Ng, J. 104
Nimmo, J. 152, 152–3, 196
Noddings, N. 188
Nordic countries: strategies for sustainable development 113
Nordström, H. K. 65
North American Association for Environmental Education (NAAEE) 254, 255
Norway: appearance as materialistically orientated 117; concept of sustainability implemented at national and local level 113; deep ecology philosophy of Arne Næss 115–16; early recognition of EfS in kindergartens 114–15; Eco-lighthouses program for kindergartens 118–19; ecological footprint of population 115; Foundation for Environmental Education (FEE) 118, 120; Framework Plan for Preschool Teacher Education 114; green flag participation for kindergartens 119; green kindergartens 118; ideas about sustainability 112–13; implementation of EfS in kindergartens 118–20; importance of kindergartens to 120–1; *Kindergarten Act, Section 2, Content for Kindergartens* 113; kindergartens inspired by deep ecology philosophy 116; kindergarten teachers 118, 119; OMEP member 215; preschool teaching of sustainable development 113–14; ROSE (The Relevance of Science Education) project 117; sponsorship and cooperation with NGOs 118; strategy for education 113; strengthening ECEfS 120–1; sustainability projects chosen by kindergartens 119; tension between tradition, environmental responsibility and individual orientation 117–18; traditions and way of life 114–15; understanding of sustainable development in kindergarten's everyday life 113; values of kindergartens 113; wider range of choices for Norwegian people 118
Nussbaum, M. 198
Nutbrown, C. 294

OECD (Organization for Economic Co-operation and Development) 81, 311
Ofsted (Office for Standards in Education, Children's Services and Skill) (UK): analysis of inspection reports 232–3; assessment of outdoor experience for children 235; recommendation of Chew Valley Lake project 237; recommendation of Emscote Infant School 241–2
O'Gorman, L. 270
Öhman, J. 281
OMEP (Organization for Early Childhood) 3–4, 4, 215–16, 216–19
Organization for Economic Co-operation and Development (OECD) 81, 311
Ottander, C. 280–93
'Other,' exploitation of 50
Our Common Future 28
outdoor play: children absorbed in creative activities and discovery 251; children developing relationships with natural world 228; development of competence 251–2; experience of the natural world 228–9; fewer opportunities for children 229; free and natural 251; importance of 226; less time spent by children 228; natural play 226; public health response to conditions of urban poor 227; regulations that require minimal outdoor spaces 257; right to 227; *see also* play
outdoor playspace: context for ECEfS 127; Critical Participatory Action Research (CPAR) *see* CPAR; cultivation of a mode of learning 203; promotion of playing opportunities 128; *see also* Acacia Kindergarten; Banksia Childcare Centre

Pachamama 31
Palmer, S. 294–308
Papamoa Kindergarten 55
Papatūānuku 54, 55, 56
participation rights 25–6
PCK (Pedagogical Content Knowledge) 289, 290
Peckham (open air school) 227
Pedagogical Content Knowledge (PCK) 289, 290
pedagogy: barriers to children's social action 202; challenging the construction of children as vulnerable and incompetent 203; children's understanding of environmental and

social changes 201; critical awareness 197–8; elements of 197; freedom of expression 199, 202; motifs 199; neglected component of education discourse 197; pedagogical foundations 197–8; public pedagogy for sustainability 203–4; social justice storytelling 198–200; stories as catalyst for social change 198; story-tailoring 199, 205; storytelling for sustainability 198–202, 204–5; view of children as citizens 202; view of children as welfare dependents 202; 'Walking Neighbourhood' project 203–4; 'walk in the shoes of another' 199; *wide-awakeness* 198
Penetito, W. 52
Phillips, J. 67
Phillips, L. G. 194–207
Pick, A. 251
place: conversation between people and 51; critical pedagogies of 51–3; education 52; models of education 52; particularities of 51
play: natural 251; romance of 196; *see also* outdoor play
playspace *see* outdoor playspace
Plumwood, V. 50
The Polar Bears' Home: A Story about Global Warming 299
Pramling Samuelsson, I. 4, 210
Principles and Big Ideas of Science 289
professional capital 295–6, 301–3
Project Approach: constructivism 158; effective educational method 159–60, 176; importance of parental participation 160–1; integrated development 159; phases of 160; three key participants of 160; transformative forms of early education 161; Transformative Project Approach 176–7
The Project Method 159
public pedagogy 203–4
Pyle, R. M. 228–9

Rainforest Project: children as change agents for sustainability 162; children's concern about polluted water and native animals 171–2; children's learning as project unfolded 172–3; class book 174; collaboratively-constructed poster 174; conclusion 174–5; context of 169–70; existing environmental practices 169–70; extended list of topics 171;

organization of puppet show incursion 172–3; role play by children 172; shared experiences of children 170; sharing picture books 171; starting the project 170–1; synthesizing phase 171
Redcliffe Children's Centre and Maintained Nursery School: approach to education for sustainability 234–5; background of 233–5; context 233–4; demographics 233–4; forest experiences 234, 235
Reed, E. 251, 252
reflective practice: commitment to 63
Reggio Emilia schools 202
relatedness: self-determination theory 117
rights of children: agentic participation rights 25–6; biocentric/egocentric rights 29–31; collective rights 26–8; conceptualization of active participation 26; dimensions of 23–31; Earth Charter 28, 32–3; expanded rights framework 23; expanded thinking about 21, 22; focus/refocus on rights and values 32; holistic standpoint 33; images 25–6; individual child rights 22; intergenerational rights 28–9; narrow conceptualization of 22; resistance to children as holders of rights 40; rethinking philosophies to connect with the natural world 32; rethinking the socio-constructivist frameworks 33; revision of 22–3, 23; supporting rights as foundational 24–5; *see also* learning for sustainability
Rights of Nature 30–1
Ritchie, J. 49–59
Rivkin, M. 248–65
Roberts, C. 296
Roberts, J. 296
Robinson, K. 274–5
Roche, J. 196
Rogers, R. 228
Rogoff, B. 150–1, 182
Rose, D. B. 50–1, 52
Rose, J. 290–308
ROSE (The Relevance of Science Education) project 117
Rousseau, J.-J. 196
Rowe, B. M. 30

Sageidet, B. M. 112–24
Sandell, K. 281
Sauvé, L. 271

Schools for Sustainable Development
    (Sweden) 211–12
Science (Sweden): adult guidance in
    children's science enquiry learning
    experiences 288; association of science
    and nature 285–6; belief in nature
    experiences 282; broadening the
    perspective of teaching and science in
    preschool 289–90; collaboration and
    critical discussion 290; combined
    Science-Creative Arts year 284;
    differences between school and
    preschool learning 288; division of play
    and learning 289; education for
    sustainability and science in the
    preschool curriculum 281–3; EfS roots
    in environmental education 281;
    emergent science 283, 289;
    environmental teaching in preschools
    282; implications for early childhood
    teacher education 288–9; lack of
    evidence of planned educational
    interventions 285; National Agency for
    Education 281–2; nature experiences as
    science and environmental teaching
    285–6; opportunities for children to
    become agents 282; preschool teachers'
    epistemological beliefs 284; preschool
    teacher students' competence and
    confidence in EfS and science teaching
    283–5; rigid traditional culture of rote
    learning of science 287, 288; science
    goals in curriculum 281–2; skills to
    promote preschool children's enquiries
    skills 289–90; standards of science
    teaching in preschools 283; stronger
    cooperation between student teachers
    and students 291; study on how EfS is
    interpreted and implemented in
    preschools 282; sustainability on
    preschool curriculum 281; teachers'
    understanding of learning cultures in
    preschools 291
SECP (Sustainable Early Childhood
    Project): active engagement 152–3;
    active research process 146–7; children
    as active participants 152–3; community
    engagement 150–2; data collection 147;
    disengagement of children from
    community life 152; division of roles
    154; family engagement 153–5; guiding
    vision 147; key findings and outcomes
    149–50; limitations of study 148; MAD
(Make a difference) 154; objectives of
    study 147; participating services 147–9;
    research contexts 146; teachers' lack of
    involvement in the environmental
    community events 151; teachers/parents
    view on participation of children
    151–2; teachers' risk aversion to
    environmental events 152; thematic
    networks 150
Selby, C. 74
self-determination theory 117
The Sense of Wonder 248, 249, 252
settlers: rural 50–1; urban 50
Shove, E. 197–8
Sideris, L. H. 249
Silent Spring 249, 254
Singapore: also known as 'City in a
    Garden' 98; Botanic Gardens 106;
    challenges in implementing early
    childhood environmental education
    103–5; changes to educational system
    101; child-centred approaches 104;
    collaboration between green agencies
    106; community partnerships 97;
    Confucian ideology 104; critical
    learning areas 101; Curriculum Guide
    102, 104; 'Discovery of the World'
    learning area 102; educational policies
    in support of early childhood
    environmental education 101–3;
    environmental awareness in early
    education policy 102; environmental
    education programs for children 99;
    Framework for Kindergarten Curriculum
    101; high ownership of computers and
    electronic media 100; Kindergarten
    Curriculum Guide 101; known as 'Garden
    City' 98; 'Learning Journeys' program
    105; National Green Plan see National
    Green Plan; National Parks 105–6;
    outdoor learning 103, 104, 104–5;
    pedagogical principles 102–3; plan for
    sustainability 98; preschool preparation
    for achieving academic skills 103;
    rationale for environmental education
    100; revised Framework 102, 102–3;
    teacher-centred approaches 104; 'Teach
    Less, Learn More' initiative 101;
    untapped partnerships for early
    childhood environmental education
    105–6
social justice storytelling 198–200
South Korea see Korea

Sterling, S. 134, 146, 194
Stets, J. 271
Stuhmcke, S. 158–79
Stoermer, E. F. 29–30
story-tailoring 199, 205
storytelling 198–202, 204–5
Studies of Society and Environment
    (SOSE) 268
Summers, M. 269
Sundberg, B. 280–93
sustainability: advocates for broad societal
    change 6; ambiguities of 41; children's
    participation in 195–7; children's
    understanding of 231; combined with
    early childhood education 257–61;
    concept of 9; core dimension of 40;
    development of interdependent systems
    194; dimensions of 210–11; distance
    moral 42; diverse interpretations of 195;
    education for 7, 21–2; environmental
    socialization 250; ethical 28; failure of
    mainstream education 89; fairness and
    justice for all 28–9; global imperatives
    for 6–7; global issue requiring urgent
    addressing 34; integration with the Arts
    see Arts; learning for 40–1; meanings and
    practice of 183; new ways of thinking
    required 6; rationales for early childhood
    education 204; role models for 250;
    storytelling for 198–202, 204–5; threats
    and dangers highlighted 6–7; UNICEF
    calls for 21; unsustainable economic
    systems 6; welfare of future generations
    29; world citizen 42; see also learning for
    sustainability
Sustainable Early Childhood Project
    (SECP) see SECP
sustainable schools framework 231–2
Suzuki, D. 56, 57
Sweden: background to Swedish preschool
    209; bricolage 209; change in student-
    teachers' perception about children's
    capabilities 302; children as global
    citizens 211; children's moral
    development 211; children's physical
    needs 212; children unfamiliar with
    sustainable development 216;
    contemporary thinking about ECEfS
    209–11; content knowledge 212;
    democratic values of preschools 210;
    dimensions of sustainability 210–11;
    Diploma of Excellence 212, 213; early
    childhood education traditions 210;

educator's report on OMEP project
    217–19; empirical research into
    sustainability issues 210; fundamental
    democratic values 212; Green Flag
    Program 217–19; models of exemplary
    practice in ECE 301; National
    Curriculum for the Swedish Preschool
    210; nature 212; OMEP project 215–16,
    216–19; pedagogical documentation
    214–16; preschool curriculum 211–13,
    214; preschool education 209; preschool
    ownership 209; professional capital
    301–3; recurrent purpose of preschools
    208; research project 214; respecting
    children's rights to be involved 216–19;
    Schools for Sustainable Development
    211–12; science in preschool see Science
    (Sweden); seven concepts linked to EfS
    216; shared thinking about sustainability
    219; sustainable development 212;
    Swedish National Agency for Education
    212; teachers' reflective practice of
    children's rights 302; Using Again
    project 217
Swedish National Agency for Education
    212
systems theory: description of 134;
    framework for SECP see SECP

The Tailor 205
Tallberg Broman, I. 208, 210
The Tbilisi Declaration 8
teachers: in Acacia Kindergarten 132;
    applying Indigenous philosophies 55–6;
    Arts and Humanities integrated subject
    in Australia see Arts and Humanities
    subject; in Banksia Childcare Centre
    131–2, 138; critical awareness of risk 72;
    embedding Indigenous perspectives in
    mainstream curricula 68; environmental
    community events 151; examining the
    everyday practices of the learning
    setting 204; higher education programs
    304; initiating relationships with local
    Indigenous people 54–5; introduction of
    new concepts 92–3; issues with fear
    70–1; in Japan 84, 86–7, 90; limitations
    on non-Indigenous practices 71–3; in
    New Zealand see Christchurch; non-
    Indigenous 49; in Norway 113–14, 118,
    119; practices appropriate to individual
    cultures 92; preparation for Arts and
    sustainability curriculum integration

268–9; qualifications of 8; qualifications required in Japan 80; reinforcing the principles of UNCRC 34; report on OMEP project 217–19; in sciences *see* Science (Sweden); seeking in-depth, local Indigenous knowledges 55; supporting children as agents of change 33–4; in Sweden 214; translating concepts of sustainability into relevant everyday practice 304

Te Tiriti o Waitangi 54

Te Whāriki: contribution 190; principles 181; strands 186; Treaty of Waitangi 192n1

theoretical framework (CPAR): hierarchical nesting of two systems 134–5; outdoor playspace physical context 134–5, 137–8

Tilbury, D. xv–xvi, 270–1

Torres Strait Islanders: children learning culture and history of 73; embedding Indigenous perspectives 67; First Peoples of Australian lands and territories 66, 70; right for all children to engage with 64, 66

transcultural spaces 5

transformative learning theory 297

Transformative Project Approach 176–7

Transnational Dialogues in Research in Early Childhood Education for Sustainability 314–5: background of participants 2; requirement to enlarge 2; self-funding researchers 1

Tranter, P. 253

The Treasure of Trash: A Recycling Story 300

Treaty of Waitangi 192n1

Treaty on Environmental Education for Sustainable Development and Global Responsibility 28

UDHR (Universal Declaration on Human Rights): principles of 24

UK Forestry Commission 227

UNCRC (United Nations Convention on the Rights of the Child): definition of 40; inadequacy in twenty-first century 22; narrow conceptualization of rights 22; participation rights 25; protection rights 25; recognition of children as rights holders 24; requirement to enlarge 3; rights and respect for 46; right to play 227; survival and development rights 25

UNDRC (United Nations Declaration of the Rights of the Child), special convention for protection 24

UNESCO: Decade of Education for Sustainable Development 2005–2014 (DESD) 7, 9, 82, 89, 281; definition of the four interdependent pillars of sustainability 194; education for sustainability 311; Growing up in Cities program 257; international meetings 3, 4; promotion of environmental education 8–9; seven Rs 298; World Conference on Education for Sustainable Development 4

UNICEF (United Nations Children's Fund): calls for sustainable living 21; Child Friendly Cities Initiative 257; Convention *see* UNCRC (United Nations Convention on the Rights of the Child)

United Kingdom: children's engagement (research theme 3) 299–300; early childhood practitioners as agents of change sustainability 297–301; Early Years Foundation Stage (EYFS) 294, 295; Early Years Professional Status (EYPS) 296; Early Years Teacher 296; ecojustice 297; generating human and professional capital for a sustainable society 301–3; generating professional capital for sustainability 295–6; identification of sustainable practices (research theme 1) 298–9; impact of social and welfare services on ECE 295; initiatives built around the seven Rs of UNESCO 298; integration of ECE into the educational experience 296; learning from Swedish experience 302–3; new approaches to ECE 302–3; operationalizing transformational leadership approach 297; practical engagement in learning 295; professional capital 295–6, 301–3; professional development (research theme 5) 300–1; questionnaires 298; research context of studies 297; studies on the promotion and implementation of ECEfS 297–303; sustainability and the wider community (research theme 4) 300; sustainable practices in early childhood education services (research theme 2) 299; training of ECE teachers 296–7; transformative learning theory 297; value of active

engagement 295–6; *see also* England
United Nations: population growth 99
United Nations climate conference 41
United Nations Conference on the
    Human Environment 82
United Nations Convention on the Rights
    of the Child (UNCRC) (UNICEF) *see*
    UNCRC
United Nations Decade of Education for
    Sustainable Development 2005-2014
    (DESD) 7, 9, 82, 89, 281
United Nations Declaration of the Rights
    of the Child (UNDRC) *see* UNDRC
United Nations Environment Program
    (UNEP) 311
United Nations Millennium Development
    Goals 311
United States Congress 253
United States of America (USA): Admiral
    Burke Park redevelopment 260–1;
    ambivalence towards urgency of
    sustainability 253; Boulder Valley School
    District 258; Cedarsong Forest
    Kindergarten 256; Children, Youth and
    Environment Center for Community
    Engagement 258; Civic Area
    redevelopment 258–60; combining early
    childhood education with sustainability
    257–61; curriculum based on
    surrounding land and seasons 256;
    Department of Community Planning
    and Sustainability 258; Department of
    Parks and Recreation 260;
    Environmental Protection Agency
    (EPA) 254; Federal Interagency Task
    Force on Environmental Education 254;
    Forest School Teacher Certification 256;
    Fragile Families and Child Wellbeing
    Study 257; Growing Up Boulder
    program 257, 258, 258–60; Horizons
    School 260; 'Leave No Child Inside' bill
    254; limited role of the federal
    government in education 254; Lucy
    School (Middletown) 255; Mother
    Earth School 256; National Education

and Environment Fund (NEEF) 254;
    Natural Learning Initiative (NLI) 257;
    nature-based preschool 255–7; North
    American Association for
    Environmental Education (NAAEE)
    254, 255; regulations requiring minimal
    outdoor spaces 257; United States
    Department of Education 254;
    Waldkindergarten 256
Universal Declaration on Human Rights
    (UDHR): principles of 24
UN Regional Information Centre for
    Western Europe 26
Urban Redevelopment Authority (URA)
    (Singapore) 98, 100–1

Vadala, C. E. 250

wairuatanga 52
Waite, S. J. 228
Waldkindergarten 256
'Walking Neighbourhood' project 203–4
Walking Respectfully project 69–70
'walk in the shoes of another' (storytelling
    motif) 199
Wann, T. 195
wellbeing: natural caring 188; response to
    and respect for 188
Where the Forest Meets the Sea 171
Whitebread, D. 230
whiteness (racial identity): attached to
    particular values and privileges 69
White, R. 252
wholism 116
wide-awakeness 198
Wilson, R. A. 86, 105
world citizen 42
World Conference (OMEP) 4
World Conference on Education for
    Sustainable Development 4
World Watch Institute 99
Wright, S. 267, 268

Young, T. C. 146–7